THE ALL-DAY KINDERGARTEN AND PRE-K CURRICULUM

Grounded in theory and research, *The All-Day Kindergarten and Pre-K Curriculum* provides an activity-based and classroom-proven curriculum for educators to consider as they plan and interact with pre-k and kindergarten children. Allowing young children the opportunities to become independent, caring, critical thinkers who feel comfortable asking questions and exploring possible solutions, the Dynamic-Themes curriculum offers children the skills they need for responsible citizenship and academic progress. This book describes a culturally sensitive pre-k and kindergarten curriculum in the context of literacy, technology, mathematics, social studies, science, the arts, and play, and also discusses:

- How to use the seven integrated conditions for learning to meet and exceed content learning standards.
- How to organize for differentiated instruction and to integrate multiple forms of assessment.
- How to teach literacy tools and skills in fresh ways.
- How to work with families, colleagues, and community.

Building on Fromberg's groundbreaking earlier work, *The All-Day Kindergarten and Pre-K Curriculum* presents a practical curriculum centering on how young children develop meanings. This is a fantastic resource for pre- and in-service early childhood teachers, administrators, and scholars.

Doris Pronin Fromberg is Professor of Education at Hofstra University.

THE ALL-DAY KINDERGARTEN AND PRE-K CURRICULUM

A Dynamic-Themes Approach

Doris Pronin Fromberg

Routledge
Taylor & Francis Group

NEW YORK AND LONDON

First published 2012
by Routledge
711 Third Avenue, New York, NY 10017

Simultaneously published in the UK
by Routledge
2 Park Square, Milton Park, Abingdon, Oxon OX14 4RN

Routledge is an imprint of the Taylor & Francis Group, an informa business

Library of Congress Cataloging-in-Publication Data
Fromberg, Doris Pronin, 1937-
The all-day kindergarten and pre-k curriculum : a dynamic-themes approach
/ Doris Pronin Fromberg.
p. cm.
1. Kindergarten–Curricula–United States. 2. Curriculum planning–United
States. I. Title.
LB1180.F76 2011
375'.001–dc22
2011015111

ISBN: 978–0–415–88152–4 (hbk)
ISBN: 978–0–415–88153–1 (pbk)
ISBN: 978–0–203–80420–9 (ebk)

Typeset in Bembo by
Keystroke, Station Road, Codsall, Wolverhampton
Printed and bound in the United States of America on acid-free paper by
Edwards Brothers, Inc.

Melvin Fromberg has survived with grace
the postponement of many outdoor hikes
and entertainments this year.

CONTENTS

PREFACE

I feel privileged to spend time in many early childhood classrooms. In each one, I learn from children's actions what they pay attention to, what they care about, and what they learn. I also have seen what many teachers do to help capture and keep children's attention, and help them learn new stuff. You, too, would be able to see that pre-kindergarten and kindergarten children are able to learn content effectively when they work and play in Activity-Based Learning Environments (ABLE).[1] To play on words, youngsters pay attention when they feel *able* in ABLE environments that *enable* them to make connections, see relationships, and build a sense of their own abilities and competence. This book provides many examples of how professional early childhood teachers can organize content-rich classrooms with ABLEs.

This book presents ways to teach so that young children make connections between their experiences in order to build concepts and skills. It is about how to match teaching with how youngsters learn. In particular, Dynamic-Themes focus on the connection-making process of learning, a reflection of how our brains function to create meaning and strengthen memories. Part II of the book includes many activities that share underlying Dynamic-Themes.

This book does not separate child development from "methods" of education. That is because sensitive teachers typically integrate an understanding of how young children develop with the sequence of activities and resources they offer children. They recognize that children build meaning when they engage in seven *integrated* conditions for learning—comparisons (induction), surprise (cognitive dissonance), social competence (social and emotional well-being), physical engagement, play and imagination, revisiting, and a sense of competence.

This book's ethical commitment to young children is how to plan activities that retain their curiosity and thirst to learn more. This book intends to be an antidote to scripted lessons with 48- to- 72-month-old children seated for long periods of time while they fill in linear, rote worksheets that test their memory of isolated information, or try to guess what they think their teacher wants them to do.

"Words are the source of misunderstanding," said the *Little Prince* (St. Exupery, 2000); so there is a need to sort out some words to help us communicate. In order to avoid misunderstanding about the words and labels of educational ideologies, it is worth defining particular practices in the early childhood field in relation to this book's Dynamic-Themes approach. The field practices a variety of educational ideologies that include primarily behaviorist, maturationist, cognitive-developmental, and dynamic systems.

The *behaviorist ideology* views the learner as an empty vessel for the teacher to fill. The unit or theme or topic typically refers to a teacher-directed set of plans. The *unit* plan, focused on vicarious subjects, such as transportation, circus, zoo, or a specific holiday, usually includes a related song, craft activity, story, and possibly cooking activity. The teacher-directed unit focuses on imparting information. It usually begins on Monday and ends on Friday.

The *maturationist ideology* views the learner as capable of developing when the teacher adapts to the learner's natural progress. The *emergent* curriculum follows the interests and pace that children appear to indicate, with an emphasis on the outdoor, natural environment.

In contrast, the *cognitive-developmental ideology* views the learner developing in identifiable stages that the teacher matches. The British use of *topics*, less-and-more teacher-directed, sometimes resembles the *project* curriculum (Helm & Katz, 2011; Katz & Chard, 2000). The topic or project, such as pizza, birds, ponds, or airplanes, includes the teacher's judgment about children's interests in relation to their development. More child-centered than the unit, the topic or project typically includes a variety of related activities that the teacher plans in greater depth than the unit and involves no fixed time span. Children engage in activities and could absorb important information that the teacher might not have predetermined.

The main theory guiding the selection of activities in this book is a *dynamic systems ideology—the Dynamic-Themes* approach. The holistic Dynamic-Themes approach views the learner primarily as a connection-maker that the teacher accommodates with challenging activities to which children could feel committed. Teachers select and sequence experiences in which youngsters can engage actively and that have the potential for children to build meaningful, natural connections between ideas that are trans-disciplinary.[2] Children are able to build the connections because different experiences share similar underlying images, as do analogies. When you perceive the image that underlies one surface form of an experience, it is easier to perceive and connect with a similar underlying meaning in a different surface form. Part II expands this viewpoint.

Young children engaged in the integrated, inquiry approach of the content-rich Dynamic-Themes curriculum use skills in the arts, technology, literacy, and mathematics in order to communicate and represent their learning. Your plans for related experiences might weave throughout the year or take place during different amounts of time, as relevant.

This is a book, therefore, about curriculum and meaning from the child's viewpoint. "Curriculum is a complex idea containing multiple components, such as goals, content, pedagogy, or instructional practices. Curriculum is influenced by many factors, including society's values, content standards, accountability systems, research findings, community expectations, culture and language and individual children's characteristics" (NAEYC/NAECS/SDE, 2003, p. 6). You will notice that this comprehensive statement ends with individual children's characteristics.

Research is clear about what works and how youngsters learn (Bowman, Donovan, & Burns, 2001; Crosser, 2005; Fisher et al., 2011; Galinsky, 2010). This book builds on a variety of curricular research to integrate content in a caring, activity-based learning environment. In summary, there is a strong integrated rationale about how young children develop and learn; and how to consider their possible perspectives and concerns. When children learn in these ways, you could claim that you are meeting, perhaps exceeding, the intent of learning standards.

Another main focus of this book is how you might plan for the meaningful and relevant learning of today's young children. Children's developmental capacities and ways of learning are situated within their specific, diverse socio-cultural and personal event knowledge. The discussion that follows—about Society; the Nature of Knowledge; the Nature of Learning; and the Nature of Teaching (Pedagogy)— looks at the contexts that inform the practice of early teaching and learning in an activity-based learning environment.

Society

The education of young children in this century needs to take into account their societal context. On the one hand, electronic technology—in the kaleidoscopic forms of television, the miniaturization of computers, the interactivity of computers and computer games, the ubiquity of cell phone technology—contributes to the multi-sensory and accelerated pace of communication. On the other hand, inequitable access to these kinds of cultural tools, often based upon socio-economic differences and individual family cultures, adds to the educational continuum of capacities and responsibilities, as well as predispositions, attitudes, and behavior toward others. Here is some relevant information about young children:

- Young children come to school with different access and exposure to events. For example, 47% of children were read to seven or more times per week; 53% less often; and 9% were not read to at all (Fields, Smith, & Lugaila, 2001). Their economic situation affected the vocabulary exposure of very young children, privileging children from more affluent backgrounds (Hart & Risley, 1995; Heath, 1983; National Early Literacy Panel, 2008). Youngsters who begin school with significantly smaller spoken vocabularies typically display achievement lags through the primary grades and beyond.

- During the first decade of this century, there was pressure for kindergartens to include preparation for testable discrete language and mathematical instruction that had previously resembled the practices of later primary grades. Vocabulary development within scripted test-preparation settings that focus on phonics is limited in comparison with possibly varied, content-rich middle-class homes. This practice underutilizes the growing brains of youngsters (Gopnik, 2009; Gopnik, Meltzoff, & Kuhl, 1999).

- 70% to 80% of children have had one year of preschool and 45–55% have had two years of preschool experience (U.S. Department of Commerce, Bureau of the Census, 2002). 41% of 3s and 66% of 4s attend preschool (National Center of Educational Statistics, 2004).

- 7.6% of children live in poverty and 11.4% did not have health care in 2003 (U.S. Department of Commerce, Bureau of the Census, 2004). The 2010 health care legislation should afford relief in children's health care.

- Immigrant 4- and 5-year-old children made up approximately 7% of the pre-kindergarten or kindergartens in 2007–2008 and up to 21% of their homes were linguistically isolated (Urban Institute, 2011).

- Both parents work outside the home in 69% of households, as do most single parents. Almost 50% of marriages end in divorce.

- One report claims that children spend more time in sedentary activities, such as television and computers, than their overall time in school (Sigman, 2008a). As many as 10.4% of kindergarten children were obese at the start of the century, in part as a result of diet, but also possibly because of sedentary activities and reduced access to the outdoors (Ogden, Flegal, Carroll, & Johnson, 2002). The situation expands as children age, with 24% of urban children being obese (MSNBC.com, 2004). In less than a decade, the number of obese young children had increased to 12.4% (Centers for Disease Control and Prevention, 2009).

Nature of Knowledge

Regardless of societal pressures for test preparation, pre-kindergarten and kindergarten children have a broad range of developmental possibilities, based upon the development of their brains and muscles as well as the experiences they have had. Therefore, this book deals with how to educate young children in ways that match their development with adults' conceptions of knowledge. Indeed, the philosopher John Dewey (1933) contended that the teacher's work is to help students move toward humanity's fund of knowledge by using the ways in which students can learn; to help make that which is "strange" become "familiar." Even so, different viewpoints define the nature of worthwhile knowledge in different ways. This book supports editorial positions, as follows:

- Worthwhile knowledge for young children centers on the imagery underlying concepts—in science, social science, literacy, mathematics, and the arts—which reflect the ongoing emergence of fresh insights.
- Young children who engage in active learning of such concepts will have strong motives to apply mathematical skills and will feel like reading to find out more, as well as represent their experiences in writing and the arts.
- Social interaction among children is an important condition for learning.
- For young children, representations in 3- and 2-dimensional arts reside on the continuum of literacy.
- This century reflects the changing nature of knowledge. Isaac Newton's model of separate, deterministic subjects has been eclipsed by Albert Einstein's focus on knowledge that resides in *relationships* (Isaacson, 2007).
- The teaching-and-learning process is both interactive and negotiated. It is a joint construction.

Nature of Learning

Another premise of this book is that children who feel successful, competent, and empowered to focus their experiences will become more capable of intellectual achievements and caring citizenship. Psychologists (Bruner, 1966; Damasio, 1999; Goleman, 1995) and other researchers have found that the brains of children who feel anxious or fearful are flooded by coping with these feelings and are unable to focus on intellectual issues (Payne & Kounios, 2009; Sandkuhler & Bhattacharaya, 2008; Tognoli & Kelso, 2008).

During this century, there has been an increasing recognition that the nature of how children learn and the nature of knowledge have begun to intersect (Jukes, McCain, & Crockett, 2010). In effect, rather than a discrete, isolated accretion of data, young children's brains are capable of recognizing patterns and making many *connections* across neurons. Indeed, after being receptive to particular exposures, they are able to expand on those initial experiences based upon future associations (Bransford et al., 2002; Davis & Sumara, 2006; Fauconnier & Turner, 2002; Klingberg, 2006; Piaget & Inhelder, 1973; Wormeli, 2009). Therefore, it makes sense for teachers to enrich, deepen, and re-conceptualize curricular experiences.

Nature of Teaching (Pedagogy)

Professional teachers of young children recognize the contexts for learning—society, knowledge, how youngsters learn—that influence the nature of pedagogy.

Giving priority to supporting conceptual learning and the flexibility of young brains, it makes sense to view curriculum knowledge as integrative—the images, analogies, or perceptual models that children experience directly that cut across the artificial boundaries of separate subjects. In order to help youngsters perceive Dynamic-Themes, professional teachers negotiate plans with children based upon the particular situation, their estimation of children's concerns, and the nature of knowledge. In a supportive fashion, teachers offer children the skills that they need for responsible citizenship and academic progress; and they offer them in contextual, caring, and playful ways. This kind of focus on a meaning-rich intellectual education includes necessary academic tool skills.

Preview of Chapters

The book has four parts that include many ways of working and activities that you could adapt to your children. Part I: The Setting, describes ways in which competent teachers organize all-day pre-kindergarten and kindergarten classrooms that cater to children from diverse backgrounds. Chapter 1 includes a "simulated visit to an all-day kindergarten and pre-kindergarten" that focuses on the interactions of a few children and their teacher. [**Procedural note:** Whenever "pre-kindergarten" is mentioned, the activity might also be relevant for some kindergarten children. When children alone are discussed, both age groups might participate and learn. The mention of kindergarten children alone suggests a more challenging activity.] Chapter 2 describes how to set up and organize the center-based classroom of the teacher in Chapter 1. Chapter 3 discusses how young children develop and learn when their teachers use seven *integrated* conditions for learning. Chapter 4 focuses on 3-dimensional learning, in particular, as a fundamental base of early learning.

Part II: Content: Connecting Experiences with Dynamic-Themes presents examples of activities from which young children are able to learn concepts and build imagery that cuts across historically separate subjects. The underlying images of Dynamic-Themes serve to connect the experiences. The introductory section defines the Dynamic-Themes, and it is followed by three chapters dealing with cyclical change, dialectical activity, and synergy. Chapter 8 presents some interdisciplinary ways to affect children's interpersonal concepts and behavior by outlining activities that focus on the *transformation* of attitudes.

Part III: Learning Tools, Skills, and Ways to Represent Experiences recognizes that children need practice in order to learn skills and build fluency. Children absorb practice when teachers provide an engaging and playful variety of activities. This part discusses how various literacy tools, skills, and ways to represent experiences support the meanings that children develop in integrated ways. Chapter 9 begins the discussion of literacy learning in the 2- and 3-dimensional arts. The visual and motor arts also form the general foundation of literacy development. Chapter 10 builds on the arts continuum of symbolic representation into the language that children speak, write, and read. Chapter 11 presents examples of experiences in which young children are able to participate and raises questions about the future of teaching practice. Chapter 12 focuses on mathematical literacy.

Finally, Part IV: Planning, Assessment, and Community Connections pays attention to the societal systems that influence learning and teaching, including issues of assessing and documenting, planning, and providing continuity of experiences for children within the school, family, and community. Chapter 13 provides a vision of scheduling and planning for the year. Chapter 14 discusses practices and policies related to assessment. Chapter 15 considers a range of ways that teachers involve families and their communities in supporting the education of young children.

ACKNOWLEDGEMENTS

I thank Routledge editor Heather Jarrow, who has provided thoughtful support and wisdom throughout the development of this project. Routledge editor Alex Masulis has provided sensitive guidance and knowledge. Philip Parr provided careful and insightful copy-editing. Routledge personnel in all phases of the work have conducted themselves with outstanding professional expertise. Keystroke personnel Maggie Lindsey-Jones, Philip Parr, Matthew Winkworth and Emma Wood provided skilled copyediting support. Diana Stiklickas, a talented Hofstra graduate assistant, provided technical support.

Sections of the introduction to Part II, and Chapters 3, 5, 6, and 7 have been adapted from Fromberg, D.P. (2002). *Play and meaning in early childhood education.* Boston: Allyn & Bacon.

PART I

The Setting

The chapters in this section provide a context for young children's education in the all-day kindergarten and pre-kindergarten. Chapter 1 describes the center-based setting and how a few children move within it. Chapter 2 shares ways in which professional teachers maintain a civilized environment. Chapter 3 provides a framework of integrated procedures that can help youngsters build meaningful connections between ideas. The many activities throughout the book include these procedures. Chapter 4 highlights the distinctive physical basis that serves as an essential foundation on which young children build much of their learning.

1

AN ALL-DAY KINDERGARTEN AND PRE-KINDERGARTEN

Introduction

Think about a classroom as an artificial environment, a box in which as many as 25 pre-kindergarten or kindergarten children and their teacher dwell during a 5- to 6-hour school day. In this environment, the simplistic image of a teacher as a stand-up entertainer who changes focus every few minutes cannot compete with the adrenalin pumps of constantly changing television images and computer games. This book discusses ways to consider why, what, and how it makes sense for teachers to deal with the complex ways in which young children can make sense of a complex world. It also deals with how they can learn many of the concepts, facts, skills, and attitudes needed in order to become intelligent citizens.

Therefore, let us begin by looking at two children between 48 and 72 months of age, first from the children's perspective and then from the teacher's. We will then consider what learning in an all-day pre-kindergarten and kindergarten looks and feels like, particularly as teacher and child interact. These relative views will be elaborated throughout the book, for they provide the best means of imparting a deeper understanding of what an all-day experience can be. [**Procedural note:** As you read, note that whenever there is mention of a pre-kindergarten child, the activity might also include kindergarten children. When there is mention of a kindergarten child, few younger children might be capable of the activity. The mention of children or youngsters alone suggests that both groups might be capable of the activity.]

The 4- and 5-Year-Old

The Child's View

Imagine yourself to be a 4- or 5-year-old, beginning school. You were born 48 or 63 months ago and have spent your time at home or in preschool and child care with some of the following people: your mother, father, older sister, babysitters, grandparents, and teachers. You find toys and pictures in the supermarket. You have waited a very long time as your mother shopped or held her place in line in a city office.

You try to capture birds with your jacket and bring a bowl of milk to the stray cat near your house. You were hit by a swing in the park, and your teenage babysitter tried to stop you from telling your mother this when she was resting after work. New flowers in spring thrill you. Puddles are an invitation for splashing through.

You watch the older children trying to burn ants off a worm's back. You recall that "One time my father drank so much and he was drunk and he fell asleep in the living room with all his clothes on" (Anonymous, 1978, p. 16). You believe that "It's a long time before you die. Everything has to die. People go around and dig and find skulls, and they say, This is the skull of a man. We saw skulls at the museum. There was a huge dinosaur skull . . . You turn into dust when you die" (Nalim, 1978, p. 20).

When thunder or gunshots waken you at night, you feel your heart beat faster as you race to your parents' bed. Getting hugs from them is one good thing about thunder and gunshots. Jerry told you that he heard gunshots on Wednesday and his brother told him to duck.

You go to your neighbor's apartment to see if he can play ball with you, but he tells you he cannot come over because he cannot bear to part with his best friend, who is visiting. You ask your grandfather to play with you because you feel so lonely and there's nothing to do. It feels good when he tells you what a great checkers player you have become.

You feel puzzled to see your older sister's face contort with disgust when she takes the spoon you have handled. More often, she wants to take what you have long before you want to give it to her.

You will miss your friend Stanley if his family moves away. He taught you to count to 100 and shared your horror when the baby doll's paint came off in the water. You play card games together, and he taught you how to stack the deck in his favor. You talk about favorite television shows together and race to your grandmother's side because the commercial tells you to tell your mother to go right out and buy it. You can sing every commercial you hear and ride a tricycle or a two-wheeler. You ask your father why your living-room floor is covered with linoleum while Eileen's has a soft carpet.

You feel guilty when you eat more candy than your mother said you could have. You don't understand why your mother not wanting to send the dentist on vacation is a reason not to eat candy. You watch the older children sneaking cigarettes in the park while their heavy schoolbooks sit on the ground. You cannot understand why they tell you not to pick up the shiny crack vials in the schoolyard. Everybody wonders why you keep collecting round red pebbles and shiny colored glass in a shoebox.

You have been delighted by *Curious George*, the peddler and the monkeys, and other storybook characters; you can look repeatedly at the pictures in the monster book (*Where the Wild Things Are*), *Cars*, and *The Trek*. You point to each word in the comic book, one at a time, without actually reading. The big kids on the block "play school" with you and showed you that c-a-t spelled cat as you copied their writing. They are shocked that you connected c-a-t, for cat, with r-a-t for rat and m-a-t for mat. Everybody said that you would learn to read when you go to the big school. You wonder if your teacher will be a smiling person.

The Teacher's View

As a teacher, you have considered that each child has had many experiences, some different from others, and that each child needs a different amount of time to satisfy his or her need for repetition in order to gain mastery—whether the task is tying shoelaces, riding a bicycle, pouring liquids, writing a name, comparing quantities, putting together a puzzle, or learning to care about friends. You have seen young children who readily repeated skills again and again and felt satisfied in doing so. They have devoted their entire attention to solving a problem. As you have walked with young children, you have seen, heard, and appreciated what might otherwise have been a lost world of novelties. You have caught a glimpse of the connections they made that sometimes felt poetic.

Your work has made you aware that young children learn most effectively when they can have physical contact with concrete materials that they can compare and imagery that represents contrasts. The children's direct involvement is the basis for their motivation. When you have been able to provide such direct involvement, you have been able to help them build on the strengths of their experiences. The children's ways of working have been an effective vehicle for carrying out the school's intellectual and socio-emotional purposes.

Young children's ways of learning and the teacher's ways of teaching are largely social, affective, aesthetic, and physical. Yet schools are the single institution charged with the major task of intellectual development. For all-day early education, the issue is not either intellect or socialization. The issue is helping young children achieve intellectual and personal success by using experiential means, through concrete and imaginative activities that are largely physical, aesthetic, affective, and social. The bulk of this book is devoted to elaborating and representing this issue through varied ways of working with children during an extended school day.

The most caring teacher can hurt children unless she or he is skilled in translating the human fund of knowledge into activities in which children can feel competent (Dewey, 1933). Researchers who study the human brain point to the importance of positive emotion in helping thinking to take place (Damasio 2003). Wedding *what* is taught with *how* it is taught is more important than either content or method alone. The value of early education derives much more from its ability to help the child build contrasting images than from isolated instances of information processing, skills building, memory cramming, or verbalization. After all is said and done, little remains of the bits of information. What remain forever are the residual feelings and attitudes that ultimately dictate how individual human beings will behave and interpret experience in life. This view concurs with Whitehead's (1929) belief that wisdom lies in the use of knowledge. Use implies action. If you think back to the most satisfying residues of your own early education, you are likely to find active participation—sometimes painful, sometimes pleasurable, sometimes actively stimulating—serving as a window back in time. The early childhood classroom within this framework is a time that is valuable in itself, rather than only as a preparation for next year.

As teachers, we know that children enter school with many rich experiences, even if they are disturbing rather than harmonious ones. We need to harness these experiences and build upon them, because they are sources of strength for the children and the basis for building a sense of personal, intellectual competence.

Simulated Visit to an All-Day Early Childhood Classroom

As we move together through an imaginary visit, we can see how a center-based, activity-rich organization works. The center-based organization helps children build concepts as well as positive attitudes toward education. This section attempts to share an image of what learning in a classroom looks and feels like after the first eight weeks of the year.

Arrangement of Space and Materials

Space is subdivided by furnishings into a series of areas similar to booths at a fair or a set of studios/laboratories rather than desks lined up auditorium-style. Children can reach materials that are set out invitingly in transparent containers on low shelves. Activities needing water are close to the sink. Children mostly work in small groups as the teacher circulates and visits each area in turn. A closer look at each area follows.

Socio-dramatic Center   *Socio-dramatic activity is the collaborative oral playwriting in which young children develop their sense of story, awareness of audience, and the voice of a writer.* Kneeling side by side, two children take wooden blocks off the shelves in the socio-dramatic area. This area also contains a hospital section and a store-front/puppet stage made of large hollow blocks. Literacy materials that are integrated include labels, signs, notices, appointment books, bills, receipts, and advertisements. Nearby, boxes, shelves, and a pegboard enclose an area containing a woodworking bench, carpentry tools, and pine lumber in a basket.

Mathematics Center   Four kindergarten children take turns tossing a die onto a mat as they play a game on the floor with the Dienes multi-base arithmetic blocks in base 3; they are adding blocks within base 3. The area, enclosed on three sides by shelves, houses mathematics–related materials. There is a balance scale with labeled boxes of beads, pine cones, sand, buttons, cotton balls, beans, discs, a yardstick, rulers, and other items. There are Cuisenaire rods, rulers, card games, and board games, some of which appear to be teacher-made. Transparent measuring cups of varying shapes sit in a tub. There are paper pad books, pencils, markers, scissors, and tape. In addition, there are picture books that include references to quantities. Some of these materials merge into the socio-dramatic center, the art studio, and the science laboratory.

Science Laboratory   At a table that holds a pan of water and a water dropper, two children sort materials into two piles on the basis of whether they do or do not absorb water. Nearby, two children are changing the newspaper in a guinea pig's cage. Atop low shelves, tadpoles at various stages of development swim in an aquarium, while a salamander adds color to the terrarium. A magnifying glass, a sand egg-timer, paper, pencils, markers, and scissors sit next to picture books that include references to tadpoles and guinea pigs.

Arts Studio   Near the sink and easel stocked with aprons, paint cups, brushes of different sizes, and a pencil, two children are weaving jersey loops at a table, while another child writes her name with a pencil at the top of a crayon drawing. She uses a teacher-made name card attached to her own photograph as a model. (The teacher explains later that almost all the children can write their names independently but that this child is developmentally delayed. The photograph helps the child find her own name or that of others in the class independently when she wants to write.) In addition, there are pencils and markers of different widths as well as paper, scissors, a hole punch, glue, and tape. A table for six adjoins the easel. This art studio stocks a rotating variety of media that include abundant involvement of children in 3-dimensional projects, such as clay, sculptural materials, small constructions, woodworking, and collages. Paint, crayons, markers, and pencils as well as papers and objects with various textures are present at different times. There are contrasts of color, shape, size, and texture available at different times. Ink pads for printing activities are present. The art studio resides on a continuum that leads to and merges into a writing center.

Writing/Drawing and Individual Manipulatives Center   Children are seated at several tables that face a wall and two room dividers. Adjacent shelves house pencils and markers of different widths, lined and unlined paper, and a stapler, tape, and scissors. Four children are writing in personal books that they have illustrated. One child is working on a puzzle, another on a card-matching game. Two children on the floor are playing checkers that are set on a mat. Two other children are sitting on a section of floor marked with tape where they read the stories to each other that they have written and illustrated. There is an unoccupied child-size canvas chair labeled "Author's Chair."

Library Center At the opposite side of the room from the sink, arts area, and science area, there is a corner created by bookshelves and a storage cabinet. Book jackets hang on a bulletin board. A box of spaghetti and the book jacket for *Strega Nona* (de Paola, 1975) are hung from two lengths of blue yarn attached to the ceiling. Books are displayed with the front cover visible in order to attract attention. One child is seated on a carpet square, one is seated at a small round table, and two are sitting together in a soft, slightly battered armchair. All are reading different books, with two wearing earphones as they read. There are two mats on the floor upon which two children lie with books. One of the reclining children holds a stuffed toy. There is also a large booth-like box in which the top of a curly-haired head is visible. This center is stocked with high-quality fiction, poetry, non-fiction, periodicals, and catalogs. It is a place in which the teacher advertises and celebrates literature by displaying the covers of books and book jackets. Children have had ample time to observe and question within real experiences before they seek answers in books, periodicals, and other print sources. A puppet frame or a flannel board is set up from time to time.

Computers/Interactive White Board (IWB) Table and Listening Center Near electrical outlets, several computers sit on a table, with two children seated at two of them, quietly talking about what they are doing. (Before using the computers, they have signed their names on the computer clipboards.) Three children are playing a counting game at the electronic IWB table. There also are earphones for two children to listen to computer stories and/or stories with books or a variety of musical selections. Educators remind teachers that the computer controls and CD-Rom changers "should be at the children's eye level, on a low table or even on the floor" (Clements & Sarama, 2009a, p. 287).

Thematic Center The theme in this area changes every few weeks as relevant. Drawing and literacy materials are present. Sometimes, planting activities take place here. At other times, children compare their baby pictures with those of other children and the teacher. Sometimes, they sort and sequence photographs of a class trip. They also compile class-made books about a particular theme, such as "Friends and Enemies" or "From Pumpkin Seeds to Pumpkin Sprouts: Our Pumpkin History Book" (Dynamic-Theme: Cyclical Change). This center integrates subjects so that children, for example, could store the cycle of adopting a tree across the school year (taking photos, samples of leaves and buds, and bark rubbings) with a photo of pumpkins in the fall that have contributed seeds for planting in the spring. This center might contain photographic timelines with simple captions that chronicle two or three life stages of children or their teachers. Another thematic center includes a globe and "Celebrating Differences and Similarities."

Teacher's Instructional Center   A pre-kindergarten child who has made his own picture book with felt-tipped colored pens dictates narrative as the teacher records his brief comments beside each picture. They are seated at a curved table in the corner, with the teacher's chair positioned so that she can observe the entire classroom. From time to time, the teacher circulates around the room and invites small groups or individuals to meet her at this table. She uses such meetings to model new skills and provides activities for children to pursue independently while she works with other children.

Some centers—such as blocks, socio-dramatic, arts studio, drawing/writing, science laboratory, computers, listening center, and library—are permanent with refreshing, different contents. Others are temporary or revisited, such as water play, ramping, cooking, woodworking, or thematic contents.

Notice that there has been no mention until this moment of basal readers, textbooks, or worksheets. So-called "adopted" programs offer several deficits:

- They do not adapt to the variety of children's past experiences or present learning needs.
- They disenfranchise the teacher as a professional by providing scripted, uniform delivery.
- Workbook pages test but do not teach.
- Scripted materials limit possibilities for expanding experiences.

The Teacher's Activities

When the picture book maker returns to the writing area, the teacher helps another child begin a two-sided sewing card in the arts center. She also obtains additional gummed paper for a collage maker, adjusts wire for a hanging mobile construction, and hangs a child's finished 12-by-18-inch painting on a bulletin board that contains an unoccupied oak tag frame.

When she sees that everybody seems reasonably occupied and can be expected to continue their activities for a while, she sits in the mathematics area with four children, the balance scale, some standard weights, and a blindfold. The weights, while all the same size, are marked differently according to their densities. The teacher explains that she is isolating the weight from its appearance and helping these children develop seriation skills, ordering first two, then three, then five weights.

She further explains to the visitor that she plans parallel activities with other materials. For example, they have also placed first three, then four, then five pictures in sequence based upon size. Later they have matched them, using one-to-one correspondence. The teacher had mounted pictures that have included seriating shoes, then aligning with socks; and dogs with feeding bowls of different sizes.

However, the teacher continues to note that the published materials are teaching conveniences. The children have many seriation experiences in their everyday lives, such as comparing sizes of berries, toys, sticks, houses, body parts, and people. This teacher has also constructed a series of cylinders using discarded paper rolls, plastic containers, lids, and buttons. She reflects that the longer school day makes it possible for her to provide, in varied forms, several experiences with a concept and to plan alternatives for those children who need them. She has time to work with small groups in mathematics board games, playing phonemic games, and, for those who need it, sorting pictures on the basis of their contrasting initial sounds.

Table 1.1 summarizes the way in which one teacher alternated direct, planned teaching and circulating around the room. While she circulated, she engaged in a variety of organizational and fleeting teaching functions, which are listed within each time period. As she circulated, she nodded at children and occasionally took a photograph of youngsters at work.

While each teacher plans ahead and prepares materials, some of the most valuable learning takes place in a teacher's spontaneous awareness of a "teachable" moment. Re-planning on the spot, doing "fleeting" teaching, asking an interested and helpful question, and matching the child's need with an appropriate activity or bringing two children together are some of the skills that the teacher uses. In this respect, the teacher in an all-day program has more opportunity for learning a great deal by being a sensitive observer, listener, recorder, and assessor of children's readiness for a range of experiences.

TABLE 1.1 The Teacher's Flow Map

Activity	*Circulation*
8:50	8:52
Children arrive together	Store personal materials
Greeting (shakes each child's hand and looks for	Assist with materials
any unusual health sign or behavior)	Appreciate
Store personal effects, sit on floor facing chart paper	Question
	Answer questions
9:00	9:15
Children formally shake hands with a child on each	
side, look at each other, and say, "Good morning, Tim."	
"Good morning, Al."	
Whole-group planning chart; review of the day's	
schedule, setting picture-label cards into pocket chart	Assist with materials
Meeting area (record activities for the day and who	Encourage
begins where)	

TABLE 1.1 Continued

Activity	Circulation
[**Procedural note:** After asking each group to plan aloud (or by drawing) what they plan to do and recording their names, the teacher sends one group at a time to their first activity.]	
	Observe Answer questions
9:27	9:40
Science area (water activity) Pre-K: Children explore pouring items of equivalent size but different shapes Kgn: Children use an egg–timer to race boats attached to balloons after the teacher demonstrates and asks them to make predictions	
	Redirect social behavior Assist with materials Appreciate children's art work and writing Take a digital photograph of a block construction Question; writes child's comment on her hand–held computer Fleeting teaching
[**Procedural note:** The teacher collects individuals for the 9:45 group as she circulates around the room. She knows that speaking to one child at a time will keep down the sound level.]	
9:45	10:05
Teacher's instructional area (writing group)	Record keeping Assessment of 3 children's drawing/writing
Pre-K: Children dictate a statement as the teacher writes verbatim on their illustration	
[**Procedural note**: The teacher sits beside each child so that the child can observe the writing at the same baseline rather than upside down.]	
Kgn: Children read what they have written.	
	Fleeting teaching Display child's work Help children plan ahead Encourage Assist at snack table
10:14	10:30
Mathematics area (balance scale: seriation; recording findings)	Help children plan ahead Mediate; highlight a contrast

TABLE 1.1 Continued

Activity	Circulation
	Redirect social behavior
	Encourage questions
	Appreciate
	Do record keeping about 4 children
10:32	10:35
Add items for seriation	Close-down, 5 minutes' notice, circulate, begin with socio-dramatic and arts areas

[**Procedural note:** The teacher staggers notice of cleanup time and then cleanup time in order to: keep down sound level; respect their need to plan closure; and assess what individuals might share with the group.]

Activity	Circulation
	Appreciate
	Answer questions
	10:40
	Redirect children to meeting area; cleanup details
10:50	10:50
Whole-group sharing	Do record keeping
Clap syllables in the names of 5 children	
11:05	
Leave for gym class (indoors or outdoors, weather permitting)	
11:40	
Whole-group read-aloud story (teacher reads); meeting area	
12:00 Lunch in school lunchroom, then to playground	
	12:50
	Assist with books for silent independent reading
12:52	
Teacher's instructional area	(N.B. Science, socio-dramatic, woodworking, and art areas are closed.)
(small-group reading instruction)	
Pre-K: Children sort objects that rhyme into small drawers Kgn: Children play a board game with a spinner that uses cards based on a modeled set of contrasting words (Chapter 10 provides details)	
	1:10
	Redirect reading groups
	Update record keeping
	Close-down notice to form a puppetry group

TABLE 1.1 Continued

Activity	*Circulation*
1:12	1:24
Socio-dramatic center	Assess
(puppetry group and tape recorder; play	Encourage
development and values discussion)	Appreciate
1:28	
Teacher's instructional area	
Pre-K: Sorting rhyming miniature objects into	Take first turn after saying
some pairs, e.g., a carpenter's box	bee–tree; head–bed
Kgn: Reading group phonemic skill instruction game	Take first turn after reading
(Chapter 10 provides details)	the model chart; provide
	ongoing coaching as needed,
	then circulate while children
	continue the game
	Observe; fleeting teaching;
	provide additional drawing
	and writing materials
	1:35
	Refocus reading group by
	taking a turn, then circulate
	1:52
1:54	Observe
Teacher's instructional area	
Pre-K: Demonstrates concentration/memory/pairs	
card game, with labeled picture pairs shaped like carrots	
Children place the "carrot" pairs into the "hungry	
rabbit's basket"	
1:56	
Kgn: Individual reading with three children in turn,	Re-plan
alternating circulation)	Answer questions
	Do record keeping
1:58	2:05
Second child	Appreciate, question, re-plan
	Do record keeping
2:10	2:15
Third child	Appreciate question, re-plan
	Do record keeping
	Close-down, 5 minutes'
	notice
	Appreciate
2:20	
Whole-group activity; meeting area (teacher	
reads poem from large chart)	
Lists children's comments	
Sing sea songs (teacher plays guitar)	
2:50	
End of day	

Observing the Child's Day

So far, our visit has looked at the teacher's flow of activity, but now let us replay the day by following two children through their experience of it. As teachers, we need to pay attention to the way children perceive their day. In this way we have a better chance of learning what activities children are asking for through their behavior as well as their overt requests.

Terry, a Hesitant Child

Terry entered the classroom with a stone-like expression, shook hands with minimal eye contact, put a small bag in the shopping bag hung from a name-bearing hook, and brushed past several children until he sat down near the chart paper. When the teacher made eye contact and smiled, Terry nodded grimly in return.

During the group planning, Terry stared at the chart paper, picked at a fingernail, and moved slightly away from another child. When it was time for four children to select a place in the socio-dramatic center, the teacher invited Terry, who shrugged and nodded.

When everyone had dispersed, one group at a time, to their respective areas, Terry remained close to the teacher and told her his plan for starting to build an animal maze, until she walked with him to the socio-dramatic center on her way to the science laboratory. As he began to remove blocks, the teacher smiled encouragingly and moved on. When another child's building grew closer, they merged their constructions. The other child chatted amiably, and Terry offered brief suggestions. Half an hour later, they were cheerfully pouring and drinking juice at the snack table near the sink.

Terry's building partner went to paint at the only open easel, and Terry went to the reading corner the long way around, past the games and media area, the teacher's instructional area, and the science and mathematics areas. As he circulated, he would stop to watch what was happening, listen to a conversation, and pick up and examine various objects along the way.

Table 1.2 shows Terry's movements for the entire day. As we analyze what he did, several patterns become apparent:

- Terry alternately engaged in an activity and then circulated, observed others, and touched materials.
- When not engaged in a clearly social activity, he appeared to seek time alone, for example on a mat or a designated private space, distancing himself from close contact with others.
- Terry made eye contact with the teacher, noting and sometimes returning her smiles.
- He seemed to alternate active and sedentary activities independently.

TABLE 1.2 Terry's Flow Map

Terry's Activity	Teacher Contact
8:50	
Shakes hands with the teacher upon entry	
Stores personal effects; moves name card	
to the "present" pocket chart; sits on floor	Makes eye contact
Faces chart paper for planning session	Smiles
9:00	
Listens	Makes eye contact
	Suggests activity
	Walks alongside Terry to the area, chatting about his plans
9:20	
Socio-dramatic center—blocks; places his	Observes
name on a Velcro spot	Smiles encouragingly, asks a question
9:25	
Parallel play with another child	
9:30	
Builds with other child	Stops at blocks, appreciates, questions
9:55	
Snack table—brings snack from closet;	
shares raisins with other child; conversation	
with other child	
10:05	
Tours the room—observes others;	Passes, smiles, and says, "Think about what
examines and handles materials	you might do next."
10:08	
Reading area—lies on mat with a book	
10:20	
Goes to toilet, then returns to mat and book	
10:30	
Finishes second book and brings a puzzle	Stops to look at Terry's book; discusses
to the mat	briefly
10:50	
Whole-group sharing	Asks Terry and other block builder to
Chatting alongside block building	talk about their structure; writes out
companion as group gathers	large labels for parts; Terry places labels on parts
11:05	
Gym class—passes ball over head; Terry	Gym teacher says, "OK, Terry!"
blushes as he takes the lead position	
Laughing as he participates in vigorously	
shaking parachute with entire group	
Jogs around outside of gym	Gym teacher makes eye contact
11:40	
Drinks water at classroom fountain	

TABLE 1.2 Continued

Terry's Activity	Teacher Contact
Listens to story	Makes eye contact
Silent during discussion	
12:00	
Lunchroom—keeps distance from others at food line; eats quickly, then slowly, looking at children across the table	
12:25	
Playground—jogs; asks aide for a ball; bounces and plays catch with another child; after ball is replaced, the children roll themselves along incline and giggle	Aide provides ball
12:52	
Teacher's instructional area with five other children	Teacher models word games, plays with children, gives feedback as they play together
1:10	
Plays word card games twice with other children	Leaves group, with writing follow-up
1:20	
Copies words from cards into personal notebook, which remains in teacher's area	Appreciates
1:28	
Goes to toilet	
Easel—paints two pictures; hangs them on rack to dry	Observes quietly
2:00	
Washes paint from hands with lots of suds	2:02
	Unties smock in passing
2:05	
Table games area—observes children; when they finish a game and one leaves, the other invites Terry to play a board game with dice; they play, with comments (the game requires adding the dice in order to move the game piece)	2:15 Stops, observes, appreciates Asks a question
2:20	
Whole-group meeting	Leads discussion
Terry offers addition to list; sings along with group, taking deep breaths	Appreciates and asks Terry to tell more about undertow
2:50	
Keeps distance as group gathers to leave room	Smiles and nods

It is important to notice that the flexible structure of this setting made it possible for Terry to choose many activities independently. In turn, the teacher could see when Terry needed the social potential of the socio-dramatic center and adapted her plans by suggesting and encouraging his activity. It was comfortable for him to receive her suggestion because there were many other times when he could make independent choices.

When a teacher schedules and plans most of a child's time, there is less opportunity for that child to feel capable, independent, and responsible. When a teacher changes activities frequently in other, more rigid settings, children learn not to invest their energies in school activities because the activities change too soon. There is a sense that just as they begin to get involved in something, they are interrupted.

By contrast, in this setting Terry could invest attention because his teacher had allowed for long blocks of time. When some people say that young children have short attention spans, therefore, we need to ask ourselves, "To what?" Young children can spend as long as an hour doing something to which they feel committed. The all-day scheduling provides an opportunity for this kind of active scholarship.

Pat, an Impulsive, Sociable Child

The crash of a paint can, the clatter of a long-handled brush, and calls for help from Pat punctuated the arts studio. At that very moment, the teacher was helping a group of seven children in the nearby science area to organize materials for experimenting with water absorption. She made sympathetic eye contact with Pat, whose pained expression was noticed by other children in the area. One child who was coming from the water fountain brought a large sponge and handed it to Pat, who recoiled for a moment after accepting it.

By the time the teacher had disengaged herself from the science area activities, Pat had artfully smeared paint over several square feet of linoleum floor beyond the newspapers that were spread under the easel. The teacher helped her rinse the sponge and brought more newspapers to cover the wet area. Her sympathetic, matter-of-fact, helpful attitude helped Pat to relax about the mishap. Pat eventually carried fresh paints to the easel, and the teacher returned to the science laboratory.

Pat painted one picture and hung the painting to dry. She gave her hands a fast splash of water and a casual wipe on her jeans on the way to the snack table. She stopped off to pick up an apple from the shopping bag labeled with her name and immediately entered into a brisk discussion of a television character's pratfalls with the other children at the snack table.

Table 1.3 traces Pat's movements in this classroom.

TABLE 1.3 Pat's Flow Map

Pat's Activity	Teacher Contact
8:50	
Shakes hands with the teacher	8:52
Playfully tackles another child	Engages in conversation, nods, smiles
Approaches the teacher with some news	Makes eye contact
about home and stores personal items; moves	
name card to the "present" pocket chart;	
sits next to another child and converses;	
turns toward chart paper for planning	
session after teacher begins the whole-group	
meeting	
9:00	
Listens, comments to adjacent children	Makes eye contact
occasionally, and raises hand to choose	Responds to Pat's comments; asks
the art studio	other children to respond to Pat's idea
9:30	
Art studio—drops paint materials, cleans up,	Makes eye contact
paints, speaks to child on the other side	Assists with materials
of the easel from time to time	
9:50	
Snack area	Assists with materials
Speaking animatedly with another snacker	
Cleans up	Invites Pat to join her in the
	mathematics area
10:14	
Mathematics area	Helps children plan ahead
(balance scale: seriation; recording findings)	Mediates; highlights a contrast
	Asks children to predict, estimate,
	explore, and compare
	Redirects social behavior
	Encourages questions; appreciates
	Does record keeping about 4 children
	Leaves the children with estimating and
	comparing game with a die
10:32	10:35
Laying out materials with partner and	Close-down, 5 minutes' notice,
outlining chart on sequence	circulates, beginning with socio-
	dramatic and arts
	Appreciates
	Answers questions
	10:40
	Redirects children to meeting area;
	clean up details

TABLE 1.3 Continued

Pat's Activity	Teacher Contact
10:50	
Ambles to whole-group sharing with mathematics partner and chart, partially completed	Asks Pat and partner to show group their chart and explain their next steps Does record keeping
11:05	
Goes to toilet, then joins the last of the children on their way to the gym	
Gym class—jogs around gym and joins the end of the ball-passing group, chatting to child in front; races to take a place next to mathematics partner for the parachute, laughs hard, occasionally dropping an edge	Gym teacher redirects Pat
11:40	
Slides into space in front of teacher and tells her about the parachute	Teacher smiles, listens, questions, and comments appreciatively
Listens intently to story; comments during discussion	
12:00	
Lunch room—chatting and jostling with other children; talks throughout the meal, sucking noisily at the straw in the milk container	
12:18	
Playground—climbs on apparatus with several others, pretending space travel	Aide cautions holding on with both hands
12:50	
Reading area—shares armchair with mathematics partner as they look together at a book, pointing, and commenting quietly	Assists with books for silent, independent reading Nods encouragement
1:10	
Goes to toilet, then puts on earphones at media center	
1:25	
Looks up as teacher places hand on shoulder; listens	Gives notice for instructional group by circulating
1:28	
Teacher's instructional area with 4 other children (reading group phonemic skill instruction game)	Teacher takes the first turn after reading the model chart and provides ongoing coaching as needed, then circulates while children continue the game 1:35 Refocuses the reading group by taking a turn, then circulates

TABLE 1.3 Continued

Pat's Activity	Teacher Contact
1:50 Pat uses materials in the writing area and writes new words in her notebook. She writes in her log section, using invented spellings. 2:09	
Brings notebook to teacher's instructional area Takes a drink of water and heads directly to another child who is playing with Tangrams; comments and makes suggestions 2:20	Nods, smiles, and says, "Think about what you might do next."
Joins whole-group activity, shoving in closer to the teacher; contributes to the discussion and sings along, swaying with the children on either side 2:50	Comments, records children's comments on chart, appreciates, and asks questions
End of day	Smiles and holds eye contact

This flexible schedule gave Pat the opportunity to bounce along, expressing her enthusiastic, chatty exuberance in many ways. She sought out contacts with others, and these were often available. Her needs to be social, to be noticed by the teacher, and to have ready access to personal routines were met in this setting. But even sociable Pat took some time alone with the earphones and a book in the reading area. The teacher, recognizing and accepting Pat's social activity, provided a balance in the reading group, where individual work, manipulation of materials, and sharing were involved.

Less reflective, seemingly more confident than Terry, Pat went directly to such activities as the easel and "Tangrams" (Elementary Science Study, 1976). For both children, the classroom offered intellectual challenges as well as exploratory, joyful activities.

Reflections

As you reflect on this experiential, all-day visit, imagine hearing what is happening. There is conversing: children with other children, and the teacher with individuals and small groups of children. There is a rather steady buzz of meaningful sound. Occasionally, you hear a dramatic exclamation or the clatter of fallen materials. As a visitor, you feel welcome but not necessarily noticed. Children seem to be involved in their activities and with one another as the teacher listens responsively to children's comments. The teacher seems to be enjoying the children and the active pace.

Sometimes you see individual children or the teacher observing, perhaps while walking around. Sometimes you see a child lie on a mat with a book, savoring a few moments of solitude, or sit alone to write, draw, read, or manipulate objects. At other times, children seek out one another or the teacher.

Teacher and children learn from one another. They live in relation to one another, the behavior of each one influencing the actions of the others. This is a shift in emphasis from the traditional setting in which children are loyally polite to the teacher as an "authority," or where children are "honest" and become "problems." Maria Montessori's (1965) pioneering conception can serve us well: the children should not learn for the love of the teacher or for fear of the teacher, but for the love of the learning. When children have the opportunity to learn for the love of the learning, they experience a sense of power, competence, and well-being. Chapter 2 describes how teachers might organize classrooms so that children can feel joyful in school and learn for the sake of learning, in fulfillment of their natural sense of curiosity and their need to make connections.

2

ORGANIZING FOR INDEPENDENCE

Introduction

If you look at any group of children, even a group labeled as homogeneous, it is apparent that youngsters arrive with different experiences, capacities, and needs. This chapter focuses on how you could organize the learning centers discussed in Chapter 1 in order to work with children who have different needs.

Beginning with the first days of school, you and your 18 to 25 children come to share an understanding of how to live together in the artificial box called a classroom during a full school day. The way you organize a classroom during the day reflects what you value about individual children's commitments to meaning. It is useful to look at how you and your children decide on the procedures that follow:

- Choices—what children will be doing.
- Space—where they will be doing it.
- Pacing—when and for how long they will be engaged.
- Social activity—how and with whom they will interact.

Beginnings: Choices

As an exemplary early childhood teacher, you need to make thoughtful plans for activities and provide educational materials ahead of time. You would also filter the activities and materials that children bring from home for use in school, after sharing criteria with families ahead of time.

Young children are quite capable of making relevant choices from among the activities that you provide. When they choose what they will be doing, they feel committed to the activity and take responsibility for their actions. Therefore, beginning with the first days of school, you should help children make informed choices. For example, during a brief whole-group greeting, children: (1) hear about and see the location of the three or four activity centers in which they will engage; and (2) understand the routine of raising their hand to indicate that they are ready to have you see what they have done. After you circulate to talk about and appreciate their activity, you can (3) remind them how to replace materials or transition to the next center. For example, "What will you do next? There is space at the library, art studio, puzzle table, and building center." When you repeatedly model questions about procedures and planning, they being to ask themselves questions: "What will I do with this activity?" "What will I do when I finish this?" "What will I do next?" "Where is there space?"

As the school year progresses, you would adapt the plans for different children. A real choice is an informed choice. An informed choice is an activity to which children are receptive and that they can pursue at a level of challenge or possible success. For example, you might say, "These are the activities with which we can begin the work period." Box 2.1 lists several things to think about when you plan with children to make choices of which they are capable.

BOX 2.1 DEGREES OF CHOICE IN PLANNING

- *What:* Children self-select an activity, from those that you prepare: "What would you like to do to start your day?" "How will you begin?" [*Plan*]
- *How many:* "We can have four people at the science laboratory water table." "Who else would like to join Deborah?" "How will you begin?" [*Plan*]
- *Either–or:* You might invite some children to select from among a limited range of choices: "Ben, would you prefer to begin with the weather station or the woodworking?" "Eden, you haven't been in the art studio or the socio-dramatic center for a while now. Please choose one or the other." "What will you do first?" [*Plan*]
- *Now or later:* When a child has not engaged in a particular activity in recent times: "Do you want to finish the project you began yesterday now or later today?" If the child reasonably prefers to do something else, then you might offer the choice of now or later: "Alec, you had some writing to finish. When do you plan to finish it today?"
- *Now is the time:* "You have not painted for a long time. Today, you can begin to paint at the easel or the table." Alternative: "Please join the Cuisenaire group with me to start the morning. We are doing some guessing games." Or, "Mel, we will be starting the day with a bingo card

game. You are ready for it now after doing so many games with dominoes. " (Even at the level of "now is the time," it is possible that if Mel has a pressing need to work in a different center, you respect his plan and feelings and include him in the card game with another group at a specific time.)

Notice in Box 2.1 some ways that you can help children *plan* what they will do. Then, they *do* it. You can follow up by talking about what they accomplish (*review* or *revisit* it). Early childhood educators appreciate the HighScope/Perry Preschool curriculum practice with pre-kindergarten children as they engage in the meaningful practice of "plan–do–review" for part of each day (Schweinhart et al., 2005, p. 36). This practice also supports the development of dual-language learners (Espinosa, 2010, p. 47). After routines are well established, children can plan their activity period beyond the first activity. Each child could fill in their

IMAGE 2.1 Velcro System for Available Center Space

individual plan for what they plan to do in each of the centers present on a preprinted picture-and-word outline of centers for the day (Bodrova & Leong, 2007, p. 61).

Where there is limited space in a center, some pre-kindergarten and kindergarten teachers use various signals to ensure that children have enough access to materials. Some provide a limited number of felt patches on which the children can place their Velco-backed name/picture cards. Others fix a limited number of hooks on which children may place their name/picture that is hung from a yarn loop. Still others use clothespins marked with each child's name that fit on a marked piece of cardboard in each center. Some teachers post a number card with a specific number or marks and numerals so that a child who wants to enter an area can match the marks, one-to-one, against the number of children already there. Children are also able to see if a center sign indicates that the center is closed. Some kindergarten teachers attempt to keep track of center use by asking children to place a mark next to their own name in the area (e.g., computer center) or on a personal record sheet of centers. It is noteworthy that most pre-kindergarten children are capable of independently and smoothly using the system of Velcro patches or hooks within the first month of the school year.

As a rule, after six to eight weeks during which you consistently plan together and circulate, reminding children of how to manage their activities, children can carry on without your continuous supervision. After building a foundation of routines, you will be able to engage in small group and individual interactions with children for brief periods of time, confident that the other children are productive

IMAGE 2.2 Necklace System on Hooks for Available Center Space

and safe. In any case, it is important to position yourself so that you can see the entire room. However, if you were unable to monitor ongoing work, even after several months together, you would not send a child who has trouble sharing to the carpentry bench, which requires close teacher supervision. [**Procedural note:** The most important support for this system takes place when you take the time to *circulate* before and after each brief instructional time in order to keep in touch with the entire class as individuals and small groups work together].

When routines and traffic patterns flow smoothly, you could offer children additional choices. For example, children are able to vote on which favorite books to re-read first. When possible, you might ask children to choose between a sequence of events as well as one or another board game or software topic. All legitimate opportunities to make choices help to empower children and to make them develop a stronger connection to the school community. It simply feels good to feel respected and trusted. *The opportunity to make choices also helps youngsters build self-regulation, independence, and resilience.*

Space Supports Independence

How you organize the space in your classroom communicates how independent and responsible you really want children to be. It also communicates what kinds of activities you value and how children will spend their time. For example, if the chairs and tables are lined up in one direction facing a whiteboard/chalkboard, it would seem that you expect children to focus on you and the board or materials on their individual desks rather than on cooperative work with others. This placement also signals that a major activity will be to sit at assigned seats and work with paper and pencil for much of the day. This kind of setup means that materials are in areas other than where children will use them. Therefore, traffic jams take place when children need to acquire materials independently, or you or a monitor will need to distribute materials to passive recipients who need to wait. Waiting, in turn, is an invitation to mischief.

Exemplary programs arrange space differently, placing materials where children will use them. This way, books are in the library center, writing/drawing materials and children's individual writing/drawing notebooks are in the writing/drawing area, art supplies in the art studio, science materials in the laboratory, and so forth. Children can find old newspapers where potential messes are likely. Children work in the area where the materials reside. From time to time during the year, you could change the focus or size of one area or another in order to highlight new concepts or underutilized materials. Active work centers are located at a distance from those parts of the room in which children can concentrate and reflect.

Children can get materials independently when the materials are in the center where they work. The only time they would need to ask you for help might be when materials run low unexpectedly or when unanticipated events suggest the need for things that are not present.

There is no designated "front" to the classroom, just as there are no assigned seats or tables. Children should store their personal materials in a number of ways, other than in desks, as is outlined in Box 2.2.

BOX 2.2 PERSONAL STORAGE WITHOUT INDIVIDUAL DESKS

- Cubbies/lockers
- Clothing closets
- Center-based storage, e.g., drawing/writing notebooks in the writing center
- Shopping bags hung from clothes hooks or the backs of chairs
- Storage drawer cabinets
- Shelves marked with children's names and photos
- Teacher-created "mailboxes" made of empty ice cream cylinders or large cans nailed together
- Transparent shirt boxes
- Empty commercial tea containers

You can use a variety of furniture to create spatial divisions, nooks, and areas that define functions. You can place low bookshelves, screens, and your desk perpendicular to the wall, which creates areas in which children can feel part of a smaller group, focus on a particular activity, or even find a place to be alone. Consider the design of a classroom as a variation on L-shaped arrangements or a configuration resembling perpendicular Es (i.e., set back to back).

When children see areas for limited use, they can be more independent because it helps them answer the self-directing questions "What will I do next?" and "Where will I put this when I finish?" Limited-use centers have labels for everyone to see, such as "Art Studio" or "Cyclical Change Center" or "Science Laboratory" or "Writing/Drawing." Labels also help parents and other adults who enter the room to understand what is going on.

When you establish a center for limited purposes, it is useful to ask yourself what you would need to use if you were a child in that area. Writing/drawing materials, for example, are available in more than one "writing/drawing" area. In addition to content, consider the needs for privacy, participation, and social activity when placing furnishings and materials.

A good environment invites children to learn. Therefore, you can be a legitimate merchandiser of significant activities. Some advertising techniques you can use include those listed in Box 2.3.

BOX 2.3 ADVERTISE INVITATIONS TO LEARNING

- Create an aesthetically attractive setting with such things as incandescent lamps, dried flowers, mirrors, draped fabric, or funny hats. Contrast a focal figure against an uncluttered ground.
- Use a redundant product image and name, including different colors, print size, and negative space; attach meaningful objects to a stuffed toy or driftwood.
- Change the packaging, name, or location of a product or a service: for example, from chemicals to "mystery powder"; from a coffee can to a gift-wrapped box; from along a wall to a central location. Change the props in the socio-dramatic center to reflect a class experience, such as a food shop, post office, or medical facility.
- Add cardboard, miniature figures, photographs, rulers, graph paper, or tickets to the block building area.
- Enlarge an underutilized area or change the location.
- Add a prestigious material, such as mechanical colored pencils or flashlights.

Space should be comfortable as well as inviting. Since young children feel comfortable on the floor, legitimize it for them. Arrange for the school, parents, or local businesses to provide mats or carpet remnants. Also consider using commercial carpet in the block-building center, in order to cut down on noise. Other ways to make space inviting include providing a variety of seating arrangements beyond institutional chairs. Some classrooms include one or more soft armchairs or a donated couch. Occasionally a small set of stairs for sprawling, a window seat, cushions, or a five-sided packing crate are also present.

Pacing and Routines

When children engage in different activities, or when they are doing the same thing, you can expect that different children will need different amounts of time to finish their tasks. As you circulate throughout the classroom, you will notice who is nearly finished and who may need more materials, a more varied activity, or additional tasks. When you anticipate children's attention spans, you can help individuals or groups to re-plan for their next activity or for a new phase of the current activity. In this way, modeling the need to re-plan or breaking down a task into sub-parts, you also reinforce the children's independent involvement.

For children who have problems with focus or special learning needs, you simply re-plan more frequently. For such children, initial planning might also include locating a space in which they can focus without distractions, such as a study carrel arrangement with folders or a cardboard box, or simply seated facing a wall. When working near other children, these children need sufficient space in order to avoid unintended destruction and spills. Some children who are labeled as having an "attention-deficit hyperactivity disorder" can benefit from such planning and monitoring. If you notice a few children who appear to be distracted or are distracting to others during group meetings, you might reflect on whether the group meeting is too long or the content less than relevant. You can also plan separately for an alternative activity with an individual child before a large-group meeting. It is supportive of the potentially disruptive child and helpful to the focus of the whole group when you plan ahead of time for individual needs. The other children recognize that individuals have different needs. However, if others are also distracted during the whole-group meeting, then you need to use a more relevant backup plan to engage the group fully.

During the full day, there might be whole-group planning times at the beginning of the morning and afternoon, and perhaps a shorter gathering around eleven o'clock. Also, at the close of a center time, it is useful for children to share (*review/ revisit*) what they have done with the whole group, a small group, or another child; they can learn from one another as well as provide a time for you to assess their accomplishments. Then again, you will do frequent mini-planning with individuals and small groups throughout the day, as you circulate during center-time blocks.

Successful all-day teachers find that it is critical to plan at least two long blocks of center-based activity time each day. During these times, children can engage in different degrees of choice and self-pacing. With enough time, children can feel encouraged to make longer-range plans and increase their relative sense of personal control.

Some activities occur at the same time each day, but others depend on the pace of groups or the needs of individual children. Successful teachers anticipate routine occurrences and develop strategies for handling them in ways that minimize demands on the teacher's attention and help children to be increasingly independent.

Cleanup Time

From the first day of school, children are able to learn how to replace equipment or materials independently so that they can find them again and so that other people can use them. Teachers help children build independence by suggesting that they repeatedly ask themselves the question "Where will I put this when I finish with it?" During the first days, a teacher might suggest that only "very capable" helpers can assist in replacing materials while explaining the need for keeping materials and equipment in their correct places for the next users. Replacing materials can then become a prestigious activity. Teachers outline places on shelves where blocks fit and the places on pegboards for woodworking tools or musical instruments. In these ways, cleanup becomes a matching activity—part of spatial and geographic development. You could color code the backs of puzzle pieces that go together and label book boxes by topic. If you notice a child's hesitancy at cleanup, try to focus on the positive and ask whether she plans to begin by replacing the larger or smaller blocks.

You can show respect for the children's need to concentrate by circulating with the reminder "Finish what you are doing because it will be cleanup time in a few minutes," then following this with "Now is the time to put away the materials." Alert those children who have the biggest cleanup job to do first, and leave those who have little more to do than finish looking at pictures or reading a sentence until last. This way, you are less likely to have children with little to clean up wandering aimlessly and getting into mischief.

This brief procedure also serves to keep down the sound level of the room because you are addressing only the few children who need a message rather than calling across the classroom. Within this procedure, you also have enough time to appreciate what children are doing without the children feeling under pressure of time.

When you circulate, this is also a good time to assess what future help or instruction children may need. After most children have finished their work and before cleanup, you can take a few moments for the whole group to focus briefly on the different accomplishments of small groups and individuals, appreciating efforts and progress as well as finished work. You can encourage children who are less inclined to take risks to try new kinds of materials by pointing them toward work in progress and projects in various stages of completion.

In summary, Box 2.4 presents some teaching activities that can take place while you circulate.

BOX 2.4 TEACHING ACTIVITIES WHEN YOU CIRCULATE

- *Fleeting teaching*—Bring another element to compare.
- *Assessing, evaluating*—Consider what intentional teaching the child might need next when you plan a small-group session.
- *Record keeping*—Keep in mind four-for-the-day or any number in order to make note of a child's activities.
- *Appreciating*—Sometimes, bonding with eye contact, a nod, a smile, a "thumbs-up," or physical nearness is sufficient. It helps to focus on the following: describe what the child is doing/has done, e.g., "That was hard and you did it. Pat yourself on the back!" "What did you do first?" Focusing on the activity and the content helps the child to build self-motivation and independence.

- *Redirecting*—When children are distracted, re-focus with a question: "I wonder what might happen if . . .?"
- *Re-planning*—"When you finish hanging up your painting, what do you plan to do?" or "We will begin your number game group at my table." By bringing children together for small-group instruction while you circulate, you also keep down the volume in the room and respect the scholarship of those children who are concentrating and thinking important thoughts.
- *Mediating*—When children are pushing or using angry voices, ask, "What might be some ways to work this out in a friendly way so that you are both satisfied?"
- *Socialization*—Suggest that a gregarious child sit beside a more reticent child.

Taking the Initiative

One kindergarten teacher begins the year by explaining to the children what it means to take the initiative and develops a badge for a child who does so: "I took the initiative today!" (Kuhn, 2009). The system recognizes any child who notices someone *voluntarily* "taking the initiative," reports it during reflection/review time, and offers a "high five in the sky" to individuals taking the initiative. Some examples of taking the initiative include such helpful acts as the following: independently picking up, stacking, or packing scraps from the floor; helping a friend hang up a completed painting or removing an apron; and helping to put away materials without being asked, even if the child had not used the materials. Only another child can nominate someone: "I have an outstanding friend announcement: Kai took the initiative."

Buddies

Some teachers arrange for pairs, trios, or quartets of children to be buddies. The idea is that, when the teacher is working with a small group or individuals, any child who needs help would first ask their buddies. This process helps to build a sense of community as well as a sense of self-regulation and a wholesome independence from adults. If no buddy can help, or if there is an emergency, the child can come to the teacher for help. When one teacher who uses a buddy system wears a sign around her neck—"Ms. Smith is busy"—that is the signal that the buddy system should be in operation. At the same time, she will sit where she has a full view of the classroom.

Snack

Just as many teachers respect children's need to pace themselves differently when they engage in scholarly tasks, they respect different needs for food, privacy, rest, and toileting. When it comes to snack, more and more all-day teachers set out a snack table around midmorning. Often a few children prepare and set out the snack with the teacher, and they can eat their snack when they need it, much as they would at home. Some teachers also place a "menu" sample, picture, or picture-with-word instruction, such as a picture of four carrot sticks. As children become able, teachers place two picture-with-word cards indicating two items on one card and one item on the other.

The practice of integrating snacks during center time eliminates the time spent in transition from an activity period (close-down, transition, and startup) and permits children to move at their own paces. Change and transitions create time for disorder and trouble while also reducing time for scholarship.

Since children learn this snack routine very quickly, there is not usually a problem of mass attack at the snack table. Children learn that they will first wash

IMAGE 2.3 Snack Table Center: Children Pour Juice, "Take Two" Crackers, and Spread Homemade Peanut Butter

their hands and that the snack will still be there for them as others vacate the chairs. In those places where children bring a snack from home, consider listing for parents those foods that you recommend for their nutritional value, such as fruits, vegetables, cereals, and baked goods that are free of sugar, artificial color, and flavoring. Some teachers ask parents to contribute a rotating set of specified raw materials from which some children can prepare their own nutritional snacks for the group.

If you plan a separate snack time for the entire group, consider sitting at a table in order to have conversations with the children. In preparation, children can count the number of napkins to set out (supporting counting) and place name cards at each chair (supporting reading).

Toileting

Toileting should also be self-directed rather than scheduled. At most, before reading a story aloud, you could suggest that anybody needing to use the toilet should do so before the story begins, in order not to miss anything or disrupt the attention of the group. It is a message to you that the story might be inappropriate or too long if children need to leave for the toilet during the reading. In a related way, it is essential that all children use the toilet before leaving on a trip outdoors. Some children benefit from practicing handwashing while thinking of the words to "Happy Birthday" after using the toilet.

Transitions

When everybody needs to get a jacket from the wardrobe or cubbies for outdoor play or at the end of the day, you might invite children "whose names begin with the same sound as Sam's and Sally's" or those "who are wearing red today" to get their clothing at the same time. This practice cuts down on stampedes and traffic jams, and it provides a gender-neutral way to address people (other than "boys and girls").

There are some unavoidable occasions when children must wait briefly for others during transitions from one activity or area to another. Box 2.5 describes some constructive devices that might be employed during such times.

BOX 2.5 TRANSITIONS AND WAITING

- After cleanup or other times when children need to gather, one or two children might be lagging. When you want to get the attention of a few laggards in order to prepare for the next activity, consider singing, "Franny wears a blue shirt, blue shirt, blue shirt, all day long." This sometimes helps Franny or a different child to focus on joining the group.

- Recite a brief poem from memory that fits the mood or occasion.
- Lowering your voice, say, "I have a secret in my pocket. What might it be? I have something that I can use to go shopping and it rhymes with honey/opens a door and rhymes with bee/something that came off my coat and I didn't have time to sew on yet." [**Procedural note:** Lowering your voice can attract attention during transitions as well as during group discussions.]
- Provide a word and ask children to create a sentence: "What could we say about chocolate/birthdays/sleep/airplanes?" "What could we ask Sponge Bob/Pokemon character?" Provide a few words that rhyme and ask children to add to the list.
- Play "Simon Says."
- Begin a finger play.
- Sing a song.
- Say you are thinking of a number and ask the children to guess it (Clements & Sarama, 2009a, p. 54).
- Clap syllables, and ask children to guess whose name fits.
- Ask children to "Think about something that makes you happy."
- If preparing to leave the classroom, display an unusual photograph or piece of art, change it frequently, and ask the children to imagine, for example, "What if you were part of the picture. Where would you like to be?" or "What might have happened just before this photograph was taken?" or "What might have happened just after?"
- Before leaving the classroom, offer an image of how children might stealthily move through the school: "Let's imagine that we are walking on marshmallows/cotton/eggshells; that each of us is inside a bubble; that we are invisible." [**Procedural note:** To avoid a crush of everybody moving at once, invite children by their birthday month, by catching a ball, or if they are not wearing sneakers, a more demanding concept that helps build inhibitory skill.]

Emergency Signal

There are times when you need the immediate attention of the entire group, especially when there is an emergency. When you share a signal, and use it only rarely, children are likely to respond right away.

From the first day of school you can demonstrate: "When you see my arms up like this, or anybody else's arms up (as in the 'halt' position), then look to see where I am and raise your arms for others to see. I will use this signal only when we have to do something very important right away or when there is an emergency. Let us see how everyone does this. Wow, you learned that signal really quickly."

Raising both arms has the effect of stopping activity and producing a quieter atmosphere. Also, using a body signal eliminates the problem of trying to find a piano, bell, or light switch that may not always be at hand, such as when you are outdoors. Moreover, it eliminates the need to shout across everyone, thereby keeping a calm atmosphere.

Schedule

The hours as well as the length of the all-day pre-kindergarten and kindergarten need consideration. In one school district, for example, the bus company dictates that the early childhood center must begin at 9:30 a.m. However, many of the children tend to wake up very early and have already been active for two or three hours before school begins. Then, by afternoon, they seem to need more time on their own (S. Terens, personal communication, 1984). It makes sense to start the school day when children are most active and social, and to send them home earlier.

It is also advisable to pace the day so that, after the initial planning and activity period, more active choices alternate with more sedentary ones. Professional teachers notice that children are able to concentrate better after active play rather than quiet activity (Baines & Blatchford, 2011). It is not wise to string several whole-group listening activities together any more than it is to over-stimulate children with whole-group large-muscle activities one after another.

When you schedule long time blocks in which children can choose among varied activities, they will naturally develop the stimulation sequence that they need, just as Pat, one of our case examples in Chapter 1, did. Such scheduling can relieve the pressure in the half-day schedule to "fit in" the varied program components while helping with boots and sweaters in two classes. The longer school day makes more relaxed scheduling practical, both outdoors and inside. It is also important to plan lunch, recreation, rest, and relaxation in consistent ways that sustain the wholesome pacing of activity throughout the day.

Lunch

Your school may provide food for children at lunchtime or may simply offer milk and juice for sale. It is important for someone to escort the children to lunch if they do not dine in the classroom. [**Procedural note:** If you are not the escort, then it is helpful if the escort spends some time with the children in the classroom in order to smooth the transition.] During the first week of an all-day schedule, you might be the one to do this in order to provide a smooth transition.

An alternative to the cafeteria arrangement in any school is to have children take turns bringing and serving food "family-style" at their tables when lunch is available in the school. If children bring lunch from home, they might take turns serving milk or juice and setting the table, even if only with napkins. These activities reinforce one-to-one correspondence and number concepts. It is also preferable for children to sit at smaller tables rather than at tables for 20 or more. This encourages conversation and a sense of belonging.

Recreation/Recess

Following lunch, and before rest, many schools have a recreation period in the schoolyard or gymnasium, depending on the weather. As each child finishes lunch, it makes sense for them to have access to an area containing equipment that suits their size and capacities.

Some schools have tricycles, climbing apparatus, and large hollow blocks, both indoors and outdoors. Other equipment for large-muscle use might include a sandbox, gardening tools, balls, hoops, and ropes. When a school plays music for free-form dancing during indoor lunchtimes, some interesting choreography can take place among both girls and boys. The gym teacher or an aide could lead group games, and ball-and-rope games.

When there is enough constructive activity available and several adults who can circulate, converse with children, and appreciate their efforts, children are likely to be constructive and civilized. It is worthwhile to teach lunch-room aides to use positively worded suggestions and instructions, and to speak to nearby children rather than shout to those at a distance. If constructive activities are not present, children might seek stimulation with one another, sometimes in asocial ways.

It is worth asking whether the children perceive that what they are doing at lunchtime is relevant and stimulating. If you find yourself in a school with a tradition of requiring children to stand in line for any length of time, consider finding a teacher ally who can help you plan and implement more appropriate alternatives. Then, children can return to class ready to concentrate and focus their energies constructively. It is this sort of activity—wondering about what is happening and acting on your values—that makes you a professional.

Rest and Relaxation

Even though teachers and children find ways to pace themselves with ongoing active and sedentary pastimes during the all-day schedule, teachers find that it is important to plan ahead and pause for rest, relaxation, and quiet recreation. Let us look for a moment at 4- and 5-year-olds at home. After lunch, what do they usually do? With rare exceptions, it is unusual to find such children taking a regular afternoon nap at home. Consider also how a family deals with inter-age planning when there may be a baby, toddler, pre-kindergarten or kindergarten child, and older children at home. Clearly, whoever needs a nap takes a nap. Whoever does not need a nap either engages in independent activity, plays near an adult in the home, or does things with an adult or another child. If somebody is taking a nap, others at home would either move to another area or keep down the volume and avoid sudden noises in order not to wake the sleeper.

These observations may seem quite obvious; nonetheless, some teachers find themselves engaged in lengthy debates about rest-time naps and the discipline problems that arise during this period after lunch. In schools where caring people think about these matters, there is usually a flexible rest time. You, the teacher, also need time to yourself. In some settings, there is a classroom area with mats for the few children who may fall asleep after the others have put away their mats. Often, the quiet/rest time for kindergarten children is about 20 minutes (30 minutes for pre-kindergarteners).

Some children lie on their mats in a dimmed room and listen to recorded music. One week might be Mr. Mozart's week; the next might be Mr. Brahms'. You can see children lying down, sometimes with a stuffed toy, listening and keeping time to the music. In other schools, children might sit or lie while reading a book, playing quiet board or card games with one other child, or doing a puzzle. In summary, different individuals have different needs for quiet time and privacy, so it is sensible to make arrangements to meet these needs throughout much of the day.

Legitimate Social Activity, Privacy, and Participation

The school setting is, at best, contrived. Because of this, it is especially important that you carefully consider providing for private experiences as well as for social participation.

Human beings' need for privacy some of the time and social participation at other times is a personal one. A child at home with one or two siblings often has a favorite place to be alone. Whether this is an armchair, a space behind a couch, underneath a table, or in a bathroom, it is important that it is there.

Young children in school might create privacy spaces under a table or by building walls with "big books" and sit within this construction to read. In your classroom, too, consider how to create places where a child can feel alone when he or she feels the need. Box 2.6 lists additional places for privacy.

In quite as conscious a way, you will need to plan for social interaction that is constructive and for activities that lend themselves naturally to cooperative work. Significant learning, after all, takes place when children interact with one another as well as adults (Piaget et al., 1965; Piaget 1976).

Spontaneous social interaction creates opportunities for repetition of ideas and techniques that children need to learn. Indeed, the oral repetition for children that takes place in cooperative learning situations increases information storage and extends memory (Johnson, Johnson, Holubec, & Roy, 1984; Slavin, 1992). Teachers in exemplary early childhood classrooms plan for significant, independent, small-group learning opportunities.

IMAGE 2.4 Building Privacy with Books

BOX 2.6 PLACES FOR PRIVACY

- Crannies in the reading area.
- Carrels (sometimes created with cardboard cartons) facing a wall or space divider.
- A listening center with earphones, facing a divider.
- A pup tent or tepee in the classroom.
- A carpet square under a table.
- A cushion in a corner.
- A blanket-lined packing crate or a blanket draped over a table.
  [**Procedural note:** Teachers should discuss with the group the courtesies of privacy for individuals who are using these or similar facilities.]

There are also a number of occasions during the school day when participation in *whole–group activity* is reasonable. In addition to periodic planning periods for the whole group, other occasions for the whole group to be together are listed in Box 2.7.

BOX 2.7 WHOLE GROUP ACTIVITIES

- Story time—read-aloud
- Celebrations and special delights
- Special resources or visitors
- Discussions of group-process issues
- Plays and performances
- Music, singing, and movement education
- Sports and outdoor activities
- Sharing work
- Mini-lessons to launch new concepts
- Lunch
- Rest time/independent reading time
- Field trips
- In some classrooms, snack time is a whole-group activity.

You will find additional ways of providing for privacy, participation, and cooperative work throughout the book. Chapter 13 provides additional details about planning and scheduling issues.

Reflections

A professional teacher in an all-day pre-kindergarten or kindergarten program spends the majority of time instructing small groups and individuals, and circulating among groups. In well-organized, effective classrooms, it is reasonable to expect that teachers spend less time on procedural distractions and more time on activities that help children build the mental models/images of Dynamic-Themes.

If you work with an aide, you would share your organizational purposes, plan together, and review events, sharing observations of children. In order to foster consistency and complementary work between adults, it helps to decide each day on territory to cover in the classroom and responsibilities for each of you to perform. By thinking about your placement in advance, you can avoid overlap or neglect of some areas in which children might need redirecting. During an activity period, you might ask the other adult to work in a single area in particular ways or to circulate so that you can focus on one area. During a whole-group story, you might ask the aide to sit beside specific children who need help focusing.

If you plan to work with learning centers, here are a few tips. Consider reducing the number of transitions between shorter time blocks and increasing the duration of fewer, longer center-based time blocks. If the first period of the day is a whole-group activity, then analyze how you might increase the time for integrated small-group and individual activities, while reducing the whole-group time at the day's start. In general, how might you reduce whole-group and increase small-group and individual study? At the same time, reduce the number of single-subject occasions, while increasing the integrated use of time blocks to support the children's development of connections. Also, consider what new learning-center focus you might add, enlarge, reduce, furlough, retire, or revisit.

Reduce one transition at a time. Add one choice at a time. If there are individual desks, group them to create a combined, larger table surface. If there is assigned storage, create personal storage. Store materials where children use them. If there is assigned seating, create an activity time during which space fits function and children move to where the function takes place.

Organization and content blend together to contribute to the quality of learning experiences children have in school. Creating a focus on learning centers begins on the first day of school with a few areas, to which you gradually add in the days and weeks that follow. As you do so, circulate frequently to support consistent routines and traffic patterns. Such provisions can help the children to become more independent within the classroom organization. In these ways, you provide a forum in which to create a caring and secure community. As you circulate— essential to helping children establish independent activity—among these centers during the first month or two of the school year, you will have numerous contacts with each child. You can assess what they can do, for how long they might do it, how they interact, and the help they need. You will then be in a good position to plan systematically for activities in which you work more intensively with small groups for up to 15 minutes at a time before circulating again.

In the chapters that follow, you will find numerous activities to support the content-rich images of Dynamic-Themes within the all-day kindergarten and pre-kindergarten organization discussed in this chapter.

3

SEVEN CONDITIONS FOR LEARNING IN EARLY CHILDHOOD

Introduction

Professional early childhood teachers, both intuitively and intentionally, use the seven integrated "conditions for learning"—comparisons (induction), surprises (cognitive dissonance), physical experiences, social interaction, play, revisiting, and a sense of competence—to help children expand their learning and build new meanings. Researchers who study the development of young children in a variety of socio-cultural contexts identify these integrated conditions for learning. For example, teachers can help children learn when they figure out what else children might be able to do (the children's *Zone of Proximal Development*; Vygotsky, 1978) with teacher support—a process of *scaffolding*. The term "scaffolding" refers to the teacher's role in supporting each next step that can help children make progress. It is similar to "guided interaction," which also views the relationship between teacher and learner as significant (Plowman, Stephen, and McPake, 2010). Therefore, each of the seven conditions for learning involves some perceivable *relationship* between teacher and children, and the *relationship* that children might perceive between activities that helps them make meaningful, fresh connections. And teachers who use the integrated conditions for learning are able to simplify activities or offer more challenges as they interact with children.

In this chapter and throughout the book, you will find descriptions of ways in which you can adapt instruction. There now follows a description of the conditions for learning in early childhood, with some examples.

Comparisons: Learning with Induction

Induction takes place when children can *compare* objects and ideas. If only one object or idea is present, then children need to depend upon memory and rote learning instead of building new connections and meanings. Contrasts between activities provide the *contrasting* figure–background relationships that help children to perceive, collect, and consider both 2- and 3-dimensional data. The *figure* represents a fresh concept that stands in *contrast* with the *background* that represents what children have already experienced. For example, children develop concepts of polarities (large–small) and relative sizes by manipulating blocks of different sizes.

When you provide systematic contrasts, children have the opportunity to perceive the movements created by the changes between specific properties, objects, sizes, poems, or stories. Exemplary teachers often provide several pairs of items for the children in order to model contrasts. For example, it is particularly helpful to highlight mathematical images when you describe the *connections*, "thus guiding induction" (Gelman, 1999, p. 52). The notion of teaching by using stories, for example, that include "binary opposites" (Egan, 1988) is also consistent with inductive processes in development such as trust–mistrust (Erikson, 1977).

In addition, the development of spoken grammar (syntax) and reading depends upon the *induction* of *contrasting patterns* of words in sentences and *contrasting patterns* of phonemes in words. Inductive experience is a natural way to acquire basic learning about the transformational nature of learning to speak, read, and write (Brown & Bellugi, 1964; Ferreiro & Teberosky, 1982). For example, when kindergarten children compare their writing with and without spaces between words, they are able to see the need to provide spaces between words so that readers are able to decode the meaning of print (Calkins & Louis, 2005, p. 36). Some examples of simple, concrete contrasts for younger children and English language learners are provided in Box 3.1.

BOX 3.1 CONCRETE CONTRASTS HIGHLIGHT COMPARISONS

Color Identification

Use colored cubes (or crayons) of the same size, with only one color contrast: e.g., blue and red.

Teacher (holding flat in an open palm, with a playful tone): "This is blue. This is red."

(Hands to a child, saying): "Here is the blue. Here is the red."

"Please give me the red. Please give me the blue."

"Please take the blue. Please take the red."

If the children can complete this playful exchange, plan to introduce blue with yellow, or red with yellow, always keeping a single new contrast.

[**Procedural note**: If children can already identify colors and their continuum of hues, there would be no need for this elementary activity. Therefore, it would be useful only for the individual child or two who needs support. Most typical pre-kindergarten and kindergarten children are likely to be able to identify basic colors by name. They do not require a time-consuming didactic experience with a whole-group "color of the day" or "color of the week" activity. For the child who cannot sort or name colors, the typical "color of the day" activity might even be confusing: what property is the naive child to focus on when confronted by faded *blue* jeans, navy-*blue* stripes on a shirt, a royal-*blue* crayon, Amy's *blue* eyes, and Alan's light *blue* shirt?]

Shape Identification

Use two wooden or cardboard forms of the same color and size, but different shapes: e.g., circle and square; triangle and circle. [**Procedural note**: Use only with individuals who need to learn to label a particular contrast. The general principle is to provide a new "figure" against a known "background." As a general practice, effective teachers analyze tasks and provide a fresh variable against a known background of experience.]

Size Identification

Use two objects of the same shape and color, but different size: e.g., a large oval and a small oval. [**Procedural note**: Use only with individuals who need to learn to label this contrast.]

In these examples, each inductive experience involves a *relationship* between the ideas or things that children *compare*. Detailed descriptions of additional inductive phonemic games appear in Chapter 10.

Moreover, the notion of "blending," making connections between images, is the basis of many important human experiences, such as pretense, fantasy, humor, expectation, prediction, analogy, and problem solving (Fauconnier & Turner, 2002). An example would be: "When children know the *−ay* rime and recognize *say*, they use this knowledge to pronounce *day*: They identify the *−ay* rime and blend *d* with *ay* to decode the world. This strategy is called *decoding by analogy*" (Tompkins, 2011, p. 111). Children who learn within the inductive process and the surprises of cognitive dissonance, discussed below, securely own their knowledge.

Surprising Experiences: Cognitive Dissonance Builds Meaning

Learning takes place within the powerful transitional area that resides in the *relationship* between what you expect and how experiences help you to confirm, disconfirm, or revise your initial perceptions. (The phase transition between not-knowing and knowing is the space of time within which meaning develops.) *Surprises take place when your image of what you have expected to happen changes after you have a direct experience. Surprise/cognitive dissonance,* the three-part process that entails *expectation–experience–comparison,* complements inductive experiences. *Surprise/ cognitive dissonance is the central feature of learning new meanings* and ensures the acquisition of new perspectives. You will notice that many learning activities in the chapters that follow integrate the learning condition of *surprise/cognitive dissonance.*

When children make predictions, they have the opportunity to wonder and consider real questions that exist for adults as well as for children. Box 3.2 provides examples.

BOX 3.2 EXPECT, EXPERIENCE, AND COMPARE

Magnets

- *Expectation:* Pre-kindergarten children often imagine that larger is always stronger. When their teacher asks them to imagine whether a small bar magnet or a large horseshoe magnet would attract more paper clips, the children typically expect the larger magnet to attract more clips.
- *Experience:* Pre-kindergarten children became transfixed while counting as they add one clip at a time to each magnet.
- *Comparison:* Children are surprised and delighted to notice that the smaller bar magnet can attract 14 clips while the larger horseshoe magnet attracts only 11 clips. [**Procedural note:** It is helpful to limit the quantity of clips: e.g., "We have thirty paper clips." It is also helpful to create a survey chart before the experience as children "vote" on which might be the stronger magnet before the experience. As they view the addition of each paper clip, the chart provides a visual comparison. (It is worth noting that young children are "magnetized" by the addition of each paper clip.)]

Buoyancy

Young children often imagine that larger objects will sink and smaller objects will float, for example when a large piece of Styrofoam is compared with a

---

small metal washer. One way to extend this activity is to raise the questions: e.g., "How might we help a sinking object float? How might we help a floating object sink" (Barrett et al., 1999, p. 46). [**Procedural note:** Create a before-chart and an after-chart. There is a variety of ways to represent these events.]

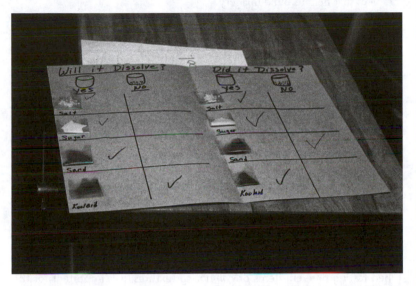

IMAGE 3.1 Did it Dissolve? Before and after Surprise/Cognitive Dissonance Charts

Additional experiences are detailed in Chapter 6. Keep in mind that this habit of thinking—expect–experience–compare—also strengthens reading comprehension, discussed in Chapter 10, because cognitive dissonance helps children build concepts. The capacity to keep past, present, and future in mind also strengthens self-regulation.

Physical Experiences: Hold, Move, Touch, Feel, Smell, and Compare Concrete Materials

Physical engagement with concrete materials, along with the other conditions for learning, strengthens perception. When children handle contrasted objects, use their bodies in space, and observe events directly, they build images of how things work as well as ways of knowing and creating in the sciences, mathematics, and the arts. The spatial *relationships* and physical *changes*, rather than the sensory experiences alone, build important meanings.

Young children enjoy repeating physical activities while trying to confirm their findings as they collect data and solve problems. For example, while children are engaged in block building and other constructions and explore ramps/inclined planes, you can encourage them to confirm their findings even when they may appear to be "correct," in order to help them build up their own critical thinking skills. Predictability as well as surprise can satisfy young children. In these ways, they build images of how things work. Box 3.3 includes concrete physical experiences that help to build imagery.

BOX 3.3 PHYSICAL CONTRASTS AND COMPARISONS

Mystery Box

Fill a box with unseen 3-dimensional items. Provide a card that depicts the outline or picture of each item in the box. Use items such as a key, pine cone, cotton ball, small box, and a small toy. Children pick a card, feel inside the box to find the item, then place it on the matching card. This use of imagery connects the 3-dimensional (concrete) with the 2-dimensional representation (visual), a step along the path to reading.

Physical Contrasts and Comparisons

When tasting different items or *comparing* textures, it is important for the teacher to provide *contrasts* and verbal harmony—naming the sensations as needed. For example, provide contrasts such as warm–cool; rough–smooth; hard–soft; and, later, ordering "harder than"–"harder than that"–"hardest." [**Procedural note:** Physical activity without comparisons is merely isolated sensory activity, a rote labeling activity, rather than an opportunity to perceive and extend concepts. The sensory touching itself is not educative and may actually camouflage a concept. It is the process of *comparing* the underlying *relationship* that helps children experience meaning.]

Ongoing research on the brain recognizes that physical activity contributes to concept development (Payne & Kounios, 2009). It is worth noting that the youngest children begin to learn about the world through gross motor contact that emerges into finer coordination of their muscles (useful for drawing and writing), which, in turn, helps build their perceptual and cognitive imagery. Physical activity is so fundamental to early learning that Chapter 4 focuses on hands-on learning ties to concept development. In addition, movement activities provide a sense of well-being and good health by helping to prevent obesity. Chapter 9 includes additional discussion of movement education.

Social Interactions: Feedback from Friends and Enemies

Social interaction provides an opportunity for *contrast* between a personal perspective and the perspective of others. Other children provide natural sources of feedback and incidentally help each other reflect on how others perceive their actions.

Pre-kindergarten and kindergarten children also provide each other with alternative perspectives to consider, possible occasions for *cognitive dissonance*. Children are able to spend more time considering intellectual issues when they engage with their peers in planning, constructing things or ideas, and problem-solving; there can be a positive influence on their capacity to learn new ideas and develop wholesome self-concepts as they do so (Dyson, 1987; Espinosa, 2010; Johnson, Johnson, Holubec, & Roy, 1984; Piaget et al., 1965).

Children who interact with others have an opportunity to reach beyond themselves and to appreciate that others may define situations differently, a process that develops a "Theory of Mind" (Astington, 1993; Astington & Pelletier, 2005; Blair & Razza, 2007; Harris & Kavanaugh, 1993; Leslie, 1995; Perner, 1991). Theory of Mind refers to the capacity to be aware of one's own thoughts, beliefs, deceptions, intentions, and feelings as well as those of other people. This capacity develops between about 2 and 4 years of age through interaction with others.

In effect, children, as well as adults, provide one another with feedback and coaching. The feedback during social interactions helps to teach about the motives of other children and can serve to balance self-involvment with sharing and taking turns.[1] The transition that defines the *relationship* between a personally centered view and a de-centered view reflects a growth of meaning (see Piaget et al., 1965). For example, Piagetian research finds that the youngest children tend to perceive breaking four cups accidentally as more worthy of punishment than breaking one cup intentionally. As they de-center after experiences in many situations, they come to understand that motives are more significant than the number of cups; recognizing motives grows with the youngsters' Theory of Mind.

From these contacts, children also help one another build self-regulation (inhibitory control) that researchers find supports mathematical as well as language development (Blair & Razza, 2007; Diamond, Barnett, Thomas, & Munro, 2007; McClelland et al., 2007). This is important, because pre-kindergarten children who are more able to delay gratification are better able to cope with stress and show more cognitive as well as academic competence when they became adolescents (Shoda, Mischel, & Peake, 1990). Additional discussions of Theory of Mind and self-regulation appear below and in Chapter 14.

You can plan for children of varied backgrounds and attainments to work together on content-rich projects so that they experience a playful form of learning; youngsters have an opportunity to appreciate one another's contributions at the same time as they extend their learning together. Such activities help children to focus on content that builds upon their earlier experiences, perspectives, and understandings as a basis for expanding their content knowledge.

Socio-dramatic activity, discussed below, provides particular opportunities for the development of social competence. During their socio-dramatic activity, children represent implicit meaning in explicit forms in ways that reveal their Theory of Mind. During the process of improving their perspective taking, they also de-center from themselves. Chapter 6 includes specific activity ideas that support this social feedback proces; and there is discussion of ways to build sensitivity to others in Chapter 8. Children's behavior, especially their socio-dramatic play, reveals how they intend to influence the thinking of others or how they respond when recognizing the intentions of others.

Play and Imagination

Play empowers children to use their imaginations while they engage in pretense with objects and others. Exploration precedes play. Children obtain information by exploring "What does this object do?" and engage in play by finding out "What can I do with this object?" (Hutt, 1976, p. 211). During play, children can feel powerful; in general, a personal sense of power to choose can support their sense of competence and builds self-regulation, which is essential to learning.

Research findings, listed below, indicate that it is valuable for teachers to provide time and space for pre-kindergarten and kindergarten children to explore imagery and pretense, and to make choices.

• Children whose parents engage in pretense with them at home are more perseverant and patient than others (Singer & Singer, 1979; Singer & Singer, 2006). These high-fantasy children also score higher in imaginative storytelling and make more analogic statements than low-fantasy children (Fromberg, 1999, pp. 39–40).

• Children who use unstructured toys engage in more extended collaborative socio-dramatic script-building than those who use high-specificity props (McLoyd, 1983; Wanska, Pohlman, & Bedrosian, 1989).

• Children who play first with realistic toys find it harder to use their imaginations than children who play first with unstructured toys (McGhee, Etheridge, & Berg, 1984).

• Mill-worker families in Piedmont tend to provide high-specificity toys for their children; and these children find interpretive and creative thinking more difficult in their later school years (Heath, 1983).

• Young children demonstrate their capacity to distinguish between fantasy and reality within different contexts; this capacity to adapt is a valuable foundation for building self-regulation (Wyman, Rakoczy, & Tomasello, 2009).

In addition, children demonstrate their developing capacity for pretense with increasing use of symbols as they: (1) substitute objects for objects that are not present; (2) simulate actions with objects not present; (3) behave as if they were someone or something else, for example an animal or a physician; and (4) engage in both of their imaginary roles with imaginary props. Socio-dramatic activity in particular supports the collaborative development of imagery and pretense.

Socio-dramatic Activity, a Form of Collaborative Oral Playwriting

Socio-dramatic activity takes place when two or more children, or a child and an adult, engage in pretense with actual or imaginary objects. During socio-dramatic activity, children extend their imagery and capacity for pretense. Children represent a seemingly infinite variety of play themes based upon their experiences (event knowledge), within the underlying rules of the socio-dramatic activity (script theory), a kind of grammar of play. Learning takes place in the *relationship* between children's event knowledge and their seamless engagement within the play's framework of rules. Children scaffold (support and build) each other's participation and learn from seeing the experiences that other children dramatize. In these ways, *socio-dramatic activity is a form of collaborative oral playwriting.*

BOX 3.4 PLAY INFLUENCES DEVELOPMENT: RESEARCH ABOUT SELF-REGULATION (EXECUTIVE FUNCTION)

Researchers have found that socio-dramatic activity can have a positive influence on the development of *language, cognition, social competence, and some forms of creativity and problem solving* (Brown with Vaughan, 2010; Singer, Golinkoff, & Hirsh-Pasek, 2009; O'Brien & Bi, 1995; Gitlin-Weiner, 1998; Fromberg, 1999; Roskos & Christie, 2002; Smilansky, 1968; Dansky, 1986).

Researchers connect experiences with pretense to the development of "executive function" skills, a combination of "(i) inhibitory control (resisting habits, temptations or distractions), (ii) working memory (mentally holding and using information), and (iii) cognitive flexibility (adjusting to change)" (Diamond, Barnett, Thomas, & Munro, 2007, p. 1387).

There appears to be a relationship between executive function and the development of Theory of Mind (Blair & Razza, 2007; Carlson, Mandell, & Williams, 2004).

Kindergarten teachers prioritize *self-regulation* (as contrasted with specific skills or information); self-regulation is an outgrowth of play experiences.

Socio-dramatic activity serves as a lymphatic system for development that lubricates the relationship between fantasy and reality. Inasmuch as the dynamics of such complex imaginative activity are:

1 rule-bound (Bodrova & Leong, 2007; Vygotsky, 1976) as well as
2 self-directed (a sense of power),
3 young children extend their learning and
4 reduce their impulsivity in the service of
5 the self-imposed rules of the play.

The discussion of script theory below outlines the process of socio-dramatic activity.

Script Theory

Script theory (Nelson et al., 1986; Schank & Abelson, 1977) outlines the underlying "grammar" of socio-dramatic activity. Children demonstrate their capacity to use the underlying socio-dramatic play structures (script theory), a kind of "play grammar of experience," when they act out imaginary events with other children or an adult and represent their variety of experiences (event knowledge) in both predictable and emergent ways.

The cultural interpretation of play contends that play functions in advance of development. One process, the Zone of Proximal Development, suggests that play serves as a bridge between objects and thoughts. Children use objects and situations symbolically as a "pivot," for example when a stick substitutes for a horse (Vygotsky, 1976). In a similar fashion, young children move into and out of the play frame (Bateson, 1979). The play framework facilitates an implicit choreography as one child enters into and "becomes" a role while another responds in a complementary role.

Children continually clarify what is inside and what is outside the play frame. Their engagement reflects their capacity to communicate about their communication (meta-communication) in advance of their years (Bateson, 1971, 1976, 1979). For example, young children step outside the play frame (meta-communication) to suggest, "You be the big brother and I'll be the baby," and then seamlessly step inside the play frame and behave in relation to the big brother (imagery). They demonstrate their capacity to classify what is and what is not play within this oscillating process. In these ways, the children subordinate themselves voluntarily and meaningfully to the "rules" (grammar/script) of the pretend play. When they use their imaginations they engage in private speech which helps to build self-regulation, the "inhibitory control" of executive function.

The more children play, the more they learn about the rules of engagement by interacting with others who provide models and feedback. In these ways, play leads development. You can see this taking place as the surface behavior of children's play becomes a vista through which to view their deeper understandings. An example of the transformational generative nature of script theory follows:

Child 1: "Wah! My leg is broken."

Child 2: "Stop moving. I need to put on this bandage."

A different Child 2 might respond: "I've told you not to jump off the roof. Bad, bad. Now I have to get some splints."

Another Child 2 might respond: "Don't move. I'm calling 911."

And yet another Child 2 might comment: "Poor baby."

Thus, different children, or the same child at a different time, might respond in numerous ways to such a session of "Let's pretend."

Each response reflects a child's event knowledge, his or her unique past experiences, and the influence of other children. There is a strange attractor between the shared play theme and each child's distinct past event knowledge that is apparent in each child's personal response. However, whatever the response, all the players implicitly agree that this collaborative, oral playwriting is relevant and meaningful to them. Thus, script theory involves the *relationship* between the underlying rules of play, a planning process (meta-communication) and the variety of surface forms of imagery that children create together. In these ways, socio-dramatic play is predictably unpredictable as the players flexibly adjust to one another. It is noteworthy that adjusting to change is part of self-regulation and executive function.

Children both use and expand their event knowledge and solve problems together as they develop oral scripts with others. The feedback that children receive during interactions with the physical world and others during play, and their other daily life experience, helps them to develop a meta-cognitive Theory of Mind. In this sense, play is an act of creation that integrates physical experiences, emotion, and logic. [**Procedural note:** Pre-kindergarten and kindergarten teachers support vocabulary development by providing props and labels that represent different topics, such as medical clinic, supermarket, restaurant, post office, or hairdresser's. To stimulate imaginative thinking, the props can be suggestive rather than replications. Drawing and writing materials are also present.]

Revisiting

Revisiting experiences can build fresh connections. Brain researchers, using *functional Magnetic Resonance Imagery* (fMRI), confirm that young children learn by combining structures of neural networks in a stimulating environment with amazing *plasticity* (Bowman, Donovan, & Burns, 2001, p. 56; Gopnik, 2009, p. 122; Sylwester, 2000, p. 11). You can build on these connections within the classroom. Quite simply, the more children can perceive connections, the more they will learn. Young children absorb even those things that we would rather they did not notice. We might imagine that the more you use a muscle, the stronger it will become—up to a saturation point, like an overly watered plant. However, if you do not use the muscle, it will likely weaken, just as a plant would wither. In the brain, *pruning* describes a similar process. Therefore, your content-rich and engaging activity-based learning environment simply makes sense.

Educators find that revisiting events with photographs encourages children to sequence and talk about activities at different times (Edwards, Gandini, & Forman, 1998). Youngsters are also able to return to activities or materials after weeks or even a few months and approach them with fresh perspectives. In addition, you can recycle or furlough props, equipment, materials, or animals. During the intervening time, additional experiences influence the original perceptions that help concepts to grow; the intervening experiences put an earlier experience into a fresh *relationship* (Piaget & Inhelder, 1973). Therefore, it is not necessary to begin a project on Monday and finish it on Friday, never to reconsider the topic again. You can weave related activities throughout the school year. Examples are presented throughout this book, especially in Part II.

Sense of Competence: Building Independent and Powerful Thinkers

A sense of competence enables learners to face challenges. When children are worrying about their competence or coping with a sense of inadequacy, their intellectual capacities recede (see Bruner, 1966, on coping and defending; Damasio, 2003, on the brain's connection between emotion and cognition; Espinosa, 2010, p. 46, on the resilience of dual-language learners and immigrant children that grows from a sense of positive expectations; Goleman, 1995, on emotional intelligence; and the National Scientific Council on the Developing Child, 2004, 2005, 2008).

Youngsters are more likely to feel potentially successful in acquiring *meaning* when they can experience a sense of *challenge*, comparing some degree of risk with a reasonable chance of meeting the challenge. The degree of challenge, the underlying *relationship* between challenge and risk, can help children focus on new learning. When you provide reasonable choices they are likely to attempt new experiences and develop their capacity for self-regulation. *Meaning* is the result of this choreography, as follows:

> An individual child's self-concept and motivation can strengthen or limit the efficiency of ties between existing memories (event knowledge), to *integrate* a fresh connection (learning), or to *generate* a fresh connection (creativity). More than just concepts or ideas alone, therefore, children's ability to develop new meaning also depends upon their emotions and motives. Some meaning involves more powerful or weaker emotion. Self-concept and imagination also influence the oscillating strength of emotion. In the face of a challenge, self-concept and imagination could influence the particular way an individual dynamically gauges risk in relation to the chance for success. Thus, human beings selectively grasp specific meanings with different degrees of perceptual strength or motivation. Motivation is both an emotional and cognitive reaction to meaning, and it also influences how much attention we pay to particular experiences. Therefore, meaning is not

"delivered." Rather, children construct meanings in unpredictable ways when they engage in focused interactions with others and the physical world. *Like music, meaning is a direct, personal experience.*

(Fromberg, 2010, p. 50)

Thus, the dynamic process of developing meaning is wedded to a sense of competence. Figure 3.1 represents the mutually interactive, varying forces that a sense of competence can influence in the process of acquiring meaning. In turn, meaning is central to educational experiences, discussed throughout the remaining chapters of this book.

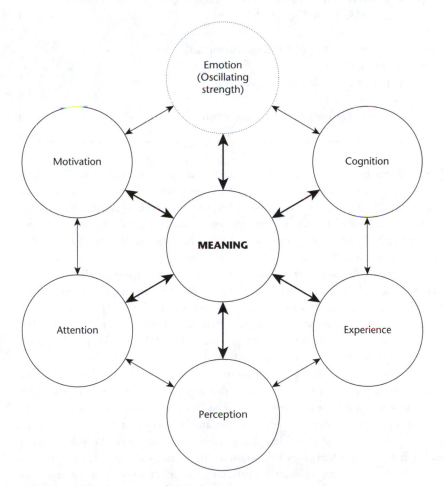

FIGURE 3.1 The Dynamics of Meaning

Therefore, you have a better chance of matching instruction to young children's capacity to learn when you engage in the following practices:

- appreciate children's efforts and focus on children's specific positive effort, progress, and accomplishments;
- offer children thoughtful choices;
- control variables by creating fresh figure–ground *relationships*; and
- take a matter-of-fact attitude toward moving along the *abstraction ladder*.

The abstraction ladder in Box 3.5 outlines a sequence of complexity.

BOX 3.5 THE ABSTRACTION LADDER (ADAPTED FROM HAYAKAWA, 1949)

- concrete–concrete (3-dimensional objects)
- concrete–visual
- visual–visual (2-dimensional pictures)
- visual–symbolic
- symbolic–symbolic (numbers and words)[2]

[**Procedural note:** The abstraction ladder can serve as a way to control variables when you sequence activities. For example, young children who have had enough experiences with concrete, 3-dimensional equipment and materials are likely to be ready to match concrete materials with pictures (visual), and so forth. If you expect children to use symbolic representations (such as reading words or using numerals), you would imagine that the children have had related past experiences with visual representations. If you perceive that a child is struggling with symbolic activity, it makes sense to move along the abstraction ladder and help the child respectfully build preceding experiences with visual–symbolic or visual–visual experiences—or visual–concrete experiences. These considerations mesh with concerns for differentiating instruction. Such adaptation is also part of the practice of "Response to Intervention" (RTI) (see Owocki, 2010), discussed in Chapter 14.]

As a professional teacher, you have an image of what concepts and skills children need to learn and the steps in reaching those goals. You understand that their potential sense of success will serve to motivate their attention to learning content. Strong meaning can develop when you match the content with an engaging sequence of activities that children can perceive as challenging. In order to help children feel competent, it is important to focus not only on pre-determined products, but upon the youngsters' process of connection-making, efforts, and progress. "Learning takes place best when children are engaged and enjoying themselves" (Hirsh-Pasek, Golinkoff, Berk, & Singer, 2009, p. 3).

Connections for the Present and Future

This Dynamic-Themes conceptual curricular approach is consistent with "learning twenty-first-century skills" (Yelland, Lee, O'Rourke, & Harrison, 2008, pp. 2–4) and an astrophysicist's projections of a future that needs people who can do the following:

- envision more than one answer to a question;
- take imaginary leaps and act on them;
- adapt to rapid change; and
- work collaboratively with others (Kaku 1997, 2008).

Therefore, it is important for citizens to develop the capacity to use knowledge for flexible and adaptive thinking and action as well as social competence in team endeavors. These capacities fall within the seven integrated conditions for learning in early childhood.

Reflections

The seven integrated conditions for learning in early childhood—comparisons, surprises, physical experiences, social interaction, play and imagination, revisiting, and a sense of competence—have in common the nature of *relationships* that children might perceive between objects and between each child and other people. The dynamic connections within these relationships provide opportunities for children to perceive new meanings, and are integrated throughout this book. The next chapter focuses on how young children build concepts and relationships that begin with physical engagement with equipment and materials. By working with the integrated conditions for learning, we can envision an integration of learning through play, value-added content through playful learning, and a recycling of fresh event knowledge into exploration and play.

4

HANDS-ON LEARNING TIES
TO CONCEPT DEVELOPMENT

Introduction

This chapter focuses mainly on the conditions for learning that deal with direct, hands-on, 3-dimensional constructions and social interactions, although other conditions for learning—induction, cognitive dissonance, imagination and play, revisiting, and a sense of competence—are integrated with children's activities in the physical world. Moreover, when you see young children engaging in 3-dimensional constructions and social interaction, you have a chance to assess their cognitive, physical, and socio-emotional competence.

Early learning begins when youngsters make connections between themselves and objects; between objects; and between themselves and others. Their brains build connections and find patterns within these experiences; and the connections and patterns are the mental images within Dynamic-Themes. When you see the connections that children make during their hands-on activities, you can plan related, next-step experiences. When you use this dynamic conceptual approach to plan activities, children can feel motivated to learn and apply mathematical and literacy skills as well as represent their understandings through varied forms of literacy, including the arts (Fromberg, 2002; 2010; Lonigan & Shanahan, 2008; Piaget & Inhelder, 1976; Schwartz, 2005; Seefeldt, 1992; Vygotsky, 1978).

Hands and Brains Connect

The brain's plasticity supports the rapid connection-making that young children experience as they interact with people and materials (Eliot, 2009). "The hand and the brain need each other—the hand provides the means for interacting with the world and the brain provides the method . . . The use of the hand to manipulate three-dimensional objects is an essential part of brain development" (Brown with Vaughan, 2010, p. 185).

This chapter applies the hand–brain connection by looking at what, why, where, when, and how 3-dimensional and interactive experiences take place in pre-kindergarten and kindergarten classrooms, and what you might do to support children who are actively engaged with their physical and social environments.

What are 3-Dimensional Equipment and Materials?

Three-dimensional equipment, materials, and experiences help young children learn about visual–spatial phenomena. Early childhood classrooms typically integrate some 3-dimensional materials and equipment with which children explore, manipulate, engage their imaginations, play, and create new forms. These activities also support design technology, discussed further in Chapter 11.

Equipment

Among 3-dimensional equipment (typically for long-term use and re-use) are the following:

- *Unit wooden floor blocks*, typically made of both solid and hollow wood; and sometimes of cardboard or dense plastic foam. The classic set of wooden blocks consists of rectangles that have a ratio of 1:2:4:12 and also includes a variety of other shapes. Some noted educators recommend 750 blocks for a typical kindergarten (Isenberg & Jalongo, 2006); others recommend 472 (Wellhousen & Kieff, 2001); still others 150–200 in 10 or more shapes along with other equipment (Chalufour & Worth, 2004.) Accessories include miniature vehicles, commercial or homemade traffic signals, labels, and writing materials; Post-it notes; miniature people (include careers that are gender-neutral as well as different ethnicities and abilities); and animals. To support children's themes, teachers add props such as photographs, drawings, blueprints of constructions, hats, steering wheels, career uniforms, a stethoscope, cash register, hoses, and so forth. As relevant, teachers add pulleys, ropes, or ramps as well as nonstandard and standard measuring tools.
- *Large hollow blocks*. When children use large hollow blocks outdoors or indoors, they are able to create structures into which they themselves can fit and pretend. Some schools provide large interlocking blocks with bolts.
- *Homemade floor blocks*. When the cost of unit floor blocks limits purchase, fill milk cartons with sand and tape them shut.
- *Table blocks*—commercially made KAPLA blocks ($4\frac{1}{2} \times \frac{3}{4} \times \frac{1}{4}$ inches); Cuisenaire rods, made of wood or plastic, are 1 cubic cm lengths of ten graduated sizes from 1 to 10 cm, with each increasing size color-coded;

colored wooden cubes; related Developmental Learning Materials cards, sequenced, in a ring binder; parquetry blocks.

- *Bowling; pendulum bowling.* Games of aiming, rolling, throwing balls of varied sizes; and catching beanbags.
- *Unifix cubes, Lego and Electronic Lego Robotics (Lego Mindstorms), Duplo, Tinker Toys,* and *Lincoln Logs* consist of interlocking pieces of wood or plastic. These valuable building materials, however, control construction in ways that limit the exploration of gravity, balance, tension, and stability (see Chalufour & Worth, 2004). It is noteworthy that pre-kindergarten children spend extended time alone and with others at large-scale Lego tabletops.[1]
- *Marble Railway (Childcraft)* and *K'Nex Arch Bridge Technology* construction materials extend generic block play.
- *3-dimensional wooden puzzles* (kindergarten).
- *Polydron™* and *Geofix™* construction materials that permit kindergarten children to build interlocking 3-dimensional forms.

Materials

Among 3-dimensional materials (typically consumable) are the following:

- *Woodworking.* Pre-kindergarten children are able to explore, plan, measure, and use tools to construct 3-dimensional objects. They hammer nails into a board and create designs with rubber bands and/or yarn (Kohl, 1984). (Chapter 11's section on "Design technology" extends this discussion.)
- *Clay* (as well as plasticene and homemade or commercial play dough). As youngsters manipulate the malleable material, they enjoy using accessories such as tongue depressors, pine cones, popsicle sticks, styluses and so forth. Young children remain attentive to manipulating and building with the malleable material for an average of 19.7 minutes (Haskell, 1984). (See Box 9.6.)
- *3-dimensional collages, mobiles, and stabiles.*
- *Pipe cleaners/Wikki Stix (waxed wires)/wires/foil; toothpicks and play dough constructions.*
- *Popsicle sticks, wooden tongue depressors, and flat wood scraps with wood glue.*
- *Sewing and weaving items.* (See also Chapter 9's section on Creating Visual and Plastic Arts.)
- *Clear plastic hoses, funnels, and containers* for water.
- *Cardboard flats* to use with wooden blocks and other equipment.
- *Movement education accessories—wooden or plastic hoops* offer topological activities. (See also Box 12.3.) [**Procedural note:** When you appreciatively label the actions as children do them, you are building their vocabularies as well as their spatial awareness.]

Why are 3-Dimensional Experiences Important?

Imagery, Visual–Spatial Skills, and Scholastic Achievement

Children develop the imagery that supports visual–spatial skills when they build with varied 3-dimensional materials. Human beings need to use their visual–spatial skills in order to develop concepts in mathematics, chemistry, physics, engineering, and the arts (Casey et al., 2008; Clements & Sarama, 2009b; Kean, 1998; Isaacson, 2007; Pollman, 2010; K. Smith, 1991; Wolfgang, Stannard, & Jones, 2001).[2]

For example, as a child, the architect Frank Lloyd Wright played with blocks (Wright, 1932). The theoretical physicist Albert Einstein played with blocks and jigsaw puzzles. Moreover, Einstein attended a Pestalozzi-inspired school that encouraged imagery and construction activities (Isaacson, 2007). Researchers find that early block building influences later mathematical achievement (Chalufour et al., 2004; Pasnak, 1987; Wolfgang, Stannard, & Jones, 2001). Other researchers have found that young children also comfortably integrate literacy materials with their block constructions and play (Christie, 1991).

Social Competence

There also are opportunities for young children to develop social competence and self-regulation as they interact with one another during block building in particular. *Social competence* and *play and imagination* are among the seven integrated conditions for early learning, discussed in Chapter 3, which effective early childhood teachers implicitly and explicitly practice.

Geographic Mapping

Children who manipulate objects in space also strengthen their geographic imagery. Moving beyond exploration with the equipment, children begin to represent both real and imaginary places. (See Boxes 8.7 and 8.8.)

Where do 3-Dimensional Experiences Occur in Classrooms?

From the first day of school, provide space for construction experiences, even on a table. With many small materials, it is helpful for a table to have a lip around the edge to contain the pieces: for example, a quarter round of wood or a tray. Montessori schools place materials with many pieces on separate floor mats.

Space and provisions themselves become an invitation to learning. Children can independently locate and replace blocks on accessible shelves with outlines of different block shapes; the block outlines facilitate cleanup. The outlines also help builders to connect 3- and 2-dimensional representation. It is useful to place the floor block-building area away from traffic by using walls, bookshelves, or low room dividers to mark the area. It helps to place it adjacent to other socio-dramatic activity in order to facilitate movement between the areas, and prevent intrusion into more sedentary classroom areas.

Some teachers bemoan the limited space in a classroom as a reason to limit block-building or other socio-dramatic area. One way to use space efficiently is not to assign personal desks, although this is a controversial concept for some teachers (see Box 2.2). Then you can view all furniture as resources to use for construction and interactive experiences. Moveable furniture provides opportunities for whole-group meetings at tables or desks or on extended floor space. You can develop safe routines in which two children move furniture against a wall: for example, legs of furniture facing down, two children together move a table to a designated space. You can also show how to carry a chair by holding the back with two hands.

When have Teachers Scheduled 3-Dimensional Experiences?

Some teachers feel compelled to provide largely whole-group and sedentary activities. However, even they are able to allot 45 minutes daily for children to participate in 3-dimensional and interactive experiences during an activity center time block. It is notable that some kindergarten children need at least 30 minutes in construction activities before they are able to focus on more sedentary work (Paley, 1984). With the all-day schedule, some teachers are able to schedule 60–90-minute activity times at least once, and sometimes twice, a day. They use the time to provide customized small-group and individual instruction while most of the children engage in independent activities. Of course, they plan carefully with the children and circulate frequently to provide support.

The mathematics, science, floor block-building, and socio-dramatic centers typically provide construction opportunities. Thematic centers for a month or six weeks also add opportunities. Thematic centers might include a weather station, props for a medical facility, or a garage. To expand vocabulary and concepts, it is important to rotate thematic props, such as a veterinary surgery, farm, food market, restaurant, post office, toy store, and hairdresser's. For example, one kindergarten group, fascinated by their teacher's new hairstyle, created a "fashion beauty shop" with a price list, appointment book, bills, and receipts. Some children use floor blocks to create a community with signs and roads. After a trip to a local family pumpkin farm, children are able to represent a farm with blocks.

In order to provide focused and meaningful experiences, the section below discusses some specific ways that you might help expand and extend construction activities.

How Does the Teacher Match Children's Developmental Phases?

Your role in the development of young children's interaction with 3-dimensional equipment and materials is to nurture, expand, and help children extend their learning. Sensitive teachers interact without intruding, and maintain children's sense of empowerment and voluntary engagement. In these ways, they "scaffold" experiences within the vision of Vygotsky's (1978) Zone of Proximal Development and the NAEYC's (2009) notion of "intentional" intervention. In effect, *the scaffold is an interaction between your (1) assessment of a child's learning potential in relation to (2) a learning pathway and (3) your invitation and challenge that provide a relevant next-step experience.* Therefore, it makes sense to scaffold in thoughtful ways that strengthen children's sense of competence rather than either direct or ignore children's block building.

Harriet M. Johnson (1933) was one of the first scholars to describe a developmental sequence of block building among young children. She also observed that children who have not had experiences with block building may need to move through preceding phases, although more quickly than younger children. More complex constructions develop with more time and experience (Hanline, Milton, & Phelps, 2001).

Preparation and Adaptation

Here are some ways in which teachers provide preparation and adaptations to the block building:

- Plan time in the daily schedule.
- Allocate space to invite participation away from traffic and sedentary activities.
- Limit or add materials or props to support children's themes, to help focus themes, or sensitively expand themes.
- Limit the number of builders in relation to space and materials in order to avoid crowding which could lead to frustration and aggression.
- Provide a loose-leaf book of photographs depicting a variety of architectural structures.
- Place a clipboard and sketching materials.

A routine might see children: (1) plan a construction by discussing or drawing an image (this is also the first step design engineers use before they build and then try out alternatives to learn what works.); or look at photos in a binder which they can revisit (e.g., bridges or the Chrysler Building); (2) take out blocks; (3) build; (4) share their work with others; (5) clean up or leave for extended building at another time with teacher agreement, or sketch/photograph the children's building to place on a bulletin board, add to a class "Book of Buildings," or place in a child's portfolio folder to revisit and share with families. Saving constructions over time becomes a record of progress.

Phases of Children's Block Building

Professional early childhood educators recognize that children who engage in pretense and block building make progress in symbolic development. However, some young children first need opportunities to *explore* equipment before they are able to use it for *pretend play*. Therefore, look at how children use blocks in order to identify their phase of development. (The term "phase" describes a flexible, oscillating process of progress while the term "stage" connotes a contained set of behaviors.) It is noteworthy that phases 1–8, outlined in Box 4.1, represent a synthesis of similar developmental progress in block building and spatial development that scholars have identified for a century (Bullard, 2010, particularly chapter 11; Clements & Sarama, 2009b, pp. 152–154; Cross, Woods, & Schweingruber, 2009, particularly chapter 6; Erikson, 1977; Hirsch, 1996; Moyer & von Haller Gilmer, 1956 citing Krotsch, 1917; Johnson, 1933; MacDonald, 2001; Piaget & Inhelder, 1976; Provenzo & Brett, 1983; Reifel, 1984; Scarlet, Naudeau, Salonius-Pasternak, & Ponte, 2005; Schwartz & Copeland, 2010; Wardle, 2003). Box 4.2 suggests some sample matches between children's developmental capacity in block building and the teacher's interaction and scaffolding.

Verbal Harmony

Sensitive teachers simply provide verbal harmony, a process of describing aloud what children are doing. When children hear teachers describe their emerging and new forms, additional new forms emerge and they "take more time in their block building as they do so" (Goetz & Baer, 1973, p. 216). [**Procedural note:** It is relevant to comment during later phases with comments that might also fit the earlier phases.]

BOX 4.1 PROGRESSION OF PHASES IN BLOCK BUILDING

Phase 1: Random Exploration e.g., Carrying, Heaping, Dumping

Scaffold: The teacher, in an appreciative tone, describes what children are doing: e.g, "You are finding out what the blocks can do."
"You worked hard."
"How many blocks did you put on the shelf during cleanup?"

Phase 2: Horizontal or Vertical Rows, and Choosing to Repeat their Buildings: e.g., Linear Building

Children explore balance, intuitively figuring out the practical working of the physics concept of critical mass.

Scaffold: "Talk with your building group about what you plan to build. What will be your first step?"

"The two of you really know how to cooperate."

"That building is growing taller by the minute. What else might you use?"

"Look at this: Here's a block/prop. Where might you use it?"

"How might the other children help you use it in that building?"

"Which wall is taller? How many blocks high is this side? How many blocks high is the other side?"

Alternatives: "Here is a rope/meter stick/yard stick."

Phase 3: Connecting and Bridging Blocks

Scaffold: "Which block might fit there?" Offer a choice of two blocks.

"Would the cylinder or arch be just what you are looking for?" [**Procedural note:** This moment and cleanup time are opportunities to build vocabulary by naming the shapes.]

As the teacher engages in parallel building: "How might you help me figure out how to connect these towers?"

"What might happen if you add that to the top?"

"What do you plan . . .?"

"What happened?"

"What might happen if you tried . . .?"

"Which blocks would fit across that part?"

"Wow! How did you do that?"

Phase 4: Creating Enclosures: e.g., Deliberate Placement

Scaffold: "What might you put inside your building?"

"What might you put next to it?"

"What other blocks could help make the walls/roof stronger?"

"Susan might have some ideas to help with that part."

"What did you put inside your building?"

"What else could fit inside your . . .?"

"Children might be provided with cardboard ceilings, so they [could] make the walls fit the constraints of the cardboard's dimensions" (Cross, Woods, & Schweingruber, 2009, p. 195).

"What are some other combinations of blocks you could use to build your floor/roof?"

Phases 5–8

Scaffold: "This looks much more complex than the one you made last week."
"Please tell us about your building."
"What did you do first?"
"What problems did you have to solve?"
"You figured out how to fix some parts. Please tell us how you fixed them."
"What help could you use?"
"Ed had some ideas that might help you do more with that."

Phase 5: Forming Patterns or Symmetrical Structures

Scaffold: "You have a pattern here [describing]. What might come next?"

Phase 6: Engaging in Role Playing and Pretense: e.g., with Prop Substitution

Scaffold: "Who played what part?"
"Please tell us about what happened."

Phase 7: Realistic Representation

Scaffold: "That reminds me of our trip to . . ."
"Wow! You put prices on those blocks: one cent and three cents. How many stickers could you put on them in order to help your customers?"

Phase 8: Fantastic Representation

Represent imaginative or fantastical objects (Reifel & Greenfield, 1982).
Scaffold: "You really know how to build with your imagination."
"What might the heroine do next?"
"How could he solve that problem without lying, by telling only the truth?"
"What signs/labels do you need?"
"Where might you use this sign?"
"What tickets could you use?"

[**Procedural note:** Wait for children to provide labels for their constructions; do not ask for them. Avoid any question that could be answered by yes or
no. Do not use judgmental terms such as "beautiful," "great," or "good work."
Instead, enthusiastically describe what children have done and share *why* someone
might make a wonderful judgment. In this way, the children focus on the reasons
for accomplishments rather than depend upon you to validate their work.] Adults
can do additional things to scaffold children's 3-dimensional experiences; these are
discussed below.

Fantasy and Pretense

Young children benefit when teachers help them to extend their complex
imaginative activity (play). Sensitive teachers become pretense partners only after
children have had the opportunity to solve some of the technical building
problems. Some teacher comments could include the examples in Box 4.2.

BOX 4.2 SOME EXAMPLES OF TEACHER COMMENTS TO SCAFFOLD IMAGINATION

- "Let's pretend that this is . . ."
- *Enter pretense.* The teacher "becomes" a role and enters the play: e.g.,
  "My store is on fire. Please help me to put out the fire on the climbing
  frame. How could you use this hose?"
- *Expand imaginative narrative.* The teacher "becomes" a popular media
  character and enters the play with a construction idea.
- *Puppets* can help children enter a pretense framework.

A psychologist identifies at least two styles of block builders—"patterners" and
"dramatists" (Gardner, 1982). In a similar view, a technology author identifies two
styles of children who use Lego Robotics—"engineers" and "storytellers" (Bers,
2008). *Patterners* (and engineers) are object-oriented. These children focus mainly
on the act of construction during which they engage in minimal social interaction.
Dramatists (and storytellers) are pretense–oriented. These children spend little time
building and use minimalist construction to engage in socio–dramatic pretense.

Sensitive teachers would *scaffold* each style differently. The patterners/engineers
might welcome technical support: e.g., "How might this triangle/rope help you?"
The dramatists/storytellers might welcome a teacher becoming a character in the
builders' fantasy theme: "Imagine that you and [a book character or popular media
character] took a walk and found this building: What might you/the character ask
the builders?"

Thus, hands–on experiences and constructions are the concrete foundations for learning that lend themselves to connections with other forms of representations and experiences, discussed below.

Connecting Block Building with Symbolic Representations, Trips, Interviews, and Books

Symbolic Representations

Pre-kindergarten children are able to make pencil drawings of their buildings using a clipboard (prestigious in the young child's culture). You can provide support by asking: "How could you begin to sketch your building?" If you sketch a child's building, you might say, "I would like to sketch your building. What was your first step in building?" If you compare a photograph, you might say, "Your building reminds me of a building we saw on our trip, similar to this photo. What do you think?" You might also ask, "What other ideas do you have?"

Trips Beyond the Classroom

You could connect block building to a field trip beyond the classroom: e.g., "How might we use the blocks to show the trip that we took?" Some kindergarten children are able to use blocks and accessory materials to represent and dramatize their first-hand experience of harbors (Imhoff, 1959; Mitchell, 1934; Spodek, 1962). Box 4.3 outlines some things to think about trips.

BOX 4.3 TRIPS BEYOND THE CLASSROOM

- *Pre-trip:* "Imagine what we might see on the trip." List questions to answer: e.g., "What buildings might look similar/different?" "What progress can we see at the construction site?" "How is that different from our last visit?"
- *During the trip:* Use clipboards with paper and pencils for drawing. Take photographs with a digital camera. One educator suggests taking a "literacy walk" to notice print items, such as signs and house numbers (Owocki, 2010, p. 174).
- *Post-trip:* Sequence photographs and drawings. Discuss events: "What did you like best?" "What surprises did we find?" "What other questions do we have?" "How might we find out more about that?"

If you have limited funds for trips, plan virtual trips. For example, museums such as the Smithsonian Museum of Air and Space and the National Museum of American Art offer video conferencing. As your imagination matches your children's interests, many things could become possible.

Interviews Incorporate Social Studies, Building, and Literacy

When youngsters interview people who work with 3-dimensional constructions, they also begin to associate meaningful experiences with the community workers rather than merely rote verbalizing about generalized "community helpers."

Interviews lend themselves to: (1) preparing questions; (2) writing invitations and thank-you notes; (3) recording events in a class book with drawings and text (either with invented spelling or by dictating to an adult or older child), and other block-building representations.

Books

Teachers also can connect block building to books that deal with builders and buildings. You might see children refer to a book as a guide to their building. Some children also spontaneously use blocks to represent locations in a story or poem.

Equitable Access to 3-Dimensional Experiences

Equitable access to play opportunities for children is significant. There are ways that teachers can be sensitive to gender, cultural and individual differences, and special learning needs (Fromberg, 2006). When teachers sit near the block-building area, girls are likely to participate (Serbin, 1978). Also, during group planning, you can invite girls as well as reticent boys to use block building and other 3-dimensional activities. If you place block building adjacent to other socio-dramatic props, girls and boys are more likely to collaborate. One researcher finds such "border work" to be effective (Thorne, 1993). Consider which children you can invite to be more physically active and who you can engage in talking about their constructions. Pictures on equipment packages also attract children, with girls generally more open to packages that depict either boys or girls. Therefore, gender-neutral packaging or presentation can provide for greater acceptance by all children.

Assessment

Three-dimensional activities provide a vivid window into assessing children's understandings. Assessment takes place when you see how children make progress in the phases along the pathway of block-building development. At the same time, "many theorists stipulate that play is likely to have delayed long-term [positive] effects on development" (Christie, 1994, p. 210). Therefore, experienced teachers trust the value of 3-dimensional construction as a source of important early learning and assessment. You will find additional discussion of assessing play in Chapter 14.

Reflections

In summary, 3-dimensional experiences integrate the following concepts and lend themselves to representation in 2- as well as 3-dimensional forms:

- *Social studies representations* include the continuum of mapping in geography; the economic concept of conservation of natural resources; and the development of a Theory of Mind.
- *Science and mathematics imagery* develop and are represented through experiences that explore physical science concepts as well as quantitative relationships and concepts.
- The continuum of *literacy and the arts* develops. Children's drawings and 3-dimensional constructions blend into representations with both spoken and written language forms. Labels for block shapes, buildings, and signs for constructions provide additional experiences.

Your role is to support and thoughtfully scaffold children's experiences, not participate in disguised academic training. In addition to valuing conceptual growth, an important purpose of teaching young children is to increase their motivation, interest, and positive attitude toward education and the school enterprise.

PART II

Content: Connecting Experiences with Dynamic-Themes

Each chapter in this part presents activities that demonstrate the use of specific Dynamic-Themes as a way to cluster activities. The discussion below describes Dynamic-Themes and how they can represent the scope of school subject matter.

Each evening, I would provide my mother with several elements which she would then weave together into a bedtime story. Sometimes, I would offer an elephant and a mosquito at the beach; at other times, a farmer, rabbit, and a cabbage patch. I took great delight in hearing about the problems that would arise in each story and how the problems were resolved. Only years later did I realize that my mother told me the same underlying story each night, albeit with different surface elements: in effect, problems arise and are resolved so that the protagonists live in peace and harmony—the end. (However unprepared such a message made me for academe, the sense of hope and optimism has proven to be valuable.) In these examples, the deep forms (my mother's plots) are predictable, and the surface forms (my elements) can be unpredictable.

The Dynamic-Theme *underlying* my mother's stories was that protagonists resolve their problems and live in peace and harmony. My different *surface* story elements carry my mother's underlying meaningful message across the bedtimes of my early childhood.

Another example of a Dynamic-Theme is the relationship of the daily weather to regional climate. The weather in the north is predictably colder in winter than in summer but more unpredictable from week to week.

It might be easier to understand the *relationships* between underlying forms and their surface representations if we capture snapshots of the dynamic nonlinear processes in the examples of Table II.1.

In Table II.1, the underlying forms share transformational relationships in which finite patterns can generate infinite possibilities. In these examples, the underlying

TABLE II.1 Sample Relationships Between Underlying Forms and Surface Variety

Underlying Forms	Surface Variety
A musical scale offers a limited number of notes	but there are many ways in which the notes can be related to one another in their sequence or through different rhythms.
An underlying alphabet	changes into different meanings as the letters are combined to create different words.
An underlying set of grammatical rules	changes into different meanings as words proceed in different orders.
Children use an underlying set of rules	to represent a variety of emergent meanings during play. (Grammar of play/script theory.)
An underlying set of images in the physical world, such as cyclical changes or synergy,	takes unpredictable forms within physical or social environments. (Analogical grammar of human experience.)

forms are predictable, and the surface forms are unpredictable. *Meaning occurs within the transformation (shift) between the underlying and surface forms.*

The term "Dynamic-Theme" is hyphenated to indicate images that are both *connected* and in *motion*. For example, the Dynamic-Theme of *cyclical change* underlies such diverse phenomena as human, animal, and plant history, population shifts, shadows outdoors, weather, evaporation–condensation, phases of the moon, and electric circuits. The perceivable *movement* of both change and time underlies and *connects* these phenomena.

The Dynamic-Theme of *contrasts and conflict/dialectical activity* is apparent in play with magnets; ramps; sharing scarce resources; human negotiations; and voting. The perceivable *movement* of tensions and polarities underlies and *connects* these phenomena.

The Dynamic-Theme of *the whole exceeds the parts—synergy*—is apparent in cooperative games, cooking, ecology, mass production, and construction crews; the perceivable *movement* of collaborative processes underlies and *connects* these phenomena.

From a child's standpoint, connections and movement are consistent with how our brains function in the process of building meanings (Tognoli & Kelso, 2008; Sprenger, 2008). The emerging process of interconnected neural networks of the brain support these flexible and transformational processes (Payne & Kounios, 2009; Sandkuhler & Bhattacharya, 2008). The local (underlying) neural networks radiate collectively and globally (surface) within the brain (Kohonen, 1989). Children more easily perceive relationships when activities include the *comparison/induction* and *surprise/cognitive dissonance* conditions for learning, described in Chapter 3.

From a teacher's standpoint, Dynamic-Themes function as conceptual orga-nizers (or conceptual maps, mental models, perceptual models, images) with which to plan experiences that can help children integrate learning across subject matter. When you carefully sequence and pace activities with different surface forms that share an underlying image, it is easier for children to integrate perceptions and create meanings. Different children can have equivalent experiences because they represent the same underlying imagery in more and less complex ways of different surface forms. *The underlying image (Dynamic-Theme) helps children to make connections between new experiences and eases the transfer of learning to perceive fresh connections.*

Analogies help children absorb the connections between their personal experi-ences (Fromberg, 2010). Some elements of an analogy are similar and some different. For example, a horse does not look like a book. However, both a horse and a book can take you places. Both can move quickly or slowly. The *contrast* between how they are similar and how they are different has the potential to create a fresh insight.

Because young children's analogical thinking and imagery are so powerful and fluid, they are able to experience relationships directly and intuitively. They readily "blend [images that are] evident in such experiences as pretense, fantasy, humor, expectation, predication, analogy, and problem solving" (Fauconnier & Turner, 2002, p. 57). Like Dynamic-Themes, analogies can create similar images and help us make connections between different experiences.

Dynamic-Themes: An Analogical Grammar of Early Human Experience

Youngsters implicitly experience the Dynamic-Theme as a connection-making process, an analogical "grammar of experience." When you plan several activities that help children implicitly experience a Dynamic-Theme, children are able to make the transition between not-knowing and knowing.

Pre-kindergarten and kindergarten children access Dynamic-Themes by using their imaginations and by making connections between concepts, in effect using analogous thinking. Each teacher and group of children negotiates and constructs their own "fingerprint of experience." These fingerprints may differ on the surface from group to group but they share similar underlying meanings. Meaning is lymphatic. Reality is complex and nonlinear, and the "knowledge of reality or meaning does not lie in the Subject or the Object, but in the dynamic flow between them (Udall, 1996, p. 49, citing Bohm)." Dynamic-Themes reflect this complex and nonlinear nature of reality.

Children are likely to devote their attention to ideas that have significance in their lives, and emotional experiences often underlie and define the degree of significance of ideas. When you match activities to youngsters' underlying emotional, perceptual, and sequential experiences, they are more likely to make fresh connections and build new images.

Effective kindergarten and pre-kindergarten teachers offer children immediate personal involvement with materials and equipment rather than a lengthy introductory discussion. Children construct and represent meanings in many forms by employing the same tools that scientists, social scientists, and artists use. However, youngsters do not divide the world into chemistry, physics, history, geography, and art. You can help children to connect the similar underlying images that represent different disciplines when you soak their environment with various surface activities that represent the underlying regularities of a particular Dynamic-Theme.

When we are born, life comes to us as a whole rather than as separate subjects. The development of disciplines, or domains of knowing, helps to focus our thinking. Nevertheless, we are continually making connections. For example, geology and physics now have specialties in geophysics; other domains have developed as biochemists, sociolinguists, and psycholinguists. Making these connections across "adjacent" disciplines or experiences is the basis for building new knowledge.

Teachers who want to "cover" separate subjects, even in an all-day schedule, might feel that they do not have enough time. However, you can use time efficiently when you plan activities with Dynamic-Themes that integrate learning across subject matter areas. Table II.2 addresses this particular issue within activity-based learning environments by showing how each Dynamic-Theme can provide coverage with relevant activities. The listing of sample images that cut across typical school subject matter accommodates the linear character of print.

The intersection of particular Dynamic-Themes and activities in Table II.2 previews several of the chapters in this part of the book.

Overview of Chapters

Each chapter presents a variety of related experiences. Chapter 5 focuses on the Dynamic-Theme: cyclical changes; Chapter 6 on contrasts and conflicts (dialectical activity); and Chapter 7 on how the whole exceeds the parts (synergy). Chapter 8 includes activities that employ the conditions for learning discussed in Chapter 3. Multicultural education is an interdisciplinary field, comprising the disciplines of history, geography, economics, political science, sociology, psychology, and anthropology. Each of these disciplines uses distinctive tools that can help students make connections. The social studies of history, geography, economics, and political science that appear in school learning standards are discussed in turn as a context for planning integrated activities. The subject matter of the social studies shares with multicultural education the potential to influence the egalitarian (anti-bias) attitudes and behavior of human beings toward one another.

TABLE II.2 Sample Dynamic–Themes Activities Cut Across Disciplines

| Disciplines | Dynamic–Themes | | | |
	Cyclical Changes	Contrasts and Conflicts/ Dialectical Activity	Indirect Progress	Whole Exceeds the Parts–Synergy
History	Hear oral history. Compare past customs and artifacts. Create a personal timeline.	Narrate and compare conflicting events.	Compare experiences of being lost and other incongruent events.	Compare surprises and explosive events.
Geography	Map city: country population shifts. Trace garbage recycling.	Map wind action and erosion.	Create and use obstacle courses.	Map immigration and change in children's families. Run relay races.
Economics & Sociology	Survey food cycle, group memberships, and changing groups.	Survey action vs. reaction, scarcity, and group conflict.	Play with short-term sacrifice. Role-play social leverage and values differences.	Experience socio-dramatic activity. Make cooperative products.
Political Science	Narrate political shifts and rule changes in school and current events.	Narrate human conflicts and values. Humorously invert reality during discussions.	Attempt to influence school administrators or elected officials.	Role-play voting and outcomes. Vote.
Physics	Observe and record seasons. Map shadows outdoors. Create electrical circuits.	Observe gravitation, interactions of forces, and aerodynamics by varying shapes of materials.	Explore levers. Experience centrifugal force with objects and other people.	Explore physical actions and reactions. Assemble simple machines.
Chemistry	Observe evaporation and condensation.	Observe and change solubility of materials. Mix oil, water, and color.	Identify substances by using household materials.	Cook representative food products: e.g., popcorn. Make butter.

TABLE II.2 Sample Dynamic-Themes Activities Cut Across Disciplines

Disciplines	Dynamic-Themes			
	Cyclical Changes	Contrasts and Conflicts/ Dialectical Activity	Indirect Progress	Whole Exceeds the Parts—Synergy
Biology	Make seasonal returns to sites of outdoor educational trips. Raise plants and animals. Classify dinosaurs. Survey human growth.	Observe interaction of environment and life forms. Control variables and compare.	Study nutrition of plants. Control variables.	Study growth and reproduction of plants and animals.
Mathematics	Classify varied objects. Measure time and change.	Classify object differences. Measure polarities.	Measure physical progress. Estimate quantities. Play games that include strategies that sacrifice pieces.	Measure transformed changes. Combine shapes and sizes.
Arts	Create present-time aesthetic experiences: e.g., bark rubbings of younger and older trees.	Play with counterpoint in music, dance, and visual arts.	Experience movement education exemplars: e.g., partners, group contra dance.	Contrast melodies with choral and ensemble work. Collaborate in movement education, visual arts, and dance. Mix colors. Create murals.
Language	Listen to literature about the past, mythic monsters, and poetic cycles. Record past and present.	Select poetic forms and literature about oppositions. Do related composing. Compare different descriptions of the same event.	Select poetic forms and literature about indirect progress. Compose.	Select poetic forms and literature about collaborative elements. Co-author.

5

DYNAMIC-THEME EXPERIENCES

Cyclical Changes

Introduction

When 4-year-old Laish talked about ancestors, his mother asked him what the word meant. He thought for a moment and responded, "Sabre-tooth tigers are the ancestors of tigers."

This verbal youngster dramatically shows us that he has some sense of time about a subject that we typically do not expect to be part of early childhood classroom study. Other 4-year-olds build a similar sense of ancestry when they learn about their parents' connections to grandparents. In a parallel way, their life experiences of waking and sleeping and the sequence of events in your classroom add to their sense of time and cyclical change.

Time, and change across time (cyclical change), is the focus of this chapter. Duration and change through time is an underlying perceptual experience. Rhythmic flow is the emotional experience that underlies cyclical change.

The Dynamic-Theme of cyclical change is present in the disciplines of history, geography, economics and sociology, political science, physics, chemistry, biology, mathematics, the arts, and language. The arts, literacy, and mathematics are integrated in most activities presented below.

Examples of experiences clustered around cyclical changes are described below. However, not all children need to participate in all experiences. You would make selections based upon your particular children and community resources. (Guidelines for adapting to socio-cultural customs and diverse learning needs are discussed in Chapter 8 and Part III.) [**Procedural note:** Many experiences for young children tend to be interdisciplinary. Therefore, the broad headings of Physical Knowledge Activities, Social Activities and Animal Studies, Quantitative Activities, and Representational Knowing and Arts, below, represent an integrated

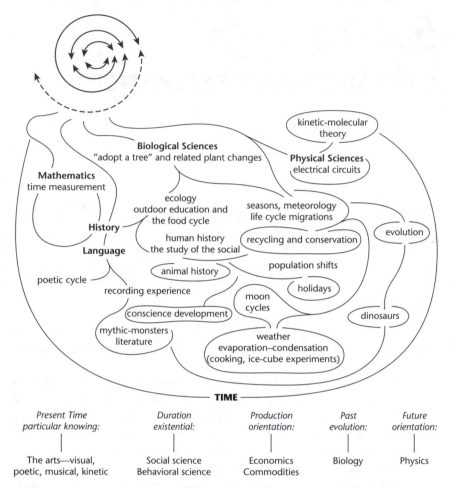

FIGURE 5.1 Cyclical Change Dynamic-Theme

emphasis rather than separate subjects within this chapter and the ones that follow. Note, also, that many kindergarten children can benefit from activities that pre-kindergarten children engage in. Use of the term "young children" accounts for either age group.] Figure 5.1 presents a model of this Dynamic-Theme.

Any experience of time and change builds toward the imagery of cyclical change. It is necessary to plan a series of several activities that represent cyclical changes in order to perceive the underlying Dynamic-Theme. The activities described below highlight the integration of *physical, inductive,* and *surprise/cognitive dissonance* conditions for learning. Children also *revisit* events and sites while engaging in *social interaction* in *playful* ways that build their *sense of competence.*

Physical Knowledge Activities

Adopt a Tree and Related Plant Changes (Biology, History, Mathematics, Literacy, and the Arts Included)

Pre-kindergarten children are able to "adopt" a tree in the school yard. They can visit their tree at different seasons throughout the year and view photographs during each season. These are some of the things they can do with their tree:

- make observational drawings over time (*revisiting*), selecting varied media;
- take turns with a partner to make bark rubbings on paper with one child holding the paper in place while the other rubs (*social interaction*);
- *compare* bark rubbings from older and younger trees;
- *compare* their tree with one that another class adopts;
- mark the shadows of the tree at different times (*revisiting*) during the day and year, play with catching each other's shadows in relation to the tree's shadow, and outline a partner's shadow (*social*) on the pavement with chalk;
- dictate cinquains about their tree in different seasons (*revisiting*);
- collect leaves in the fall, and compare the leaves of their tree with leaves from other trees;
- use their tree as a snowball target (in northern climates in the winter), a maypole around which to play games and dance (in the springtime), and a shady spot for story time and sing-a-longs (in mild weather) (*revisiting*);

IMAGE 5.1 Adopt a Tree Bulletin Board

- record their seasonal activities with photographs and drawings, make *comparisons*, and add dictated or invented spelling comments to their "Tree History Book";

- dictate and engage in invented spelling, writing about what they might see, and wondering what if they were to "become" a tree at different seasons or in different locations (*imaginative play*);

- measure the circumference of the tree trunk with yarn and, late in the school year, with tape measures marked by both inches and centimeters. Employing the *surprise/cognitive dissonance* condition for learning, they begin to estimate the circumference of the tree by: (1) (*expecting*) asking how many hand spans or cubit spans (elbow to middle finger length) would circle the tree; (2) (*experiencing*) placing their collective hands around the tree; and (3) *comparing* their predictions and their findings. Keep *comparison* charts of their findings; and share their findings with other classes (*social; sense of competence*).

The Food Cycle and Gardening (Biology, Economics, Geography, History, Literacy, the Arts, and Mathematics Included)

Adults refer to activities such as gardening and collecting as play (Fromberg & Bergen, 1998). Planting and gardening offer other opportunities to perceive cyclical change. However, the point of such activities for young children is the experience of any change over time, not necessarily plans that demand the demonstration of a full cycle. *Young children's learning is, after all, legitimately episodic because they are satisfied without a formal beginning, middle, and end.*

Planting seeds can demonstrate cyclical change, especially when children scoop out pumpkin seeds in the autumn, dry them, and save them for spring planting. Some teachers arrange for each child to plant their own pumpkin seeds in individual used milk containers in order to provide a beribboned presentation for Family Day in May. In the interest of good feelings, teachers sometimes surreptitiously plant "replacement" containers for those children whose seeds have not sprouted. Imagine the *surprise/cognitive dissonance* of one child's teacher during the following exchange (J. Koch, personal communication, 1996):

Daniel: Teacher, this is a miracle.
Teacher: What do you mean, Daniel?
Daniel: My seeds grew even though I ate them.

It is important to grow plants in order to observe changes and to learn about the factors that influence change, such as water, light, and so forth. Bulbs, flowers from seeds, and vegetable seeds can grow rapidly in a window box or outdoor garden. Sprouts grow quickly from alfalfa seeds, mung beans, sunflower seeds, mature green peas, and avocado pits, as do such plant cuttings as carrot tops, turnip tops, and sprouting sweet potatoes. A related activity includes placing celery in one color of dyed water and a white carnation in a different color. Children are able to observe the color rising within the plants' capillary systems.

Kindergarten children can keep a log of changes they observe. Teachers would need to help pre-kindergarten children note periodic changes. [**Caution and Procedural note:** (1) experiences and questions come first; (2) discussion and information take place after children see events unfold; (3) books come after experiences in order to answer questions that children have or to confirm their findings.]

Electrical Circuits (Physics Included)

Kindergarten children create electrical circuits with clamps and a battery that powers a light bulb, buzzer, or bell to use in their socio-dramatic play centers. They are able to use protected wires of varying lengths as they play with constructing and then using the circuits. (Adults usually find that the light bulb is the least disruptive form for classroom use.) The electrical circuit is another form in which young children can directly experience cyclical change. (This is also an example of design technology, discussed in Chapter 11.)

Moon Cycles (Physics, Geology (Earth Science), and Literature Included)

Young children participate in checking the cycles of the moon and kindergarten children are able to represent them in a journal. They take care always to view from the same position. They compare the night sky and the morning sky when both the sun and the moon are present, experiencing some *surprise/cognitive dissonance*.

Social Knowing and Animal Study

Human History (Biology, History, Geography, Sociology, and Economics Included)

Timelines are *playful* when they are collections of each child's photographic history from infancy to the present, with accompanying captions. Children also measure themselves at the start and near the end of the year. Whether they create a photographic timeline of class pets or a school trip, children can have equivalent experiences of cyclical change that different experiences represent. After all, *different children doing different things at different times may have the equivalent experience of change over time.*

You could also invite a grandparent or community elder to bring photographs to school. It is important to prepare visitors to discuss such issues as "how things used to be" before television, computers, or when they lived on a farm. It is also very exciting to bring in a baby who can be the subject of observation and measurement at different times throughout the school year. Again, recordings include photographs, yarn strips to measure the length and girth of the baby, drawings, and language experience/shared writing. Some families might share a newborn's footprint that children can compare with the later outline of the baby's foot. Families that save children's baby shoes or other clothing are able to share some samples for comparison with current clothing items. There might also be audiotapes of vocalizations or videotapes at different times.

Children enjoy marking their height at different times during the school year, charting with nonstandard direct (particular length of yarn) or nonstandard discontinuous (numbers of blocks) measures and then standard measures. Each kindergarten child might have a personal notebook in which to record his or her weight and height early and then later in the year.

Population Shifts (Geography, Economics, History, Geography, Political Science, Literacy, and Mathematics Included)

After children visit different locales, they are able to compare rural, suburban, and urban areas. Some kindergarten teachers and children could create a Venn diagram of city and country attributes. A book such as *The Little House* (Burton, 1988) shows cyclical change and lends itself to opportunities for dramatic play that might also stimulate additional local trips.

Holidays (History, Economics, Geography, Sociology, Chemistry, the Arts, and Literature Included)

Schools less typically relate holidays to the weather and cyclical change. On the surface, "holidays differ from outdoor education or the weather. On the deeper level, they represent cyclical changes of passing-through struggles in human lives" (Fromberg, 1982, p. 195). A discussion of the Dynamic-Themes that underlie holidays across cultures appears in Chapter 8.

Recycling and Conservation (Geography, Political Science, Mathematics, and Literacy Included)

Trace garbage recycling and the water cycle. Everyday events, rather than artificial or trivial "units," can contribute to experiencing the Dynamic-Theme of cyclical change. Dripping water faucets (see the Political Science section in Chapter 8 and Box 8.3) represent aspects of cyclical change (*cognitive dissonance*). Consider also what accessible experiences your community offers to trace the recycling of bottles and cans.

Animal History (Biology, History, Mathematics, Literacy, and the Arts Included)

Gerbils and guinea pigs lend themselves to the study of change in similar ways. Some groups predict the weights, record their predictions, weigh their gerbils using balance scales, and then record their findings. Children compare their predictions and findings over time (*surprise/cognitive dissonance*). Such activities lend themselves to multiple forms of representation that include drawing, writing, and photographing. [**Procedural note:** Remind children to wash their hands after handling animals.]

Land snails or *hermit crabs* offer another form of study that can extend to *comparing* habitats. The terrarium of the land snail begs *comparison* with the hermit crab's aquarium, the tadpole's pond, and the lizard's desert habitat. Land snails, for example, can begin their visit to a classroom with each child receiving a transparent "salad bar" container with air holes added. Each container includes wet paper towels, twigs, pebbles, and two snails. Children observe the snails with lenses, flashlights, and offerings of unsalted and unprocessed foods. Box 5.1 outlines their activities with land snails.

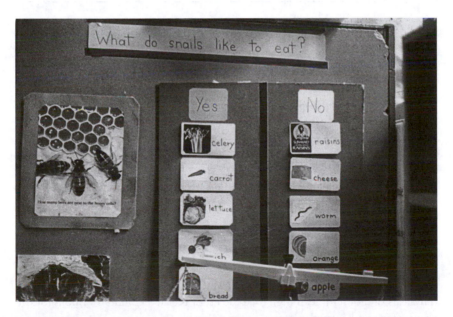

IMAGE 5.2 Yes–No Survey of Snails' Diet (Picture–Word Format)

BOX 5.1 STUDY OF LAND SNAILS

- Observe and describe the snails' interactions within their physical environments and with one another.
- Observe new generations of snails appear.
- Observe snails die.
- Explore and play with the snails.
- Represent activities in a variety of symbolic forms:
    - vote on names for the snails, place votes on a graph, and count the votes
    - draw
    - create yes–no surveys of foods that snails do and do not eat
    - language experience/shared writing describes observations of the snails
    - write with inventive spelling (kindergarten)
    - tell imaginative stories about the snails and, along the way,
    - *inductively* learn about cyclical changes.

[**Procedural note:** In studying an animal, whether a land snail, hermit crab, butterfly, fish, or guinea pig, there is a powerful learning process in the following format:

- First simply observe.
- Second, share only observations.
- Raise questions.
- Share likenesses and possible findings.
- Children raise new questions.

Suggest that children consider "What might happen if . . .?"]

In addition, teachers as well as children who are able can read books about the animal. The use of books would take place *after* the process of observing and talking about events. Nonfiction books serve as a dramatic part of *surprise/cognitive dissonance* after children have experiences and talk about them. When used after real experiences, books help to enrich the brain connections that children make during the multisensory experience of handling, seeing, smelling, and listening (physical condition for learning). (See the list of Related Children's Books for this chapter for good examples.)

Tadpole eggs appear in ponds during the spring. Youngsters appreciate raising tadpole eggs and then feeding tadpoles on crumbs and fish food in an aquarium. When the peeper frogs develop, you would transfer from the water to a terrarium. *Eggs and Tadpoles* (Elementary Science Study, 1974) offers an array of interesting ideas for teachers and children to pursue.

Butterfly gardens are commercially available (Insect Lore) and pre-kindergartens use them successfully. Educators (Worth & Grollman, 2003) report that children who had direct experiences with a butterfly's life cycle found discrepancies in the popular book *The Very Hungry Caterpillar* (Carle, 1970).

Hatching chicks in an incubator provide equivalent experiences. Local 4H clubs will often supply a school with eggs and an incubator.

Mealworm study is another exciting activity that exemplifies cyclical change. Mealworms are available at local pet shops. [**Procedural note:** If you anticipate that a major transformation might occur very fast or when school is not in session, consider photographs and books as relevant.]

Dinosaur study generates some controversy in early childhood education because they are now extinct (Kamii with Houseman, 2000). Dinosaurs, nevertheless, appeal to young children's imaginations because of their multisyllabic, prestigious names, and they perhaps serve to help young children come to terms with issues of conscience, power, and monsters. In addition to small models, there are huge museum replicas that some children might visit. Box 5.2 outlines some dinosaur model study activities.

BOX 5.2 DINOSAUR MODEL STUDY

- Classify vegetarian and carnivorous dinosaurs by comparing limbs, tails, and footprints.
- Classify other animals' tails, paws, ears, size, teeth, skin textures, mobility, and adaptation patterns.
- In the spirit of a guessing game, kindergarten children can *play* with estimating and comparing the heights of different dinosaur models with Unifix cubes and then build cube towers to compare their estimations (*surprise/cognitive dissonance*). [**Note:** This type of activity helps children tumble into number operations.]
- Count how many cubes taller, how many shorter, and how many cubes tall altogether for each dinosaur model.

The concept of a *fossil* becomes accessible with plaster-of-Paris hand- or footprints. Printing with sponges, vegetables (and later with words) adds to the fossil concept. Feeling the soil during different seasons, making predictions, attempting to create footprints, and then comparing the attempts can add to the study.

Fossil study might lead to the study of varied rock formations and the roles of heat and pressure. Kindergarten children, for example, are able to recommend various ways in which they might sort the rocks they collect by testing hardness with their fingernail or a steel nail.

Children also experience *surprise/cognitive dissonance* by predicting and comparing their findings: "How long might it take for grapes to dry into raisins?"

Quantitative Study

Time (Biology, Physics, Chemistry, Mathematics, the Arts, and History Included)

Related activities that represent cyclical changes might include some of the following: count the number of birds at a *bird feeder* at different times during the school day by children moving pegs from one box to another; and survey *heartbeat rates* before and after running for one minute.

Children create the concept of a *sun dial* by marking the passage of shadows outdoors on an oak-tag clock-face. Then they compare the oak-tag markings with a working, analog clock-face (*surprise/cognitive dissonance*). They *play* (condition for learning) with creating *shadows* in front of or behind themselves. They try to hide their shadow, jump on it, and chase it. *Play* (*physical* condition for learning) with shadows prepares children to begin to grasp the concept of time in relation to the sun. Some playful activities appear in Box 5.3.

BOX 5.3 SHADOW EXPLORATIONS

- Play with light from the sun to make shadows.
- Make funny-shaped shadows . . .
- Who can make the longest shadow?
- Who can make the shortest shadow?
- Can you hide your shadow?
- Can you jump on your shadow?
- Stand upside down and make a shadow.
- Can you make a shadow with four arms and four legs?
- Can you move without your shadow moving?
- Can you stand with your shadow in front of you?
- Can you stand with your shadow behind you?

(Richards, 1992, p. 15; see also Malaguzzi & Petter, 1996; Ritz, 2007, pp. 279–289)

Bird watching and feeding, and recording findings across the seasons, add to the concept of cyclical change. In addition, youngsters attempt to imagine their own growth and have difficulty sorting out the concept of time. They do, however, notice plants and animals that die, food that decays, and metal that rusts. They hear about the death of elderly people and sometimes younger people. They also engage in socio-dramatic and pretend play concerning the related themes of ages, roles, and death; the pretend play also may involve solitary use of toy figures or dramatizing a drawing.

The Weather (Chemistry, Geology, Economics, Geography, History, Mathematics, Literacy, and the Arts Included)

Attention to the weather can integrate the study of earth sciences and social sciences in ways that do not need to create a daily calendar ritual but that do extend possibilities for learning. It is worthwhile to take the weather more seriously than the usual preoccupation with "Today is Monday. It is cloudy and raining. We will have lunch inside." It is relevant to look for a basis to plan beyond how things have always been done.

Children learn about *temperature* through direct daily experiences. For example, create the rain cycle in a terrarium or by inverting a transparent container over items drying in the sun. Children also see examples of the *evaporation and condensation cycle* by observing cooking activities. (Additional activities appear in Chapter 11.) On another note, challenge children to consider reversing parallel physical events, such as envisioning how to reverse food color or get toothpaste back in the tube (Krogh & Morehouse, 2008, p. 249).

Representational Knowing and Arts

Movement

Movement education offers a forum for using personal analogy as another way to raise consciousness about *temperature* (see the Temperature section in Chapter 11). The aesthetics of viewing a snowfall through the window, dancing the fall of snowflakes, or taking a walk around the school on crunching snow are aesthetic ways of knowing the impact of temperature.

Folk Songs

Folk songs that deal with planting include *Garden Song* (Mallett, 1975), which includes, "Inch by inch, row by row / This is how my garden grows" and selected parts of *The Field behind the Plow* (Rogers, 1982, pp. 88–89): "And watch the field behind the plow turn to straight dark rows / Put another season's promise in the ground." **[Procedural note:** Poetry and songs offer incidentally repeated exposure to rhymes, expanded vocabulary, and language with complex grammar.]

Assessment

You might assess the sequence of emotional and perceptual development of cyclical change as children demonstrate their capacities, as follows: (1) accepting events; (2) receiving and sorting events; (3) anticipating change; and (4) creating change over time. When you plan activities with *surprise/cognitive dissonance*, children's *surprise* reaction signals their learning.

Consider several facets of content assessment shared by Dynamic-Themes in general. At the most concrete level, you can assess children's comprehension of content by observing how they use materials in particular ways, how they make connections, and what they say. They sometimes reveal a different degree of understanding when they draw an image of events, so you just might ask on occasion. They show their understanding when they make connections by sorting related items. They also show their understanding when they use humor; by playing with what something is not, they show that they understand what it is.

Children demonstrate a deeper level of understanding when they sort or connect related items or processes based upon analogy: for example, they recognize analogies based on some shared similarity or relative intensity (see Wormeli, 2009; Pinker, 2007). Additional discussion of assessment is integrated within the pathways of learning and teacher scaffolds across chapters that follow, particularly Chapter 14, in which Table 14.3 includes an evaluation scale for conceptual development.

Reflections

It is apparent that there is insufficient time across a school year to participate in all of the experiences in this chapter. Within your particular situation, however, you would plan those activities that match your children within their particular environment. Urban, suburban, or rural areas offer different possibilities and resources. Personnel support for trips just beyond the classroom and funds for purchases are other considerations.

A representative range of several activities from among those described in this chapter will provide an underlying experience of the image of the cyclical change Dynamic-Theme. Moreover, activities dealing with cyclical change help youngsters trust that change and good things can take time. Youngsters learn to trust that activity for its own sake, rather than immediate gratification, can be comfortably engaging. These kinds of middle-term and longer-term experiences could contribute to building self-regulation.

Children in different years who work with you might have equivalent experiences of the dynamic changes, just as different groups of children within a particular year who engage in a different mix of experiences might have the equivalent experience of cyclical change. The point of their experiences is to provide the armature around which they may build future associations.

6

DYNAMIC-THEME EXPERIENCES

Contrasts and Conflicts
(Dialectical Activity)

Introduction

When Albert Einstein was 4 years of age, his father gave him a compass (Isaacson, 2007). Einstein credited his imagining the theory of relativity with his early curiosity about how an unseen force could control the movements of the hand on the compass. In general, he envisioned that the conceptual developments in his adult years began as "pictures in his head," similar to the iconic imagery of many 4-year-olds.

At a "Physics of the Universe Summit," physicists discussed how "a refrigerator magnet can hold itself against the pull of the entire Earth" (*New York Times*, January 10, 2010, p. D2).[1] It is noteworthy, therefore, that kindergarten children are also beginning to consider the interactions of the same contrasting forces of gravitation and magnetism as they explore various materials over time, imagine the "pull" of unseen forces, and discuss other forces, such as somebody pushing a door closed (Fromberg, 1965). Young children are receptive to the underlying imagery of contrasting forces when teachers intentionally plan activities with physical contrasts. A description of related activities appears in the Interaction of Physical Forces section later in this chapter. [**Procedural note:** Within this framework, it is important to keep in mind that *different children at different times might have equivalent experiences*. The precise form and content that you offer children will depend upon the particular interactions that take place and which you are able to adapt within your comfort zone and your range of resources.]

Struggle/challenge is the emotional experience that underlies conflict/contrast (dialectical activity). Polarities and contrasts are the underlying perceptual experience. This chapter outlines some ways in which teachers can plan to saturate engaging activities with images of contrasts and conflicts to which young children

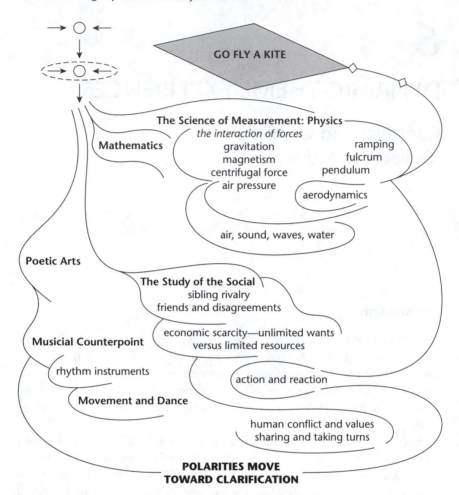

FIGURE 6.1 Contrasts and Conflicts (Dialectical Activity) Dynamic-Theme

are receptive. Figure 6.1 presents a model of this Dynamic-Theme. The chapter continues with a description of activities that help young children experience contrasts and conflicts/dialectical activity within social and quantitative knowing, representational knowing and the arts, and physical knowing.

Social and Quantitative Knowing

Scarcity (Economics, Mathematics, Sociology, and Sciences Included)

The issues of supply and demand integrate social, economic, and scientific threads. For example, children sometimes want to use equipment that other children are using. Young children deal with the dissonance between what they want and what they can have or can acquire on their own or with the help of others. Teachers repeatedly encourage children to wait their turn and to share materials with others. All human beings experience the contrast between what they want and what they might have or are able to do. Each person can jump only so high or run so fast or reach so many targets with a ball or beanbag.

Wants and Needs

Through *social* (condition for learning) feedback, human beings learn to work out many of the differences between what they want and the resources they might have. Some teachers use puppets to help *play* with some of these issues. Kindergarten children might also role-play to represent conflicts and alternative ways to resolve them; for example, "What are some other ways he could solve the problem without lying?" Teachers read stories that deal with sibling rivalry and acceptance or rejection by others. They discuss with children how these stories relate to the children's lives. Some thoughts about dealing with role-playing are outlined in Box 6.1.

BOX 6.1 ROLE-PLAY TO RESOLVE ISSUES OF WANTS AND NEEDS

- Using a photograph, you might wonder out loud: "There are many possible ways to figure out what is happening here. What do you suppose *might* be happening?"
- "What else might be happening?" "What else?" "What ideas do other people have?"
- "What might you wish would happen to help them?" "What else?"
- "What might be some ways to work things out so that everyone leaves feeling good?" "What else?"
- "When did something like that happen to you?" ". . . to somebody you know?" "Tell us what happened." "What do you think about how things turned out?" [**Procedural note:** The use of "might" signals that more than one interpretation is possible and welcome. The question "What *is* happening?" suggests a single correct interpretation. Children learn that you respect their ideas and that there might be more than one way to solve problems.]
- "Let's pretend that one person becomes this person in the picture and two other people talk to him using Bob's idea." "Please raise your hand if you want to play this role." "What would you say to him first?" (See also Box 8.9.)

Voting (Political Science, Mathematics, Sociology, Multicultural Education Included)

Voting is one way that children can experience contrasting (dialectical) viewpoints. Through many varied experiences, in which teachers respect children's choices, children come to appreciate differences and the value of taking turns. Some examples of play with voting follow.

During a national election, children become aware of candidates' names and families' preferences. They enjoy role-playing voting, looking at posters, marking ballots, and then tallying the results. Beginning in pre-kindergarten, teachers and children survey the children's preferences. For example, selecting a colored sticker, a few 4-year-olds at a time are able to place their favorite color on a grid. Two pre-kindergarten children are able to circulate during an activity time and alternately carry a clipboard and mark under "yes" or "no" others' preferences for a type of snack, for example candy corn or pretzels. (Box 12.8 and the pages that follow provide additional activities and procedures.)

When children participate in voting and surveys, they can see a graphic representation of: (1) their prediction/estimation; (2) selection activity; and (3) comparison between the prediction and the outcome. The contrast between the prediction and the outcome is a *surprise/cognitive dissonance* (condition for learning), the moment of meaningful learning.

Fairness (Political Science and Mathematics Included)

The issue of fairness also provides an experience in the contrasts and conflicts/ dialectical activity Dynamic-Theme. A creative pre-kindergarten teacher (Mardell, 1999, pp. 103–105) discussed with the children that some had turned 4 or 5 while others were still 3 years of age. Only one age group on alternating days could vote on snacks; the other age group complained about fairness. A lively discussion ensued about ways to organize fairness.

Representational Knowing and the Arts

Movement Education and Angular Momentum

When children spin as they dance, they explore moving faster when they bring in their arms, which conserves angular momentum (*physical* condition for learning). Children intuitively learn to spin in dances and games, and they *compare* (condition for learning) streamlined vehicles with their kites. Their *play* includes activities in Box 9.3.

Counterpoint in Music, the Arts, and Literature

Children can listen to counterpoint in music and play with rhythm. They see dialectical images in visual arts, such as Picasso paintings, compare painters who use different styles to represent similar themes, and create rhythmic-movement activities that involve syncopation and opposites. They hear the same music interpreted by different performers and hear folk tales retold with different interpretations. They discuss the differences and vote for their favorite versions. Kindergarten children are able to engage in choral speaking and round singing that creates a *contrast* and *conflicting* counterpoint experience. Teachers read aloud biographies of the same person written by different authors and children *compare* the accounts. They enjoy the multiple viewpoints and argue about the nature of truth and the interpretation of events.

Sound

Youngsters play with sound as they imitate animal noises as well as the sounds of people in their lives. They begin to sing and play with pitch, dynamics, and volume. Pre-kindergarten children intentionally alter how loudly they shriek, sometimes to the point of throat strain. They enjoy pounding on their chests as they speak in order to hear the vibrations. They put their ears on the chest of a speaking adult, and giggle at the tickle of the vibrations.

They directly experience sound when banging on pans and using rhythm instruments. They play with various informal noise-making materials and more formal rhythm instruments. They shout in each other's ears and speak on the telephone. They construct their own listening devices that include paper cups and strings, tubes, and funnels. They rub a fingertip around the rims of glasses, and tap a spoon on glasses filled with varying amounts of water—often in restaurants, often to the limits of adult tolerance. In addition, kindergarten children enjoy part singing; pre-kindergarten children create rhythmic clapping to chanted jingles and rap messages. Some youngsters begin to play musical instruments with systematic instruction. In short, they play with sound by using objects as well as their own bodies and voices. Schools typically offer opportunities for counterpoint with group singing and group playing of rhythm instruments.

Physical Knowing

Magnets (Physics Included)

Toddlers use magnets to collect spilled paper clips and other objects. Pre-kindergarten children predict which objects a magnet is likely to attract. They: (1) predict; (2) sort; and (3) compare their findings. *Surprises/cognitive dissonance* emerge when children predict that the magnet will attract all shiny, smooth, and hard materials but find that it does not attract all similar-looking materials: for example, copper is not attracted. (See also Box 3.2.)

Kindergarten children enjoy predicting, repeating various approaches to "trick" the magnets, and comparing their results. They are also able to magnetize blunt-tipped embroidery needles by moving a magnet along them in a single direction while holding the eye. They then observe the attraction of opposing ends and attempt to "trick" their magnetized needles. These early images of attraction and repulsion establish a thread that later connects to the imagery underlying electro-magnets and the behavior of subatomic particles. The underlying Dynamic-Theme (*contrasts and conflicts/dialectical activity*) becomes the basis for building connections among images over time.

Waves: Play with Water, and Sound (Physics, Mathematics, Geography, Chemistry, and the Arts Included)

Help children explore and play with the properties of water using a *surprise/cognitive dissonance* format. For example, they: (1) predict; (2) observe and sort materials that absorb or shed water into separate "yes" and "no" containers; and (3) compare their predictions with their findings.

The classroom does not duplicate the random exploration of the at-home bathtub. Rather, teachers sequence the interaction of water and air while providing contrasting variables, such as shapes of openings, methods of movement of drops of water, and the flow of water (Chalufour & Worth, 2005). Other professional

IMAGE 6.1 Yes–No Sorting: Does it Absorb Water?

sources offer additional examples of water play (Elementary Science Study, 1971; Richards, Collis, & Kincaid, 1995; Worth & Grollman, 2003). Some teachers and young children (1) predict; (2) act; and (3) compare their findings when they explore floating with whole fruit, peeled fruit, and cut fruit in salted and/or sugared water (Brooks, 2011). They compare what happens when they place either a whole orange or orange slices in the water. Others compare the floating of raw and cooked vegetables, one variable at a time. These activities integrate the *surprise/cognitive dissonance* condition for learning.

Kindergarten children figure out how to float objects that would otherwise sink, a form of construction play and design technology. They use aluminum foil and plasticene to create "boats." They *predict* how many paper clips they could place, one at a time on their boat before it sinks, and *compare* their prediction with their observation. They also *play* at blowing directly on the water and through straws into the water to make waves and move their boat.

Pre-kindergarten children *play* with water wheels and pour higher or lower streams of water to create different degrees of force. They enjoy filling containers to the point at which they overflow. Some children play by adding a spoonful at a time to a nearly full container. Kindergarten children can also control the water with an eyedropper. When they add one drop of water at a time to a container that looks full, they "dare" and test when it will reach its capacity. Children, after exploring how to control drops (sometimes with teacher modeling), count how many drops of water might cover a penny, look at what happens when they blow on drops and how drops combine on wax paper, and so forth (Worth & Grollman, 2003; Brooks, 2011).

Youngsters enjoy making predictions and watching the water molecules mount. *Surprise/cognitive dissonance* is an important component of phase transitions, the bridges to understanding. Youngsters also enjoy comparing how water molecules behave with soapsuds. They incidentally learn the terms "molecules" and "surface tension" in the context of *playful* activities.

Air Play (Physics, Chemistry, Mathematics, and Geography Included)

Pre-kindergarten children actively sort those things that are easier or more difficult to blow with their own breath or with a drinking straw. They delight in blowing the paper covers off drinking straws—a way of learning about air that some adults do not appreciate! Ask children to predict and compare the relative ease with which they might blow different objects by puffing through a drinking straw. Box 6.2 describes these activities. Professional sources offer additional ideas for activities involving balloons and inflatable toys (Chalufour & Worth, 2005; Zubrowski, 1979, 1990).

BOX 6.2 THE FORCE OF AIR CREATES MOVEMENT IN PRE-KINDERGARTEN

- Youngsters mark floor squares and predict which objects they might propel beyond one, two, or more squares.
- They blow up balloons with their own breath and with manual balloon pumps.
- They play with air- and water-propelled rocket launchers outdoors.
- They blow marbles through mazes.
- They use straws to create sand art and air-propelled paintings.
- They partially insert a drinking straw in an otherwise sealed ziplock bag, and take delight in seeing one object at a time set on top of the bag—such as a small book, doll, or wooden cube—tip over when they blow through the straw into the sealed bag.

Bubbles

Bubbles provide another focus for *play* with *contrasts and conflicts*, beginning with soapsuds. Youngsters enjoy blowing bubbles in their glass of milk, feeling carbonated water bubbles tickle their nose, and seeing bubbles appear in their water play. Teachers of pre-kindergarten children who can blow out rather than suck in liquids can add detergents to water and encourage bubble play with various objects, such as whisks and eggbeaters. Children can also blow bubbles by using wires and wands of different shapes, plastic mesh, and plastic berry containers. They: (1) *predict* the shape of bubbles through wands of different shapes; (2) blow bubbles; and (3) *compare* their findings with their predictions (*surprise/cognitive dissonance*). They enjoy exploring how to make bigger or multiple bubbles, and how to collapse or sustain bubbles by using a wet or dry finger (Zubrowski, 1979; Ritz, 2007). They blow and follow bubbles, try to catch them, and aim them (Davies, 2003, pp. 190–191). Children wonder about and discover the effect of color added to the bubble solution.

Young children also imagine themselves contained within a bubble, "become" a bubble, dance as if they are bubbles, and walk as if bubbles are on the ground. This use of personal analogy lets children *play* with ideas and represent their understanding of concepts in ways that you can assess. Kindergarten youngsters' play includes the activities in Box 6.3.

Colloquial language mocks the notion of "blowing bubbles" as a trivial activity. However, advanced mathematicians in recent years have studied bubbles in a bid to understand their geometry and their role in aspects of the universe itself.

BOX 6.3 THE FORCE OF AIR CREATES MOVEMENT IN KINDERGARTEN

- Kindergarten children blow up balloons and let the air out, feeling the flow on their skin and hearing the sound of the exiting air.
- They use a balloon pump and can see that a smaller balloon containing the same amount of air as a larger balloon travels farther because the air exits more forcefully.
- They compare the propulsion of a balloon filled with air and one filled with water.
- They observe a toy boat propelled by air escaping from an attached balloon; they create racing games with boats and make *predictions* about the speed of different boats; they wonder whether the location of the balloon makes any difference and then see what happens. (Note that, after a lengthy ready–get set–go process when they use a timer to time their race, kindergarteners immediately pocket the timer in order to focus on the boats. Their behavior helps their teacher assess the limits of their capacity to multi-task.)
- They also can draw pictures on the balloons before blowing them up and then compare the pictures afterward, learning about topology while taking delight in the contrasting transformations.

Kites

Pre-kindergarten children also see commercial kites and play with those they make themselves. Kindergarten children play with the different aerodynamic properties, a form of design technology, also including the activities in Box 6.4.

BOX 6.4 KITES

Children
- vary the shapes of materials and the direction of propulsion;
- build on their play with the propulsion of paper straws and paper planes;
- try to propel their constructions farther by varying the size of the straw, the opening of the straw, the length of the string, and the shape of the construction, one variable at a time;
- add a paper clip or two to different places on their constructions;

- vary the type of material, including paper, cloth, and plastic; and
- consider the angles of construction and wonder why heavy airplanes can fly (see Atkinson, 1995).

Ramps and Related Activities (Physics, Chemistry, and Mathematics Included)

Young children enjoy exploring inclined planes by dropping, rolling, pushing, and pulling objects. The activities listed in Box 6.5 follow the format of direct involvement with, first, having an *expectation* and making a prediction between two objects with one variable; then engaging in the activity and, sometimes, finding a *surprise/cognitive dissonance*.

BOX 6.5 RAMPING/INCLINED PLANES

- *Expect.* Using two parallel ramps with different inclines, children predict which objects (e.g., identical miniature vehicles, cylinders, spools) will roll farther along the path, based upon the angle of the ramps. They place carpenter tape or a colored Post-it note on the floor where they predict each item will stop.
- *Experience.* Using a meter stick to hold the same starting point across both ramps, they release the meter stick and joyously observe the rolling items.
- *Compare.* They place a different color of tape at the final resting place of each object, discuss their findings, and sometimes repeat the process in order to verify their findings and test new ideas.

[**Procedural note:** *Recommended:* It is useful to enter into the activity directly: e.g., "This ramp is higher. This ramp is lower." "I wonder which truck will roll farther?" "Let's put tape where you think it might stop." "Let's see what happens when . . .?" "What are some ways we can fix the way it rolls?" "What if you wanted the truck to go slower/faster/farther?" *Not recommended:* Teacher-talk in an introduction or a recitational quiz can have the effect of reducing children's focus and willingness to participate.]

Ramping Variations

- Children play with different loads in their trucks.
- They vary the ramp surfaces, comparing one texture contrast at a time, such as nylon, other fabrics, aluminum foil, sandpaper, and plastic wrap.
- They measure the prediction and the result. Some groups are able to use a meter stick (or a "railroad track," or pumpkin shapes, or multiple shoe shapes) alongside the path to compare the distances that objects roll and collate their findings on a class chart. The class chart represents three rows: *Farther, Closer, Same*. Children place their colored Post-it notes in the row they predict, then compare their findings. Kindergarteners are able to record their findings in personal notebooks.
- At different times, they discuss what variables contribute to the distance that objects roll, such as height of ramp, nature of object, degree of thrust, and ramp surface texture.
- Pre-kindergarten children are also able to make predictions, collect objects in the classroom to place on the ramps, test their expectations, and sort the objects into smiling-face or frowning-face containers.
- They are able to create a series of ramps and boxes by predicting the distances that a ball would roll into a basket in which the ball could rest. Some kindergarteners enjoy the activity so much that they are able to combine their electrical circuit activity with the ramping. They embellish this concept by having their ball roll over a switch that closes an electric circuit in order to turn on a light. They are also able to embellish this activity with transparent plastic cylinders as well as cardboard cylinders. This is a form of design engineering.
- Firmly stuffed cloth bowling pins provide a different goal for objects rolling down a ramp.
- Different groups of children can compare their strategies and observations. They contrast the textures and angles of the objects before and after attempting to roll them down ramps of various heights. They vary one height at a time. Some children use a chart with a smiling and a frowning face next to a picture of each object and place copies of their own photograph under their predictions.
- Kindergarten children are able to use boxes with elastic or string to pull blocks and toys up a ramp.
- They also use open cardboard tubes as ramps.

Teachers offer children the chance to build structures with wooden ramps and marbles that include baskets as goals for the marbles (DeVries & Sales, 2011; see also Kamii & DeVries, 1993; Zan & Geiken, 2010).

IMAGE 6.2 Ramps: Predicting and Comparing Distance with a Ruler or Sneakers (Permission for the sneaker insert provided by Jaclyn Rosenzweig)

[**Procedural note:** Children need time to explore how objects function on inclines before you can expect them to imagine alternatives and manipulate variables. By kindergarten age, young children have had many experiences in the resistance and nature of propelling objects and themselves across many surfaces as varied as an inclined plane while holding an adult's hand, a slide in the park, or attempting to pull a wagon uphill or down an inclined plane with more or less load. They have built wooden block structures and figured out by trial-and-error how to align blocks for their preferred angle or inclined interfaces. These direct physical *play* experiences are the platforms upon which more complex *physical* learning rises. It is important to use vocabulary in the context of events.]

Kindergarten children play at bowling and using a *pendulum*, varying the direction of the bob as well as the length of the string. They can vary the force and become aware of the degree of arc that they need to bring down their targets. They consider how heavier or lighter, longer or shorter twine can influence their aim. A few children are able to survey the heights of the bob before and after the arc, while many children simply play with their aim and make intuitive adjustments. Related games with balls and the contrasts of density are detailed in Box 6.6.

BOX 6.6 REBOUNDING GAMES

Ball Games and Rebounding

Young children have many experiences in dropping and bouncing balls of various sizes and densities as well as objects such as empty containers, aluminum foil, and objects of different sizes and shapes.

- *Expect*. Children predict the distances of rebound.
- *Experience*. They toss and observe the balls and other objects.
- *Compare*. Children seriate, then propel objects, and record their findings in ways that they can understand. For example, pairs of kindergarten children are able to measure the distance of rebound using yardsticks, prestigious folding carpenter rulers, and measuring wheels.

Liquid Density Game

Another form of "rebounding" relates to the density and solubility of liquids. Pre-kindergarten children take delight in mixing oil and water, ketchup and milk, juice and syrup, soap liquid and poster paint.

- *Expect*. Will items such as a penny, marble, key, sponge, or wooden bead move more quickly through oil or water or shampoo or syrup? [**Procedural note:** Youngsters enjoy the image of objects "racing" to the bottom of the container.]
- *Experience*. Children observe each item within two liquids.
- *Compare*. They represent the findings with stickers on drawings of the containers. Youngsters learn to appreciate the resistance of objects traveling through liquids of different densities. Kindergarten children are able to predict and seriate the densities and progression of objects through liquids of various densities; and create drawings and photographs to record their predictions and findings.

[**Procedural note.** Control variables by contrasting two liquids at a time within the range of materials.]

Fulcrum Play (Physics, Music, and Economics Included)

Children delight in exploring balance on a seesaw as they (1) walk along while holding an adult's hand and (2) experiment with different objects to see how to create or tip the balance. They use rocking boats with gusto; they also create their own balance scales.

Sit with a small group of blindfolded children and ask them to compare the weight of two objects at a time. The children then look at the objects without the blindfolds on, and test their *expectations* by using a standard balance scale. Kindergarten children also enjoy predicting how many pennies and then, in turn, how many other objects could balance the weight of their guinea pig. They are also able to *estimate* the relative weight of dry to wet sand and *compare* their findings after using a balance scale. Using containers of different shapes, they employ the balance scale to test their guesses about which containers could hold the same amount of water. Kindergarten children, using a suspended wire hanger, create mobiles and explore ways to balance the parts.

When youngsters compare their predictions with their findings, *surprise/cognitive dissonance*—a fresh perception—takes place. Teachers who provide more opportunities for *surprise/cognitive dissonance* afford children more opportunities for transformational and constructive learning. Teachers who support transformational learning are teaching in nonlinear ways. Young children, in turn, experience such learning as *play* when they can control an open-ended process.

Interaction of Forces (Physics, Mathematics, Social Studies, and the Arts Included)

Gravitation can contrast with air pressure, magnetism, and centrifugal force. There are many activities in which children directly feel these contrasts. Beyond sucking and blowing, young children appreciate their own power in keeping objects submerged in bath-water. They experience *conflict* in the disparity between what they want and how others comply with their wishes (social studies). They enjoy the predictability of seeing objects fall to the ground and wonder after their expectations are not fulfilled. They enjoy playing with dropping objects such as a shuttlecock, feather, wooden bead, card, piece of paper, marble, and rubber ball. They are able to discuss their observations, and you can invert reality by asking, "How could we make it fall up?" Figure 6.2 outlines a planning map for studying the *interaction* of forces. The important aspect of this work centers on the *interaction* (*contrasts and conflicts/dialectical activity* Dynamic-Theme) of the forces.

The sub-sections that follow describe experiences with gravitation, magnetism, air pressure, and centrifugal force. The experiences took place over the period of a school year in a half-day kindergarten class in which many children were space travel enthusiasts. The teacher worked briefly (15–20 minutes) with half the class at a time, once a week, while the remainder of the class was with the assistant teacher or special subject teacher in another activity.

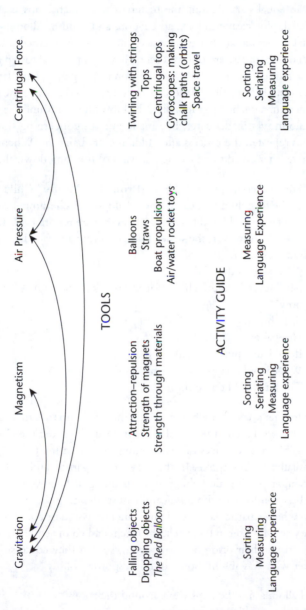

FIGURE 6.2 Conceptual Planning Map: Interaction of Forces in Physics

Gravitation   First, children predicted and compared what might happen if they dropped a variety of materials, one at a time, and then two at a time, from the same height. One child appointed himself as referee by holding a meter stick to be sure that there was an equal start. Among the materials were such items as a feather, shuttlecock, pencil, pipe cleaner, block, air balloon, and helium balloon.

Since gravitation was a familiar experience, the activities focused on helping the children become more aware of this force. They dropped and tossed a variety of objects and *contrasted* finding out why objects stop moving up. They played with ordinary balloons and helium-filled balloons. They attempted to solve the problem of getting a paper cup attached to the helium balloon off the ground. Seeing that one helium balloon was inadequate, they made guesses concerning how many would work and repeated the process after adding extra balloons. When the cup finally rose, the teacher asked them to suggest ways of bringing down the cup.

Child 1:   Hey, we could put wood in it. [**Procedural note:** "Child 1" refers to the first child to speak in each dialogue. Each number represents a different child in different episodes that are reported. Within each episode, however, the same child's contribution is indicated by the same number.]

Teacher (T): What would that do?

T: (after several children have placed a block in the cup) What happens now?

Child 2:   Weight.

Child 1:   How about a ladder?

Child 3:   If we had a pin, we could pop it.

T: What would happen to the balloon?

Child 4:   The air would come out.

Notice that the teacher accepted each suggestion. She was in no rush to feed a single "right" answer that would end the speculation. Instead, she asked the children to describe the possible consequences of their actions. She used the terms "gravity" and "force" casually, as they spoke. In this way, she began to build a pattern of guessing, observing, repeating, describing, and explaining that allowed the children to deal with a basic outlook of the physical scientist: defining the limitations (or context) within which a particular natural phenomenon could or could not occur.

In an ancillary activity later in the week, the teacher asked the children to dictate statements concerning their prior group meetings, so that they could share them with a youngster who was absent. Some of the responses follow:

Child 1: The balloons and the cups went around the room.

Child 2: 'Cause they had helium in them.

Child 3: They lifted the cup up.

Child 4: Four balloons.

Child 5: We counted to four.

T:	We had balls, too. What kind of balls?
Child 6:	Little balls.
Child 7:	(Moving hands) they were shaped like this.
Child 8:	Like a capsule.
T:	(Reads back what is written.)
Child 4:	They went up, up, up, up, up.
T:	What made them come down?
Child 8:	The air came out.
Child 7:	Gravity.
Child 5:	Because they have no motors.
Child 6:	They don't have propellers or wings.
T:	A bird can have wings and he can come down. Why does he come down?
Child 1:	There's nothing to keep it up.

[**Procedural note:** By recording the children's statements "for the absent child," the teacher was able to assess what the children perceived.]

As they continued to be receptive to these exposures, the children added to their information and began to apply it. In contrast with these earlier experiences, notice the wider scope of their comments five weeks later, during an activity period when they are looking at pictures of space travel on a bulletin board.

Child 1:	That's a rocket!
Child 2:	My friend has a cardboard rocket that goes round and round.
Child 1:	Hey, that rocket's upside down.
Child 2:	I'm not crazy. That rocket is upside down.
Child 3:	He's flying.
Child 4:	He's standing on his head because there's no gravity.
Child 5	There's no gravity in space.
Child 6:	If you get very far away, the gravity can't pull the rocket down.
T:	What if you were up in space where Meg said there's no gravity? How could she be kept from flying around?
Child 7:	She wears a gravity belt.
Child 5:	If she didn't have one, she would be flying around.
T:	What if she were flying?
Child 2:	Just like upsy-daisy.
T:	What if she tried to pick up her mommy?
Child 8:	She could pick up her mommy.
Child 3:	Because there's no gravity.

Magnetism   The teacher selected the force of magnetism as another focus for activities since it *contrasted* with gravitation. Another consideration was that children can see and feel the effects of this force directly, thereby possibly strengthening their concept of force. [**Procedural note:** Only after many focused observations of each phenomenon did the teacher "invert reality" by asking, "How can we make a paper clip *fall up?*"]

The teacher worked with two groups of four and five children at adjacent tables. She had set out the materials with enough magnets for most of the children. She limited group size so that there would be a maximum opportunity for children to use the materials. Also, in this way, she could be in touch with both groups. At other times, she worked with eight children as one group, rather than the entire class, in order to stimulate wider participation in discussion. She provided magnets of different sizes, shapes, and strengths along with a variety of magnetic and nonmagnetic articles. The teacher suggested that they guess into which pile each article might be placed. She encouraged the children to separate the objects into piles of those that the magnet attracted and those that would not be attracted. After they finished sorting the objects, the children listed for each other the articles in their respective piles.

When the teacher asked what attracted materials were made of, some children variously mentioned metal and iron. However, after they saw that several magnets did not attract a metal ring, children were left with a new classification to ponder until a later activity. New words such as "repel" and "attract" were added to the children's vocabulary in a functional way.

Another classification activity with the magnets was to differentiate them by size and strength. The teacher asked children to notice which magnet an object was attracted to first when she moved magnets of different sizes toward an equidistant object on the table. She asked them to guess which magnet might be stronger than a larger magnet to suggest ways of testing the magnets. In another activity to measure the relative strengths of magnets, the group used paper clips. They saw which magnets could attract more and fewer paper clips, and they represented their findings on a survey chart. (See also Box 3.2.)

Approximately two months later, the children spontaneously applied these experiences to a situation with a gyroscope during a center time in an attempt to change its direction of movement.

Child 1:   I don't think the magnet will do anything.
Child 2:   (Indicating the gyroscope) I don't think it will spin. The inside will but not . . .
Child 3:   (As child brought a magnet) Nothing happens. I'm going to use all the magnets.
Child 4:   'Cause it's going too fast.
Child 1:   Maybe it's not metal or something.
Child 5:   Maybe it's not iron, not iron, not iron . . .
Child 6:   You sure it isn't the broken one?

The children certainly were able to use their knowledge of magnets independently in this new situation. Independent work with the magnets during center activities with other children as well as discussions with the teacher contributed to this facility in applying their knowledge.

In a variety of events, the teacher encouraged children to *predict* with each additional material, to test each in turn, and to *describe* and *compare* each occurrence. Children held their breath at the veritable dramas during such occasions. While to an adult it may seem to take a long time to figure things out, the children derived a direct, aesthetic satisfaction from these experiences.

Air Pressure   Children can see and feel the force of air pressure directly. When the teacher planned the viewing of an astronaut's rocket launch, which relied upon jet propulsion, she felt that kindergarten children who had been exposed first to the use of air as a propelling force might bring more associations to that later experience. She thought about what materials could offer experiences with air pressure. For example, she decided against using pressurized cans because children could not feel the pressure build up. Since they had used plastic bottles and squeezed air out of them at other times, she added model rockets designed for children to use outdoors because they required a combination of water and air pressure for their propulsion. The children could pour the water, attach the parts of the model rocket by themselves, and then feel the air pressure build up as they pumped.

Initially, the teacher encouraged the children to select balloons, blow them up in whatever ways they chose, and play with them. Some children blew them up and asked the teacher to seal them. They would pat and throw the balloons up and down and follow them around the room. Other children, who had difficulty blowing them up, tried to fill them with water. Still other children blew them up and let the balloons loose to enjoy the sight of them deflating and the sound of the air escaping. This last play became popular, and the children also placed the deflating balloons against their cheeks. One child said to nobody in particular, "Can't see air, but you can hear air."

The teacher planned activities with balloons, drinking straws, and toy boats. She asked the children to tear off an end of the paper that covered the straw, to suck at the straw and describe what happened, and then to blow out and notice what happened. The children had a grand time and compared this activity with others they had had.

Child 1: It stuck on.
Child 2: Kind of like a magnet.
Child 1: When I blow up paper it's like a balloon.
Child 3: He was the pump.

She asked the children to *predict* in which direction an untied balloon would move if it were released. The children pointed in a variety of directions and later *described* and *compared* the actual course. They repeated the procedure several times, and the teacher remarked, as she had done before, "Now you have to do things several times to see where they're going." In this way, she was trying to make them aware of the need for repetition and tentativeness when studying natural phenomena.

Then they discussed the plastic boats. A hole was drilled in the rear of each boat. A transparent dropper, from which a rubber cap had been removed, was set through the hole so that an end of the dropper would be below the water line. The teacher attached a balloon to the opposite end of the dropper that sat in the boat, and rubber bands held the apparatus together.

Children blew up the balloons in the boats through the dropper, set the boats in a large water-filled tub, and gleefully watched the boats being propelled by the air that was escaping from the balloons. As they repeated their activity, they talked together about jet propulsion.

Child 1:   What would happen if it had two balloons?
Children: It would go faster.
T: What if we put three balloons?
Child 3:   (a child who rarely spoke, smiling) It would go faster.
Child 4:   Round and round.
Child 1:   Let's do it.
Child 2:   If they were on the sides it would go . . . (Makes a zigzag motion.)
Children: (Laugh.)
T: That would be good to try. Hal thinks it will stay pretty still, wouldn't go in any direction.
Child 3:   That's the problem. We really don't know.

The children seemed involved and comfortable in expressing conjectures, "not knowing," and extending the discussion. Yet, through the discussions and introduction of new materials, they continued to be active and inflated the balloons. The physical involvement with the materials was similar to their ongoing use of magnets. The physical involvement with materials appeared to help them keep their thinking focused. They were simultaneously able to manipulate materials and expand ideas.

Centrifugal Force   An understanding of orbits in nature requires some idea of centrifugal force. Therefore, the teacher planned classroom experiences in which children could feel and see the effect of centrifugal force. To equal lengths of string, they attached a spool, cardboard square, small plastic toy, cork or other small object; they then created a twirling motion by hand at the top of the string. As they did, they saw each object swing around and spin away from the hand. The dialogue in Box 6.7 shows how the children and their teacher interacted as they explored this force by *predicting*, *observing*, *comparing*, and attempting to *understand* their findings. Notice the integrity of the children throughout these interactions. Children are saying what they actually see. They are not simply trying to guess what the teacher might expect a single "right" answer to be. At the same time, their teacher was able to assess the limits of their understanding.

BOX 6.7 KINDERGARTENERS EXPLORE CENTRIFUGAL FORCE

Predicting Stage

T:	(Holds strings from which cardboard squares are suspended.) Look at what we have here.
Child 1:	A merry-go-round.
Child 2:	(Holds strings apart.) If it would stick out like this, it would look more like a merry-go-round.
T:	How might we make it go out?
Child 3:	Sticks.
Child 4:	Glue it out.
Child 2:	You can push it around.
Child 5:	You can blow it.
Child 1:	You could twirl it.

Observing and Comparing Stage

Child 6:	It's going faster.
Child 2:	I saw the string going with it.
Teacher:	Is the cardboard under my hand?
Child 1:	At the sides.
T:	(Holds a yardstick.) How far off the ground is it?
Child 6:	Eighteen.
Teacher:	Yes, just about. Let's see if it goes down closer to the ground.
Child 7:	No, higher.
Child 5:	Lower.
T:	Let's measure and see.
Child 1:	Twenty-four.
T:	Is twenty-four more than eighteen?
Children:	(Nod.)
Child 4:	'Cause your arm is higher.
T:	Let's measure if it goes higher without an arm moving. (They repeat the procedures until all are satisfied that they are repeatedly seeing the same thing.)

Explaining Stage

T: What might make it go up?

Child 1:   Air.

Child 8:   Your hand.

T: Does it go out by itself?

Child 8:   When you twirl it the air holds it up.

T: Is it moving faster or slower?

Child 4:   No, faster.

T: When it goes faster, what else is happening?

Child 2:   It's going outer.

T: What makes it go out?

Children 2 and 4:   Air.

T: Remember, when we drop things, what's the force?

Child 3:   Gravity.

T: (Mentions forces of magnetism and air.) The force that makes the spool go out is centrifugal force. This is the center, and the force that's moving it out is centrifugal.

They followed a similar procedure after the teacher added some transparent tops to the materials that children used during activity periods. These "centrifugal" tops contained colored water, colored oil, and grains that separated into three rings when they were twirled. The children enthusiastically used some of them and acquired great skill at keeping numerous tops twirling simultaneously.

Meeting with half the class for a discussion, the teacher distributed the tops so that three or four children shared each one. The children identified the three materials in the tops—water, oil, and beads—and then compared the materials with regard to weight and color while the tops were at rest. Then, with the tops spinning, they described the color of the outside, inside, and middle rings and observed that the rings were always in the same order. That in turn led them to think about which of the materials was heaviest and which was lightest. Their interchanges suggest that the children were becoming more careful observers. They seemed able to challenge the observations of others and to offer explanations for events based upon prior activities in the classroom. Their numerous earlier experiences with differentiating and ordering relative weight were essential to this activity. Over the next weeks the teacher planned several related activities, listed in Box 6.8.

BOX 6.8 KINDERGARTENERS EXPLORE ROTATION, ORBITS, AND PROPULSION

1   Children observed the rotation of clay spheres on pencils in the presence of a flashlight.
2   They heard the story *Follow the Sunset* while a globe lit by a projection lamp was nearby. A globe had always been present in the classroom, and children had often referred to it. The teacher's purpose was to highlight the notion that the Earth moves continuously. This activity preceded a look at a large model of the sun and planets in motion.
3   They used chalk to follow the path of a gyroscope spinning on the floor.
4   They launched their own toy rockets outdoors.
5   They watched a space launch on television.

Children were beginning to apply some of their learning and to try out their growing vocabulary, sometimes more accurately than at other times. They brought in newspaper clippings about a space ship's orbit and discussed why the path was not straight up. The children were able to relate the path to the "round" Earth. The youngsters communicated excitement. To summarize, they were receptive to activities that dealt with the interaction of opposing forces, such as gravitation and magnetism, centrifugal force and gravitation, and air propulsion and gravitation. The images and connections they formed along with their growing vocabulary were relevant to their capacity to learn at this time of their lives. The *comparisons and contrasts* between forces contributed to their perceptions.

Measurement

In dealing with the physical world, we often deal with quantities. The children repeated their manipulations of concrete materials and measured changes when possible: for example, when they used the meter stick to study centrifugal force. The use of this tool was possible only because they had had prior experiences in the classroom measuring and seeing numbers written. They also frequently used rulers at the woodworking bench. In addition, they had compared the weights of objects in a pan balance scale.

At the teacher's request, the children suggested ways that they could make boats sail. The children mentioned pushing, blowing, and fanning the boats, in addition to jet propulsion. They predicted and measured how far the boats would move and how long it would take when they compared the methods of blowing, fanning with cardboard, and jet propulsion.

Then they compared which methods took the longest and shortest time to move the boats their greatest distance. As they repeated each procedure, the teacher wrote their findings on a chart so that they could compare times and distances. The children were physically involved and attentive as they coordinated their manipulations of materials and their discussion of events.

Depth of Study

The study of the interaction of forces in the physical world can spread over half or all of the school year, depending on the density of activity to which the children seem receptive. When they engage in related activities, rather than isolated one-time events, they can integrate new perceptions in individually meaningful ways.

For example, look at erosion as an illustration of forces. You can speak of and observe the interaction of air, temperature, water, soil, wind, rock, and human-made structures. You can notice the relationships between forests, fires, rainfall, climatic conditions, and landforms, tying in human use of land as an interactive element. You can observe eroded sites; directly witness erosion during and immediately following rain, flood, or a thaw; and compare pictures taken before and after land development for construction, pictures taken before and after fires, and pictures taken before erosion and at a later seashore or riverbank visit. You can read about mudslides and avalanches in both adventure stories and newspapers. You can create structures in the classroom or on school grounds and play at eroding them. You can view videotapes as possible substitutes for the real thing, but they are insufficient by themselves. Therefore, if children were growing up on an Iowa plain, for example, without direct access to mountainous terrain, their teacher would attempt to plan a series of related experiences that reflect the interaction of human beings and nature in their own locale.

Measuring tools may differ. The plains child might measure wind, drought, or flood damage. The interplay of different tools and varied data can provide a large number of experiences of comparable quality. Here again, the nature and purpose of experience is to *use* knowledge to gain understanding and cultivate collaboration, with absorption of information being an important by-product, not the only end, of learning.

Assessment

You might assess the sequence of children's emotional and perceptual development of the *contrasts and conflicts/dialectical activity* Dynamic-Theme when children demonstrate their capacities as follows: (1) impulsive negativity; (2) active resistance; (3) passive resistance; and (4) increasingly subtle resistance followed by increasingly influential resistance. When you assess children's progress along the continuum, you are able to adapt to the capacities of different children.

Within an activity-based learning environment, it is also possible to assess children's acquisition of meanings by hearing their comments as well as observing their capacity to explore materials independently in a social setting. In the activities described above, children's comments show that they are able to make connections between forces and interactions, raise questions, and indicate what they needed to find out. They are able to do so with integrity. The children also seek out the materials during activity choice times when they continue to explore the materials and discuss their observations with one another and adults. When you document students' participation, comments, questions, and connections, you are in a position to assess their achievements. In particular, when children connect ideas and apply their knowledge, you can evaluate the facts that they have acquired. You would certainly augment these observations with interviews in natural-appearing settings. Children readily recount events to somebody who was not present: "What would Brian have seen if he had been here when we . . .?" "What else did you see?" "What do you remember about . . . [select a variable]?" "What might happen if [variable] were [this] instead of [that]?"

When you keep records and digital photographs of events, you provide opportunities to celebrate children's progress and achievements. Youngsters also enjoy seeing the tangible progress they make in many strands of learning mid-year and later in the year. Seeing their progress adds to their *sense of competence* (condition for learning), possibility for success, and positive expectations within the educational enterprise. Additional discussion of assessment is integrated within the pathways of learning and teacher scaffolds across chapters that follow, particularly Chapter 14, including Table 14.3, which includes an evaluation scale for conceptual development.

Reflections

When you plan activities that share the underlying *contrasts and conflicts/dialectical activity* Dynamic-Theme, there is the potential for children to make connections and transfer learning as they build on prior images across subject matter domains. Young children experience the Dynamic-Theme *intuitively* and with *surprises/cognitive dissonance* within the conditions for learning that include *social* contacts as well as their activities in the *physical* world. Above all, their *sense of competence* and their ongoing young right to curiosity are crucial to their perseverance within school.

7

DYNAMIC-THEME EXPERIENCES

The Whole Exceeds the Parts (Synergy)

Introduction

The *whole exceeds the parts/synergy* Dynamic-Theme is defined by "cooperation" and "interdependence" among the parts of an experience. Cooperation among the parts of an experience can result in a transformation. Cooperation and transformation are the underlying perceptual experiences of this Dynamic-Theme; and a feeling of being flooded is the underlying emotional experience.

Children can see when objects or events interact and emerge as new forms. They accept these observations as if "That's just the way things happen." As youngsters develop, they begin to sort out accepting transformational events as a reality, and when experience and logic fail, as if magic is at work.

Experiences that represent an image of *the whole exceeding the parts/synergy* typically take place within the physical and social world as well as the arts. In this chapter, activities that emphasize physical knowing are presented first, followed by experiences that emphasize social knowing and the arts. It is worth mentioning again that *different children doing different things at different times might have equivalent experiences with synergy*. Figure 7.1 presents a model of this Dynamic-Theme.

Physical and Social Knowing

Food Preparation (Chemistry, Literacy, and Mathematics)

Prepare or cook food products that dramatically change form, such as eggs, butter, homemade ice cream, muffins, fruit salad, yeast dough, and popcorn (in a visible air popper). With your assistance, kindergarteners are able to measure changes in volume, shape, and weight before and after cooking. Pre-kindergarten children observe the drying of foods such as apples and green pears; they can *estimate* how

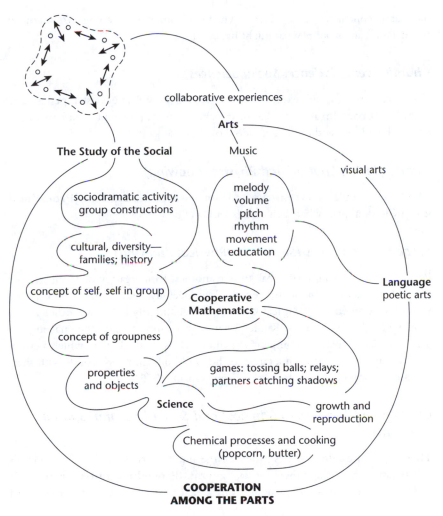

collaborative experiences

Arts

The Study of the Social

Music

visual arts

sociodramatic activity;
group constructions

melody
volume
pitch
rhythm
movement
education

cultural, diversity—
families; history

concept of self, self in group

**Cooperative
Mathematics**

Language
poetic arts

concept of groupness

properties
and objects

games: tossing balls; relays;
partners catching shadows

Science

growth and
reproduction

Chemical processes and cooking
(popcorn, butter)

**COOPERATION
AMONG THE PARTS**

FIGURE 7.1 The Whole Exceeds the Parts (Synergy) Dynamic–Theme

long it might take for a grape to become a raisin and *compare* their findings with actual events (*surprise/cognitive dissonance*). Their experience of surprise/cognitive dissonance feels like *playing* a guessing game to them. [**Procedural note:** As relevant, create a picture–word recipe or prediction chart to add literacy and mathematics to activities.]

Combining Materials (Chemistry)

Melt wax and old crayons to create candles and fresh recycled crayons. Dissolve substances and observe what happens when a drop of colored water enters a transparent container of clear water or when you combine two colors. [**Procedural note:** *Predict* and *compare* what might happen.]

Chaotic Events (Science, Social Sciences)

Compare surprises and explosive events, such as volcanoes, stampedes, and tornados. [**Procedural note:** Compare two 2-liter transparent soda containers, one with and one without a Tornado Toy Tube.]

Games (Social, Spatial, and Physical Knowing)

Children assemble jigsaw puzzles and simple machines together [**Procedural note:** Children plan what each child's part will be.]

Large Muscle Games (Social and Physical Knowing)

Partners or small groups toss a ball to one another. Kindergarten children are able to run relay races. Pre-kindergarten children gleefully share a rocking boat; they enjoy noncompetitive "Musical Chairs" and voluntarily help each other find a chair when the music stops. Kindergarten class members enjoy the challenge of playing collaborative, noncompetitive games such as "Stand Up" in which a group tries to stand up together in a circle as they hold one another's hands with their backs facing the center of the circle (Fleuegelman, 1976, p. 65).

Chasing and Tag Games (Physical and Social Knowing, Spatial Relations)

These types of outdoor games provide large muscle activity and build children's collaboration in sharing power by taking turns. [**Procedural note:** Discuss with children the need for safety by designating areas that do not interfere with others.]

Square Dance and Folk Dance (Geometry, Counting, and the Arts)

When kindergarten children engage in simple figures of square dances, the group collaboratively *transforms* into different combinations of children with each figure. They also count steps as they shift together from moving forward and then backward during circle folk dances.

Cooperative Shadow Games (Spatial Relations and the Arts)

Collaborative shadow-catching games with friends outdoors continually shift children's focus. Friends make their shadow shake hands, enclose an object on the ground within their shadows, help each other draw around their shadows, and create a shadow with six arms. (See Box 5.3.)

Reproduction (Physical Knowledge, and Biology)

Reproduction of plants transforms seeds, cuttings, sprouts. Children are intrigued with the transformations of animals such as butterflies, tadpoles in an aquarium, hermit crabs in a mixed environment in a terrarium, and dipsosaurus dorsalis lizards in a desert terrarium. (The Dynamic-Theme of *the whole exceeds the parts/synergy* is represented from the ecological standpoint of these habitats. Reproduction and growth also represent the Dynamic-Theme of *cyclical change*.) [**Procedural note:** Comparing more than one environment offers the potential for additional *surprises*.]

Ecology (Physical and Social Knowing and Literacy)

Ecology deals with understanding the interdependence of people, the environment, animals, plants, and seeds. The conservation of water is discussed in Box 8.3. Box 7.1 describes a related collaboration in the comparison of mass production and individual work, an economics concept that engenders the *surprise/cognitive dissonance* condition for learning.

BOX 7.1 MASS PRODUCTION

- *Expect.* Children predict if individual or shared preparation would construct and fill more baskets for a party or create more sandwiches.
- *Experience.* During the same time frame, half the group works as individuals and the others create an assembly line.
- *Compare.* Participants experience surprise when they find that the assembly line produces more baskets or creates more sandwiches. (Adapted from Robison & Spodek, 1965.)

Social and Multicultural Knowing

Socio-dramatic Activity (Social Knowing, Literacy, and Mathematics)

Socio-dramatic play is a powerful collaboration. You can vary the themes and props with artifacts from different cultures and businesses. Children's continuous collaborative transformations of activities during socio-dramatic play serve as a kind of lymphatic for youngsters' development, just as lubricating oil is essential for the functioning of an automobile. (See also Chapter 3.)

Drama (Social, Multicultural Knowing, Literacy, the Arts)

Kindergarten children make masks and minimalist costumes together for play productions and enact the plays. [**Procedural note:** You might need to take a role at the start in order to model and support the dialogue and action, before gradually withdrawing as children become increasingly able.]

Quilts and Murals (Arts, Literacy, Mathematics, Geography, and Economics)

Children make cooperative products, such as a mural or a tablecloth for a family breakfast, or assemble a thematic quilt from pieces of paper or cloth that they illustrate. Some kindergarten children enthusiastically create a mural of their ideal community. Pre-kindergarten and kindergarten children typically participate in mural making from their own baseline viewpoint. A few children might notice the upside-down appearance when the mural is hung; this provides an opportunity to consider possible future solutions. *Seven Blind Mice* (Young, 2002) is a neat fit after this kind of experience because the characters are able to see narrowly, only from each one's perspective, therefore missing the whole picture. This book deals with perspective-taking and the wisdom of seeing the whole before coming to conclusions. Children who create quilts that demonstrate the assembly of the same shape or pattern, as well as the combination only of squares, also explore the mathematical concept of the parts in relation to the whole.

Global Holidays (Social, Historical, Economic, Political, and Multicultural Knowing)

Teachers plan with children meaningful projects that look at holidays across cultures in order to transform attitudes from self-involvement to a shared sense of human experience. There is expanded discussion of this in Chapter 8.

Posters (Social Science)

Classes display photographs, posters, and books depicting human beings around the world engaging in similar pastimes, such as nurturing, cooking, working together, playing games together, and traveling in trucks, automobiles, and boats together.

Buddies (Social Knowing, Literacy, and Mathematics)

Beginning in pre-kindergarten, teachers help youngsters organize a buddy system of pairs or groups of four. This strategy encourages collaboration and respects children's capacity for independence. Other forms include playing with partners and small groups as well as kindergarten pairs-share for drawing/writing or book sharing. [**Procedural note:** In book sharing, two children "sell" each other reasons to look at a book that they enjoyed.]

Construction Site (Sociology, History, Economics, Literacy, Mathematics, and the Arts)

When a class adopts a construction site, there are opportunities to document the events unfolding there with photographs, drawings, and invented spelling. Children note the multiple roles of construction participants by interviewing the workers (for example, one electrician could also be a father, husband, brother, son, book club member, and bowling league member). Thank-you notes after interviews integrate literacy experiences. [**Procedural note:** It makes sense to plan with the construction personnel and the interviewees ahead of time.]

Together, your group can create a timeline, draw, dictate, or write with invented spelling about the workers' collaboration. Counting days and weeks to record progress of construction phases applies mathematics. (Note that the changes from start to finish of the construction also reflect the Dynamic-Theme of *cyclical change*.)

Family Trees (Sociology and History)

Some kindergarten children ask families to help create family trees. Books that deal with similar family themes appear in the Related Children's Books list for Chapter 8. [**Procedural note:** Teachers should be sensitive to the particular community and alternative family structures.]

Family Involvement (History, Geography, Multicultural Knowing, and Literacy)

Children and their families create an immigration map, timeline, and museum of family artifacts, and engage in multicultural festivals. (This activity, expanded in Chapter 8, represents the Dynamic-Themes of *synergy* and *cyclical change*.)

Quantitative and Spatial Knowing

Collaboration continues to be the underlying feature in experiences that emphasize quantitative and spatial knowing, as follows:

- *Cooperative mathematics activities* (quantitative knowing). Two to four children play cooperative mathematical games, such as board and card games. Pairs of kindergarten children measure with a measuring wheel; youngsters make nonstandard measures of a partner's height and limbs. Chapter 12 describes many collaborative activities.

- *Traffic surveys* (quantitative knowing). Two or more children are able to undertake surveys. For example, pre-kindergarten children might learn "How many trucks/cars pass our classroom window?" They use a three-minute egg timer and take turns moving pegs to keep a tally.
- *Constructions* (quantitative knowing). Children plan with others and build structures together with wooden floor blocks.
- *Hiding games* (spatial knowing, geography). Pre-kindergarten children play collaboratively by hiding objects in games that move from simple hide-and-go-seek to kindergarten treasure maps.
- *Mapping each other* (spatial knowing, geography). With your help, children are able to use a large sheet of paper to outline a partner's body for "mapping," and then complete the project by drawing or making a collage.

Representational Knowing and Arts

Young children express themselves physically through a variety of art forms. Play activities, in themselves, reveal children's Theory of Mind as well as their event knowledge. In addition, children draw, build, paint, sculpt, dance, pantomime, dramatize, speak, and write in order to represent their experiences.

Cat's Cradle (Social, Spatial, and Representational Knowing)

Kindergarteners' string figures, such as Cat's Cradle, require collaboration. Although one person holds the figure while another manipulates it, more than two kindergarten children are able to play by taking turns around a circle of three or four individuals. Several players together can serve as a support system for one another. [**Procedural note:** The teacher or another child initially demonstrates the activity.]

Movement Activities (Social, Spatial, and Physical Knowing)

Movement education includes collaborative dance development, such as partners "mirroring" each other's movements. Kindergarten children are able to collaborate in simple circle- and folk-dances where pairs of children create different grouping arrangements (physical and representational knowing). (See also Boxes 9.2 and 9.3.) Pairs of children also take turns and collaborate to stretch lengths of knitted or plastic bands into different shapes, accompanied by music.

"Parachute" (Spatial and Social)

Outdoors and in the gymnasium, groups of children play with a gigantic parachute (or a sheet or tablecloth) in various ways, such as gleefully running under the parachute before the other children lower it.

Music (Social, Multicultural, and Mathematical)

Groups collaboratively create chants, melodies, and poetic songs, and engage in part singing. They might also participate in rhythm band activity. *Scaffold* this by asking the children to listen to a particular rhythm or pattern and invite them to build upon it or create their own patterns.

Orchestra (Social, Mathematical, Literacy, and Visual Arts)

Pre-kindergarten children appreciate viewing duets, trios, quartets, quintets, and orchestras. Older children or adults can bring musical instruments, play duets, trios, and quartets. Children interview musicians, and compare the sounds of individual instruments with the combination of sounds. They also observe Internet sources. They count musicians, write invitations and thank-you notes, and make illustrations for related class books.

Folk Songs (Music and Literacy)

Poet-composers create songs that focus on cooperation and transformation. Contents that embody collaboration include the song *Wonderful Friends* (Wyatt & Seeger, n.d.): "When I think of the ways that I've grown / I know that I couldn'ta made it alone, I owe a lot to the sharing, caring, daring wonderful friends that I've known."

Visual Art Collaborations (Social, Spatial, Physical, and Representational Knowing)

Pre-kindergarten children work together at the computer with graphics software. [**Procedural note:** An adult often opens the program and, for those who need it, models the process.] They also combine colors with food dye, paint, and overlaid plastic discs. Children who view reproductions of a visual artist's body of work are able to consider the distinctive "wholes" of the artist's style along with the holistic styles of other artists' work. Children's drawings and paintings are evidence that they are able to grasp the underlying visual analogies (Dynamic-Themes) underlying an artist's distinctive body of work. Chapter 9 expands this discussion.

Collaborative Class Books Circulate (Representational Knowing, Literacy, and History)

Youngsters contribute to class books with shared topics, such as family activities, changes in the school yard, friends and fights, giving and taking, wishes and dreams, science splendors, artist's studio, and so forth.

Puppet Shows (Social and Representational Knowing, the Arts, and Literacy)

Kindergarten children plan together; create simple puppets from paper plates or bags; and present puppet shows. [**Procedural note:** Teachers find that children need help in planning and presenting puppets so that the puppets have voices rather than only physical interactions.]

Role-Playing (Social Knowing and Literacy)

Other collaborative experiences include role-playing stories and interpersonal issues ("what if?") that include drawing, writing, or graphing. When there are issues about sharing and caring for one another in the classroom community, teachers sometimes augment the role-play with topical books, such as *Have You Filled a Bucket Today?* (McCloud, 2006). (See also Chapter 10.)

Assessment

You might assess the sequence of emotional and perceptual development of *the whole exceeds the parts/synergy* when children demonstrate their capacities, as follows: (1) feeling of being submerged by results; (2) first stirrings of connection with others; (3) increasing perception of connections between objects; and (4) increasingly effective collaboration with others. It is reasonable to expect that your assessment of the connections that youngsters make will take place over time. Table 14.3 includes an evaluation scale for conceptual development.

Reflections

This chapter, along with Chapters 5, 6, and 8, presents many relationships between activities and concepts that cross formal disciplinary boundaries. Planning the juxtaposition of several activities with *the whole exceeds the parts/synergy* Dynamic-Theme in mind provides a way to connect your understandings flexibly with children's potential for engagement and connection-making in the service of meaning. After children engage in several activities that represent each Dynamic-Theme, there are reasonably equivalent opportunities for them to *induce* the underlying image as they construct a mental model. Over time, you can see how formal learning standards fit your thoughtful plans. Indeed, you might find that the children could exceed minimal expectations.

8

SOCIAL STUDIES, MULTICULTURAL, AND EGALITARIAN EXPERIENCES

Introduction

When his grandmother repeatedly exhorted Mel to eat his food, the very slender 5-year-old repeatedly claimed he wasn't hungry or was uninterested in the food. When his grandmother said, "It's a shame. You should eat your food because there are children in India and Africa who are starving," he responded, "Who are they? Tell me their names."

In this scene, Mel's language indicated he had developed a sense of critical thinking that involved perspective taking. He was unconvinced about his grandmother's assertion. He was also seeking accurate information to confirm her claim, an indication that he was capable of critical thinking.

Perspective taking, trying to understand what others might think or intend, is important in social and cognitive learning. When we consider and appreciate that other people have similar feelings, needs, and wants, it is possible to develop a sense of caring, fairness, and ethical behavior.

Multicultural education is like a tree that has many branches. All parts of the tree need nourishment, although some parts manage to absorb more sun, moisture, or nutrients. The society in which young children live is similar to the tree. All human beings are connected. All children need nourishment and support. As with the various parts of the tree, some children have had more advantages than others.

Multicultural education addresses the need for all children to experience an equitable access to education regardless of their ethnicity, gender, families, ages, abilities, language, beliefs, and customs. Multicultural education is part of the study of social experiences and the social sciences. It is an integrative study that encompasses history, economics, geography, sociology, anthropology, and political science. This chapter begins with a discussion of multicultural education and then discusses aspects of the learning standards that address history, geography, economics, and political science (civics), which are integrated in multicultural education.

Multicultural education can mean different things to different people. This book does not focus only on how people of diverse ethnicities differ from one another, although differences are interesting. It does not focus on a tourist approach, looking only at how people from diverse cultures and regions eat, dress, dwell, play, work, and conduct their daily lives. Instead, this book focuses on how all human beings need similar support, consideration, and respect. Therefore, the focus is on the study of social life, and the concerns and needs that people share across the globe.

The book's intention is to look at *how teachers might influence children's attitudes, predispositions, and behavior toward other people*. This might happen when children have direct experiences that help them to find fresh perspectives. The *surprise/cognitive dissonance* condition for learning new perspectives can occur when children have an opportunity to (1) anticipate, (2) have a real experience, and then (3) find a *surprising* fresh insight that connects what they anticipated and what they experienced.

There are several ways in which teachers can influence attitudes toward others, in addition to simply modeling support, consideration, and respect. Five ways that teachers attempt to influence attitudes, using a Dynamic-Themes perspective, are discussed in turn. Teachers:

- select clusters of children's literature that *celebrate similar underlying human themes* (Dynamic-Themes), *albeit with different surface forms*;
- commemorate holidays across the globe based upon shared human purposes;
- provide an equitable environment, including materials;
- plan two-way bilingual experiences; and
- share intergroup experiences that can affect attitudes.

Rather than a "tourist" or "token" view of culture, the focus of this chapter is on intentional plans to *transform* interpersonal attitudes so that children can build egalitarian interactions (Nieto, 2010; Ramsey, 2004; Sleeter & Grant, 2009; Sleeter, Grant, Nieto & Fettes, 2007). The discussion of multicultural resources then moves on to look at social studies from the perspectives of the disciplines of history, geography, economics, and political science in ways that match the thoughtfully active means by which young children learn.

Multicultural Dynamic-Themes in Children's Literature

There are many wonderful trade books (as contrasted with textbooks) for young children (see Box 10.3). Many of these books depict the lives of people across the world and across time in ways that can touch the reader or listener. There are many books available to teachers about people in different settings, some of whom look different from one another on the surface, but who share the same underlying concerns or personal experiences. (See the list of Related Children's Books for this chapter.)

When young children learn about others who share similar personal experiences, they can begin to identify with and respect others who may look different, dress differently, and appear to lead different lives. You can support children's growing capacity for perspective taking when you read aloud in sequence related books that depict shared human experiences. Some examples of shared human themes (underlying Dynamic-Themes) in high-quality literature appear in the outline that follows. As you select books, think about the following comment: "The first step in building an anti-bias library is to ask yourself: Can all the children in my classroom find themselves in [our] book collection?" (Derman-Sparks & Edwards, 2010). Your next question might address how to help children find reflections of themselves in human beings in general. The *induction* and *surprise/ cognitive dissonance* conditions for learning are the processes by which youngsters are able to build egalitarian attitudes.

- *Rites of passage.* Young children can identify with the rites of passage of people of different ages in different countries. Issues include learning to read and write; obtaining a first library card and a first umbrella; losing a tooth; attending school for the first time; and voting in an election for the first time.
- *Learning to speak English as a second language* (a particular rite of passage). Children from different countries value their own name and struggle with the transition to speaking English.
- *Dealing with a new baby.* Families from different cultures share issues that deal with the integration of a new baby, twins, an adopted baby, and interracial adoption.
- *Wholesome family relationships.* Family traditions and artifacts across cultures that appear different on the surface reveal wholesome, caring, underlying interactions across generations.
- *Modern families.* Warm family relationships across cultures embrace serial families, single-parent families, and interracial memberships with dignity.
- *Economic issues affect families.* Children and families around the world work to overcome adversity, sometimes at the expense of personal sacrifice, sharing scarce resources, valuing family connections, and striving for civil liberty.
- *Loss.* Young children in different environments, of different ethnicities, deal with feelings relating to issues of material and personal loss and resolution.
- *Overcoming obstacles.* Adults and children around the world deal with overcoming personal, ecological, cultural, and political issues.
- *Friendship.* Children across cultures share concerns about the ups and downs of friendship.

- *Emotions and bullying.* Children in different situations try to cope with verbal and physical abuse, bullying, and angry feelings.

[**Procedural note:** Some teachers store those books that deal with the same shared theme together in separate boxes.]

- *Follow-up activities.* You can connect each theme in a cluster of books to children's lives by thoughtful questioning and listening. Youngsters are able to identify with things they have done and are able to share their thoughts about the books. For example, pre-kindergarten youngsters are able to talk about their losses thoughtfully after hearing *Where Can It Be?* (Jonas, 1986). After hearing stories about feelings, children can develop drawings to illustrate what they like about themselves or about events in their own lives that represent strong feelings. In addition, plan with children and adults to inter- view family and community residents to tell the story of their immigration experiences, as outlined in Box 8.5.

In addition to continuing to use related books to build children's perspective taking and a sense of shared human experiences, the next section discusses how holiday celebrations can support these underlying Dynamic-Themes with the *induction* and *social interaction* conditions for learning. *Revisiting* themes with different surface forms also adds to the integration of egalitarian attitudes.

Holidays: Dynamic Themes in Shared Global Human Experiences

Some teachers treat holidays as the center of the social studies curriculum. Some settings engage in a form of calendar worship that moves from one holiday celebration to the next. Often, there are uniform crafts, such as pasting collage faces on pre-cut orange pumpkin shapes or collages on pre-cut green fir trees. Such uniformity reduces opportunities for children to feel empowered to create their own forms of art work and adds little to their knowledge base.

Schools less typically have seen holidays as related to the weather and *cyclical change*. On the surface, "holidays differ from outdoor education or the weather. On the deeper level, they represent *cyclical changes* of passing-through struggles in human lives" (Fromberg, 1982, p. 195). Holidays, however, can merit significant attention. After all, they exist to celebrate and commemorate historically important events, and reflect opportunities to touch on ideas related to geography, econo- mics, political science, sociology, chemistry, the arts, and literature.

Seasonal holidays address the themes of new life, energy, growth, and cele- bration in the spring, the celebration of plentiful food in summer, harvest and remembrance in autumn, and brightening the world with light and warmth in winter (Kindersley, 1997).

Harvest Festivals Celebrate Survival

Harvest times might reflect a more significant focus than recognition of a season. Human beings across the world commemorate a good harvest because it means that the community will evade starvation and can look forward to survival. So, in looking at holidays, it is significant to think about *why* we celebrate them. In that way, we can bring together the appreciation of holidays across cultures that mark significant shared human experiences.

It is remarkable that people across the globe and across time appear to mark holidays by *celebrating similar underlying human themes, albeit with different surface forms*. Some Dynamic-Themes that connect a sampling of people's shared experiences across borders are discussed below.

However, it is important to be sensitive to the feelings of different groups within a class whose perspectives about the same holiday might differ. For example, some families might not celebrate *any* holidays. Also, because of their treatment by early European immigrants, some Native American Indians value neither the historical roots of Thanksgiving in the U.S. nor Columbus's voyage, and they might view them as times of sad remembrance because they represent the roots of oppressing indigenous peoples.

Beyond Thanksgiving, some teachers and children also celebrate a plentiful harvest with Kwanzaa (Africa). Fewer schools commemorate other harvest festivals, such as Trung Thu (Vietnam), N'cwala (Zambia), Timoleague (Ireland), or Divali (India), which celebrate prosperity. Within Thanksgiving in the U.S., it is possible to commemorate the survival and the peaceful strivings of the Iroquois nation as well as an occasion for families to gather and share a bountiful meal.

It is interesting to realize that these occasions, as well as similar ones in different cultures, occur in different months of the year. However, if you consider the goal of highlighting the shared experiences of people's lives, it is important to provide the potential for children to see the *connections* between these holidays. Many countries celebrate by focusing on particular foods, such as eating rice cakes and being thankful to ancestors (Korea's Chusok Festival). Other foods are important in the Native American Cherokee Green Corn Festival and the New Yam Festival in Ghana and Nigeria. Some cultures include singing and dancing in their celebrations.

Some classrooms celebrate harvest festivals with cooking, baking, and community events, outlined in Box 8.1.

BOX 8.1 CLASSROOM FEASTS CREATE COMMUNITY

- Children enjoy creating vegetable soup and listening to books about feasts. You might read related books, such as *Stone Soup* (Brown, 1947) and *Pumpkin Harvest* (de Paola, 2009).

- Youngsters can prepare butter by taking turns shaking sweet cream and then spreading the butter on toast for a snack.
- Children make fruit salad together and serve it at special family breakfasts. [**Procedural note:** Pre-kindergarten children are able to use plastic knives.]
- You can prepare picture–word recipe charts for various food preparation activities.
- You might ask children to dictate comments about those things for which they feel thankful to include in the class e-letter (or newsletter) to families.

[**Procedural note:** In maintaining a focus on shared anti-bias human experiences of significance, teachers should not focus on feather bands or pre-cut turkey crafts.]

Youngsters are also able to engage in *role-playing* around the Thanksgiving theme that reflects the important role of colonial women (D. Barnes, personal communication, 1981).

Sacrifice, Repentance, Commemorate Inequities and Renew a Sense of Hope

Some holidays contrast with harvest commemorations by remembering occasions of shortages; practicing sacrifice; and repenting sins. For example, Lent (Catholic), Ramadan (Muslim), Yom Kippur (Jewish), as well as Hindu and Buddhist holidays modify diets or practice fasting as a form of repentance or highlight compassion when remembering shortages.

Some schools engage in food pantry and toy donations in order to engage in sharing. Others send art supplies, children's art work, and greetings to those in need after an earthquake or flood. An international pen pal project for orphanages in India and Eastern Europe provides contacts for "giving and receiving through art" (Haugen, 2007).

Independence, Overcoming Tyranny, and Celebrating Freedom

Throughout the year, many nations, from Afghanistan to Zimbabwe, celebrate independence from other countries or freedom from oppressive governments. Again, food is part of the celebration. For example, Haitians eat formerly forbidden soup and Israelis eat matzo, their "bread of affliction" and tri-cornered pastry that duplicates the shape of an oppressor's hat.

Children can follow up with *social*, *physical*, and *playful* activities, such as those listed in Box 8.2.

BOX 8.2 COMMEMORATING INDEPENDENCE

Many countries celebrate Independence Day with a parade and fireworks. Children energetically participate in parading with flags. Some children might consider creating individualized collages, similar to coats of arms, representing their community.

Earth Day

The United States, South Korea, Costa Rica, China, and India, along with 170 other countries, commemorate Earth Day to raise awareness about how human beings impact the climate and global warming. Teachers plan activities to help children learn about conservation of natural resources through recycling projects, as well as reading books. For example, they plant vegetable gardens and window boxes together. Youngsters are also able to learn about conserving water in a toothbrushing activity, described in Box 8.3.

BOX 8.3 WATER CONSERVATION SURPRISE/COGNITIVE DISSONANCE

Materials: A *transparent* two-gallon container. Toothbrushes. Toothpaste. Cups with water for rinsing. A sink with running water.

- *Predict.* Four children at a time predict how much water might flow into the container while they are brushing their teeth. Each child places a tape at the height that she/he predicts.
- *Experience.* Children brush their teeth at the sink while the water fills the container.
- *Compare.* Children compare their predictions with their findings. In order to conserve water after the activity, some groups decided to water plants.

The toothbrushing activity provides a dramatic outcome. It is noteworthy that the two-gallon container often fills close to the top, providing a real *surprise/cognitive dissonance* condition for learning when children can see that their tapes predicted that they would use much less water. After the surprise, parents often report that their children remind them to turn off the faucet when brushing their teeth. (This type of parent feedback demonstrates an important aspect of assessment—the use of knowledge.) This activity is an experience that transforms attitudes and subsequent behaviors.

Prominent Citizens, Heroes, and Heroines Take Risks for Their Beliefs and Labor

Many U.S. schools celebrate St. Patrick's (Ireland), Martin Luther King Jr., and Presidents' days. Most countries celebrate variations of Heroes' Day (Namibia), Memorial Day (U.S.), and Remembrance Day (England). Canadian Aboriginal Louis Riel Day commemorates a Metis leader who led and lost a revolution; this holiday is a symbol of First Americans' quest for independence.

Children begin to learn about historical and popular figures with the experiences outlined in Box 8.4.

BOX 8.4 LEARNING ABOUT HISTORICAL FIGURES

Comparing Biographies of the Same Historic Person

Kindergarten teachers read biographies written by different authors about the same historic person. Children then discuss the different perspectives that each author emphasizes about the person. Then, they vote on their favorite biographer. For example, many biographies have been written about Mary McLeod Bethune; Marie Curie; Mahatma Gandhi; Michael Jordan; Martin Luther King, Jr.; and Abraham Lincoln.

Role-play: Martin Luther King, Jr. Day

Pre-kindergarten children thoughtfully role-play the Rosa Parks bus boycott during January when the U.S. celebrates the birthday of Martin Luther King, Jr. They concentrate on creating seats on the bus and take roles as the bus driver and passengers.

Honoring and Celebrating Parents and Caregivers

Some celebrations honor parents and caregivers from March through June in the U.S., Europe, the Middle East, and Asia. Some groups sensitively develop an extension to the study of heroes, heroines, and nearby heroic caregivers. They create a class book "about men and women in the children's families and neighborhoods who help make a better life for people. Ask families to suggest people. With their permission, get or take a photograph of each one and write a few sentences about the person. When you read the book to the children, invite them to add other sentences" (Derman-Sparks & Edwards, 2010, p. 147).

Equitable Setting and Materials

Gender-neutral Poster and Practice

There is a poster that suggests to teachers "101 Ways to Line Up Other than by Sex" (Project Sex Equity in Education, n.d). This poster recommends, among other ideas, calling children together by the color of an article of clothing or type of shoe that they wear. It is an attempt to create a gender-neutral environment. This contrasts with the ingrained folklore of schools where teachers reflexively call for "boys and girls." Some teachers practice the alternative of addressing children as "class," "everyone," "people," "students," "friends," and so forth.

Posters and Photographs

There is a variety of ways in which early childhood teachers sensitively create an environment that supports equitable attitudes toward others. Posters abound on the Internet that depict children around the world holding hands. Other posters depict elderly people as well as people in wheelchairs engaging in productive work. Similarly, there are images of both men and women engaging in non-traditional professions. You would place such posters that contain lots of detail at children's eye level so that they can think and talk about them. There are also posters depicting people living in different climates and habitats, such as the desert, tropics, plains, mountains, or polar regions.

Current Events

"Clip newspaper photos of familiar people, places, and events; write simple captions; and post them near the door so children and families can see and discuss them at drop-off and pick-up times" (Epstein, 2009, p. 77). You would select items that represent global elements and an egalitarian, anti-bias orientation.

Art Supplies

Also consider art supplies. For example, when African-American and Caribbean-American kindergarten children are drawing self-portraits, you might see Sam color his face brown. You might also hear Ben, an African-American child, inform Sam that he, Ben, was not brown but white. Perhaps "multicultural" crayons, pencils, paints, paper (and clay) that included an array of skin shades would help Ben to find an alternative. With well-developed school–family trust, this is an occasion to discuss the incident with Ben's mother. Also, having children look together in a mirror can be useful in developing a sense of identity.

Socio-dramatic Props

The contents of the socio-dramatic centers offer another opportunity to consider representing a variety of materials that can support diversity. You would include dolls, puppets, and block-building accessory figures that represent family and occupational figures of different ethnicities engaging in non-traditional occupations. Other provisions include a variety of figures that represent physical abilities/disabilities; skin tones; ethnic clothing; and anatomical features. Also include multi-ethnic food models and utensils that represent different cultures; and clothing that represents different occupations. In addition, families can contribute clean, empty, multilingual packages that children can use in their socio-dramatic play. [**Procedural note:** Change props and themes every month or two in order to provide a variety of equitable experiences.]

Music, Listening, and Singing

Rhythm band instruments from around the world are available. There are also CDs and audiotapes with music from different regions. A listening center provides opportunities for individual choices. You might introduce folk songs from around the world, including some in languages other than English.

Globes and Maps

It is useful for each classroom to have a globe of the world as well as a Mercator projection. However, many teachers find it useful to consider the perspective of a Peters projection map of the world. (The Peters projection shows how all the continents could fit within Africa's land mass.) Also consider having photos of the Earth from space in order to provide another perspective. Although young children view such items as informational, it is a beginning exposure to which they are receptive. Moreover, many children are already aware of road maps and GPS units in their family vehicles.

Playthings

There is a puzzle in which each peg presents a sign-language letter, a sign-language rug as well as a Bingo game (http://www.harriscomm.com). Among their offerings, school supply companies are sources for alphabet rugs, flags-of-the-world rugs, and globes.

Inter-ethnic Experiences Affect Attitudes

Pen Pals

Children in different neighborhoods and countries are able to communicate in a variety of ways, including the following:

- dictate letters about their activities; share information and questions;
- create illustrated "class books," sometimes with photographs;
- engage in communication through interactive video [**Procedural note:** Real-time activities require planning between the teachers and with the children in order to use the time efficiently and for a particular purpose.];
- dictate/write fan letters to diverse living authors and artists after hearing their books and viewing their art productions.

Pair Interviews and Introductions

A few pairs of kindergarten children practice interviewing one another by developing questions about their families, preferences, and activities. Then, using positive terms, each child introduces their interviewee to the class. Sometimes, kindergarten children and their teacher can extend this activity with a graphic organizer that shows their different connections to people and activities.

Interview Community Workers, School Personnel, and Family Members

Occasionally, adult interviewees demonstrate musical instruments, and share songs, dances, and games from their cultures. Children appreciate seeing hats and head wrappings from across the world, and are able to learn to create wrappings. When asked, the interviewees can share cultural birthday celebration activities, such as a piñata or pin-the-tail-on-the-donkey. It is also useful for older interviewees to bring photographs that represent their early years and the physical settings and technologies that were part of their lives (*cyclical change* Dynamic-Theme).

Children's parents as well as other community residents can visit to discuss their travel tales and work. For example, a letter carrier in uniform might arrive with his bag and a hand-held computer. Children prepare questions to ask and the letter carrier is prepared to talk about how he learned to do his job. He can also come prepared to discuss his other roles, such as being a son, a father, a grandson, and a neighborhood baseball team player. A gifted teacher uses thoughtful procedures to interview community workers, many of whom are parents of the children in the class. Each weekly or bi-weekly interview culminates in the children's development of an illustrated class book that circulates among their families, who report feeling a sense of community with interviewees (Rogovin, 2001). Interviews demonstrate the interdependence of workers within a community (*the whole exceeds the parts/synergy* Dynamic-Theme).

When interviewees discuss the reasons for coming to the U.S., such as the contrast in economic opportunity or the urge to escape oppression, children can build the imagery (*contrasts and conflicts/dialectical activity* Dynamic-Theme) on which to develop other historical, economic, geographic, and economic concepts. Box 8.5 suggests additional activities.

BOX 8.5 INTERVIEWS WITH IMMIGRANT RESIDENTS

When you plan ahead together, interviewees bring photographs, documents, family artifacts, memorabilia and hand-made toys. Children participate in the preparation for an interview by suggesting questions they would want the visitor to answer. [**Procedural note:** It is effective when several different visitors from different countries and with different experiences or from different generations interact with the children. The similarities in the immigrant experience across different people can help to influence children's attitudes toward the underlying humanity of the participants.]

Inviting more than one visitor from a profession or culture averts tokenism, because not all people within a group are the same; this practice can avoid the development of stereotypes. It is a particularly useful experience when the visitors come *before* children read related books; then, the books take on more meaning. In order to provide ethnically diverse and gender-neutral models of careers, concerned teachers invite women as well as men of different ethnicities who work in science, engineering technology, and mathematics; and men as well as women of different ethnicities who work as nurses and artists.

Family Museum and Immigration Timeline

Teachers, with family involvement, can create a multicultural museum. Children help create an invitation for families to attend a special breakfast or evening dessert event, to accommodate working families. Families bring articles that represent their family traditions and set them out on tables with labels. Families might bring photographs; documents; medals; special clothing; uniform items or badges; jewelry; recipes; family Bibles; family trees; traditional toys; and handcrafted knitted, quilted, embroidered, and woodwork objects. Everyone *inductively* (condition for learning) appreciates the underlying similarities of family keepsakes, and helps community members to meet and increase their comfort with one another. Families take home their valuable items.

A few teachers create a multicultural museum thematic center in the classroom for several weeks with items that families feel comfortable to leave in the classroom. Families also indicate their own or their ancestors' countries of origin with Post-it notes on a map. You should be sensitive to your particular community's immigration stories when planning this activity.

Class Quilts

Quilts lend themselves to a variety of representations. Children can create a square to represent their family traditions. They could use heavy paper stock or oak tag and markers. You could then punch holes in the corners and tie them together with yarn.

Classroom Mural of Handprints

Using a variety of washable paint colors, including multicultural colors, all children contribute a handprint and discuss the beautiful result of their collaborative project.

Rice and Bread Across the World

Children cook, bake, or eat multi-ethnic breads and explore rice dishes that represent different cultures. They begin with the ethnicities of children in the class, thereby celebrating the favorites of class members.

Apple Seeds

After surveying their favorite apples, children are able to *predict* how many seeds they might find in apples of the same color. When the apples are cut across the center, they remove and count the seeds in each apple. The discussion can turn to how people who look different might have similar insides.

Games and Toys Across the World

Tangrams (Asia) and kalah/mancala (Africa) games are discussed in Chapter 12. A related book is *More math games and activities from around the world* (Zaslavsky, 2003).

Talking Stick

Children take turns speaking in a group when they hold the classroom "talking stick" or a special stuffed toy. This is a Native American Indian/Canadian First People custom that formalizes taking turns to speak in a group. It also helps to support inhibitory practice as well as political socialization, discussed below within the context of social studies standards.

Passport

Kindergarten children create passports to support role-play. They use their passports to travel on airplanes—constructed in the floor block center—to pretend visits to countries from which their families originated or which their families have visited.

Two-way Bilingualism

When young children learn the meaning of words in a language other than their own they can feel closer, and perhaps less superior, to the speaker of the other language. For example, some people treat English language learners as if they are generally less competent. Therefore, it can be helpful when a child who is learning English becomes the "expert" who teaches both you and the other children some names of classroom objects in their native language.

Poems, Songs, Books, and Labels

Hearing poems, songs, and books in both English and another language adds to the appreciation of meanings across cultures. Label features in the room in the children's presence, such as "window" and "door" in both English and another language. Children learn words that represent their body parts. Youngsters enjoy using courtesy words, such as "hello," "goodbye," "please," and "thank you" in a language other than English, including sign language. [**Procedural note:** Teachers typically use one word in context on a given day, and the children look for opportunities to use the word—providing a sense of empowerment that they enjoy.] A bilingual class book can capture these experiences (see Schiller, Lara-Alecio, & Irby, 2004).

Movement Education

Integrate a word in another language together with English that describes the speed or direction of a movement.

Food Preparation with Picture–Word Recipes

Cooking and food preparation offer opportunities to use pictures with words in more than one language as well as vocabulary related to measuring: for example, *uno mas* or *encore* (another time); *plus* (more); and *tzvei* (two) (see Haskins, 1991).

Games

Play a familiar game, such as Lotto, Pairs, or "In and Out the Windows," in two languages by substituting a word, such as *"ventana"* for "windows."

Bilingual Buddies

Pair English language learners with a buddy in their own or another class who is bilingual and already proficient in English. The buddies provide companionship and support for one another; and share labels in their first language.

Guest Storyteller

Invite a family member and/or community member to read a familiar story in their language (other than English). Sometimes, the visitor might teach the children a simple song in their native language, such as "Happy Birthday," or provide the words for a familiar game. In addition, books and computer games within the Dora the Explorer website (http://www.PBS.org) offer both English and Spanish versions. Moreover, when Dora the Explorer plays Candyland on the computer, children can hear both English and Spanish comments. Bilingual books and computer programs provide additional opportunities for two-way bilingualism. [**Procedural note:** Provide a variety of models within any culture to avoid stereotypes and bias.]

Family Involvement for English Language Learners

Use picture books and photo albums to make up stories with the children. These can be told in any language and encourage participation of all children. Parents and other family members can also use these books to engage in extended conversations about shared experiences, family customs, recent outings, and/or different kinds of animals. These shared book readings are also an excellent time to explicitly point out vocabulary in both languages.

(Espinosa, 2010, p. 97)

The activities discussed above contribute to the kind of holistic multicultural education that aims to affect egalitarian attitudes, predispositions, and behavior among people. The holistic approach to multicultural education includes aspects of national learning standards as well as school subject matter defined within the four disciplines of history, geography, economics, and political science. The discussion that follows outlines U.S. national learning standards and looks at how scholars use tools in these four disciplines to help them learn about concepts and sequence activities, and also how children can use the tools.

Social Studies: Translating National Standards into Activities for Young Children

Tools, by their nature, imply some form of active participation. Young children are able to use some of the tools in their activities that social scientists use.

As the discussion continues with a look at four social science domains, it is helpful to consider how activities for young children align with themes recommended by the National Council for Social Studies. The themes are Culture; People, Continuity, and Change (history); People, Places, and Environments (geography); Individual Development and Identity (psychology); Individuals, Groups, and Institutions (sociology); Power, Authority, and Governance (political science); Production, Distribution, and Consumption (economics); Science, Technology, and Society; Global Connections; and Civic Ideals and Practice. These themes are represented throughout this part of the book and in Chapter 11.

When you think back to your own social studies education in school, you might find what many adults notice. The most memorable, "best" social studies experiences are often the following: role-playing; creative dramatics; field trips; cultural festivals; dioramas; mock trials; cooperative learning; simulations; and researching a topic of personal interest. The author has never met anyone who has said that they found reading textbooks aloud, memorizing dates, answering factual questions in a quiz, or filling out worksheets to be worth remembering or enjoying.

You can plan with children a variety of ways to use the tools of social scientists in memorable, worthwhile activities that integrate the conditions for learning. There are many practical experiences in this part of the book that meet national guidelines and standards for achieving skills and concepts.

History

Youngsters become historians when they use the historian's tool—the interpretation of events—to understand what happens across time. Activities that represent the Dynamic-Theme of *cyclical change* deal with the nature of how events change across time.

Young children have a general sense of the time during which they have lived. Of all measurements, time is the most complex. Even so, youngsters are capable of imagining other times and places in their own ways. They are able to *compare* and interpret what happens and changes across time by comparing documents, photographs, artifacts, oral histories, and diaries. (See Box 8.4, which outlines activities to help children appreciate historical figures.) Activities such as those in Box 8.6 encourage diverse interpretations as well as critical thinking about history.

BOX 8.6 PROMOTE CRITICAL THINKING TO INTERPRET EVENTS

- Ask children to dictate or tape-record their own biographies and compare them.

- Read stories by different authors on the same topics, such as friends or babies.
- Present more than one edition of a story or tell a story from the point of view of a different character (Cullinan & Galda, 1994).
- Listen to different singers render the same song: for example, *City of New Orleans* sung by Judy Collins, Arlo Guthrie, and Willie Nelson. Discuss why different children vote for or rank their selections differently. [**Procedural note:** To avoid children copying one another, provide a picture–word paper ballot.]
- Poll children about a presidential election or other timely, controversial event.
- Use pictures, puppets, or flannel-board figures that interact in ways that suggest varied interpretations.
- View several brief films that show varied human patterns of life around similar needs.
- Use a diorama with figures that move in relation to it (Lavatelli, 1970). These materials involve changing perspectives and promote the beginnings of reversible thinking.
- View different photographs of the same subject, then draw, write about, tape-record, or photograph similar subjects and discuss their different renderings.
- Elicit analogies and compare the outcomes from different children; each sincere contribution is legitimate.
- Highlight the multiple interpretations of driftwood, art forms, mystery boxes, and incomplete data.

The digital camera can be your good friend as you record the sequence of events when children visit community sites or interview community workers. *Revisiting* some of these events through the sequence of photographs, a current timeline, becomes a concrete, accessible activity.

Photographic Guessing Activity

In a similar way, some teachers use personal photographic timelines. Sensitive to community possibilities, you might ask families to loan baby photographs of their child that they can *compare* with current photographs. Teachers place current digital photos backed with Fun-tak on a bulletin board and children attempt to match one another's baby photo with their current photo. Teachers and school administrators might also participate. In these ways, it becomes easier for children to experience how people change over time.

Children and teachers engage in a game to try to match contemporary with past photographs. Classes in the school attempt to match photographs of teachers from their early childhood years with their contemporary photographs. After each class submits their votes, all classes receive some form of recognition, such as new library books, colored pencils, and board games. Note that the activities involve the *comparison/induction* and *surprise/cognitive dissonance* conditions for learning.

You might let children know that "You are a historian. You are comparing the past and the present." You could imagine together, "What if there were no TV or electricity or automobiles? What might people have done?" Children see films and photographs of people in the past who dressed differently and lived with different technologies.

In addition to activities mentioned about cyclical change, *Fast is not a ladybug* (Schlein, 1953) is a classic non-fiction book about time as a relative phenomenon. For example, it is apparent that some changes occur more quickly than others. The Earth, for example, changes abruptly during an earthquake but more slowly when glaciers melt; geographers study the Earth.

Geography

Geographers use the primary tool of mapping. Their main social studies focus is how human beings affect their environment and how the environment affects us.

When kindergarten children interview somebody from another country, they are able to locate the visitor's country on the globe and a map. In this way, the map becomes meaningful. Children ask about how the visitors traveled; how long the trip took; and if there might be another way to get to them, such as water, land, or air. It becomes a playful adventure to try to trace the route on the globe to see if one or another means of transportation would have been possible. As they consider distances and routes, they are actively using the *comparison/induction* and *surprise/cognitive dissonance* conditions for learning.

Field Trips

A variety of ethnic restaurants and other businesses in some areas are happy to play host to young children and their teachers. Children can interview owners of different ethnicities and ages. They often ask about their childhoods and immigration experiences, as relevant. Some urban or rural schools that lack transportation or businesses in walking distance invite business owners to the school. [**Procedural note:** Prepare interviewees ahead of time with the kinds of questions that the children might ask. If children do not raise some questions, you might raise them instead: for example, "Where were you born?" (Locate the country/ state on the globe with a Post-it note and add a note to the school's location.) "How did you travel here?" "Tell us about how that place is different from this town." "Why did you come here?" "Tell us about the people in your home when you were growing up." "What is your work?" "What do you do?" "How did you prepare for it?" "What do you enjoy the most about your work?" "What do you like to do after work?"]

Young children also progress toward a fuller understanding of geography after they create 3-dimensional constructions and drawings. They learn that they can represent the physical world in a variety of ways. When children create self-portraits at various times during the year, or draw pictures in general, they are engaging in forms of mapping. Mapping develops with block building, a matter of scale.

Box 8.7 includes some examples of concrete experiences (including *surprise/ cognitive dissonance*) that can help pre-kindergarteners build imagery that leads to mapping. When children engage in building this type of imagery, you communicate that it is important to imagine and think first.

BOX 8.7 IMAGINING LEADS TO MAPPING

Imagining a Color Map of Cubes

In an opaque paper bag, place varied colors of same-sized wooden cubes.

Teacher (shaking the bag, with a playful tone): "What do you suppose might be in this bag?" (After children offer some ideas): "Could there be mashed potatoes in this bag? Could there be cotton balls? Could there be marshmallows?"

"Let's see" (holding up one cube and placing it on the table). "What do you notice? What else do you imagine might be in this bag?" (Hold up another cube and place it next to the first on the table.) "What else do you imagine might be in this bag?" And so forth.

Attribute Blocks (Variables of Color, Size, and Shape), A More Complex Mapping Activity

Using an opaque paper bag, repeat the Imagining a Color Map activity with "attribute blocks" and lay out each one as children identify and label the attributes. After a few colors, sizes, and shapes have been organized on the table, ask: "What else do you suppose might be missing, might be left in the bag? Let's find out" (removing one at a time as children identify items.)

Additional experiences in constructing community models (including *physical* and *surprise/dissonance* conditions for learning) are outlined in Box 8.8.

BOX 8.8 MAP AND COMMUNITY CONSTRUCTION

Pre-kindergarten children are able to:

- Match cubes and patterns of colored cube with increasing complexity. [**Procedural note:** Begin by placing each cube directly on the corresponding square on a card. After some practice, children can construct the patterns of cubes directly on a cloth or tray, while using the cards as references. A similar sequence can occur with pattern blocks. A ring binder helps to keep the cards in sequence.]
- "Map" the outline of their bodies on discarded wallpaper rolls or paper. [**Procedural note:** You might trace the outline of the child's body for the child to draw/paint/collage the area. This is sometimes an early experience of completing a representation across several days.] Children appreciate hearing you say, "You made a map of yourself. You are a geographer. Geographers make maps and read maps."
- Sit back-to-back as a pair with identical contents of a farm or doll furniture or tabletop blocks/Cuisenaire rods and take turns instructing one another about where to place each item. Then, they compare their findings, a process of feedback (*surprise/cognitive dissonance* condition for learning) about accurate communication.
- Hear about different countries or towns and observe adults locating family origins on maps.

Kindergarten children are able to:

- Map any room of their choice at home. [**Procedural note:** Any room, rather than "their room," because many children do not have a room of their own. A child's rendition of a map provides a form of assessment about their perceptions (see Fanelli, 2001).]
- Work in small groups to map the classroom.
- Use blocks to represent their understanding of harbors (Imhoff, 1959; Mitchell, 1934; Spodek, 1962) and other land forms.
- Develop a street map when relevant to their school's location.
- Enjoy simple treasure-hunt maps.
- At different times, place an 8 × 11-inch paper in urban, beach, and suburban environments and collect in separate bags, with your agreement, what they find under the paper. Then, they compare the contents. [**Procedural note:** You would scan the areas beforehand to be sure about safety and use plastic gloves.]

- Help you label the classroom walls north, south, east, and west, and play movement games using directional terms.

Set the Rules for Building a Community: A Guessing Game

After visiting a variety of locations in the community and interviewing visitors who engage in a variety of occupations, kindergarten children are able to use color cubes and colored loops to plan and develop towns. (See also Box 12.2).

In addition to field trips and other activities, you can add to children's image of mapping and land forms with photographs and books, such as *Blueberries for Sal* (McCloskey, 2010). Keep in mind that other books present both land forms and the Dynamic-Theme of *cyclical change*, such as *Round Trip* (Jonas, 1983) and *The Little House* (Burton, 1988). Young children are also able to consider different kinds of dwellings in which they might live, including apartments, houses with different architecture, mobile homes, tents, yurts, hogans, houseboats, and so forth; a relevant non-fiction book is *Homes around the world* (Lock, 2009). The creation and use of classroom tents is a popular project; the youngest children are satisfied with a blanket covering two sides of a table.

Teachers and children are able to build enclosures and mazes with blocks for toy vehicles. One educator recommends that you should build a series of different mazes with unit blocks at different times (MacDonald, 2001). You can describe how the car moves as children use a toy car to move through the maze; and children have opportunities to coach one another.

Directions and transportation are part of the study of how humans interact with their physical environment. In turn, the impact of transportation on the economy brings us to the discussion of economics education.

Economics

Economists deal with the main issue of scarcity: we all want more than the resources we have or need. There is a disparity between wants and needs, represented in the *contrasts and conflicts* Dynamic-Theme. Economists collect information about resources of both goods and services in order to set priorities and try to predict and avoid shortages.

Young children experience the emotional aspect of scarcity. In general, they learn through social and emotional means before concepts develop. Ethical questions about a fair distribution of resources arise on a regular basis. Daily interactions lead to talk about sharing (the economic concept of supply and demand) and taking turns. These are cognitive attainments and involve the youngsters' developing Theory of Mind and capacity for inhibiting their impulsive behavior.

Youngsters also see that the exchange of money and credit cards buy food and playthings. They are less clear about why people receive change when they exchange money for purchases. For example, they would typically expect that a larger coin would have more buying power than a smaller coin. That is because they are not yet consistently able to conserve quantity which requires holding on to more than a single variable at one time. They are also less clear about payment for services, which are less tangible than goods.

A direct experience of the *surprise/cognitive dissonance* condition for learning that represents the economic concept of wants and needs (scarce resources) appears in Box 8.9.

BOX 8.9 EXPERIENCES OF SCARCE RESOURCES (WANTS AND NEEDS)

Packing for a Trip

Invite kindergarten children to role-play packing a bag for a trip. "Let's imagine a trip that you could wish to take." (Many children select Disneyland.) "Here is your backpack. There are lots of choices to make in packing." [**Procedural note:** Lay out the contents of two huge bags. There are many more objects than could fit into the backpack. The bags contain *necessities*, such as a comb, toothbrush, toothpaste, clothing, and sneakers, but also *wants*, such as traveling board games, an iPod, cell phone, stuffed animals, a doll (or other prestigious toy), jump ropes, and hats with superhero logos and sports team logos.]

Each child in a small group selects a different color of Post-it note to place on all the items that they plan to pack. In this way, more than one child might select the same item(s). (Keep carpenter's tape handy if some items need better adhesion.) "Place your Post-it notes on all of the items that you want to pack. More than one person can choose the same items and will have a turn to pack."

- *Expectation.* Children place their Post-it notes on all of their choices.
- *Experience.* Each child has a chance to pack selected items into the backpack.
- *Surprise/cognitive dissonance.* The limited space requires that they prioritize. Then, they need to consider what they really *need* and set aside the things that they merely want.

See also Box 7.2.

Game of Honor

Here is another activity that integrates *surprise/cognitive dissonance* as well as the economic concept of scarcity. Provide some children with a medal, sash of honor, or prestigious mechanical pencil. Other children typically protest. This is an occasion to discuss their feelings of exclusion and possible ways to empathize with others as well as distribute privileges fairly. (After such activities, you might read aloud relevant children's literature—see the Economic Issues Affect Families section of the Related Children's Books for this chapter.) In addition to learning about the fair distribution of resources, the issue of who decides on the distribution of limited resources connects to issues of government and politics, discussed below.

Political Science/Civics/Government

A central concept of political science is the study of power. Children emotionally understand the issue of power—who gets what, when, and how (Lasswell, 1958). You could provide opportunities for them to make choices and vote on issues that arise in class. Among such issues are surveys of favorite books, foods, and priorities. Kindergarten children are able to explore and share different ways to ask different, influential questions in preparing and shaping their surveys (Whitin & Whitin, 2010). In this way, they add to their perspective taking and build the images that might influence their capacity to consider propaganda and advertising claims in the future.

After children experience the *surprise/cognitive dissonance* of role-playing the Game of Honor, the children who do not receive the medal or mechanical pencil typically ask when they will receive the prestigious item. When they hear "We don't have any more" they complain, "That's not fair." This is the moment to discuss the issue of fairness. "What would be a more fair way to give out the goodies?" "How might there be a way to share them?" "What rights does everyone in this class expect they deserve?" Children are usually able to resolve the issue by taking turns. Of course, you would help all children eventually have a turn to be "honored." You would be able to use concepts of sharing and taking turns to describe the way government works and how people vote for those who will help them by making fair decisions, and so forth.

Youngsters are able to develop a discussion about what services the government provides for everyone. You might invert reality and ask them to imagine, "What might happen if there were no schools, roads, firefighters, police, safety rules about food, medicine, or working conditions?" It is noteworthy that this "political science" activity crosses into the economic issue of scarcity—unlimited wants and limited resources (wanting more than we can have). This is another example of the idea that separating disciplines of knowledge can identify particular methods of inquiry and conceptual emphases, but life is holistic. The Dynamic-Theme of *contrasts and conflicts/dialectical activity* can therefore serve as a basis for providing a broad range of connected learning by planning relevant interdisciplinary activities. Also, the underlying image of a government that provides for the general good can contribute to building *the whole exceeds the parts/synergy* Dynamic-Theme.

A related example is a pre-kindergarten teacher who dramatically was able to begin the study of fairness by reading an imaginary letter from South Africa (Mardell, 1999). [**Procedural note:** The experience of the letter, dramatically removed from an envelope, *precedes* reading about apartheid and South Africa's struggles for civil liberties.]

Kindergarten children who notice a leaky faucet are able to have an experience of political socialization. Children might know about conserving water from popular media, and you might talk with them about the subject. Kindergarten children are able to place a transparent container under a leaky faucet and collect the dripping water. They are able to create drawings and notes with invented spelling. Then, they can become empowered by inviting the school custodian to see their collection of data. You could prepare the custodian to share with the children an appreciation of their data collection with a plan to fix the leaky faucet. The children's sense of political influence and their strong research attitude can give them a sense of pride in accomplishing change—a lesson in political advocacy. To document this kind of activity beyond photographs, children can prepare a class book on the subject of the leak and their political action.

These activities demonstrate that social studies and egalitarian education can emerge from the daily interactions between you and the children with whom you work. Along with the way you organize your classroom space and schedule, it is worthwhile to consider how verbal and social interaction influence what children learn about ideas as well as about school. Children also need to decide how to

IMAGE 8.1 Report of Water Conservation Action

interpret messages in advertising—"This is the best cereal"—and appeals, such as figuring out when to "Run right over to your mother and tell her to buy . . ./ enroll you in this program/etc." The purpose of the suggestions in Box 8.6 is to help children interpret not just the past but also their present world.

Young children also need to feel competent and optimistic. Therefore, the ways in which you help them to focus on solving problems as well as welcome their attitudes, ideas, opinions, and feelings are important. (You can find specific strategies in Box 14.4.) Also important is the respectful, positive way in which you help them to support their *sense of competence* (condition for learning). (Specific strategies appear in Box 13.2.) The strategies discussed in Boxes 14.4 and 13.2 are relevant to consider within the framework of multicultural education and studies of other social science concepts. These strategies are also useful during discussions across all of the work that you do together. Moreover, they provide an opportunity for you to assess what youngsters understand, how they make connections, and how they apply the knowledge they acquire.

Assessment

Professional teachers document and assess children's concepts and attitudes as they participate in the activities embedded in this chapter. Look at their constructions, artistic and written work. Listen to their interactions, comments, and questions. Indeed, you are acting upon your assessments of children's learning as well as their possibilities to learn more (Zone of Proximal Development) each time you provide "scaffolds" to transform attitudes or make fresh connections.

Children reveal their most significant knowledge when they make connections and apply their learning. For you, the wait is not long because youngsters develop quickly. However, you would expect some delay, because significant knowledge-for-understanding, different from rote information recall, percolates a while before it rises to the surface. If you feel an earlier need to know what children perceive, they are likely to be agreeable to helping a peer. "Please tell Sam, who was absent, what you did when . . ." "Tell him what that was called." "Tell him what happened when . . ." "Sam, what questions do you have about . . .?" In this way, different children can organize their memories in their own ways in the context of helping someone else, rather than feeling that they are being formally examined and judged. In effect, retelling events for someone else is also a way to apply learning.

Reflections

This chapter has focused on the goal of forming and transforming egalitarian attitudes and behaviors between human beings. When professional teachers read books to children that show how human beings share experiences similar to their own, even though they might look different or live in different environments, then the group has a chance to experience a shared sense of humanity *inductively*. These teachers want children to feel sensitive to others' feelings and to treat others fairly. They saturate their classrooms with materials and experiences to support the goal of building egalitarian attitudes. They also celebrate holidays based upon the underlying, shared human need across cultures to commemorate significant events, such as overcoming tyranny or celebrating a successful harvest in order to support survival. When they plan and do so many significant things, trivial things are simply squeezed out of the school day.

Young children can begin to learn about concepts in the social sciences—history geography, economics, and political science—by focusing on the processes and some of the tools that social scientists use in ways young children can understand. For example, youngsters compare past and present life and try to imagine and interpret events and when they took place in broad terms, such as recently or a long time ago (history). They build an understanding of themselves in space as well as time and begin to map the world by beginning with themselves (geography). They understand the economic concepts of wants and needs by comparing situations and weighing decisions within everyday events. They figure out ways to influence events by voting or collecting data and asking administrators to fix things (political science/civics).

Although scholars approach the study of social events with distinct perspectives and tools, human events tend to overflow the borders of separate disciplines to beg for interdisciplinary, holistic considerations. Indeed, new knowledge tends to grow from boundary-breaking insights which activities connected by Dynamic-Themes have the potential to nurture.

Professional early childhood teachers can use the techniques of building imagery, role-playing, and constructions to support social learning. They engage in thoughtful questioning, juxtaposing activities in space and time in order to help children experience connections. They generally focus on a playful, activity-based learning environment. While integrating the seven conditions for learning content, teachers focus on supporting children's positive self-concepts. They serve as impresarios who create "happenings" and special moments of delight. As they do so, they integrate the literacy tools that children need to learn.

Part III, which follows, expands the discussion about a variety of literacy skills.

PART III

Learning Tools, Skills, and Ways to Represent Experiences

The definition of literacy is changing to include electronic forms of communication beyond the printed page. Children will be required to make connections and select from alternative ways of working to communicate in order to fulfill their potential.

Children who actively engage in drawing, writing, reading, music, dance, movement, drama, mathematics, design technology, and science do not necessarily become professional artists, journalists, composers, dancers, athletes, actors, mathematicians, engineers, or laboratory scientists. However, they might use

> the habits of mind . . . to think about and make sense of many of the ideas, claims, and events that they encounter in everyday life. Accordingly, . . . literacy enhances the ability of a person to observe events perceptively, reflect on them thoughtfully, and comprehend explanations offered to them. In addition, those internal perceptions and reflections can provide the person with a basis for making decisions and taking actions.
>
> (AAAS, 2009, p. 306)

Therefore, although the chapters in this section highlight the *acquisition* of learning tools and skills, the *application* always involves content. Indeed, content and the skills to represent them blend. The variety of literacy forms function as interdisciplinary connections (Gullo, 2005). Children draw, write, read, measure, sing, dance, play and imagine, and act out concepts to represent their experience.

When you envision the *connections* between literacy forms and domains, there is a chance to assess what youngsters understand. As children move their bodies, create other forms and artful products, and make connections between experiences, you are able to assess their developing control of skills along the way from (1) approximate to (2) intentional, (3) fluent, and (4) automatic.

Looking ahead, each chapter in this part focuses on a particular form of communication and set of skills. Each form has a distinct grammar made up of elements and the *contrasting* patterns of their relationships. Chapter 9 looks at ways to represent and communicate meaning in aesthetic, physical, and spoken forms; these forms of representation form a continuum with writing and mathematics. Chapter 10 looks at practical activities that young children learn as they progress from presenting meaning beyond 3-dimensional and into 2-dimensional forms. Chapter 11 looks at ways to integrate electronic technologies, design engineering, and science experiences. Chapter 12 considers the power and joy in manipulating, envisioning, and representing quantitative properties through everyday experiences.

9

LITERACY IN MUSIC, MOVEMENT, AND THE ARTS

Introduction

This chapter discusses music, movement, dance, drama, and the visual arts—universal forms of communication as well as aesthetic experiences. The capacity to have aesthetic experiences and to appreciate and create art forms is part of what defines us as human beings. When you talk about, criticize, and trace the history of art forms, you engage in an *indirect* activity, which is different from the *direct*, aesthetic experience of art. Young children do not merely have aesthetic experiences; they are also able to represent the world in 3- and 2-dimensional formats.

As children produce art forms, you can assess their images, ideas, and experiences. The physical aspect of the arts is the foundation for other, less visible, integrated learning. For example, children illustrate or act out poems (literacy). They create rhythms as they tap, clap, jump, stomp, and dance the syllables of their names (mathematics; literacy). They can graph numbers of syllables as well as add and reduce dancers or movements (mathematics). When they move faster or slower in time to music, their brains build a connection with fractions; at another time, you might plan a spinner game with fractions or give children the problem of dividing a cake or stalk of celery so that everyone can have a piece (mathematics). Dancers explore the dynamics of force, speed, and timing (physics); their brains seed the imagery on which to grow related concepts. Children solve the problems of creating masks that represent different feelings, concepts, or cultures (design technology; social studies). The digital possibilities for creative artistic representation offer yet another medium. Imagination is the only limitation to represent experiences with the arts.

In this chapter, we shall look at the nature of aesthetic experience. The framework within each section of the chapter is as follows. Within music, movement, creative dramatics, and the visual arts, there is an outline of the elements in each form and how they function together (their grammar). With these elements in mind, you might plan *contrasts* that help children create art forms (*induction condition for learning*). In turn, you are able to appreciate children's work when you consider the elements along with the pathways of their development within each form. Then, you can help them extend their skills and appreciation.

Aesthetics and Education

Aesthetic experience that includes the "formed" arts as well as ordinary life is available in some way to all people, regardless of age or intellectual capacity. Art is neither elitist nor a "frill," but an intrinsic perspective that is possible in all human activity. "Even a crude experience, if authentically an experience, is more fit to give a clue to the intrinsic nature of aesthetic experience than an object already set apart from any other mode of experience" (Dewey, 1958, p. 11). Aesthetic experience exists within, but also beyond, the "artistic" disciplines, such as music, dance, drama, and the visual arts. Daily life as well as these art forms have the potential to create joyful, aesthetic experience when we see the "familiar" in "strange" ways (Dewey, 1933; Gordon & Poze, 1980). The readiness of a consuming human being guarantees the aesthetic experience, not the form itself.

There is no guarantee, however, that we can have an aesthetic experience unless the artist successfully creates a form that can help us share some of the artist's experience, based upon our own past experience as well as our present motives for perceiving (Rosenblatt, 1969, 1978). There is an aesthetic experience for both the artist (while creating) and the connoisseur (while appreciating), a direct relationship between two human beings in a particular moment, an "I–Thou" relationship (Buber, 1958). The relationship between the producer and the connoisseur is an opportunity for enrichment and fresh "insight" into a work of art (Langer, 1953, 1957).

The sensory, emotional, surreal, and imaginative processes can reflect a rich range of Dynamic-Themes (underlying images that can connect experiences) that would be less fully knowable if only logical and linear tools were employed. Indeed, people have different proclivities for appreciating aesthetic experiences or representing meanings through various media (Gardner, 1982). In effect, some people tend to find kinetic or visual or musical or linguistic experience more accessible, although opportunities for exposure, practice, and cultural valuing could help to enrich their learning across all forms.

When you expose children to a full range of meaning-rich experiences and forms of representation in school, they have opportunities to use the artist's tools and ways of knowing as well as the tools of scientists, mathematicians, and others. You can integrate their tools across the range of children's experiences to provide opportunities for flexible thinking, problem setting and solving across media, and the creation of new connections. Many of the children's aesthetic experiences will come as they play with materials and with one another. "In a field where there are no 'right answers,' individuals learn that art can be a celebration of diversity, a celebration of individuality for its own sake" (Barnes, 1987, p. 16).

Youngsters can create insightful forms, even if those forms are somewhat episodic rather than closed. Their coordination and skills will grow. Beginning with random approaches, they create forms with varying degrees of purposefulness. It is worth mentioning that the progression from "scribbling" toward representation and realism might not suggest only that realism is better than abstraction, but that scribbling may be revisited throughout the creation of art work.

Part of your role is to recognize a child's perspective, support succeeding levels of challenge, and communicate an appreciation of small benchmarks. After all, "Creative ideas are often those that bring together ideas from different domains or fields" (Brown with Vaughan, 2010, p. 136). As children make connections, they are using their memory, resisting impulsive repetitions of familiar patterns, and engaging in adaptive thinking—all skills related to the self-regulation of executive function. Box 9.1 suggests roles (scaffolds) that you might use to support youngsters' creativity.

BOX 9.1 TEACHER SCAFFOLDS SUPPORT CREATIVITY

- *Sensitizing*. Provide a description, a kind of "verbal harmony," using relevant and expanding vocabulary, to appreciate what you perceive is a child's intentional combination of materials.
- *Modeling fluency*. Elaborate on symmetrical or unusual structures. "What might happen if . . . [e.g., you moved your arm first like this]?" "What are some other ways to . . .?"
- *Modeling originality*. Create bulletin board displays; share decorative programs; or create original work of your own, such as haiku poetry, in the children's presence (not for copying). Offer analogies.
- *Flexibility*. Ask children to create new forms or explore aloud alternative ways to frame and solve problems. "What do you think might hold that together?" "What other things could you try?" "Here, I'll tape that down so that it doesn't move." "What did you try?"
- *Elaboration*. Model a technique. Make suggestions. Raise questions: e.g., "What else might . . .?" Share and build ideas with others. (Torrance, 1952, defines creativity; see also Burton, 2001; Krogh & Morehouse, 2008)

Sensitive teachers intervene in ways that help children retain a full focus on the present, so that the children might transcend the moment. Human beings usually experience this satisfying sense of challenge, independence, immersion, and timelessness as pleasure during play, working in the arts, and personally meaningful and challenging pastimes. One psychologist calls this sort of experience a sense of "flow" (Csikszentmihalyi, 1996). The sense of flow may emerge during such varied occasions as vigorous physical activity, dance, musical experiences, immersion in a mutually satisfying conversation, feelings of affection, or the solving of a puzzle.

The all-day schedule permits time to work in greater depth in the arts and deepen all program activities as children represent their experiences in the arts. The integration of any representational forms provides opportunities for children's brains to strengthen conceptual connections, and for you to assess their progress.

Excluding Italy's Reggio Emilia schools (see Edwards, Gandini, & Forman, 1998), it is rare to find an art specialist in early childhood programs. Most early childhood teachers include art activities as a major program component and feel comfortable using specialist resources in other areas. They recognize that visual arts in particular are a major form of symbolic representation in the early years. A main role of the arts is to build on a strength that young children bring to school—their capacity for successful aesthetic experience.

Occasionally, teachers who are particularly skillful in music education will share their skills with other teachers, providing a special music time that can supplement, but should not replace, music as a regular part of classroom experience. It is unfortunate that music appears to be an area in which many teachers feel a lack of confidence; however, there are varied activities that teachers can do with children that do not require extraordinary skills. Where separate special education classes exist, programs with teachers who specialize in movement, physical education, or music include children with special learning needs.

Music

Representation through music and movement is one way in which children communicate, along with other media. Before and after:

- Mathematics instruction—children move themselves and objects through space.
- Speech development—children represent experiences in movement.
- Writing—children represent experiences in drawing.
- Reading print—children decode the meanings of human emotion and behavior.

In all of these activities, children represent their feelings, experiences, meaning, and imagination in play.

No matter how long or how well someone describes music, we will never grasp it unless we hear it directly. In this sense, music is a non-discursive symbolic repository of imagery in its perceptual immediacy, direct involvement, and connectedness. One philosopher has seen "mathematics as conceptual music and music as sensuous mathematics" (Polanyi, 1963, p. 38). There is a sense in which "only music can achieve the total fusion of form and content of means and meaning, which all art strives for" (Steiner, 1970, p. 29).

Music can communicate basic human feelings to babies before they understand the words. It has long been a part of school life. In addition to creating music, children can listen purposefully to different musical genres and music from different cultures. You can plan engaging activities to *compare* and *contrast* the elements of music.

The Elements of Music

Rhythm and *tempo* (pace) complement one another. Children learn to differentiate rhythm and tempo when you describe what is happening as they explore different rhythms with parts of their bodies, objects, or drums.

Notes (*pitch*) combine to create a *melody*. Children need help to differentiate *pitch* from *volume*. For example, they equate a *high* note with *loud* volume. You can label the higher or lower note and the louder or softer volume. Again, when they explore melodies with different emotional qualities (*dynamics (force), including tempo and volume*), you can add to their knowledge by labeling their slower or faster speed or louder or softer volume. Children come to understand the vocabulary when they experience events in *relationship* to the elements; the perceivable movement between elements in the *comparison* provides a chance for them to experience the elements by the *induction* condition for learning.

As with any grammar, the combinations of elements that conform to the rules of how they interact are predictably unpredictable. This feature of the arts makes it possible for producers to be creative and consumers potentially to appreciate the creativity of each piece. For example, "Across cultures and across language barriers, we consistently use metaphors to describe sound qualities, such as dark, light, warm, lilting, or sprightly" (Wright, 2003, p. 128, citing Worth, 2000).

When humans do not have the words to describe feelings or aesthetic experiences, music's uniquely sound-based "language" can mirror and represent the experiences. The human *brain* appears predisposed to seeking such connections and patterns.

Creating Music

Instruments   Rhythm is a kind of mathematical pattern, an intuitive inner mathematics. Individually and in groups, children explore rhythm directly by moving their bodies and using percussion instruments, including such items as drums, triangles, Chinese gongs, shakers, rhythm sticks, African rain sticks, tambourines, and everyday objects. Melodic and harmonic patterns are available

through singing and playing other musical instruments. Children directly experience the *contrast and conflict/dialectical* Dynamic-Theme through musical counterpoint, part singing, and rhythm instrument orchestration. [**Procedural note:** It is
important to intersperse plenty of free-form exploration with instruments each time
that children use them. It will be easier for you and the children to listen if you
begin with a few instruments of fine tonal quality and gradually add to this stock;
you might also reduce parts. Before the children receive the instruments, make sure
they understand your visual signal to "stop and place instruments on the floor." In
that way you can arrange to stop and share ideas after they begin to play.]

Children can classify and contrast instruments of different pitches and music
of varying rhythms and tempos. After they hear contrasting models, they can
intuitively contrast the musical concepts. With increased awareness, children might
be able to take turns providing musical accompaniment to favorite stories, poems,
or creative dramas. In addition to percussion instruments, children might look at
string instruments, comparing them with woodwind and brass instruments that
older children might demonstrate.

Music educators support a sequential improvisational process that consists:

> of different, increasingly sophisticated behaviors. Children may revert to a
> lower level when encountering a difficult musical element, a new musical
> style, or a change in mood . . . [as follows]:
>
> - exploration (loosely structured);
> - process-oriented (producing cohesive patterns);
> - product-oriented (conscious of . . . tonality and rhythm);
> - fluid (applying relaxed and fluid technique);
> - structural (. . . improvisations through a repertoire of strategies);
> - stylistic (incorporating music of a given style); and
> - personal (develop a new style).
>
> *(Wright, 2003, pp. 203–205)*

An experimental attitude on your part will encourage experimentation—for
example, highlighting *contrasts* among the variations in echoes made by the human
voice, objects, or rhythm instruments. Empower yourself and the children by
communicating your acceptance of the notion that everyone can be expressive and
creative with sound.

Song   One of the most available and versatile of all music-making instruments is
the human voice. Singing can turn an ordinary moment into something filled with
expectation and camaraderie. If you believe that you cannot sing on pitch or carry
a tune, you might notice that young children do not care. Thus you might feel
comfortable accompanying activities with a song, whether at the beginning of a
whole-group meeting or during transitions, such as, "This is the way we get our
coats, first with friends who are wearing green." When you substitute a child's

name in a song, they usually welcome the recognition, although an exception might be a child whose family culture avoids personal attention.

Folk songs[1] and contemporary songs, with their natural repetition and rhyme, are especially relevant for use with young children. For the child who is learning English, a private way to practice the new language in a group sing-along is singing, "Sing along, sing along; and just sing tra-la-la-la-la [or substitute sounds] if you don't know this song / You'll quickly learn the music and find yourself the words / 'Cause when we sing together we'll be heard." Folk songs in languages other than English offer an additional opportunity for the bilingual child or family member to teach a song or participate more fully at the same time as English-speaking children expand their range of language. You are able to appreciate the increasing accuracy with which children sing along, remembering the words.

Folk songs and other lyrics help build vocabulary and grammar. Singing also helps reduce stuttering. The format of some songs, with their repetitive structure and rhyme, lend themselves to substitute wordings that children gleefully compose, such as, "Put your finger in the air [hair, nose, etc.]." It is no surprise that children's musical creations combine easily with their socio-dramatic play and creative dramatics, increasing their richness and expressiveness. "Taking poetic license with pitch, rhythm, and expressive aspects—like holding particular words for special effect—will keep the interaction interesting and enjoyable" (Wright, 2003, p. 199). [**Procedural note:** Rather than trying to "teach" a song precisely, line by line, try to "infect" children with songs by singing them spontaneously as well as on planned occasions. The important experience for children is their feeling of belonging and participating.]

Appreciating Music

Children appreciate as well as create music. In either case, music is a symbolic form, and some elements require instruction so that they can become new "figures" standing out against a familiar "background" of sound.

You can set the tone by scheduling and creating a climate for listening. Sometimes controlling lighting or using a fragrance can set a tone conducive to listening.

You can control variables. You might contrast melody, rhythm, tempo, volume, or mode with another musical element. Play CDs or arrange for live performances in which children hear individual instruments and then the instruments in combination with others. Children feel how their vocal cords vibrate and how musical instruments vibrate. When they see music notes as another written form of sounds, some children spontaneously imitate the form on paper.

Another way to highlight and contrast unique forms is to hear brief samples of music from different cultures. Young children can distinguish between European, African, South American, Asian, Australian Aboriginal, and North American First

People's music. You can augment an activity when children hear the music before or after a story or videotape.

We are culturally conditioned to expect certain music to evoke certain kinds of images. Working with young children who are not as fixed in their connections, you may be able to keep open their appreciation by encouraging them to select, from a large collection of varied pictures, those that remind them of music they hear. When they see that you accept a variety of alternative associations, they build confidence in your support of diversity.

Movement Education

People have a veritable need to move despite the fact that, as they grow older, they have movement socialized out of them. Along the way, movement is fundamental to many aspects of experience. Children have aesthetic experiences when they move through space and observe the movement of others. In addition, experiences with movement are foundations for the development of mathematics and science concepts. Children may also apprehend the imagery of the *contrast and conflict/dialectical* Dynamic-Theme as they have experiences related to studies in mathematics and science as well as in music, movement, and the visual arts. Creative rhythmic movement is also a starting point for dramatics, a part of poetic language experience as well as an outgrowth of socio-dramatic play.

The Elements of Movement

Movement involves *direction, levels* in space, *intensity, frequency, duration,* and visual as well as *rhythmic patterns* (see Pica, 2004, p. 146). Children construct *relationships* among *what* they do, *where* (space) they move, and *how* (force/effort) they do it. Movement skills are verbs such as "strike, travel, roll . . . [and are] typically less interesting than [when] . . . modified by an adverb—strike hard, travel jerkily, roll smoothly. Skills can stand by themselves. You can roll or gallop or jump but you can't slow or high or under. Concepts modify skills" (Sanders, 2002, p. 35, citing Graham, Holt Hale, & Parker, 2001).

Young children enjoy many activities with *rhythm* and rhythmic movement. Rhythms are varying interrelations of tempo and pulsations that we perceive as patterns. These rhythmic patterns are repetitious signals that we perceive as "wholes" that are more than their "parts." Much of musical experience reflects this quality of transposing "emotive" wholes, a direct experience with the Dynamic-Theme of *synergy*.

It is valuable to do movement activities and play with rhythm alone as well as with melody. In order to keep open their opportunities for new discoveries, you can use a drum to accompany the children rather than ask them to keep in step with you. With more experience, children can try to adapt to rhythms that you or other children initiate. A variation is playing with drum echoes or clapping "conversations"; individual children take turns to provide a rhythm for others to echo. You can blend this sort of activity into clapping, then counting, the syllables of children's names.

These practices build and extend children's imagery. If possible, consider videotaping children's efforts as a way to provide them with both feedback and appreciation. To begin, you can encourage children with the invitations in Box 9.2.

BOX 9.2 CREATIVE MOVEMENT: DIFFERENT LEVELS[2]

Children can create different ways to move across the room:

- Come to me in any way you like.
- Come in a new way. Come in a different way.
- Come in a high way. Come in a low way.
- Come as if the bottoms of your feet were covered with glue/as if you were wearing a heavy crown/as if you were carrying an injured bird/as if you were very angry/as if you were on the moon/etc. [**Procedural note:** Children's movements can help you informally assess their understanding as they *apply* their learning to the activity.]

Children can isolate and variably combine parts of their own bodies, as follows:

- Move only your elbows/your shoulders/your head.

They can isolate levels:

- Move in as high a way as you can/the most curving way you can.
- Move in the flat, as if there are transparent walls in front of and/or behind you.
- Move in the deep, as if there are transparent walls on either side or both sides of you.

[**Procedural note:** Movement activities take place at different times, as children have related prior experiences. Teachers *revisit* (condition of learning) some of these activities, focusing on individuals' discoveries while continuously describing: "Rita has a new way to move," "Hal found a new level," "Sam reminds me of a storm," and so forth. "Everyone has such original ideas."]

Youngsters enjoy the challenge of "coming to you" across the room in different and creative ways. Their use of space and rhythm are kaleidoscopic. When you emphasize the validity of finding alternative ways to move, children can directly experience the Dynamic-Theme of *indirect progress*.

After such personal explorations of space, they also enjoy using props, such as hoops, ropes, scarves, costume items, balloons, and labels. You can scaffold the use of props, for example by differentiating the size of balls or targets; and have children begin by picking a target. You also can scaffold by: (1) balancing movement and sedentary activities; and (2) pairing children who can serve as models for one another. With partners as well as alone, children can explore their use of space. The activities suggested in Box 9.3 would take place over a period of many weeks.

BOX 9.3 SOME IMAGINATIVE MOVEMENT ACTIVITIES

- *Angles.* When your feet stay in the same place without moving, your body can lean. That's very special. Now try a different way to lean. Take a partner and try leaning with him or her.
- *Bubbles.* Imagine that you are inside a bubble. Show how you could move so that the bubble won't break, so that you can stretch part of the bubble, ever so gently now. As you move inside your bubble, show how you can pass other people in their bubbles without touching, then with touching.
- *Moving with a partner.* Move toward somebody. Move away from that person in a new way. Meet somebody else in a new way. (Adapted from P. Press, personal communication, 1974.) First, imagine how you will move. Partners take turn walking, skipping, tapping, or running on one another's shadows.
- *Directions.* With a partner, try moving together toward the labels on our wall, first toward the north, holding hands. Hold your partner by the elbow and move in a very tall way toward the west. ("Oh, Ari has found an interesting way to hold Jan's elbow. Betty is making a new line with her head. Jo is showing us the west side with her ear also. It's beautiful to see so many different ways.") Move toward the south with your partner in a very low way, as if there is a low tunnel. Find a new way to move together. You're leaving that tunnel in so many different ways. ("Danny, that's a new way that you never tried before—very clever idea. Evan, how original. Pam looks so relaxed and comfortable. Peter looks as if he's done a great deal of hard work.")
- *Make four elbows* (or four feet or four fingers) with other children (Copley, 2010, p. 69). Use different numbers as well as different body parts.

Outdoors, children create tallies or pips or numerals and wear their marked card as a necklace. They create a train of people in a sequence of numbers; or match someone else's card; or kindergarten children add cards together to make a particular sum, such as ten (adapted from Copley, 2010, p. 71).

- *Mirrors.* Next, let's be mirrors. Take partners and decide which of you will begin. It could be whoever is nearest the east side of the room. Now, one of you move very slowly as you hear the drum begin. Partners, try to copy that person. ("What nice new movements. Slowly, carefully now. Nicole and Sarah, move there so you have more space.") Now, the lead partner, change, and be the mirror to your partner. (Repeat.) [**Procedural note:** Variations on this activity include using hoops which children can roll to one another, with one another, move around and inside of, or jump in and out of, faster or slower, abruptly or smoothly, heavily or lightly.]

- *Personal analogy.* Everybody go to the end of the room. Now, come to me in a new way. ("That's fine, so many different ways—some high, some low, somebody sideways. Oh, it's good to see you being so creative.") Try another new way now, and move backward to where you started. Try a new way to come sideways. Find a new way to return sideways. ("So many new ideas. Martin was really following his neck. Nora, what an original way to use your shoulder.") Let's rest for a minute and talk. What were you thinking of that can move sideways? What else can move sideways? (Pointing to four children) Try to be that thing. (Repeat procedures with different groups of children.) Let's think together about some things that can move backward. Yes. Uh-huh. Interesting. What a fine idea. The objects can bend and stretch? Let's try (pointing to six children) to move backward as those things do. Become those things. Let's move as if we're in water, on mud, in a crowded hallway/bus. Become popping corn before the heat comes on. Now, begin to pop until all the pieces are touching. Become a seed. Imagine that you are in soil. Now, feel the water washing your seed parts. Show what you are doing. Now the sun is warming the soil. Show what you are doing. [**Procedural note:** Popcorn and seed images come *after* the children have related activities. You can assess what they understand when they show their learning with movements.]

It is possible to make the case that children are incidentally experiencing geographic and mathematical images when they engage in some of the activities in Boxes 9.2 and 9.3. The children's perceptions are joyful and they can feel empowered because the activities encourage them to be creative and independent problem setters and solvers. Game songs, such as *Clap, Clap, Clap Your Hands, Looby Loo*, asnd *The Wheels on the Bus*, suggest movements that you can use to pursue this purpose or to restrict it, depending upon what you intend. Some classical movement games also include *London Bridge Is Falling Down, Ring Around Rosie, Jack Jump Over the Candlestick*, and the action song *Head, Shoulders, Knees, and Toes*. Consider a game in which children balance a beanbag on different parts of the body (Edwards, Bayless, & Ramsey, 2005, p. 20; see also Sanders, 2002, p. 21 for a collection of traditional action songs and music) or touch a different part of the body to the floor (Pica, 2004, p. 88). Different children might use a different body part based upon their capacity. Another approach is to engage in practicing self-control by moving in an opposite direction, such as lowering your hands when your partner raises his/her hands.

An activity within limited space is "Simon Says," played without eliminating children. [**Procedural note:** When children are eliminated, there are many "losers" (sometimes waiting impatiently or mischievously, while not practicing the spatial game) and a single "winner." Although life outside school has competition, your classroom might be the single reliable place in the lives of some children where they can feel competent and successful for much of the time.] Children also take turns suggesting the movements. Movement activities, including action songs and games, also incidentally help English language learners to build vocabulary.

Physical Development and Coordination

Physical activity makes assessment an ongoing visible process. Sensitive teachers appreciate what children can do, encourage them to explore new contrasts, emphasize, and elaborate their movements.

Large Muscle Participation and Endurance   Children walk and dance in rhythm, jump, hop, skip, and run. They extend rhythmic patterns with fine and large muscle movements. For example, youngsters stand and sit or create a group circle or line up in different patterns. They clap, tap, stomp, and combine movements in different spatial patterns and rhythms. These activities also support mathematical concepts. You can notice when children maintain rhythm with body movement or rhythm instruments. See how children are able to coordinate following directions in an active game or dance sequence. Pre-kindergarten children can dance to music by taking three steps–stop–forward, then three steps–stop–backward, four steps sideways, and so forth. A next step would be to move in another pattern, such as four steps forward and two steps back.

A *sequence* of large motor development includes the upper body as well as the lower body muscles. There are ways to help youngsters learn to catch, throw, jump, gallop, and roll (Sanders, 2002). Children walk, run, jump, hop, gallop, and skip (first a one-footed skip; then a combined step and hop) (Gallahue, 1993, p. 26). Youngsters learn to grasp and release objects; throw; catch; kick with force.

They can balance on one foot; forward roll; and attain a three-point balance (Gallahue, 1993, p. 28). [**Procedural note:** Remember to present cues one at a time, reminding individual children when they need a cue.]

Educators cite physical development goals by the end of kindergarten as follows: "Stand for six seconds on one foot with [their] eyes closed; . . . throw and catch a small object . . . to another person . . . ten feet away; visual motor skills [such as] cutting, coloring, clay work, [and] stringing beads; and . . . skip for at least ten yards" (Hofreuter-Landini & Krulock, 2010, p. 1). Youngsters can also walk on a balance beam/board with adult support, and those who need help can walk on a board or line on the floor to integrate balance and sensory faculties.

Some teachers also introduce simple yoga stretches and poses, while everyone breathes deeply for a specific number of breaths. Such activity and other vigorous movement bring oxygen to the *brain*. Researchers also cite a connection between the brain's linguistic and movement areas (Armstrong, 2004, citing Fulbright, 1999). Moreover, with regular opportunities to practice, researchers find a positive impact on language development after children engage in large muscle play involving their "physical development, muscle development, coordination, and obesity prevention" (Zigler & Bishop-Josef, 2004, p. 9). Quite simply, the process of physical development helps children refine their movements by trial-and-error practice.

Another form of active movement is the *electronic* "Ready Set Learn! Jump and Dance Music Mat" (Discovery). This activity both challenges and responds to children's movements (Neuman & Roskos, 2007, p. 158).

Outdoors, teachers of pre-kindergarten children can chalk hop-scotch frames on pavement. Children then toss a pebble and hop. Youngsters often follow their own rules and alternate with running, climbing, and sliding. They create games with hoops by alternating hoop colors on the ground. Then they hop, jump, run, and walk through as well as around the hoops. These activities are quite different from teacher-directed physical activities. Scholars do not recommend competitive sports for young children because their sense of competence and belonging are important conditions for their learning. Not only are children continuing to develop rules and inconsistently adapting them, but they need opportunities to build a foundation of as much sense of success and *competence* (condition for learning) as possible.

When children *switch rules* in familiar movement games, they are using the *inhibitory function* that provides practice in *executive function*. Pre-kindergarteners are able to practice playing "opposites," increasing their capacity for self-regulation, by placing their hands on their feet when Simon says, "Put your hands on your head" (Galinsky, 2010; McClelland et al., 2007). In the action song *Up on the Mountain*, partners first swing each other and then become "frozen" into statues, as follows: "Up on the mountain, two by two (twice) / Let me see you make a motion two by two (twice) / Rise, sugar, rise" (Landeck, 1950). Pairs of children create a "sculpture" by releasing their hands and freezing their free-form movements at the "Rise, sugar, rise" signal—an act of *self-regulation*. You also might adapt other songs and signals. You could emphasize the variety, originality, and specific elements of these "frozen" statues. Incidentally, children may directly experience centrifugal force before they "freeze." A great deal of such tacit knowing of physical science concepts also takes place when they dance and use playground equipment, such as swings, seesaws, and slides. Thus, their 3-dimensional imagery builds in many ways.

Fine Motor Coordination   It is easier for the youngest children to use their whole hand rather than isolate fingers for eating, writing/drawing, or playing games. You might notice if some children need more opportunities to work with play dough to create small forms and use a variety of smaller writing tools as well as one-handed scissors for increasingly complex tasks. When needed, teachers scaffold children's use of scissors by providing increasingly angular cutting tasks; or using left-handed or two-handed scissors; small concrete materials; and brushes of different thicknesses for painting. In general, they offer choices of smaller items. They provide tongs, and increasingly smaller tongs, for children to pick up increasingly small items to place into categories the children select. They notice if a child places glue on the proper side of the items. They provide support by demonstrating or working hand-over-hand with an individual child. Does the child cross the midpoint in small and large muscle activities? Tossing beanbags or balls across the body into a container can help to build this skill.

In many ways, when you assess what children can do by connecting your observations to the pathways of their physical development, you have a solid basis on which to build activities. Their physical development and movement activities also include gestures, pantomime, and dramatic expressions. These physical activities blend with sounds and language to lie on a continuum with dramatic presentations. The discussion now continues with a look at creative dramatics.

Creative Dramatics: A Poetic Art

Creative dramatics grows out of children's rich experiences in music and movement activities, socio-dramatic play, and literature. This activity is at once social, emotional, substantive, verbal, and aesthetic.

The Elements of Creative Drama

The elements of drama include *roles, characters, relationships, movement, time, space, plot,* and *language.* Music and rhythm sometimes appear, too. Visual elements, such as scenery, props, lighting, and costumes, can also be elements in dramatic representations. The interaction of some or all of these elements constitutes the grammar of this domain.

In socio-dramatic play, both pre-kindergarten and kindergarten children's favored, repeated plays in the form of informal oral "scripts" may become more formalized as episodic creative dramatics. The drama retains an evolving, episodic format around this kernel of common experiences and interaction. These plays express actions, feelings, and problematic issues. It is a group authorship in flux. Such play might never be written down or, with help from older children or adults, might evolve into written form.

Music can also enter creative dramatics as children collaborate in exploring space through rhythmic movement activities and experiment with the interplay of sounds. If you notice that a few children's rhythmic movements complement one another, you might invite them to develop partner, trio, and quartet movements as you observe with the class. As they enjoy this joint effort of using space together, they sometimes begin to develop pantomimes. They might pantomime and invite others to guess episodes of trips they have taken to a zoo, a bakery, or a bottling factory. Pairs of children can plan together and "become" inanimate objects, sharing their interpretation with the group. They are able to "become" parts of cooking processes, electrical experiments and appliances, and pantomime volcanic eruptions. Some of the pantomime activity could evolve into sounds and dialogue.

As an activity grows increasingly elaborate, the emergence of dialogue marks its transformation into creative dramatics. These explorations typically would span several months, during which a few weekly sessions might last from 10 to 15 minutes. In some classes, English language learners are able to participate successfully in these collaborative processes along the movement–pantomime–speaking continuum. [**Procedural note:** The whole group would participate most of the time, with brief spectator periods.]

There are opportunities for you to assess and highlight elements, varied forms, original efforts, and growing sensitivities and skills. You can notice when children's actions become more spontaneous and authentic or when they are contrived and restrained. These are moments when you can let them know that all sincere expressions are acceptable; and you can recognize and appreciate each child in relation to his or her progress.

A contrasting source for children's creative dramatics comes from the outside, as compared with the more internal evolution just described. Some poems and cumulative folk tales lend themselves to dramatization that is heavily improvisational. Children find high drama, suspense, and glee in stories with this form of manageable threat.[3] Increasingly, children elaborate their play, adding simple costumes and props.

Creative drama or role-playing episodes typically last 12 minutes or less. Whenever young children attempt to "become" a role, they need to have a background of experience sufficient to fuel their imagination. For example, it is too much to ask some children to take on career-based roles. However, roles that fall within their experience—such as a child who is trying to persuade a parent to acquire a pet or change a rule, or persuade a sibling to share television time or a toy—are more likely to develop meaningful role-play. Box 9.4 outlines an author's theater process in which children use their own ideas to direct the action.

BOX 9.4 AUTHOR'S THEATER DRAMA

Overview:
1. Read-aloud folk tale format literature written by adults. Practice role-play with some of these.
2. Children dictate their own stories.
3. Children select actors.
4. Children tell their own story as the actors dramatize.

Methods:
1. The child dictates a story with clear sight lines as you record the words.
2. Save a copy for your record-keeping folder.
3. Write child's name and date.
4. Limit the text to one page. Refer to "next chapter" for the future, if needed.
5. The subject matter excludes unkind remarks or toilet talk.
6. React and scaffold: "That's amazing! What did you do? What will the actors do when they become the brother? Maybe you could put that in the story."
7. Reflect back what you hear: "So, what happened after . . .?"
8. Read back, pointing to what you wrote, part-way and at the end.
9. Ask the child to select actors as you review what roles need to be played. Four to six actors are enough, and imagine the rest.
10. Write the cast names on your copy of the story. Scaffold during the performance.

(Adapted from Cooper, 2009)

The next section discusses the visual and plastic arts. "Plastic" arts refers to the many different ways that children might decide to use basic materials.

The Visual and Plastic Arts

Elements of Visual and Plastic Arts

Whenever you provide a new experience for young children, you have made an implicit assessment that the children might meet the challenge. In order to make artistic assessment more explicit, it is helpful to consider the elements within the medium that the visual artist uses.

Children use the elements of *line, shape, space, size, texture,* and *color* as they create visual and plastic art forms. They are figuring out how to *compare* and *relate* these elements with one another. In the process, they explore ways to compose and, eventually, balance their work.

Their exploration of elements with varied media contrasts with the work of adult artists who face an interesting paradox. Adults need to solve the problem of marrying sophisticated technique with the pure vision of a young child in order to create an aesthetic balance and *surprise.* The art experiences that create predictably unpredictable forms take our breath away and help us perceive fresh connections.

Creating Visual and Plastic Arts

Teachers typically reserve space for the visual and plastic arts near a water source, thus cutting down on traffic and mess. Box 9.5 suggests some possible materials. [**Procedural note:** Rotate different materials so that children can experience *contrasting* colors, textures, and surfaces at different times.]

BOX 9.5 CLASSROOM ART STUDIO

- An easel and brushes of varying thickness so that children can choose their own style; each child should have a fresh set of tempera colors, at least two of their own choice, in order to provide contrasts; colored ink stamp pads.
- A pencil hung from the easel or the table painting area so that children who are able can sign their own names.
- A drying rack.
- Plastic aprons.
- Table space for six to eight chairs.
- Storage shelves, including shoe boxes of uniform size, transparent shirt boxes, huge ice cream cylinders, and/or packing crates.
- Newspapers for covering table or floor surfaces, in order to cut down the washing up of markings, glue, and clay residues.
- Glue sticks and white glue. [**Procedural note:** Are there children with possible dairy allergies to the white glue?]
- Colored pencils; crayons, multicultural crayons, and markers of different thicknesses; cotton swabs and oil pastels; papers of varied size, color, shape, and texture.
- Clay and varied accessories, including dowels of varying diameters for rolling; jar covers; cookie cutters, sticks, and a stylus for marking; and

---

plastic knives and wires for cutting; pine cones and other large, textured seeds for pattern making.

- Collage materials, including shop window dressings, discarded wallpaper books, close-out fabric sample booklets, merchants' discards, wrapping paper, candy wrappers, packaging materials and small cardboard boxes and cylinders, discarded buttons and trimmings, feathers, yarn, fabric, washers, screening, mesh, wires, wire ties, seeds, and dried onion skins.
- Scissors, tape dispensers, and hole punchers.

Outline and store materials on shelves or peg boards. Store scissors and markers in wood or Styrofoam holders to ease retrieval, return, and inventory. Tool carriers and a low rolling cart are also useful for many of the activities discussed below.

Clay   Molding play dough, clay, or plasticene is popular. Children find comfort in squeezing these materials. As with other skills, children progress in their ability to represent their feelings and ideas. Therefore, it is important to provide time for them to explore each phase of development before offering scaffolds. Box 9.6 suggests ways that you might support children's use of molding materials.

BOX 9.6 CLAY (OR PLASTICENE) PHASES AND SCAFFOLDS

- Squeeze and pull; *Scaffold:* Verbal harmony—"You are squeezing the clay." "See how it looks."
- Pound; *Scaffold:* Verbal harmony—"You are working hard when you thump/pound the clay." "Look at what happens. What do you see?" Invite a child who rolls to sit nearby.
- Roll; *Scaffold:* Verbal harmony—"Look at what happens when you roll that clay." "What will you do next?" Provide dowels of varying thickness: "What might you do with a dowel?"
- Connect and build with pieces; *Scaffold:* Verbal harmony—"You figured out how to connect those cylinders/flat pieces. What did you do?" "What do you plan to do next?"
- Complex sculpture; *Scaffold:* Demonstrate poke and pinch as needed. Provide props such as pine cones for texture, string or craft sticks for slicing, a stylus for poking, as relevant.

Many classrooms use masonite as clay boards. Routines for cleanup of clay and storage to retain moisture are part of the process (Wright, 2003, p. 175). In general, 3-dimensional arts, including clay, collages, sewing, and weaving, are part of design technology, discussed in Chapter 11.

Collages   Collages provide opportunities for systematic *contrasts*, such as two, then three, colors; two or three textures; two or three dimensions; two or three shapes; or two or three sizes. There is variety when children decorate paper or cardboard boxes or pinwheels. They can create collages of their likes and dislikes with cuttings from magazines or catalogs. They can sort collage materials by color, shape, and size. Their collage and craft projects provide practice in fine muscle movements that support writing.

Paper strip sculpture is a type of collage. Collages have 3- as well as 2-dimensional aspects, when children fold, twist, crumple, loop, fringe, and layer materials. For these as well as other activities you would do well to become a selective junk collector. In addition to materials already mentioned, children can use wood shavings, toothpicks, various dry beans, eggshells, and a variety of macaroni products. Making puppets and masks extends collage activities with such materials as paper plates held up by a tongue depressor, paper bags, Styrofoam, stuffed socks, covered balloons, sticks, and clothespins. "Masks are used to celebrate holidays, tell stories, or as a costume or uniform. Masks hide you or tell people about you" (Douglas & Jaquith, 2009, p. 99). Some masks and puppets fulfill children's need for a sense of power and playfulness; they may also lend themselves to sewing.

Sewing and Weaving   *Sewing* follows a sequence. Pre-kindergarten children are able to wrap colored yarn or raffia around a cylinder. Some are able to lace through holes in sewing cards that have outlines on both sides. The next step is an outline on one side of the card with increasing numbers of holes. Kindergarten children become able to engage in mesh *weaving* after they draw a design.

You could create looms with plastic berry baskets or a sewing card by stringing holes punched in cardboard food trays or paper plates.

"Cat's eye" weaving around two crossed dowels, which you tie firmly at the center, is another kind of loom that kindergarteners use with various yarn colors and beads. Kindergarten children can also weave with paper clips and paper straws, and make pot-holders with jersey loops. (Parents often find that the pot-holders with asymmetrical patterns and skipped stitches come in handy for many years!) Such sewing and weaving activities begin with patterned bead stringing and double- and single-sided sewing cards that children can use. Paper weaving, while traditional, appears to generate more frustration than fun.

Variety   Variety is important if you want to keep interest fresh and create new problems to solve in the art center. For example, at different times during the school year, you might offer string or shadow drawing, sand painting, and printing

IMAGE 9.1 Drawing and Weaving on Mesh

with a range of implements, such as textured materials, spools, jar lids, or potatoes with children's original designs. Children enjoy using luminous colors of paint and crayon on dark paper, and they also like to engage in face or arm painting, especially when they can decide on elbow-, foot-, or hand-printing. Provide paints that are more or less thickly mixed, multiple hues of two primary colors, opportunities to mix colors, and to add color to white paint (Barnes, 1987; Schirrmacher & Fox, 2008). When you provide repeated, well-spaced exposures to materials, you will observe different outcomes, due to children's intervening experiences, their growing coordination, and their ability to plan.

Now, you might welcome some ideas to minimize cleanup tasks. After laying out newspapers, plan to keep sponges, paper towels, and dustpans nearby. Other ideas to reduce washing up include placing plastic sandwich bags inside paint containers and mixing tempera paint with liquid dish soap (Matricardi & McLarty, 2005, p. xi).

Some teachers leave drawing materials in the floor block building center and invite children to record their plans or their products. Children use clipboards in order to draw what they see on trips. Both actual and imagined drawings are acceptable and offer opportunities for ongoing *revisiting* (Edwards, Gandini, & Forman, 1998). Pairs of children sometimes use their imaginations to illustrate a song. With your support, youngsters enjoy using digital cameras to take photographs of objects, parts of objects, or events during the day; most are familiar with video cameras and tape-recorders.

Donated Materials   If you run out of paper for painting, grocery bags and classified columns of newspapers can serve as great substitutes. Freezer wrapping paper or barber-chair paper rolls are less expensive substitutes for fingerprint paper. Lumber yards sometimes provide soft-wood scraps suitable for carpentry or collage; printers might provide surplus poster board and paper; and merchants might donate wallpaper rolls or fabric scraps. You could ask families to donate clean lid covers, baby food jars, cardboard tubes, buttons, keys, ribbon, gift wrappings, and greeting cards.

In general, diverse materials encourage diverse, personal use. This use is quite different from static pattern making, picture coloring, or copied cutting-and-pasting pastimes. There are unlimited possibilities to use materials artistically when you and the children learn to see the "strange" in "familiar" surroundings. When that happens, your major problem may be to find space to store everything.

The goal is that products of different children will be distinctly their own. Box 9.7 lists some ideas for a variety of art activities with which children can create their own products. [**Procedural note:** Provide a few possible activities at a time so that children can focus on exploring *contrasts*. When they *revisit* the materials weeks later, they often receive them as fresh opportunities.]

BOX 9.7 BEYOND CRAYONS AND EASEL PAINT: SOME IDEAS FOR CHILD-DEVELOPED ART WORK

- Wood and glue construction.
- Stapling/gluing together small light cardboard boxes/packaging (Styrofoam).
- Rubber bands on pegs.
- Sand/sawdust painting on black (use corn starch and food color; margarine pots/plastic dishes).
- Puppets (paper bag, paper plate, etc.).
- Stringing patterns of beads, buttons, straw pieces, or empty spools with plastic-tipped laces or blunt embroidery needles.
- Weaving—mesh (masking tape at edges for safety) (kindergarten).
- Sewing cards, figures on both sides, then one side.
- Collage themes with selections of contrasting materials as well as children's choices.
- Map of yourself with markers/paint/collage/combinations of media.
- Murals, topical subjects.
- What can you create with black squares, green and orange triangles, etc.?
- Rubber cement painting; paint with white glue and food color.
- String painting/collage—paint with string/straw; blot; fold paper over string and press.

- Blow painting—use straw to blow on a dot of paint on smooth paper or cardboard box lid.
- Painting on tables or the floor.
- Paint objects: e.g., stone, wood, pine cones, spools, paper cups/plates, package scraps, dry clay, and woodworking projects.
- Finger paint in a baking pan or other container (with increasing control of the product).
- Finger paint prints.
- Negative space painting.
- Print with ink pads: found objects; sponge cutouts; cut potato.
- Paint rollers; sticks for design; print from them (kindergarten).
- Rolled-up and taped newspapers for construction and painting.
- Crayons grouped together with tape.
- Clay, plasticene, and play dough.
- Pipe cleaners in color/wire for stabiles/mobiles.
- Mobiles, in general.
- Crumpled paper collages.
- Mosaic collage (children select a topic or you invite a topic, such as emotional faces).
- Pattern covering of small containers with yarn or paper.
- Dioramas (collage; cardboard box). [**Procedural note:** In general, sculpture requires experience with balance and gravitation.]

Art educators encourage artists to "exaggerate" and "transform" media, "and the artist, too is transformed" (Douglas & Jaquith, 2009, p. 99).

Appreciating Visual and Plastic Arts

Just as young children listen to different genres of music and literature from different cultures, they are able to enjoy and contrast different visual and plastic art products that represent different genres and cultures. After viewing Monet's, Hokusai's, Picasso's, Rivera's, and Pollock's paintings, they can create paintings that directly relate to the respective styles, *inducing* an underlying Dynamic-Theme image.

Youngsters view portraits and self-portraits of artists; and create self-portraits. Kindergarten children can draw a friend's name out of a grab bag to create that friend's portrait (M. Silberman, personal communication, 1998). Pre-kindergarten children can play concentration/memory games with fine arts cards from which they are able to *induce* the style of the artists (L. Davey, personal communication, 1993).

When teachers provide *contrasting* bodies of work done by different artists, including those in children's books, young children are able to *induce* the under-

IMAGE 9.2 Various Interpretations of an Artist's Style

lying aesthetic unity of each artist's style. This takes place without adult expectation that children will create a particular product, and it makes us aware that children do perceive the underlying imagery, and are able to identify or represent the feeling directly. *Exposure to, and welcoming, many kinds of art products is the antithesis of copying, tracing, coloring in, following patterns, or other forms of trivial "busy work."* Indeed, the arts provide an ideal time for children to feel a sense of control and strong motivation to spend time creating a product. *The Art Lesson* (de Paola, 1989) is a picture book underscoring the personal and political need of artists to create their own forms. A nonfiction work for children that focuses on some accessible elemental contrasts in visual art is *Lines* (Yenawine, 1991); it can help children to become more aware of the styles that illustrators employ in other books.

Educators recommend exposing children to the representative work of professional artists through actual or virtual visits (print reproductions and websites), and to talk with youngsters while incidentally building a vocabulary of art (Althouse, Johnson, & Mitchell, 2003; Eisner, 2009; Gardner, 1980; Isenberg & Jalongo, 2009; Wright, 2003). You can extend children's view of alternative styles by looking together at the art created by Diego Rivera and Jose Clement Orozco of Mexico, African artist Malangatana Ngwenja, African–American artists such as William Henry Johnson and children's book illustrator Faith Ringgold, and Aboriginal artist Emily Kngwarreye. Looking at the work of other women artists, such as Artemesia Gentileschi, Frida Kahlo, Lee Krasner, Georgia O'Keefe, and Mori Marika, among others, can expand your children's cross-cultural and egalitarian view. Reproductions of museum holdings are available on museums' websites as well as in library books.

A Sample Art Appreciation Program

One study found that, after seeing contrasting samples, kindergarten children are able to use the vocabulary of artistic genres, such as portrait, landscape, seascape, still life, and family themes (Silberman, 1988). They are able to *compare* the similar, underlying features within one artist's work (a Dynamic-Theme) as well as compare the different styles of different artists. Children can choose their own style for self-portraits using markers, crayons, and/or colored pencils along with a mirror or photograph. You might integrate landscapes into their study of seasonal changes and use objects in the environment to create still life art. After looking at seascapes, the children can use wet paper with sharpies. [**Procedural note:** Kngwarreye's pointillism and use of swirls and lines can provide an interesting comparison with Seurat and Van Gogh.]

The Teacher's Role in Assessment and Scaffolding

You can see children making connections when they wonder if Columbus saw a swirly sky like Van Gogh's *Starry Night*. In assessing progress in drawing, at the beginning of the year you might ask children to create a self-portrait or family portrait (people who live in their home). Then, you and the children can compare portraits they create mid-year and again near the end of the year. Some educators (Cole & Schaeffer, 1990) suggest an interview format to help assess pre-kindergarten children's artistic perceptions:

- Pretend you're talking to me on the telephone. Please name the things in this picture so I'll be able to recognize it?
- I'm pretending I can't speak English. Can you teach me the names for the objects I point to? Are there any I missed?
- If we could, would you want to take this painting back to our classroom? What do you like the most?

[**Procedural note:** If a child does not appear to understand a question after a reasonable time, then adapt to another question. Note that suggested questions would be interspersed throughout the year, when they casually fit the moment, rather than asked all at once.]

It is clear that your assessment and understanding what children might perceive as they have diverse experiences is an ongoing process. Children's artistic representations of their experiences serve as a lens through which to *assess* the imagery that they share. For example, urban children tend to draw trees that are shorter than houses while suburban children's trees in some areas tend to be taller. Also, young children's drawings often reveal more content than their budding writing skills. When teachers have discussed the meaning of parts of their illustrations, kindergarten children have motives to expand their writing (Calkins & Louis, 2005, p. 18).

As you assess children's art work, it is useful to remain conscious of the representational continuum, beginning with 3-dimensional constructions that blend into 2-dimensional arts. In turn, 2-dimensional representations blend into the symbolic literacy of invented writing and beginning reading.

Just as there are *developmental paths* in other domains, there is a progression of representation in the visual arts. There is general agreement that drawing begins with the exploration of "scribbling" random marks and continues with controlled scribbles. Then, representation emerges with some fluctuation between "pre-schematic" representation and controlled scribbling (Lowenfeld & Brittain, 2006; Hetland, Winner, Veenema, & Sheridan, 2007). Rather than view representational work as an elitist accomplishment that marginalizes abstract expressions, the issue for young children is their increasing control of the artist's tools at their own rates.

When you see how children create sketches from memory, they also reveal what they value (Krogh & Morehouse, 2008; Walmsley & Wing, 2004). In turn, when you assess what they value, you have additional data with which to plan next steps.

Supporting Exploration

Many teachers integrate children's drawings and constructions throughout the day, which serves as a way to assess their conceptual understanding (Krogh & Morehouse, 2008, p. 340; Isenberg & Jalongo, 2009). For example, the children of Reggio Emilia use art forms to document their various theories about rain, aquifers, and physical reflections (Malaguzzi & Becchi, 1996).

Keep in mind that *exploration* is the process of finding out what things can do; *play*—a form of representation—is finding out what you can do with them. Therefore, young children need many opportunities to explore the visual arts, music, movement, and socio-dramatic and creative dramatics activity, as you encourage and highlight their original expressions and helpful, collaborative intentions.

Different children need more or less practice holding different sizes of pencils, chalks, crayons, and brushes. Occasionally, a child, perhaps one with special learning needs, will need help in applying glue. You might find it useful to hold a child's hand when he is using glue or scissors so that he can see how it feels. For children who are left-handed or have special needs, provide left-handed or four-fingered scissors. If a child is beginning to use the scissors with two hands, use masking tape or carpenter's tape to attach an end of the paper to the table, so that the child can do the cutting as independently as possible. Children find that cutting lines and curves is easier than cutting angles. Therefore, you can sequence cutting activities as children start to feel successful with practice.

It is important to offer consistent opportunities for exploration, even if the representations take place in what you might consider to be science study. If you were to offer kite-making materials during the study of wind, for example, provide children with varied materials and encourage them to try out different shapes with both 3- and 2-dimensional forms, instead of pre-cut, uniform materials. Such exploration is part of design technology. The children can appreciate the relative movement and efficiency of angles and aerodynamics from the aesthetic standpoint of design and body movement before they are ready to understand the technology and science concepts. Along the way, acknowledge and appreciate their aesthetic experiences. Talk with them about what they are doing so that they can have connections to vocabulary and you can try to figure out what they intend to create. *When you use words in context, there is no need to "dumb down" vocabulary.*

Engaging in Conferences

In order to represent experiences, children need to make decisions about the content to which they feel committed. Just as you engage in writing conferences, you would also confer about children's role-play, visual art work, movement activity, and author's theater, because they all require children to think and attempt to solve problems in representing meanings. These contacts are times to ask children to share their preferences and joys. They are also times to plan activities that might extend skills and expose children to varied media.

The purpose, after all, is to build independent skills and a sense of confidence as well as to avert frustration and defeatism. Children feel appreciated when you nod and focus on features of their work, such as: "You used yellow in so many spots." "That blue line really helps to connect the parts of this picture." "What do you want to say about your work?" "What can you tell us about your picture?" "What tools/materials did you use?" They might also be exploring a medium in a sensory way or creating a design. Therefore, do *not* ask: "What did you make?" A child might experience such a question as a "failure" or could infer that realism or a particular standard is the only acceptable form.

Children take delight in seeing their progress in representation. As you appreciate their collected work together, with careful questioning and the use of analogy, you might help children extend and plan their art work.

Planning

Any time you find yourself feeling that absolutely every child must use a particular material or create a particular product, you might suspect that a truly artistic experience is missing. Remember the teaching assumption: *different children doing different things at different times can have equivalent experiences.* Your observations also point to the need for sequencing particular skills, such as providing materials and techniques as needed, for example, to help children move from random printing to patterned printing to planned patterns, and so forth (Barnes, 1987).

Encouraging Connoisseurship

You can serve as a museum curator when you frame or mount children's art work and written work with dignity and display it on walls at the children's eye level, on the backs of room dividers, and on the spaces between windows. Before the school year begins, hang a frame (construction paper) for each child's 2-dimensional art work. With limited space, children decide which pieces to rotate for new work; this is one way to avoid clutter.

With the children, you can create attractive arrangements on which to display 3-dimensional work. You can cover boxes with contact paper, wallpaper, or cloth and stack them to provide a 3-dimensional display area for children's constructions and collections. String wire or twine across a corner, or across a room from wall to wall or corner to corner, and hang up such things as hangers and hoops for making mobiles as well as displays. One educator suggests displaying children's unit block work on a turntable that can rotate, in order to add spatial awareness (Haskell, 1984). Another way of valuing children's work is to shine a lamp on such a turntable display or on some other 3-dimensional arrangement, creating interesting shadows.

You can signal respect for children's efforts with photographs of their art work, costumed dramatic productions, movement activities with props, and other moments of them at work. Sometimes you can move a storage shelf or screen to set off a new area, so the contents of that area become a new focus for attention.

Children themselves can help create such "museums," which become an integral part of their experience of success rather than an alien form. These personally involving experiences create a readiness for trips to a school exhibition or art fair and to school- or library-based hands-on museums. School librarians, collaborating with teachers, can also develop these kinds of experiences. You are indeed fortunate if there are such collections of activities or hands-on museums nearby.

Communicating with Families

Hanging photographs, with captions, of children's construction work, painting, costuming, and movement activities dignifies their efforts and affords delight to them and their parents. Dating samples of children's art work and related photographs can help you to communicate the progress that children are making in their representational skills. In parent conferences, it is worthwhile to highlight the creative ways in which a child has solved the problem of representing 3-dimensional space in a 2-dimensional medium. There are cases, for example, of children depicting both the inside and outside of houses, or the four sides and top of an automobile (Gardner, 1982), similar to adult artists who lived in different epochs and regions but solved similar problems in similar ways (Gombrich, 2006). Such documentation, along with your interpretations, also communicates to parents and others the significance and variety of your activity.

Reflections

Western culture appears to value logical, abstract, and verbal thinking. Many schools today typically value mainly literal language and linear interpretations. The arts that share a physical basis tied to emotional forms of representation appear to merit less value (excluding perhaps the adult commitments to organized sports competitions). This dichotomy reflects the dual view of mind as distinct from body.

However, *brain* research points to the physical foundations for symbolic development. Early brain development begins with the body, aesthetic experiences, and the potential for connection making. The more varied and rich experiences children have in exploring and creating art forms, the more connections their brains can make.

This chapter has presented a case for keeping alive and integrating imaginative representations and nonlinear interpretations of experience. For young children, the arts are early forms that represent and communicate their experiences (*knowledge*). As *forms of representation and communication*, all the arts smoothly integrate throughout an activity-based learning environment. As *skills*, they are trans–disciplinary. As particular *products*, the arts reside on a continuum with other forms of literacy. Visual and dramatic arts, in particular, precede and support writing and reading literacy. Music and movement precede and support mathematics and science literacy.

Some aspects of the arts are accessible to all children. Children come to understand some of the elements involved in the creation of various performances or products. When children develop comfort with a variety of art forms, they develop the *disposition* to appreciate these forms. Moreover, they develop positive *attitudes* toward school. It is particularly important, therefore, to avoid competition, whether in performance or production in music, movement, dramatic or visual arts activities. A feeling of *competence* is an important condition for learning.

With a balanced view of the whole child, therefore, you can support the development of young children by embracing the many behaviors and forms in which they communicate with you. This balanced view frames an activity-based learning environment that values the connections within Dynamic-Themes. Each skill follows an erratic developmental path as children achieve increasing flexibility and fluency in using the skill. The next chapter continues this image with a focus on language development that shares the representational continuum with the arts.

10

LITERACY IN ORAL LANGUAGE, WRITING, READING, AND ENGLISH LANGUAGE LEARNING

Introduction

A 4-year-old and his grandmother met an elderly neighbor who offered the child a book and asked if he could read. The youngster rummaged in his pockets and said, "Of course, but I forgot my glasses" (adapted from Chukovsky, 1963, pp. 15–16).

The youngster's humor demonstrates that he understood how reading takes place and that reading conveys meaning. Indeed, language learning and teaching can be a natural part of most activities that are rich in personal meaning. In turn, language adds meaning to human experiences. Language is also a tool in communicating meaning. The repetition and practice that are necessary for acquiring the skills to use this tool fluently occur naturally in various forms that you can integrate throughout the day. *Induction* is the foremost condition for learning literacy skills in the context of daily life that includes representing the underlying imagery of Dynamic-Themes. The purpose of this chapter, therefore, is to provide perspectives that highlight a particular *inductive* framework. There is a discussion of the knowledge bases of a literacy program and a focus on what language and literacy look like in classrooms for 4- and 5-year-olds.

Meaning is present in the multiple ways that children develop and learn language skills. Language grows from the seeds of each child's unique personal culture and sprouts in their unpredictable products. All young children, including English language learners (ELLs), begin to communicate meaning with a combination of gestures, postures, sounds, and spoken language.

Language development, along with conceptual learning, follows the *abstraction ladder* (Hayakawa, 1949) in Box 3.5 and begins with the concrete–concrete (object and object); it continues with the concrete–visual (object and picture); the visual–visual (picture and picture); the visual–symbolic (picture and word); and then the symbolic–symbolic (written/printed words). Thoughtful professional educators move back and forth along the abstraction ladder as they assess and adapt to what different children need at any particular time.

It is worth noting that most certified early childhood teachers have had specific course work in reading and study about literacy learning and teaching. Among many, there are plenty of good specialized sources that focus on how to teach reading (Fountas & Pinnell, 2006; Routman, 2003; Taberski, 2000). Rather than focusing on either part or whole approaches to teaching reading, the body of researchers view the complexity of the literacy process as a combination of socio-cultural, emotional, biological, and technical issues (Neuman & Dickinson, 2001).

Beyond 3-dimensional constructions and artistic representations discussed in earlier chapters, there are four essential, integrated components in a systematic approach to early literacy learning and instruction, as follows:

1. The development of spoken language and syntax. (Syntax/grammar is the *contrasting pattern* of words in sentences.)
2. Fine-quality children's literature.
3. Writing/drawing into reading.
4. Phonemic games. (The phoneme is the smallest unit of sound to change the meaning of a word; words consist of *contrasting patterns* of phonemes.)

Each component is discussed in turn. Different children need many opportunities to practice these components with flexible, sequential, and intentional teaching. At the same time, practice takes many forms and is most effective when children have reasons to use language as a tool for communicating their ideas and feelings.

The Development of Spoken Language and Syntax: Induction of Contrasting Patterns of Words as a Way of Knowing Language

Every one of us can look around and see that typically developing children learn the language that they hear around them, yet most adults do not remember learning to speak. It just happened comfortably for most of us, without self-awareness. Theoretically, it should feel no more difficult to learn to read and write than it was to learn to speak. After we look at some basic ways in which children learn to speak, we can consider how to extend these processes as children learn other language skills.

In a nutshell, children learn to speak through the process of *induction*. First, they perceive a model that they hear repeated in daily life settings. After lots of touching, seeing, and hearing a word and object together, children perceive a *relationship* and begin to approximate the sounds, to great acclaim and appreciation. They imitate sounds, receiving adult feedback, until they are able to expand an utterance to approximate the whole word.

A similar process takes place as children begin to learn and use sentence structures (syntax) within daily life situations. A kind of rubber-band stretching takes place: children imitate adult language by reducing the sentence structure— "More cookie"—while the adult in turn expands the child's statement—"Oh, you want another cookie. Well, it's almost time for supper." With continuing interaction between adults and other children, children begin to expand their syntax, stretching toward the adult's more fluent, complex syntax.

Psychologists identify a continuing process of adult–child language "expansion/ reduction/expansion/lesser-reduction" (Brown & Bellugi, 1964). Scholars of varied viewpoints underscore the power of contrasts and analogies in the child's active construction of language and concepts (AASA, 2009; Bruner, 1966; Cazden, 1981; N. Chomsky, 1965; Clay, 1991; Ervin, 1964; H.A. Gleason, 1965; Harste, Woodward & Burke, 1984; Miller, 1969; Wittgenstein, 1958; Wormeli, 2009). As children intuitively perceive contrasts, their ability to use language becomes more flexible.

At the same time, the expansion of children's spoken language is not guaranteed but depends upon an adult modeler and child sharing language within particular situations. When teachers tap the satisfaction that new speakers experience and nurture this naturalness, children typically expand their language skills with comfort and satisfaction. The meaning they share provides a deeper structure than the mere words of an utterance (N. Chomsky, 1972). Culturally sensitive teachers also try to build upon and recognize (rather than devalue) "differences in narrative style" (Ladson-Billings, 1995, p. 55). Such teachers focus on meaning, ask for children's ideas, listen respectfully, and follow up responsively.

Throughout the process of literacy learning it is more important for young children to focus on ideas and learn language functionally than to focus merely on being aware of how they are using it. Consistent with this outlook, the HighScope Perry Preschool longitudinal curriculum research intervention summarizes their effective approach to literacy development as follows:

> The language and literacy category includes talking with others about personally meaningful experiences, describing objects, events, and relations; having fun with language, listening to stories and poems, and making up stories and rhymes; writing in various ways—drawing, scribbling, letterlike forms, invented spelling, conventional forms; reading in various ways— reading storybooks, signs, symbols, and one's own writing; and dictating stories.
>
> (Schweinhart et al., 2005, p. 36)

Oral Language and Language Education

In the beginning, significant language grows out of in-depth conversations (Cazden, 1988; National Early Literacy Panel, 2008; Shagoury, 2010). Oral language is also rich in structures which serve people as they share important meanings in many societies that do not depend upon written language. The focus on oral language is one essential starting point along the path to writing and reading with meaning.

Before and when youngsters learn to speak, write, and read, it is instructive to notice that the *playfulness* of young children is an important factor contributing to the *inductive* development of creative language possibilities. Babies learn the rules that hold language together. They frequently over-regularize these rules logically and creatively, even when they are unconventional. For example, a toddler might say, "I runned home."

Teachers can consciously use the expansion, coordination, subordination, or other alterations of *sentence pairs* in the context of playful, active, and physical social settings. Notice that if we expect children to understand words denoting relation and subordination, such as *but*, *because*, *which*, *that*, *if–then*, *or*, *and of*, *all*, *some*, and *any*, they will need to hear them *contrasted* with other words in sentences. Many of these concepts are essential to understand problem setting and solving in mathematics and other studies and they deserve our systematic inclusion in situations that make sense to children.

When researchers model the informal repetition of sentences that are syntactically equivalent but with varied content, children are able to induce a more efficient or expanded use of spoken language (Cambourne, 1988; Fauconnier, & Turner, 2002; Fromberg, 1976; J.B. Gleason, 1981; Yonemura, 1969). For example, when teachers use concrete, materials-based, playful game situations that are tied to certain contrasting pairs or trios of sentences, they expose children who need help to a planned—rather than the usual random—modeling of contrasting sentences. Examples of such "syntax model games" can be found among the works cited. Children who are learning English derive particular benefits from such contextualized playful, physical activities and language accompanied by movements and gestures. Box 10.1 summarizes the process of induction that takes place in the development of spoken syntax (the contrasting patterns of words in spoken language) as well as in learning to read (the contrasting patterns of phonemes (sounds) in words.)

BOX 10.1 THE PROCESS OF INDUCTION (CONTRASTING PATTERNS) IN ORAL LANGUAGE AND READING, AND TEACHER SCAFFOLDS

- *Repeated models of contrasting patterns* of words in sentence pairs. *Scaffold:* Teachers model language in playful and game-like situations.
- *Imitation* by children as they play the game, with children *reducing* and adults *expanding* sentences. *Scaffold:* Adults accept and appreciate

children's statements without expressed evaluation; and repeat expanded models.

- *Induction* of the syntax (or connection between the print that represents a particular meaning), evidenced by the children's use during vocal game playing (or reading). *Scaffold:* Teachers continue to listen responsively and repeat expanded models.

Within the contexts of daily activities, adults also *expect* children to be capable of speaking and of learning to speak at their own pace in their own ways.

The progress of children who are learning to speak English follows a similar path. Researchers have found that children are able to learn two languages (Esposito, 2010, p. 68). They have also found that "Many early language and literacy skills learned in Spanish clearly transfer to English" (Esposito, 2010, p. 83). Children who enter into an English–only environment appear to pass through flexible phases that are similar to those listed in Box 10.1. Box 10.2 focuses on English language learners and teacher scaffolds.

BOX 10.2 FLEXIBLE PHASES FOR ENGLISH LANGUAGE LEARNERS AND TEACHER SCAFFOLDS

- *Home language:* For a few days or longer, in an attempt to communicate, children continue to use their home language (Espinosa, 2010; Gordon, 2007; Hough & Nurss, 1992). *Scaffold:* Teacher assists with gestures and points while labeling objects and actions.
- *Nonverbal/observational period:* Children observe, speak rarely, or use nonverbal means, a period of active language learning. Children come to understand nouns and verbs. *Scaffold:* Teacher uses physical movement games, particularly during classroom routines; and concrete materials with accompanying language.
- *Telegraphic and formulaic speech:* Children produce reduced sentence structure. Children come to understand the meaning of prepositions and adjectives. *Scaffold:* Teacher nods appreciatively and restates expanded form. Teacher uses verbal harmony, describing all actions.
- *Productive language:* Children induce the vocabulary as well as the grammar and keep building statements. They continue to experiment with increasingly long, more fluent, and complex sentences. The use of articles and noun–verb agreement continue to develop. *Scaffold:* Teacher continues to model expanded forms and provides verbal harmony.

Youngsters continually increase the flexibility and scope of their speech. Folk songs and *Mother Goose* rhymes help English learners as well as native English speakers develop vocabulary and grammar.

You can see language progress in daily life as well as in games and songs when children substitute words for a familiar song. For example, the song *Fiddle-I-fee* begs for substitutions of the word "cat" in the following: "I had a cat, and the cat pleased me / I fed my cat under yonder tree / The cat went fiddle-I-fee" (Sweet, 1992). More complex substitutions for competent speakers include substituting initial consonant sounds or rhymes in familiar songs (Epstein, 2009, pp. 23, 29). The power in such humorous substitutions tickles children.

Similarly, when children have the sense that they can interchange phonemes more freely, their writing and reading skills gain more flexibility and scope. Thus, the *inductive* social processes within which young children construct their spoken language also function in their development of reading and writing skills, discussed in the next sections. (Although discussed separately in the sections that follow, reading and writing influence one another.)

Reading and Fine-quality Children's Literature

Rather than a review of the field of reading programs, this section presents one point of view about integrated literacy instruction in all-day kindergarten and pre-kindergarten. Keep in mind that you can help children develop their language skills best while they engage in activities that are meaningful to them. At the same time, learning to become an independent reader is a skill, and any skill requires practice in many different forms. In effect, children learn to read when you saturate their auditory and visual environment with written language. Specifically prepared professional early childhood teachers do not base the center of their program on rote drills or worksheets that merely test for single expected answers. Indeed, researchers find that, "Reading [and hearing] figurative language—sentences containing irony or metaphor—produces more brain activity than reading factual, literal sentences . . . [perhaps because] the brain is often forced to retrace its thinking process in order to understand some of the unusual use of words" (Sigman, 2008b, p. 8, citing Eviatar & Just, 2006, and Davis et al., 2006).

> Sometimes, teachers tell stories or ask children to close their eyes and listen to a story or imagine a situation. [W]hen the brain imagines it increases activity literally forming new dendrites and synaptic connections. Imagery therefore speeds communication within the cells and between the cells in the brain. Imagery building skills from oral word "paintings" involves a process of conscious thought that transfers to reading imagery skills. If you visualize what you hear, you facilitate the ability to visualize what you read . . . That is why storytelling provides excellent cognitive exercise—in neurological terms it is a cognitive multi-gym.
>
> *(Sigman, 2008b, pp. 32, 33)*

Therefore, it is important to allow time for children to choose between several books for you to read aloud. Let them select books from the library center where you prepare book boxes for different levels of complexity as well as topics. Note also how you might cluster books based on a Dynamic-Theme, including multicultural content, noted in Chapter 8.

Although children pick up many concepts about print from their home and community environments, including signs, labels, newspapers, television advertisements, and computer games (for some children), they need to have considerable exposure to fine-quality literature throughout their lives, beginning as early as infancy. Therefore, teachers should acquaint them with books and other forms of print throughout the day before, and in conjunction with, their earliest writing experiences.

When you provide literature for children to listen to, look through, and read, the main purpose is to enjoy its meanings and varied forms. Youngsters can experience a read-aloud as a playful experience when you set a playful, interactive, and comfortable tone. Use puppets, stuffed toys, and props, such as wearing caps when you read *Caps for Sale* (Slobodkina, 1989). Positive experiences with a just-right book can help children to build reasons to want to read. Box 10.3 offers a perspective on the criteria for selecting high-quality trade book literature for young children.

BOX 10.3 CRITERIA FOR SELECTION OF "GREAT BOOKS" FOR YOUNG CHILDREN

Criteria for Selection

- Characters have integrity, are believable, and can be identified with
- Characters represent wholesome human relationships
- Values are integral to the material
- Egalitarian values are present: e.g., gender equity, multiethnic, ageism, and ability
- There is a satisfying ending
- The content is playful and/or significant
- Language is used beautifully
- Each book contains one story
- Illustrations are integrated with text
- Illustrations are aesthetically appealing

Criteria for Rejection

- Characters are super-cute, mawkish, or contrived
- Characters promote prurience or violence

- Values are present as moralizing
- Values include stereotypes
- The ending is anxiety-provoking
- Content is trivial or exploitative
- Language is stilted or contrived
- The book is part of a series or a textbook
- Materials conform to a pre-established word list
- Illustrations are sentimentalized

The following pages discuss some examples of fine literature for children. An asterisk will identify sample books that some kindergarten children and a few pre-kindergarten children will be able to read for themselves.[1] These books tend to have plenty of repetition, integrated illustrations, brief narrative passages, high predictability, cumulative structures, and appealing subject matter.

Animals Representing People

There are many stories about human problems and feelings that are masked by animal forms. Young children can identify with these animal characters, which serve quite a different purpose than do the violence-prone and violence-immune characters that appear in some other books directed at children. One excellent example of the genre is *Charlotte's Web* (White, 1968), which is laced with life-and-death issues, while involving the kindergarten listener in an intimate friendship experience with a spider and farm animals. Teachers can read this "chapter book" to kindergarten children one chapter at a time, which adds to their anticipation. *The Noisy Book*★ (Brown, 1973), filled with repetition of the word "No" that children enjoy participating in, leaves the reader/listener with a sense of empathy for a convalescent dog and provides a satisfying ending.

At best, these animals representing people, no less than human story characters in good literature, frequently involve the reader in significant human problems. Issues of growth and achievement; security and dependency; fear, assertion, and power; and life and death are universal themes that can engross a reader. They reflect the kind of Dynamic-Theme content to which children can commit their attention. The finest stories handle these issues with care for children, providing satisfying, if not always happy, resolutions. They do not titillate children or present suspense and violence as ends in themselves.

Realistic Fiction

Anything that really could happen in a child's experience can be the subject of realistic fiction. Children have opportunities to see how other people or animals behave and feel in situations with which the young listener/reader can identify. Sometimes these situations occur at times and places other than those in which the children live. These stories can help children to see familiar events in new ways.

The best authors use mostly direct conversation that focuses the reader on a main idea in present time. Young children are satisfied with simple endings. Even if an ending comes as a surprise, a child should be able to imagine it.

Folk Tale Formats

The cumulative form of the folk tale, in which each successive event is added to the next and repeated, is frequently present in literature for young children. When the substance is appealing, the cumulative stories are most popular and easily retold. The repetition helps to make these tales readable. Children also enjoy the repetition since it offers them a sense of mastery due to their being able to predict what is coming, sometimes chanting familiar refrains. Folk tales themselves also serve children as a window through which to view the perspectives of families and cultures other than their own.

Poetry

Successful authors appeal to children by communicating appreciation for their characters and respect for their audience. A kind of sincere "eye contact" is made with children's very marrow. A.A. Milne was a master of this craft, as evidenced by *Winnie-the-Pooh* (1957) and his poetry classics *Now We Are Six* and *When We Were Very Young* (1958). He manages to touch many concerns and problems of childhood, except for the pain of major deprivation. When adults read "Sand between the Toes," with coordinated tickles beginning with "sand in the hair," both reader and listener share a rare joy. Using this poem for physical pointing—as well as using pointing to words on a poster or interactive whiteboard with many other books and songs—particularly helps children who are learning to speak English.

Children certainly appreciate poetry that they hear. Narrative poems can serve as a basis for their creative dramatics, alongside prose stories. Poetry is particularly adaptable to choral speaking, with subgroups taking turns, which helps reticent children or those who are learning English to participate. In addition, when you group together poems that have a metaphor or *imagery* (Dynamic-Theme) in common, children can experience similar images from various perspectives, a powerful *inductive* way to learn about different ways of knowing the world.

Your own enjoyment of a poem can be contagious. It is worthwhile to build a stock of familiar, favorite poems that you can integrate incidentally at the "right" moment, even if it is not story time. The daily story time, a planning meeting, or a transition time could include one or two or an entire session of poems for children to hear. Many teachers regularly present a poem on chart paper for all to see as they point to each word while reading to the children. Children ask for repetition of favorite poems, just as they do with favorite stories.

Nonfiction Trade Books

Many nonfiction trade books are written imaginatively and entertainingly for young children. Illustrations in both fictional and nonfictional works are frequently well integrated with the text and add to children's experience of the book. In *A House is a Home for Me*★ (Hoberman, 1978), for example, the use of metaphor, imagery, rhyme, and detailed illustrations adds a poetic feeling to the acquisition of information. However, as much as these features serve to capture a child's interest, the primary purpose of nonfiction is informational. In addition to information about the world in general, nonfiction trade books for young children include such topics as varied alphabet books, puzzles, riddles, jokes, magic, recipes, and games.

Periodicals and Other Print

Periodicals for young children consist largely of illustrations with just a few labels and captions. Rather than use these as a whole-group, didactic reading activity, provide several copies of newspapers or other appropriate periodicals that children can choose to read in the library center. The library center can be a place for a variety of other print forms, such as several versions of alphabet books, catalogs, and collaborative class books to which children have contributed. You can retire, refresh, and revisit different titles and print forms.

Big Books and Skill Building

By being extra-large, big books provide an opportunity for you and your group to share a detailed viewing of the conventions of print and the illustrations together (Butler & Turbill, 1984; Fountas & Pinnell,1996; Holdaway, 1979; Routman, 2003). As you read to the children, for example, point to words and spaces, emphasize sounds and directionality, and welcome children's chanting along. The big books serve as an engaging way to build reading skills. The playful textbook formats clearly provide skills practice; this contrasts with the sheer literary appreciation and aesthetic experiences with trade books discussed in the preceding sections.

Publishers of big books, such as Reading Development Resources, Scholastic, Sunshine, and the Wright Group, among others, also typically provide small copies so that children can reread the stories at other times, sometimes with audiotapes. Butler & Turbill (1984) also suggest that children use a box in order to collect a few titles that they can reread at their own level of interest and capacity. [**Procedural note:** Teachers mark the books within each box with the same symbol or color as well as topic in order to make storage and retrieval easier. For emerging readers, it helps to guide them in choosing books with similar difficulty.] Many of the stories, poems, or songs tend to have a folk tale quality, selected because of their repetitive story structures and language. Youngsters have their favorites based upon the appeal of empowerment, such as getting filthy in *Mrs. Wishy-Washy*★ (Cowley, 1990) or the sheer nonsense of *The Big Toe*★ (Melser & Cowley, 1986). An activity to *assess* if children understand the text in a big book (or any other book) is the following: photocopy each page of a book, laminate it, and hand one page to each child. As you read aloud, each child holds up the page that you are reading.

You can use big books as exercise material to practice comprehension strategies. Youngsters can focus on comprehension when a Post-it note covers a word in a sentence. A word frame can help children focus on a particular repetitive word. Sentence and word strips offer kindergarten children a chance to sequence sentences or words in a sentence in a pocket chart or on a flannel board. These activities also reinforce the concept of parts in relation to wholes, which supports mathematical relationships. Pre-kindergarten children are able to match word cards visually with the words in the book.

Together with young children or with the help of older children, teachers also create big books that replicate or create variations of smaller favorite books. Kindergarten children retell the stories, dramatize events, create murals, and kindergarten children raise related questions in their journals.

Despite the enthusiasm of teachers and children for big books, these titles are not a literature program in themselves. Children also need to hear selections from among the finest of the varied literature that you can acquire. With the thousands of new titles that appear each year, along with the classics of varied genres, children should hear and see many fine trade books.

Putting Reading in its Place

When children figure out how to read at an early age, possibilities for independent, vicarious, and extended experiences open up sooner. Reading is useful and pleasurable when children take meaning from the text that they hear and then read. It is an essential economic and cultural tool and it also offers aesthetic experiences. However, rote decoding without understanding is a meaningless exercise. This is the place, therefore, to talk about how children might learn to read in ways that can support their future, self-directed reading. It is relevant to note that a review of research on reading points to the importance of providing a focus on *meaning*, providing choices of interesting material, and welcoming collaboration among young children—not rote drill or guided reading (Allington, 2005, p. 466; Allington, 2009, p. 125; Neuman, 2010; Routman, 2003). Moreover, when children build vocabulary across the content areas, they make the most progress in literacy (Epstein, 2009, p. 25).

Some researchers, however, find that several hundred kindergarten children enter school as independent readers (Calvert, Rideout, Woolard, Barr, & Strouse, 2005; Durkin, 1966). Researchers also find a correlation between using computers at home for non-game play and early reading (Calvert, Rideout, Woolard, Barr, & Strouse, 2005, p. 601). Early readers typically have access to older children or adults who engage them in reading activities at home. At the same time, a quarter of pre-kindergarten children in a language-rich, activity-based Dynamic-Themes setting that integrates the seven conditions for learning become emergent readers by springtime (L. Davey, personal communication, 2010).

Most children in our society learn to read before they are seven years of age. Before kindergarten, young children maneuver effectively through a multitude of environmental print, from cereal box labels to television channels and computers. However, teachers are finding that about 15 percent of children display perceptual difficulties before they are expected to read, and the percentage may be higher among children exposed to prenatal substance abuse. Pre-kindergarten children and a few children entering kindergarten also need to become aware of sound itself as a conscious "figure" highlighted against their "background" experiences. For these children, instruction may recreate the earliest kinds of interactions between parent and child, as, for instance, when the parent mentions body parts, touches and labels objects, or sings *Mother Goose* rhymes or other songs.

Educators speak of "teachable moments" and "sensitive periods" when the time is ripest for learning particular skills (Hunt, 1961; Montessori, 1965). Vygotsky (1962, pp. 101, 104) contends that "instruction usually precedes development. The child acquires certain habits and skills in a given area before he learns to apply them consciously and deliberately . . . Therefore the only good kind of instruction is that which marches ahead of development and leads it; it must be aimed not so much at the ripe as at the ripening function."

Adults are likely to be more aware of sensitive periods when they are missed and children develop remediation needs; therefore, you do well when you help children in a timely way. A part of the timing issue in teaching reading during kindergarten and pre-kindergarten is that ethical educators want children to learn as much as they can in ways that make them feel human and competent. At the same time, a program that focuses on the three Rs to the exclusion of rich experiences and meaningful content places disembodied tools into a child's hands. Attempting to develop skills in such a sterile atmosphere is like dosing babies with medication that kills helpful bacteria along with the unwanted ones. We might reverse the babies' resulting digestive upsets in some cases. However, if children exposed to conent-poor early schooling learn the "school game" of feigned attention as a façade for boredom, their alienation from schooling may not be reversible.

The fact remains that learning to read is not an end in itself but a tool skill that can help to capture, support, and extend the range of possible meaning for children. It is particularly unfortunate that the pressure to provide reading instruction for low-income children of color often takes a linear direction, largely excluding *inductive* methods which can support learning and meanings that the children can value. However, fine-quality children's literature is an accessible format to add to children's community and home experiences.

Difficult as it may be to imagine, there are children who enter pre-kindergarten without positive encounters with books. For these children, for others who may have become television or video-game addicts, as well as for those who have had many positive associations with books or are already reading, it is essential to provide a meaningful, aesthetically varied, cheerful exposure to fine literature.

The library center, described briefly in Chapter 1, is a place in which you can create a comfortable environment to attract children. It is a setting that you can embellish with "invitations" to expectance and delight. As you read aloud to the entire group at least once each day, you can extend this atmosphere. You can re-read favorite books or poems that encourage children to interact by chiming in to repeated comments or refrains. Children also appreciate sitting close to you in a small group. [**Procedural note:** Routines before a whole-group read-aloud: "If anyone needs to use the toilet, do so before the group gathers. Here is where I will be holding the book. If you cannot see it, then please move now to where you can see it." This kind of routine signals the importance of sustained focus during this occasion.]

Comprehension

In order to extend the pleasures of reading and help children comprehend and connect books to their own experiences, you would read nonfiction after related experiences to help answer questions raised during the experiences. Some ways to extend experiences with either fiction or nonfiction include creating graphic organizers, Venn diagrams, and story timelines of events with the children.

Anticipating It also helps comprehension when children have some expectations about what you will be reading, so that they can have the pleasure of imagining what is to come and playfully predict (building *surprise/cognitive dissonance*) what may be ahead. Before beginning to read, you might preview the pages together, and ask them to wonder what the book might be about and what questions they might have. You might raise one or more questions, as relevant, such as: "What do you suppose we might find?" "Where might the people be coming from/going?" "What questions do you have?" "Tell us what we might like about this book." "Let's find out." At the same time, "advertise" the wonderful reactions you had when you read the book, such as how much it tells about a topic or the grand surprises that you found. Focus on impending delights.

Responsive Reading and Discussion   During the reading, you can point to words in order to reinforce incidentally the idea that spaces between words have meaning. You might ask children about what they think might happen next, when they have had a similar feeling, or what they wonder about a particular part of the story.

Such "instruction," however, needs to be subsidiary to the focus on the children's delight in books. When children hear some poems and stories, the experience itself can be sufficient. The "turned on," totally absorbed atmosphere and the children's very posture tell you when they are aesthetically captivated. It is redundant to ask, "Did you like it?" when their behavior holds the answer. Certainly, if they are fidgeting, looking around, or trying to find stimulation in one another, you have clues that the book is not relevant at that time. And, sometimes, you focus only on the shared, aesthetically profound connection to a book and savor a quiet appreciation.

The critical comprehension element in hearing stories is the back-and-forth talk between you and the children around literature that you share. You have the chance to extend ideas and language by asking children to compare parts of the story with their own lives as well as imagine. The "what ifs" are so valuable in building images and concepts.

Follow-up   At other times, however, you might want to compare books that share an underlying theme. Youngsters can also begin to build critical comprehension when they hear biographies about the same person written by different authors, as noted in Figure 8.4.

A follow-up discussion might include talk about the content as well as imagining, "What might have happened before this story [prequel]?" "What might happen next [sequel]?" When you plan, you might also list a few reading comprehension questions, such as children's favorite character. Other "essential questions" might involve such issues as sharing; fairness; truth; preferences; and "If you could become a character, to whom would you want to talk?"

Depending upon the mood set by the story, you might engage with children in a critical discussion concerning their reactions to the issues raised or actions of the characters portrayed in a story: for example, how the story relates to their own experiences and preferences as well as alternative ways in which people behave. Ideas for focus questions and techniques are integrated in the context of Chapter 8 and Box 14.4.

After children share an experience, you can help sharpen their *critical-thinking skills* by highlighting their reactions:

- What part of the story/film/trip did you like the best? Other views?
- What part did you like the least? Other views?
- Which part did you find the most exciting/interesting/funniest? Other views?
- Which character did you like the best/least? Other views? What did the character do to make you like/dislike him/her?

- What makes you agree/disagree with [name of classmate]?
- When did something like that happen to you/somebody you know?
- Think about this: what else might this character have done?
- What might have happened if he had not . . .?
- What might this character wish? When was a time when you felt the way he did? What might have made him feel that way?
- If you had been this character, what might you have done when . . .? How might you have changed what happened?
- If you could ask the characters questions, what would you want to know?
- How would you continue this story?

As you listen to the children's ideas, attempt to follow up on their content. For example, ask other children: "What could you add to Eden's idea? What do you think about what Gail said?" When you build on their ideas, there is a smooth teacher–child–child–child flow instead of only a teacher–child–teacher–child recitation. These can become crystal-clear moments for teaching and learning.

Retelling   You can assess and support children's expressive language and understanding when they retell stories or the content of nonfiction books. Children can enjoy retelling stories if there is a reason to do so. For example, they might tell a visiting adult or a child who had been absent. You also might use the imaginative device of asking a child to have one puppet retell a story to another puppet. You might energize retelling with a flannel board. Children are able to sequence photocopied pages on a flannel board as they retell a story. Pocket charts or a long ledge serve as alternatives to the flannel board. If you need a more formal assessment format, consider using a retelling rubric (available for free download and printing on the website http://www.tcpress.com; Schwartz & Copeland, 2010, p. 131).

Role-playing   Researchers have found that role-playing improves story recall and comprehension (Pellegrini & Galda, 1982). Young children, however, need guided practice in role-playing. [**Procedural note:** You can take a role yourself in order to start the process or to help sustain the action.] The repetitive folk tale format lends itself to role-play. Children can use a combination of words, gestures, and movements to role-play fiction and nonfiction.

Role-playing after children have had experiences helps them to express their understanding and to make connections with other feelings and experiences. You can begin this activity with some questions that help children to place themselves inside a character:

- Let's imagine that you could become that person. What would you want to do/say/ask/know/have happen? How might their lives become happier/ safer/friendlier?

- What might be happening in this picture? Other views? What clues helped you to think that?
- What do you think about what Robin said? What else might be happening? What clues helped you to think that?

Beyond hearing you read fine trade literature, children need to have fine literature to read as their skills develop. Some teachers provide an opportunity for all children to read/look at books directly after lunch as a matter of course. It is worth noting the criticism that most schools offer less than nine minutes each day for meaningful reading; this suggests that you should consider integrating many opportunities during the day for children to select and handle books (Anderson, Hiebert, Scott, & Wilkinson, 1985; Allington, 2002).

Author Studies Many early childhood groups also undertake author studies, reading several books by a single author, such as the classic works of Eric Carle, Ann Jonas, and Ezra Jack Keats. Author studies entail some of the experiences outlined in Box 10.4.

BOX 10.4 EXPERIENCES WITH AUTHOR STUDIES

- Teachers read aloud many stories written by the same author.
- Children illustrate their favorite parts of various stories.
- They correspond with living authors and occasionally meet and interview authors. Some author websites include video clips.
- Children vote on their favorite book by the author and represent their collective finding in a graph.
- Children create illustrations in the style of the author's books.

Children also use their knowledge of books to fuel their writing, and writing involves re-reading the writing (DeFord, Lyons, & Pinnell, 1991). The next section focuses on drawing–writing into reading.

Drawing–Writing into Reading

Space to draw and write provides an invitation to children. Think about organizing space that invites children to draw and write their way into reading. Box 10.5 presents some details.

BOX 10.5 THE DRAWING–WRITING CENTER

This is a space set aside and *prominently labeled*, "Drawing–Writing Center." Consider some provisions:

- Tables for six–eight chairs facing a wall, room divider, or carrels.
- Storage for journals, writing folders, easily accessible by children.
- A place to leave "finished" work for you to see
- A place and procedures for storing work in progress: for example, clipboards or clothespins on a line of string from which to hang papers
- Shelves *outlined and labeled* with places for the following items:
  - Writing/drawing implements, reserved exclusively for the writing center. These may change from time to time in order to highlight the center, such as special markers or stunning pencils. The assistive device of Wikki Stix wrapped around a pencil adds good grip, as needed.
  - Paper supplies and teacher-made, stapled pad books of varying sizes or shapes (four to six sheets of paper stapled together)
  - Collage materials
  - A stapler, Scotch tape, and glue (stored on their shapes outlined on a shelf)
  - Scissors, stored in a holder
  - An optional picture alphabet
  - The name and photograph of each child and adult
- *Journal.* Each child should have a journal notebook, labeled as such, with the child's name. Contents might include drawings, personal writing and, for kindergarten children as they become more able throughout the year, correspondence between you and the child.
- *Bulletin board and hallway displays.* Label displays, "Kindergarten/Pre-Kindergarten Writing—[month]" and include broadsides, an occasional pad book, or captioned drawing/writing, framed, and arranged in an aesthetically appealing format.
  - *Teacher's record keeping.* Records might include the following:
  - Dated file of samples of children's completed writing/drawing progress in the form of single sheets or short pad books. Save finished work in manila pocket folders, one for each child, or create digital photograph files.
  - Dated schedule of reserved space in the center for each child to work consecutively for *at least* three days at the start of each moderately active center time. As each reserved space is vacated, another child

> may choose to use the space. You would also invite children to write/draw within all activity centers.
>
> - *Teacher's task file.* Your personal file of sequenced ideas for stimulating writing content and for energizing the drawing–writing center.
> - *A digital camera.* Photographs of children's work and of children engaged in writing–drawing or sharing their work.
> - *Report to parents.* Bring to the parents' attention the contents of items listed above.
> - *Mailbox for each child and adult in the classroom.* People send and receive items such as drawings, messages, greeting cards, picture–word appointments, and notices to go home. (Children learn to copy their name and address.)

Writing feels like some form of drawing. Children begin with a notion of the undifferentiated meaning of the spoken sentence that extends to writing. Word cards can help build up a sense of word-ness and meaningful sentences. Children who have difficulties with fine muscle coordination can benefit from moving around word cards. You could also explicitly mention that spaces separate words which you can count together on a line of print as you write in the children's presence. Kindergarten children are able to learn that it is easier for their teacher and others to enjoy their ideas when they place spaces between words (Calkins & Louis, 2005).

As children perceive contrasting patterns of print, much of their early writing development takes place. However, there are specific skills that you will need to show them at just the right moment. The discussion that follows suggests ways in which you can support children's development of writing and reading.

Language Experience/Shared Writing

The whole point of shared-writing, or language-experience, activities is to demonstrate to pre-kindergarten and kindergarten children that what they say has meaning that helps others recall their ideas. Clearly, children who have opportunities to react, feel trust, and experience delight in school activities have more about which to talk and write; and they also have more background to bring to reading the printed page.

In the shared-writing approach to writing and reading, in the children's presence, you write down brief comments that children dictate to you or another person. You might label classroom objects and write children's comments about their paintings on chart paper or interactive whiteboard. You can save and *revisit* (condition for learning) their written comments.

Almost any everyday experience can become an "experience chart." This practice saturates the children visually with the medium of writing, in much the same way as they learned their native spoken language at home and with aural and written forms in community and media environments.

On these occasions, it is important to record precisely what the children say, so that the written form captures their spoken language, even if it is not standard English. For example, the earliest help might be merely verbal harmony, describing how you are writing a pre-kindergarten child's first name: "I am starting to write your name on the left, where there is a blue dot. First, I write the 'D,' by making a line down and then connect this curve. To write the 'e,' I make a line across and then connect the curve back the other way. To write the 'b,' I make a line down and then connect this small curve . . ." and so forth. Pre-kindergarten teachers can add second names after different children learn to write their first names. You can describe how you leave a space between each word and count the number of words together.

When key words that have unusual configurations appear often, some children sort them out. With many such experiences, some children begin to *induce* the sound structure of words, while others build a sight vocabulary.

Large sheets of paper, with or without accompanying pictures, are useful for recording with captioned pictures the procedures that a group follows, say, in a science or cooking activity. You can create labels in the classroom for doors and windows when the children are present. You might pin labels (or hang labels from yarn) on children's clothing that states their roles in socio-dramatic play. In addition, you might provide letters or words on flannel boards and magnet boards with which children can play. Different pre-kindergarten children each day are able to fill in the missing first letter on a class chart or a letter that corresponds to their name.

Plan   Some teachers model a Venn diagram or planning web, particularly during discussions before writing. For example, before developing a class book about friends, you could ask a group of children to dictate words that remind them of a friend or what they do with a friend. Whether your web looks like a daisy—with the center as "friend" and petals of "play," "like," and "trust"—or a central square with lines leading to other squares, you reinforce the notion that you think about and plan your work before writing.

Discuss and Collaborate   When you feel that a child might like to discuss a drawing or painting, you might ask, "What would you like me to write about your picture?" You could bind a group of pictures with captions or brief dictated narratives into a class book. Class books might include such topics as "Changes Outside the Window," "Friends and Bullies," "I Hate . . .," "Pre-Kindergarten Block Building Architects," and "Motors," and some youngsters are able to compose a song or write a rhyme or riddle about events in a story. Class books circulate at the reading center or overnight at home. Other dictated writing might include such forms as menus, diets, tickets, shopping lists, fantastic magical words, party plans, notices of special events, schedules of daily activities, special instructions, letters to a sick child, a thank–you note to a toy donor or senior citizen who visited the class, and invitations for parents to assist on a class trip.

Occasionally, individual pre-kindergarten and kindergarten children create "talking compositions" on audiotapes. Adults might turn an audiotape into a language experience chart. Children *retell* their stories on the tape, embellishing or varying the material; this is as close as kindergarten children come to the act of revising or editing. For them, the process itself and the satisfaction of the experiences are enough, even though they may be episodic, incomplete, or rambling by adult standards. To the children, the sense of being competent creators of language is more important than the final product. Earlier and later renditions can serve to assess children's progress in language and narrative complexity.

Writing Names and Handwriting Most kindergarten and many pre-kindergarten children are able to write their own names with practice. They enjoy writing their names to identify their own drawings. They also learn to recognize the names of other children when there are many opportunities to see them. Books about children learning to write their name, mentioned in Chapter 8, add inspiration.

Young children are highly motivated to write their own names. After children can copy, then write, their own names, some kindergarten teachers arrange a trip to the local public library where the children obtain library cards. [**Procedural note:** Many people report that when they are unsure about how to spell a word, they write it in their hand with a finger. Consider that handwriting involves fine muscle skills as well as seeing and hearing sounds. Writing practice, no less than playing the piano or typing, is in the hand, not in the air. If you provide plenty of varied practice for children to write throughout the day, there will be no need for isolated, costly gimmicks.]

Composing

One researcher contends that, for young children, "the natural order is writing first, then reading what you have written" (C. Chomsky, 1971, p. 296). She points out that the child who selects a plastic letter "r" to represent "w" in the word "wet" is reminding adults that this is the way he pronounces his "w"s. Scholars support the developmental value of such invented spelling (Calkins & Oxenhorn, 2005; Ferreiro, 1991; Newman, 1984; Sulzby, Teale, & Kamberelis, 1989). Before youngsters begin to use the alphabet, their written forms resemble the written language of their environment, whether it is Arabic, English, Hebrew, or Japanese (Harste, Woodward, & Burke, 1984).

Researchers describe a gradient of writing development in which young children increasingly create forms that approximate standard writing (Calkins &

Oxenhorn, 2005; Clay, 1991; Ferreiro & Teberosky, 1982; Harste, Woodward, & Burke, 1984; Richgels, 2001). At a later date, children can often read the same messages from their pre-alphabetic written forms. Box 10.6 outlines how children transform their early forms of writing on the way to alphabetic writing (Ferreiro & Teberosky, 1982).

BOX 10.6 PHASES OF EARLY WRITING

1   Curved and/or straight lines.
2   "Stable, graphic strings" that include a fixed minimum number of forms.
3   A "syllabic hypothesis" in which one letter represents one syllable. [**Procedural note:** Consonants typically precede the use of vowels.]
4   A *conflict* between graphic strings and syllabic hypothesis; that is, "conflicts between an internal requirement and a reality external to the child" (Ferreiro & Teberosky, 1982, p. 204). [**Procedural note:** This is a form of *surprise/cognitive dissonance*, the transition point at which learning occurs.]
5   Alphabetic writing that recognizes sound values less than syllables.

Scaffold: Teachers saturate children's environment with writing in context. Teachers describe what they are doing as they write. They sing the "alphabet" song while pointing to the letters, and play movement games with letters on the floor. They draw attention to the page numbers in books and invite children to create more than a single page of writing by providing stapled booklets.

Other scholars consider similar "stages" of writing development (Heroman, Burts, Berke, & Bickart, 2009; Hutinger, Bell, Daytner, & Johanson, 2005, citing Barclay et al., 1990, 1996). Terms, such as "transition," "temporary," and "developmental" spelling are used synonymously with invented or approximate spelling. Alphabetic writing with conventional spelling usually begins with children's initial awareness of beginning sounds, then ending sounds, and then medial vowels. Children often begin to write medial vowels when writing their own names (Sowers, 1986b).

Children who are English language learners or are reticent about writing "may be more able to write when allowed to work through picture-making" (Bridge, 1986, p. 75). This practice focuses on the communication of meanings as the priority in literacy growth. Several scaffolds include the use of pattern texts, literacy blocks, and fixed-form poetry with which children can practice alternative fill-in content (Gordon, 2007). For example, you can scaffold the counting poem "One, Two, Buckle My Shoe" by deleting some of the phrases and replacing others: "One, two. —— true. Three, four, —— store" (Gordon, 2007, p. 105). (Detailed free lesson plans and graphic materials for English language learners can be found on the "ESL Portfolio" website: http://www.people.hofstra..edu/faculty/Tatiana_Gordon/esl/index.html.)

Children have strong personal motivation for improving their own writing, especially when sharing with others (Calkins & Louis, 2005; Clay, 1991; Dyson, 1989; Ferreiro & Teberosky, 1982; Gibson, 1989; Graves & Stuart, 1985). Pre-kindergarten children begin by exploring individual letters, often of their own names. Since the act of composing, used in the sense of freedom to organize feelings and ideas in a personal way, is the single most important writing task to nurture, you can become a great appreciator of the trust with which young children present their work. Quite simply, you should appreciate the flow, enthusiasm, and sense of accomplishment that young children bring to their work.

Technical instruction should take place at times separate from when young children feel the flush of accomplishment. You can create small groups for specific skill instruction and change the composition of the groups to adapt to different learning needs.

Indeed, children learn to write much as they learn to talk—by hearing and seeing repeated models. Thus, as children have contacts with books and other print forms, reading serves to enhance writing; critical reading and critical writing support each other.

It may be helpful to think of the composing process as a set of interwoven, recursive phases: prewriting (experiencing and talking about what children might plan to write about); writing interwoven with sharing with other children; and publishing or occasionally preparing a rendition on special paper. If youngsters create a booklet of drawings and text, consisting of a few stapled pages, you might encourage them to read their work to other individuals in school or at home. One energizing suggestion is to have an autograph page for all those who heard children "read" their book (Rog, 2007, p. 56).

Prewriting-into-writing

The prewriting phase is a critical time for you to work with children in harnessing and building enthusiasm and motivation for writing. It is a time to develop ideas about which to write. Children have plenty of ideas when they participate in daily life activities that represent the underlying images of Dynamic-Themes. The "inner language" of ideas emerges as children act and talk. It is important for teachers to provide many opportunities for them to talk to you and to one another. You invite them to talk about and plan what they might draw and write.

When kindergarten children work with a partner, you could model and practice ways for them to scaffold each other's writing/drawing. For example, after children discuss their plans for writing, researchers find it useful to extend the activity when their teacher provides several stapled papers and touches each page in turn, asking what would happen next, and next (Calkins & Oxenhorn, 2005, pp. 6, 21). Box 10.7 describes additional experiences in which pre-kindergarten and kindergarten groups can engage.

BOX 10.7 SOME ACTIVITIES WITH REASONS TO READ AND WRITE

- *Literacy to build independence.* From their first day in school, pre-kindergarteners are able to move their photograph with their first name from the left side of the pocket chart to the right side to indicate their presence. As the year progresses, some children become able to move their name without their photograph. By March, most youngsters can use a card listing both their first and last names. Most of them are also able to identify the first names of their classmates.
- *Visiting a post office.* Children mail letters. They are interested in the variety of stamps and are able to make their own stamps for use with pen pals.
- *Writing their names and addresses.* The children copy their names and addresses.
- *Creating personal alphabetized word notebooks.* Some teachers provide prestigious notebooks in which children collect "personal" words, with and without drawings. An alternative is for many children or the class to create an alphabetized class book of drawings/pictures with words.
- *Pen pals.* They can draw pictures and write, using invented spelling, to children in another kindergarten room. In turn, they are delighted to receive mail from their pen pals.
- *Greeting gards, invitations, and thank-you notes.* Children draw/write to other children, family, and community members. [**Procedural note:** Some teachers provide a "project folder" of relevant words, such as "Dear Ms. Rand"; "thank you"; "please"; "come"; "happy birthday"; and "love." Other teachers create bulletin board "word walls" with frequently used words.]
- *Labels.* They write their names on their drawings and paintings.
- *Socio-dramatic activity.* They draw/write appointments, prices of items, and receipts as they are able within the various themes in the center.
- *Feely box.* Children feel unseen objects—always an attention-getting and suspenseful activity that stimulates imagination. Then they imagine "becoming" the texture (or fragrance or appearance) and share, while an adult writes (1) what they might be, (2) what they might think, (3) what they might do, and (4) the possible advantages and disadvantages of being that thing.
- *Dynamic-Theme activities.* The related activity-based experiences typically include children's reasons to write.

It is particularly helpful to plan some child-centered questions (a form of scaffolding) that might help children think about the relation of a story or event to their own experiences: for example, "When did something like that happen to you?" "What would you have done next with that character if the book could keep going?" "Who was your favorite character?" "If you could talk to that character, what would you want her to know about your family?"

Questions that help you assess children's learning across the curriculum appear in Box 14.4. In summary, the questions you raise are important in order to encourage an authentic exchange of ideas. You can see meaningful interactions when children respond to and build upon the content of one another's comments, rather than merely "answer" your questions.

Young children comfortably integrate writing and other representational activities throughout the day. The socio-dramatic area, for example, might include writing tools as props in their restaurant, hospital, or shop. They could create advertisements for their store (Raines & Canaday, 1992).

IMAGE 10.1 Beauty Parlor Price List with Invented Spelling (Haircuts $1 and 99c; Shampoo $1 and 99c; Haircurlers $2 and 99c; Permanents $3 and 99c)

Researchers have found that integrating writing materials with changing socio-dramatic play themes generates increased use of literacy skills (Christie, 1991; Morrow, 2009; Roskos & Neuman, 2001; Schrader, 1989, 1990).

Journals   The bulk of young children's writing appears and increases after several months of the school year. Some kindergarten children are able to respond personally in journals to stories that they have heard. The journal notebook contains an ongoing personal statement in which kindergarten children can write each day once you feel they are ready to do so. Different children will be ready at different times, so look for children who are beginning to use the syllabic hypothesis.

Journal writing, which kindergarten children perceive as prestigious, provides an opportunity for you to correspond with the children through their journals. For example, before the children arrive, a New York City public school kindergarten teacher would write a daily one- or two-sentence letter to each child who had a journal. She might ask about how they like something or about siblings or

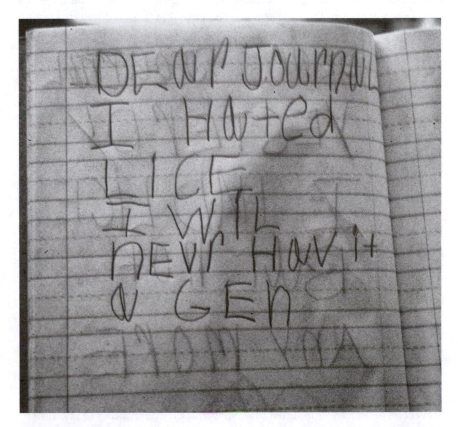

IMAGE 10.2 Invented Spelling

other everyday experiences, and the children write their answers in the journal. Often, they ask a question in return, such as: "Dear Ms. Davis, I have a sister. She is a baby. How many brothers and sisters do you have? Love, Alex." Sometimes children write in the journal and fold over a page to denote that it is private (U. Davis, personal communication, 1985). Notice that some of the correspondence might include building on the teacher's model. Acquiring a journal serves to scaffold children's writing. In addition, you can support children's writing by starting with lots of thinking and talking about things that they want to write about. Follow up with more talking and writing. In all things, *you support children's writing when you focus on their ideas.*

Some kindergarten teachers provide a growing "word wall" for those children who are ready to use frequently found words, such as "the," "is," "before," and "after." Bulletin boards ideally list such words alphabetically at the children's eye level. "Project folders" might contain similar words and also include unusual words in separate folders related to a particular project. A project folder might include words for correspondence; animal names; transportation modes; science-related terms; and so forth. The project folder makes it easier for some youngsters to transfer horizontal print to a horizontal table, instead of the word walls that create a vertical-to-horizontal transfer.

Writing Conferences

As you appreciate the process of children's writing efforts, you can highlight various aspects of writing in a conference with an individual or with several children. For example, you might reflect back what a child has written and ask the children for confirmation. You might ask what a child felt was the most important part of the story or how the child decided to write about this topic. You might ask for additional information. You might also ask if the child plans to write about a similar or different topic next time.

You might consider some of the ideas, and raise some of the questions, outlined in Box 10.8 for which you really need an answer because the contents grow out of the children's insights. Rather than expecting a single "correct" answer, you will find that the best questions may be answered differently by different children. These strategies encourage children to trust you enough to risk sharing honestly and to develop their own critical-thinking skills in relation to stories and events. When your purpose is to help children develop independence in writing, you might ask then to think about their meaning: "When you reread that piece, you changed it so that it made sense. Way to go! Pat yourself on the back." It is noteworthy that the strong body of research points to the value of "deep-level" questions to support the "deep understanding of taught material" (Institute of Education Sciences, 2007, pp. 2, 29ff).

When children are committed to the content, they have plenty to say. Instead of a cycle of teacher–child recitation, there is much more child–child interaction about ideas; children listen to each other and build on one another's statements. Look at questions as opportunities for children to contribute, share, and find out what others are thinking and how they connect ideas, rather than as times for children to "answer" questions. Examples of questions that you can use to scaffold children's thinking about their experiences before and after writing appear in Box 14.4. Questions to focus children on the specific contents of their writing appear in Box 10.8.

BOX 10.8 SOME WRITING CONFERENCE QUESTIONS

- Please read your story.
- What else could you say about . . .? Where could you write it?
- What part do you like best? When did something like that happen to someone you know? What happened after this?
- How might you feel if . . .?
- What might you say when . . .?
- What might you do when . . .?
- At what part are you not happy?
- What might you do to make the beginning of your draft set up the reader? What is the most important thing you are saying? What happened when you shared with a friend?
- What words do you think you used best?
- What is a different way to say this?
- You said that so clearly. Where could you write it so the reader can know more?
- How is the ending different from your last piece? (Adapted from Turbill, 2001).

[**Procedural note:** These types of questions offer alternatives that you might adapt if a few questions seem relevant to a particular situation.]

Children are also able to help one another with their writing/drawing when they share their work informally, at peer conferences, or in a larger group sharing time. Other children could raise important questions that help the author to clarify meanings. Sharing ideas and written work with others in these ways helps children to build a sense of audience. Then, the writing conference as a "thinking conference" serves as a "structured . . . intellectual collaboration" (Newkirk & Atwell, 1986, p. 3). In addition, sharing ideas helps build the sense of a caring community where children can feel safe.

Beyond adding to their work, a revising or editing phase is usually not relevant for young children. Occasionally, a child may add to a piece or see something months after he originally wrote it and marvel at how much more proficient his later work seems. An opportunity for self-directed revision might occur, long after a first flush of creative achievement, if a youngster prepares some favorite writing on "special" paper for a display.

Publishing

A parade of children holding their products, be they drawings with children's names or stories several pages in length, can be a satisfying "publishing" event for youngsters. You can tape a mark on the floor to designate an area for peer sharing. By sitting there, any child is inviting another to share their written work. At first, children may speak/read simultaneously to one another. After you have consistently modeled appreciation, the retelling of stories, and clarification questions, children learn to do this for one another. For example, following your model, it is possible to observe a child finish reading to the class in an "author's chair" (or on an "author's stump"); fold her arms and ask, "What did I just say?"; call on individuals to speak; then ask, "What questions do you have about my story?" There are helpful sources of ideas for teacher and peer writing conferences and publishing (see Calkins & Oxenhorn, 2005; Flemming, 1986; Sowers, 1986b).

Another way to support peer sharing suggests that "the teacher assigns the roles of storyteller and listener children in pairs by giving the storyteller a card with a picture of a mouth and the listener a card with a picture of an ear. These cards help the children keep their roles straight" (Bodrova & Leong, 2007, p. 89). This type of scaffold also helps buddies to build self-regulation as well as to share nonfiction topics of mutual interest.

In addition, bulletin board and hallway displays labeled "Pre-Kindergarten/ Kindergarten Writing—[month]" might include broadsides, pad books, or labeled drawings, framed and arranged in an aesthetically appealing format. There might be photographs with captions of children engaged in writing or sharing their writing with others. It is useful to bring to the parents' attention and the attention of other school personnel your written explanation of the value of invented spelling as a form of wholesome progress in early writing.

Phonemic Instruction Through Phonemic Games

It is worth noting that most children learn to read regardless of the methods that teachers use. However, as much as you saturate the environment with rich and varied language materials, some other children may need specific technical help in using the sound structure of print in reading English.

Phonemic instruction, which deals with the sound structure of language within the context of whole words, is another component in an *inductive* comprehensive literacy program. While retaining an atmosphere in which rich, meaningful activity continues to predominate, it is worth looking at the most efficient way to help children who need focused help to figure out the sound system of written symbols. The sooner children reach a level of reading comprehension that approaches their level of interest, the sooner reading can function as a tool. Early success breeds a feeling of competence as well as purposeful, natural use of this tool. As with any skill, coordination and comfort accrue with practice.

For these reasons, when some children need help in recognizing the sound structure of printed symbols, many teachers offer focused phonemic instruction, using the same *inductive* process that took place in the early development of spoken syntax. For example, pre-kindergarten children are able to play with sound awareness and engage in sound discrimination games with objects. *Such instruction, however, is only needed for some children who need help in discriminating different sounds and should form only a small part of their exposure to language-enrichment activities.*

A kind of baseline is that many children hear the alphabet and recite it as a chant, part of their social knowledge. Researchers remind us that the alphabetic system and its sound-based system is actually helpful in learning to decode print (Adams, 2001; Whitehurst & Lonigan, 2001). However, children can acquire the meanings represented in print at the same time as they build their full grasp of the phonology. As was the case with spoken language, these skills emerge most effectively with varied forms of repetition and practice.

Putting Practice in its Place

Scholars believe that all readers build habits through practice. One idea is that each reader develops a range of habitual responses to a specific set of *contrasting patterns* of graphic shapes (Fries, 1963). Another notion is that readers learn to exclude those graphic elements that are immaterial to meaning by acquiring a habit of expectancy in relation to symbols (F. Smith, 1978). Practice strengthens habits, and real habits are self-motivated. Brain researchers support the notion that "most children" require practice in order to read (Nevills & Wolfe, 2009, p. 77).

Practice, in and of itself, does not make learning to read occur, but it does provide the time for the *inductive*, connection-making processes that do. In effect, *it is your professional skill to dress the same skills in different, as well as appealing, clothing.* It is also professional skill to provide focused practice only for those children who need a particular skill in a timely way, and this should form only a small part of their exposure to language-enrichment activities.

Practice can take place when children hear and see the same stories again. Your own enjoyment of reading aloud certainly helps them look forward to reading. Practice can take place when you saturate engaging and varied activities with language skills. The more opportunities children of the same general age have to develop skills, however, the wider the range of abilities among them will become. Therefore, any grouping that you organize should be for a specific short-range purpose, such as playing a game that includes the particular phonemic skills of contrasting the *cat–pat–rat* and *can–pan–ran* patterns of words, or the particular interest in discussing sports books of varied complexity.

Whole and Part Approaches   Reading, as well as mathematics, deals with part–whole relationships. When lay-people and some teachers talk about learning to read, they most often refer to the practice of teaching children to "sound-out" words. The "developmental basal series" marketed by many publishers are built on the methods variously referred to as the "whole-word," "look–say," "sight-word" approach. These words may be found in controlled vocabulary passages that offer children artificial, stilted language structures devoid of committed content. Children, within this approach, begin to read by memorizing whole words that may or may not be regularly spelled (i.e., words that have a one-to-one correspondence between each letter and single sound, such as "fat" or "sun" that are spelled regularly; those that do not fit this description, such as "look," "come," "said," and "house," are irregularly spelled). The vagaries of the English language, however, mean that about 15 percent of the words we frequently use, including "the" and "said," simply do not fit regular spelling patterns (Mazurkiewicz, 1964; Tompkins, 2011). Children are more likely to recognize those words after seeing them written and if they have some sense of phonemic associations to guide them; youngsters who use invented spellings show significant progress in acquiring phonemic associations.

When basal reader-oriented teachers begin with the whole-word methods, they usually introduce "sounding-out" toward the end of the first year, or after children have achieved a body of "recognition" words. "Phonics"—different from phonemics—is the school-based instructional program for sounding-out words. In phonics instruction, children are taught isolated sounds. Also, in phonics instruction, teachers mark vowels phonetically to differentiate "a" as in "hat" from "a" as in "hate." Teachers tell the children the generalizations and expect them to memorize and apply the idea *deductively* in all cases. However, this book points to research contending that young children learn more readily with *inductive* teaching approaches.

Even when children begin seeing irregularly spelled whole words that teachers expect them to memorize, they usually notice reduced cues, such as the initial letter of the word, the outline of the word's letters that ascend above or descend below the line, the length of the word, or a nearby picture clue. The "part," or synthetic, methods vary along a continuum from the traditional "phonics" instruction, with an initial introduction of isolated sounds, to "phonemic" instruction, in which *contrasting patterns* of sounds are bound within whole words. In either case, there is support for the development of phonological awareness, involving the *comparison* of similar sounds (National Early Literacy Panel, 2008).

A Balanced Viewpoint   The viewpoint in this chapter is that children can learn to read without calling letter names first. When teachers spend 26 weeks devoted to studying one letter name each week, besides boring any child named Susan or Sam during "S-week," they provide children with a trivial focus that absorbs time which could be used for meaningful pursuits and literacy activities.

Although it does not hurt to know the letter names, which children can acquire through an alphabet song as you point to each letter or with music games on an alphabet carpet, it is not worth belaboring. In any case, most typical young children learn the alphabet easily if they have not picked it up before school.

The use of lower-case letters in shared-writing and beginning reading helps children to perceive more differentiation than with capital letters. To start out using both capital and lower-case letters is to expect an act of conservation of shape (and sound) for young children, an added burden.

Although most children will easily infer the regularities in the relationships between sound and print, some will profit from varying degrees of carefully planned and sequenced instruction. It may be that those children who have not induced the phonemic bases of the English language have had fewer opportunities to highlight the connections between spoken and written representations of ideas. They might need especially sharpened contrasts between the phonemic "figures" within the "backgrounds" of words. Whether the sources of this discontinuity reside in perceptual focus or unfortunate interactions that lead children, in Jerome Bruner's (1966) terms, to "defend" in order to "cope," a playful approach that *contrasts* whole words can help some children. The brain "seeks order and patterns that are meaningful . . . A letter-to-sound strategy, primary word walls based on the alphabet, incomplete orthographic rules, or sounding out individual letters in words are some of the teaching practices that can lead to confusion" (Nevills & Wolfe, 2009, p. 106).

You can support fluency and meaning when you provide games with contrasting patterns of phonemes within words. A successful, longitudinal research study found that, among other factors, a focus on meaning and "having fun with language" have a significant long-term impact on children's lives (Schweinhart et al., 2005, p. 36). Also bear in mind that, even with plenty of playful phonemic contrasts and story repetition, it is still natural for young children occasionally to make written or visual reversals, although most of this passes by 7 years of age.

The Role of the Teacher in Inductive Phonemic Games

You can create games that match the particular phonemic variables that the children need to learn if you are unable to find controlled variables in commercial games. Then you would play the games with those children who need help in order to *induce* the contrasting patterns of phonemes.

The children's motives for playing are the game activity rather than the phonemic learning. The games use concrete materials with controlled phonemic variables within the context of whole words; hence the opportunity to *induce* the contrasting patterns. From two to five children play together, affording many opportunities for participation. Focus on cooperation rather than competition: for example, "Let's help [the current media figure] get home." The games are part of a larger experiential setting in which children become saturated with written as well as spoken language.

There are five principles in these games that replicate some of the strategies by which children learned to speak, thus providing support to children who are English language learners. The principles that follow guide the playing.

Provide Contrasting Patterns A primary principle is to provide contrasting patterns of phonemes in whole words. The phoneme is the smallest range of sound that can change the meaning of a word. For example, the transformation of the word "mat" to "that" represents a single phonemic substitution. While two graphemes represent "th," it is a single sound, or phoneme. Each game transforms a single new phoneme because when there are too many variables, it is more difficult for children to induce the new phoneme.

Point to each word as you read the model chart. The model chart of contrasting pairs of words remains visible as a self-checking device to help children become more autonomous. You would not say, "no" or "wrong" or "almost"; nor ask another child to "help out" with the "correct" reading. If a child reads inaccurately, you would remodel, pointing to the model chart (which is always

IMAGE 10.3 Phonemic Board Game, Model Chart, Spinner, and Word Cards—"Action Figure Goes Home"

in sight): "If this is . . . and this is . . . if this is . . . and this is . . ., then this is . . ."
If the child cannot decode the word that represents the new phonemic contrast,
then you would offer the word in a neutral tone and refocus the child on the action
of the game. You take note, however, of the child's need for additional practice
with a less complex contrast at another time.

Use Whole Words   A second principle is to model the new phoneme several
times in the functional context of a word. When you avoid "naked consonants"
by verbalizing phonemes in a functional whole-word context, you might avoid
subsequent blending problems. For example, it is practically impossible to state a
consonant sound alone, It comes out as a "*b*uh" or "*k*uh" or "*s*uh." When children
who are taught to read by using phonics or sounding-out methods meet a new
word, the "naked consonants" slow them down. For example, you could witness
some children in intermediate grades distort the print "*s*uh-*t*uh-*o*-*p*uh" as "supper"
rather than "stop." They mix up the extra, voiced "*uh*" vowel sounds and do not
focus on the word's meaning. In effect, the isolated sounds can also mask meaning.

Control Variables in Sequence   The third principle is to present the simpler
and more commonly used phonemes within word patterns before the more
variable and less used phonemes. For example, the common sounds of the vowels,
as in "bat," "bet," "bit," "but," and "lot," are easier to learn than the name sounds
of the vowels, such as "bake," "beat," "be," "boat," or "rule," which require
accompanying patterns. Similarly, consonants such as the "c" in "cat and "face"
or the "g" in "gas" and "gem" are more complex than "m" or "b," which do not
require the ability to conserve sounds.

Be Flexible   The fourth principle derives from the third. For example, in case
you plan an activity that is too difficult or too simple for your small group, you
would prepare either a simpler or more complex alternative for next time. This
means preparing earlier and later model charts and word cards. To adapt during
an ongoing game, simply consider the sequence of phonemic complexity and
substitute the chart or cards.

You should also be flexible about the range of abilities in your classroom. Many
children learn to read without apparent effort by inducing the contrasting patterns
of phonemes after minimal modeling; they are able to become independent readers
rather smoothly. However, others require varying amounts of systematic help.
Your greatest contribution is to give systematic help only when children need it.
If a child can already decode, then offer that child reading selections from among
the fine literature that you collect.

Build Cooperation   Whenever possible, it is useful to avoid, play down, or
minimize competition in these games. If children can perceive their own learning

to read in a neutral, straightforward manner, perhaps fewer learning blocks will occur.

For example, there are some ways you can avoid or reduce competition with board games. Instead of each child moving a marker toward the goal, the entire group might move a single marker toward the goal. You could encourage group focus with such comments as "Look how far Sponge Bob has gone. Let's see how far he will go with the next roll of the die." A competitive atmosphere may be a signal to you that children's self-confidence is shaky or that they feel pressured. It is worth mentioning again that a *sense of competence* is an important condition for learning.

Decoding Activities

It is easiest for children to play decoding games when you read the model chart and model the game by simply taking a first turn, avoiding lengthy preliminary descriptions. Open each session by reading the new model chart alone at first, thereby showing the children a new phonemic variable contrasted several times against known phonemes in words. Then model the game by taking a sample first turn. A look at specific games will clarify this procedure.

Pairs   The game of "Pairs," or "Concentration," adapts to any skill level. It could almost be an entire sequence in and of itself. In addition, children are highly motivated to focus on the cards that are turned face down, as they try to pick a pair. For this game, it is also possible to set different tasks for children.

To become familiar with the game format, the earliest cards in a pre-kindergarten Pairs game may be simply those pictures, shapes, or colors that are the same; or pairs of animals, flowers, or outdoor–indoor picture pairs. Pre-kindergarten children are able Pairs players with pictures of objects and shapes.

Before reading words, some children might need to sort sounds that are the same. At the sound level, a set of cards could match pairs of pictures that begin with the same sound as "boy," "box," and "ball," or "milk," "man," and "mouse." The model chart would consist not of words but of rows of other pictures that begin with one or the other sound. Still another game could be pairs of pictures that end with the same sound as "hammer," "fur," and "car" or pairs of pictures of words that rhyme. Thus, to start, a few children would be using pictures to discriminate sound.

Of course, children need to learn to play the Pairs game itself. Box 10.9 describes procedures to play word games with kindergarten children.

BOX 10. 9 PROCEDURES FOR PAIRS/CONCENTRATION GAME

- Create card games that contrast a single new phonemic variable with already known phonemes. Let us say that the game involves contrasting patterns of words in which the new variable is the final consonant sound. For example, place the preprinted original pattern on an oak tag file folder in full view, standing up. The oak tag model chart (which remains visible to the players throughout the game), for example, is the following:
    - bat – ban
    - mat – man
    - fat – fan
    - cat – can
- In order to provide more practice with the new phonemic variable of the final consonant sound, there are more pairs of cards for the words in the right-hand column (e.g., eight pairs, with only four pairs of words in the left-hand "known" column).
- Model the action yourself by taking the first turn. Turn over and read each of two cards which, if they are not identical, you turn over while repeating, "I am going to remember where I put the 'pat' card and the 'can' card. I am putting them back in the same place that I found them because they are not the same. But you will try to remember where you put each one."
- The first child takes a turn and turns over two cards, tells what she or he sees, and then replaces them face down, as you have done. You might ask the child to repeat where he/she put each one. [**Procedural note:** Be sure that other players see the cards that the player turns over before they are replaced. Children can see better if they are seated in a row along the same base line, so that no one is seeing the cards upside down.]
- As the others take turns, each player tells what he or she turns up.
- Each player replaces the cards in the same locations if they do not match.
- It is an exciting moment when the cards *do* match and you can add, "You really are concentrating." The children can then place the matched pair in the groups' cooperative storage container, which you might label, "The Hungry Hippo," "The Dog's Bowl," or "The Rabbit's Bowl." Some ambitious teachers prepare cards in the shape of bones for the "Hungry Dog" or bananas for the "Hungry Monkey." However, keeping all cards the same design for different word games makes for less work. Also, it is less work to make a game easier or more complex with a different model chart of words if you adapt the game by subtracting or adding word cards.

[**Procedural note**. Children should not need to wait long for their turn, so two to four players is a sufficient group size. All cards are lined up so that children see them right side up when they turn them over. A symbol on the back of each card helps to place all the cards on the same base line for viewing. If a child is unable to read aloud the new word pattern, then you can reread the model chart while pointing to each word or read the word on the card so that the child can focus on the game. It is extremely important that the center of attention is on playing the game.]

You can increase the pairs of chances for your children to be successful by constructing two identical pairs for each of the new contrasts. The game can build gradually toward ten pairs. When playing with children who have matched pairs of pictures, you might add, to an ongoing set of pictures or shapes, a pair of cards with the common sound of "a" as in "pat" pronounced on it, with the total number of cards newly reduced for this occasion. This procedure makes for a smooth transition. When "at" is added, then "mat," with one set of four cards in each new game, you retire the "a" cards. Box 10.10 presents a possible early sequence of words in phonemic games.

BOX 10.10 A POSSIBLE SEQUENCE OF WORDS IN PHONEMIC GAMES

- a – at
- at – mat – sat – pat – fat (etc.)
- pat – pan, fan (etc.) or pin, fin (etc.)
- pat – pit, sit (etc.) or pit, pin (etc)

Adding a new variable in each game, *only as needed*:

- (Game 1) 2 × 4 =   a   a   a   a
                                    at   at   at   at
- (Game 2) 2 × 4 =   at   at   at   at
                                    mat mat mat mat
- (Game 3) 2 × 4 =   mat mat mat mat
                                    pat   pat   pat   pat
- (Game 4) 3 × 4 =   mat mat mat mat
                                    pat   pat   pat   pat
                                    rat   rat   rat   rat
- (Game 5) 3 × 4 =   pat   pat   pat   pat
                                    rat   rat   rat   rat
                                    fat   fat   fat   fat

- (Game 6) 2 × 4 =   pat – pan
  rat – ran
  fat – fan
  mat – man

Most kindergarten children who need support are able to handle and enjoy this activity before mid-year. Then, "at" alone retires, replaced by four or five different initial (onset) consonant sounds with four cards each (at – pat; at – mat; at – rat; at – fat). For example, note the introduction of "rat" in Game 4 and "fat" in Game 5. Then, the children are ready for the transformation of "at" (rime), to "an" (Game 6). The "an" pattern can build words with many of the same initial consonant sounds. In this manner, the game of Pairs continues to expand through the other simple consonant–vowel–consonant (cvc) word patterns, such as "tan," "tap," "tag," and so forth, one at a time, over a period of weeks. It is worth noting that younger children find it easier to perceive the transformation of "mat" to "man" than "mat" to "met." The medial vowel seems to be *sequentially more complex*.

The ccvc (consonant–consonant–vowel–consonant) patterns, such as the words "flat," "slit," "stop," and "plum," build in a similar way, as well as the ccvc patterns such as "felt," "soft," and "bend." Words such as "plum" and "send" are natural extensions of these sound patterns in which there is a one-to-one correspondence between sound and symbol. This sequence is loosely adapted with reference to a variety of linguistically based works (Bloomfield & Barnhart, 1961; Fries, 1963; Gattegno, 1968). (Teachers and Hofstra University students have adapted the games from the lexicon of existing children's games and played the phonemic games with hundreds of children between the ages of 4 and 12 who needed specific support.)

As children become more proficient, you can add word patterns gradually and in turn:

- Words that end in *ill*, *ick*, and *ack*
- Transformational patterns such as hat – hate; rat – rate
- Patterns in a separate activity, such as bit – bite; kit – kite
- Commonly used digraphs, such as *sh*ut, *ch*ip, *th*is, and *th*ink
- Vowel digraphs represented in patterns such as *set* – *seat*; or *got* – *goat*

For example, well beyond the cvc stage, the following model may comprise one game of Pairs:

- bet – beat
- met – meat

- net – neat
- pet – peat
- set – seat

If you try to teach several vowel digraphs together or silent-"e" transformations at one time, you impede the natural *induction* process. Presenting more than one new phonemic variable usually depends upon *deductive* applications of general principles; therefore, it is less accessible for pre-kindergarten or kindergarten children. In this way, children figure out phonemic skills *inductively* in the functional setting of a game, one new variable at a time.

Ongoing Assessment   In the course of becoming an independent reader—beyond the scope of most typical kindergarten children—a child may come to recognize some words as whole entities without really having grasped the underlying phonemic properties. There may be no comprehension problem; however, children cannot necessarily transfer the component pattern to other words simply because they acquire the sight-word. This is one of the diagnostic problems that teachers face.

Children who are independent readers may need to practice with *er*, *ir*, and *ur*, or *scr* and *thr* combinations, within the context of whole words. You can contrast these various phonemic patterns by using the game of Pairs as well as other games described in the next sub-section.

Other Card Games   Lotto/Bingo games are also helpful because the cards are open for all participants to see. These games capitalize on the fact that young children are able to match word forms before they can read them. A useful Lotto sequence includes: (1) picture-and-word–picture-and-word; (2) picture-and-word-word-and word; and (3) word–word. You can provide a model for the contrasting phonemes in these games, as you did for the Pairs game, using a preprinted model chart.

A phonemic Bingo game includes cards with a different sticker theme on each card. In order to reduce competition, you can prepare four cards with the same words in a different sequence so that all children finish the game together. Five- and six-year-old children focus on the different stickers and often insist on playing all four cards!

You could adapt several other card games in order to develop sequential skills. [**Procedural note:** Young children have difficulty fanning cards. You can use a Scrabble stand or saw halfway down a 1 × 6-inch length of wood to create a stand for the cards.] An early form of these card games uses pictures (as was the case with the Pairs game) in order to acquaint children with the game format and to help them focus on similarities and differences in the sounds. For example, in the "Go Fish," game, each player receives four cards from the deck. Then they ask each other for a card that goes with one of the pictures that they are holding.

[**Procedural note:** Before the game begins, share common labels for the group to use so that the picture of the mouse is not taken to be a rat, or the dish to be a plate.] As each child collects a pair of pictures whose labels rhyme, that pair is set aside. Otherwise, the child "fishes" for another card.

Card games serve as an opportunity for you to provide initial instruction through a brief modeling of the game, taking only a minute or two. They give you great flexibility because you can add or remove cards to make the game simpler or more complex. They also provide an opportunity for the children to play later with each other independently, usually for 10 to 15 minutes or so. In this way, the children are practicing a particular skill in a playful way.

Board Games and Adaptations   You could also create "universal" board games. Players move a token in response to different words either on cards or taped to a wooden cube that they toss. The children might also spin a dial with numbers to indicate how many boxes along the board to move the shared token. [**Procedural note:** You can flexibly reduce or increase the number of dots, cards, or items in a game.]

You can construct your own inexpensive boards by attaching together large paper bags from the supermarket with masking tape and "energize" them with thematic stickers or clip art. [**Procedural note:** When you use cards or a die for directions, you can change the "universal" board game more easily by changing the cards or a die rather than an entire board. Plan the board so that the markers move from top to bottom and left to right, without reverse-movement penalties.] Each of several concentric circles on a spinner, different sets of spinner cards, or different cards with a related model chart can direct different players within the same game. In this way, you can individualize a game.

There are many imaginative, colorful themes you can use when you custom-design board games for the children with whom you work. Among popular topics for board games are "Snoopy Goes Home," "Rainbow with a Pot of Gold," "Baseball," "Haunted House," "Space Ship in the Planets," and media characters. These materials could become part of your collected stock of other stimulating activities.

Games with Objects   You will need games with objects, particularly for those children who need help with visual and auditory discrimination and for children who are English language learners. Children can sort objects that begin with the same sound as "house" and "hat" into a brightly colored "horse" box and place objects that begin with the same sound as "feather" and "fig" into the "fruit" box. Also, they can sort objects that rhyme. Notice how the use of whole-word models that contrast sounds, rather than the isolated sound or letter name, makes it possible for children to grasp inductively how the sorting works.

Another sorting device that has prestige appeal in the child's culture is a cabinet of small transparent plastic drawers usually found in carpentry shops. Inside each

216 Learning Tools and Skills

drawer are two miniature objects that begin with the same initial sound, such as "doll" and "dog"; or rhyme, such as "bee" and "tree" or "chair" and "bear." Children, working at different times with either initial sound or rhyme, empty a few drawers onto a cloth and sort the objects into the drawers, or remove objects from a drawstring bag and sort them into the drawers. You can find selections of miniature objects in arts and crafts shops or on doll-house websites.

Educators engage in considerable debate concerning the place of phonics instruction within the whole language philosophy, because phonics practice isolates sounds from whole words and meaningful contexts. The *inductive* phonemic games described above, however, use only whole words in *contrasting patterns* within a playful game format. The game format supports children's sense of competence because you invite only some children to engage in those custom-made games that are relevant to them. In this way, you can adapt approaches and activities to different children. [**Procedural note:** Prepare model charts and word cards for each model chart weeks in advance in order to meet the needs of different children.] By the way, if you occasionally isolate a sound, you might still get to heaven if the rest of your life has merit!

The reflections of a pre-service early childhood teacher (M. Schwartz, personal communication) focus on the process of teaching with phonemic games, as follows:

> I've learned that induction is a subtle method of learning that really works. When children are not focused on the reading of words but on the game, they don't notice the learning that is taking place. Reading whole words and remodeling when necessary were sufficient ways of teaching them to read groups of words. The teacher must be careful to see that the children are not simply matching the words instead of reading them. Watching them to see if they make an effort to read each word (with or without the chart) is an important step. If the children are matching, they are not learning by induction. A good way to test for inductive learning is to place some old words in the new lesson and see if the children can read them. If not, see if they can inductively learn how to read them using the chart. The teacher must make sure that a controlled variable is present and that there is enough contrast provided to facilitate learning. I learned this when children were having difficulty with pin–pen (pen–peg would have been better because they provide more visual and auditory contrast). The teacher must remember to remodel as needed.

> Learning is evaluated by noticing the progress the child has made. Is the child easily reading words now that he had difficulty with at the beginning of the lesson? Is the child reading or matching the words? Is the child learning from remodeling? The teacher must ask and answer these questions to determine how much progress is being made. After making such an evaluation, the teacher can decide whether to go on to a more difficult lesson or go back to an easier one.

As this novice teacher describes how she assesses children's skill development by seeing how they play phonemic games, the section below turns to an outline for assessing the overall process of early reading and writing (see also Fountas & Pinnell, 1996; Taberski, 2009).

Assessment of Literacy Development

Kindergarten children demonstrate that they understand content by self-correcting their reading or their miscues to make sense, for example "house" for "home." To do so, they use short-term memory to track cues from before and after the meaning as well as illustrations; the short-term memory reflects an aspect of executive function. You might contribute by asking pre-kindergarten youngsters to anticipate "What might happen next?" "What clues did you get so far?" It is important to remain mindful about the research about children "who develop effective decoding skills and still lag in demonstrating adequate comprehension development" (Allington, 2009, p. 129). In short, do not be satisfied or lulled by decoding alone.

Writing and reading assessment are married. The first step in learning is *recognition*. Writing requires a more complex mental act of *recall*. For example, the invented spelling of young authors shows that they are wedding their early grasp of the phonemic aspect of language with visual representation (see Richgels, 2001, for a research review).

This chapter has discussed many ways in which teachers systematically teach literacy skills to small, flexible groups based upon ongoing assessment. This process also provides opportunities for different children to work together based upon their need and interest. Box 10.11 lists a variety of formats that help teachers assess children's development.

BOX 10.11 CLASSROOM LITERACY ASSESSMENT FORMATS

- Checklist of skills in oral fluency and complexity: e.g., expanding vocabulary and grammatical markers such as articles, prepositions, and adjectives.
- Checklist of skills in print literacy: e.g., understanding the concept of a word; engaging in language-experience/shared writing.
- Written products and phases of writing/drawing [**Procedural note:** Collect samples during the first month of school and compare periodically.]
- Physical coordination samples over time (handwriting).
- Book handling.
- Predicting story meaning from a preview of illustrations and ongoing

---

read-aloud.
- Story retelling with and without props.
- Role-play story after read-alouds.
- Role-play child-created story (see Box 9.5).
- Rubrics for story retelling and writing.
- Miscue record as a sign of reading with comprehension and self-correction; or merely focus on sounding-out—e.g., "monkey" for "mother." [**Procedural note:** You can create running records easily when you photocopy each page, ready for marking (Tompkins, 2011, p. 78).]
- Encourage participation in literature-based computer software.

The writing and story retelling types of products, in themselves, implicitly answer the informational questions of who, where, when, and what happened. In short, you are able to figure out next steps by seeing what children can do with support as well as by understanding the overall process of literacy development. An outline of the phases of literacy development and scaffolds appears in Box 10.12.

BOX 10.12 OUTLINE OF WRITING AND READING PHASES WITH TEACHER SCAFFOLDS

- *Pre-reader.* Reads pictures and talks about them. Recognizes own name and some signs. Explores print by writing signs that resemble English, some random letters, and mainly consonants with invented spelling: for example, "I L D F" (I like the flower), "I SR RAN SM" (I saw a radish stem). *Scaffold:* Invite children to join rhymes in poems/songs. Provide choices of books with one word on each page. Point to words in books or on posters as you read, and say what you are doing. Provide picture–word captions. Educators recommend the following scaffolds: "*Children with motoric challenges* need adequate physical support . . . Sometimes the angle of books and other picture material has to be altered to adapt to the child's line of vision. Paste cardboard tags on pages; Hot-glue popsicle sticks to pages; 'Page fluffers' [transparent adhesive buttons/sponge/weather stripping] create space between pages so the child can turn the pages more easily or with a device such as a pointer" (Nwokah & Gulker, 2006, p. 4). [**Procedural note:** Many pre-kindergarten children are pre-readers. At the end of the school year, you might expect that they will be able to write some degree of invented spelling labels and captions on their drawings.]

- *Emergent reader.* Asks to hear stories read. Youngsters see that print has meaning; increasingly recognize some sight-words, and can read names of some other children as well as classroom print. Their writing transitions from syllabic to alphabetic hypothesis, indicated phonological development: for example, "This is a GORDIN" (GARDEN), "This is a boy PEYE BASCKBALL" (PLAYING BASKETBALL), "ILSAD BY" (ILLUSTRATED BY), "DACASN" (DEDICATION). *Scaffold:* Survey together all pictures in a book before reading. Wonder together about what the book is about. Read aloud lots of predictable books and poetry, pointing to each word—and say what you are doing. [**Procedural note:** Some pre-kindergarten children become emergent readers.]
- *Beginning reader.* Points at words. Reads repetitive patterns and predictable print. Writes increasingly using vowels in words with identifiable spacing of words. *Scaffold:* Describe their accomplishments, focusing on specific strategies. Provide a card (marked on the left as the starting place) under each line of print to assist focus in writing and reading. Offer attractive choices of leveled books with different content as well as lots of repetition and predictability. Few words on each page. [**Procedural note:** If reading miscues show a focus on sound, re-focus on meaning. Some kindergarten children have become beginning readers and are able to write a few related sentences.]
- *Developing reader.* Expanding sight vocabulary with phonological strategies. Uses context clues and focuses on meaning. Writes with clear spacing between words and mainly accurate use of vowels. Looks for conventional spelling in known books and print in classroom. *Scaffold:* Offer attractive choices of short, leveled books with different content, some repetition, predictability, and a few sentences on each page. Describe the strategies they use when they read and write, focusing on meaning. Show "another" way to write, while focusing on model grammar, and have the child author compare the meanings. Children can alphabetize words by the first letter. Find pictures and words that begin with consonant blends: e.g., "drum," "story." A few kindergarten children become developing readers.
- *Independent reader.* Increasingly able to read silently. Reads with understanding, inflection, and some fluency. Writes mainly with conventional spelling and seeks accuracy. *Scaffold:* Offer attractive choices of leveled books with different content and some brief paragraphs. Discuss strategies they use as they read and write, focusing on meaning. Children can alphabetize beyond the first letter. Very few kindergarten children who entered as independent readers develop this fluency.

As you work with young children in language instruction it is important to remember not to expect instant results and to help parents, as well as next year's teacher, appreciate small steps.

The *Common Core Standards for English Language Arts and Literacy in History/Social Studies, Science, and Technical Subjects* (Common Core State Standards Initiative, 2010a) for kindergarteners includes print concepts and phonological awareness. Elements of these standards for speaking, writing, and reading are integrated in this chapter. While blending onset and rime are presented in the section describing phonemic games, the *Core Standards* include isolated sounds and place a stronger emphasis on naming letters of the alphabet.

Reflections

This chapter has discussed four integrated components of a systematic approach to literacy learning and instruction: spoken language, fine-quality children's literature, writing/drawing into reading, and phonemic games. As a tool skill, language develops after *inductive* practice (condition for learning) with meaningful activities. For young children, the practice is physical, social, and rich with meaning. Youngsters are eager to communicate and are curious about how older children and adults manage to write and read. The chapter discussed a variety of activities that can build on children's motives.

The start of early literacy and reading instruction is largely auditory and social. Many legitimate opportunities exist for children to talk to one another and to you in small groups and one to one. For example, children can choose to be members of a writing/drawing or book discussion group because they share in common such an interest as animals or motors, although they may be more or less emergent readers. This kind of format adds to inclusionary practices. For those children who need additional support, the custom-made, playful, inductive phonemic games outlined in this chapter help youngsters learn to decode as they focus on the game.

You can see young children make significant progress in the components of a systematic literacy program that focuses on meaning. With an all-day schedule, children have more time and opportunity to explore and play with language. Although you provide a library center, writing center, and teacher's instructional area, literacy activities also go on in many other areas of the classroom, school, and community. Children's activity-based engagement with Dynamic-Themes adds to their vocabulary and content knowledge and helps them build the meanings that stimulate reasons to read and write. Moreover, activities with the potential to lead to concept development provide plenty of reasons to talk, write, and read about ideas. These occasions provide literacy practice in many forms that can strengthen the *inductive* process that builds toward expanded and fluent literacy skills.

11

LITERACY IN COMPUTERS, DESIGN TECHNOLOGY, AND SCIENCE

Issues and Opportunities

Introduction

Five-year-old Benjie spent a long time transforming two empty, pint-size milk cartons into a truck. After carefully cutting, constructing, connecting, and painting the cartons, he worked on the wheels. He had cardboard disks with a center opening and repeatedly tried to create axles, but was reaching frustration level. His teacher appreciated the care and time that he had invested in the activity and asked him what methods he had tried. While explaining his various attempts, his facial muscles showed increasing tension. At that point, his teacher commented, "You certainly figured out a lot of building problems and thought of some creative ideas. I wonder if you looked at the brass fasteners." He tried the fasteners and beamed when he was able to roll his truck, albeit somewhat unevenly.

Benjie's activity falls within the domain of design technology. His teacher provided scaffolding in order to support his *sense of competence* (condition for learning). This chapter discusses design technology (DT) as a bridge between information and computer technology (ICT) and science education. Children such as Benjie are learning about the physical world from the beginnings of life. Therefore, their scientific literacy today grows within the context of computers and design technology.

In comparison with DT, electronic technologies are increasingly vicarious, including 3-D formats and virtual reality technologies. These developments are likely to influence educational contents and priorities. Therefore, this chapter discusses the nature of ICT and questions that arise today but are likely to be answered in the future as ICT continues to change and evolve. This chapter first talks about ICT, then DT and science education.

Information and Computer Technology

To begin, there are some questions to frame the discussion. Now that there are:

- iPads, iPods, digital books, digital cameras, DVDs, and 3-D video cameras, *will paper books go the way of vellum*? (Broadband is already replacing CD-Rom games (Gee, 2007, p. 96). We can only wonder about the next generation of I-pads and virtual reality technology.)
- E-mail, instant messages, and Twitter, *will the post office continue to dwindle? What might be the future of standard spelling?*
- Cellular phones, *will we see an eclipse of landline phones?* (The number of telephone booths has already declined.)
- Skype communication and interactive whiteboards, *how might geographic borders diminish?*
- Interactive whiteboards (IWBs), *how is the role of the teacher changing?*
- Document readers, *how might disaffected youngsters engage in a sense of community?*
- Assistive technologies, *how might children who have special needs increase communicative competence?* (Voice- and eye-movement activated, image-stabilization technology, and single switch options provide the potential for independence.)
- "Artificial intelligence software [with] motion tracking and speech recognition" (Carey & Markoff, 2010, p. 1), *how might autistic children mimic some social signals?*
- Electronic toys and screen-based media, *how might that impact the function of teachers and classroom organizations? How might virtual pets impact socialization?*
- MP3 players where higher and lower frequencies are missing, *how could children acclimatize to electronic sounds that preclude later expectations and appreciations of live music?* (E. Archer, personal communication, 2010)
- 3-D TV (without glasses) and handheld 3-D devices, *what will that mean for 2-dimensional forms of communication? How might young children solidify their distinction of reality and fantasy?*
- All of the above and future ICT developments, *how much seat-time makes sense for young children?* (Consider the obesity issue.) *What is the balance of large muscle activity, social interaction, and efficient interactive learning with technology?*

Electronic technology, a cultural tool that includes sound and moving images, continues to develop vistas of distance learning and virtual experiences. "Vygotsky argues that children acquire cultural tools through their interactions with the adults and older children that surround them, and use this inheritance to make sense of and act in their world" (Plowman, Stephen, & McPake, 2010, p. 42). Within any culture, however, not all high- or low-income situations are the same (Heath, 1983; Rogoff, Mistry, Goncu, & Mosier, 1993).

Compare the history of technologies before and after the printing press; then the 19th century's "factory line industrial model age" brought recorded voice and music. The later 20th century's "information age" brought video games, computers with interactive conferences, the beginnings of 3-D, and virtual reality technology.

Now, the 21st century's "digital age" expands interactive computers with virtual reality, miniaturization, and expanding access through touch-screen icons/pictures as well as audio controls. At the same time, consider major policies affecting early education. A kind of Luddite movement pushes more rote learning into the lives of younger and younger children. Naive, linear policy pressures increase to speed-up outputs of separate parts in a factory line model reminiscent of the industrial age. It is tough to recognize that many schools for 21st-century young children resemble the 19th-century factory line industrial model, although contemporary culture needs connection-makers.

Each generation wonders how each new technology will affect human behavior and imagination. On the one hand, some question the impact of electronic technologies during the early childhood years and counsel little or no exposure (Sigman, 2008a). On the other hand, others suggest that "What it means to be 'literate' in the digital age is not only about reading and writing but also about solving problems using simulations. What matters in the digital age is not learning to do things a computer can do for you but learning to use the computer to do things that neither you nor it could do alone" (Shaffer, 2006, p. 65). ICT can also serve as a path into learning for the apathetic or hesitant child. Moreover, it is a way for children to move at an individual pace, allowing some particularly creative children to soar (Clements & Sarama, 2003, p. 35).

Current debates might remind you of earlier debates over the impact of comic books and television on book literacy. Instead, you might consider how to maintain important physical and sensorial controls for young children while, at the same time, integrating the reality of electronic technology.

The Grammar of Electronic Technologies

As with socio-dramatic play, each form of communication includes its own grammar, as follows:

* *Books and comic books.* In varying degrees, the *reader interprets* description and *translates* punctuation: for example, "Good night," he said.
* *Radio.* The *listener*, with *sound* effects, *imagines* events: for example: "Don't point that finger at me."
* *Film and television.* The *viewer*, with *sound* and *movement*, needs to learn the conventions of filling in transitions: for example, a person is riding a horse when the scene cuts to that person seated at a table. Our prior knowledge helps us imagine that the person got down from the horse, walked into the house, and sat down.
* *Computers in context.* Computers retain the grammars of earlier communication technologies with the added potential for interactivity and editing: for

example multimedia authoring; collaboration and networking; the potential for personalized short cuts with "bookmarks"; and the potential for virtual trips and 3-dimensional presentations. Virtual field trips save expenses incurred when visiting museums, zoos, and geological sites, and when conducting distant interviews. The industry offers a variety of computer games that provide new ways to manipulate variables in language and mathematical study, as well as multi-media access to multi-sensory information.

It is noteworthy that each new technology changes the focus and mix of sensory participation. Half a century ago, a social scientist identified the impact of television as a change in sensory priorities, and predicted that education in the future would be built around "perceptual models" as a way to organize vast stores of knowledge (McLuhan, 1963). In a compatible way, teachers are able to use Dynamic-Themes to sequence activities so that children have the chance to perceive potential relationships and connect meanings across domains.

Within the limits of research on the human brain, this book is attempting to raise awareness of how young children are able to connect and communicate meanings. Therefore, it helps to understand how much exposure to technology young children bring to school. In the United States, nearly all young children have TV as a household staple. Many pre-kindergarten children use touch-screen iPods, iPads, iPhones, and digital cameras; some use aspects of the Nintendo Wii's interactive software when adults set up the program. Box 11.1 summarizes related research.

BOX 11.1 RESEARCH ON YOUNG CHILDREN'S EXPOSURE TO TECHNOLOGY AT HOME

- 75% of preschoolers live in homes with computers (Gee, 2007, p. 95).
- 66% of pre-kindergarten children use computers.
- 80% of kindergarten children use computers.
- Children on a particular day use the computer mainly for games, for anything from a few minutes to a matter of hours (DeBell & Chapman, 2006).
- Most 3½-year-olds with computers at home are independently able to turn on the computer, point and click the mouse, and load CD-Roms (Calvert, Rideout, Woolard, Barr, & Strouse, 2005, p. 603).

Researchers and educators have different viewpoints about the use of inter-active books. On the one hand, some educators feel that they could extend the electronic-reading of *Just Grandma and Me* software (Hutinger, Bell, Daytner, &

Johanson, 2005, p. 11). For example, some teachers invite grandparents to class; develop class books about grandparents and memories of other family members; and connect the software to other learning centers. You can scaffold a computer book as you would any other book by asking children to compare an episode to their own experiences, to anticipate events, or to role-play.

Educators also suggest that,

> although children's "reading" of the [computer] visuals and their discussions around these may have been different from what we might expect of book-based "reading" of the illustrations, . . . the children were creating meaning from these visuals and animations. This form of "reading" needed to be incorporated into both the teacher's definition of reading and her classroom practice.
>
> *(Turbill, 2001, p. 275, citing Parkes, 2000)*

On the other hand, some educators caution about the addictive quality of radio, TV, and video games (Bruner & Bruner, 2006). Researchers have found that,

> When parents and their 3-year-olds read an electronic console book together, parents spend much of the time trying to control their child's manipulation of the book rather than talking about the story . . . With traditional books, 92% of parents' talk is about the story. Not surprisingly, children understand significantly more about the story when they hear it from a traditional book than when they hear the electronic version . . . Children pick up new vocabulary without even trying, as parents talk about what the child's finger points out. With traditional books, children are not preoccupied with the "bells and whistles" but with following the story narrative, a skill that is crucial for learning and loving to read.
>
> *(Hirsh-Pasek, Golinkoff, Berk, & Singer, 2009, p. 13, citing Storch & Whitehurst, 2001, and Wasik & Bond, 2001)*

However, there is a *digital divide* for *some* children who have less access to computer technology when their parents have less education, less income, and a non-English first language (Calvert, Rideout, Woolard, Barr, & Strouse, 2005; DeBell & Chapman, 2006; Gee, 2007; Judge, Puckett, & Cabuk, 2004; Li, Atkins, & Stanton, 2006; Shore, 2008). At best, low-income families have limited access to computers in libraries or community agencies. Researchers also find that *some* high-income families are less interested and *some* low-income families more enthusiastic about providing ICT experiences for their children (McPake, Plowman, & Stephen, 2010). This last finding is a reminder to remain tentative about generalizations based on socioeconomic situations.

The computer as a communication tool depends upon the encoding and decoding of meaning, and meaning builds from experience. Therefore, teachers help all children acquire meanings across all domains of knowledge and skills. Teachers can use Dynamic-Themes to plan activities that match and scaffold children's past experiences. As with all skills, proficiency needs practice. "Neuroscientists say that repetition helps to reinforce the neuronal connections associated with learning and repetition is something machines are better at than humans" (Shore, 2008, p. 29). At the least, it is useful to identify software and seek ways to modify software that you can customize as you do with other educational games so that children can practice skills in engaging and meaningful ways.

The position paper of the National Association for the Education of Young Children recommends software that children can pace, vary, and control, offering increasing degrees of challenge (NAEYC, 1996, p. 12). Researchers concur, and note the value to youngsters when they can create mathematical transformations on-screen as well as with physical objects (Clements & Sarama, 2003, p. 38; 2009b). Other considerations include egalitarian content and "nonviolent ways to solve problems and correct mistakes" (NAEYC, 1996, p. 14). Researchers also support the need for child control when they find that attention to learning verbal content on the computer was "higher when the adult followed the child's lead for inter-active media" (Calvert, Strong, & Gallagher, 2005, p. 586). Many of these principles are the same as non-electronic teaching principles. On-screen control can parallel real-world game play and pretend play in which children control the action.

Those who resist the notion of electronic technology in pre-kindergarten soon notice that children leave the environment when they feel frustrated by the software. However, when you see a child unsuccessfully try a procedure a few times, you might take the opportunity to scaffold the moment by raising a ques-tion, modeling a new technique, or changing the level of difficulty. In a remarkably similar way, a "smart" online board game, Bring It, builds in a responsive level of challenge based upon each player's performance in order to increase a sense of progress for them (Heffernan, 2010, citing PBSkids.org). High-quality software offers parallel experiences in which players can explore, build models, and role-play (Gee, 2007; Shaffer, 2006). It is worth noting that software, no less than books, can vary in quality.

In order to help all children feel competent and successful, teachers typically try to build community (rather than competition) and problem solving (rather than violence). When children have opportunities to choose (even among software thoughtfully preloaded by you) and have some sense of control (a sense of exploration, playfulness, or reasonable challenge), they are likely to build their skills and conceptual knowledge. It makes sense, in any case, to pay attention to children's play preferences with or without electronic technologies.

Guidelines and Scaffolds When Using Computers

Computers, with or without voice synthesizers and headsets, are resources in many early childhood classrooms. When well integrated, they conform to a number of consistent criteria, represented in Box 11.2. Working with computers in an interactive way, there are times when you might stimulate children's critical–thinking skills and perhaps tickle a sense of self-awareness—for example, by using the question pair "How did you do that?" and "What might you want to do next?"

BOX 11.2 QUESTIONS TO GUIDE SOFTWARE SELECTION FOR COMPUTERS AND INTERACTIVE WHITEBOARDS IN AN INTEGRATED EARLY CHILDHOOD CURRICULUM

- How can children set their own problems and explore alternative ways of solving them? [**Procedural note:** Alternative methods or possible solutions offer opportunities for you to engage in discussion.]
- To what extent are children able to control the pace and content?
- How does the pace help children to focus and think before acting?
- What opportunities support the use of children's imagination?
- When children find problems to solve, what are the opportunities for alternative ways of solving them? How do they have opportunities for critical thinking?
- Which children are "accustomed to 'reading' information from left to right, right to left or up and down?" (Cooper, 2005, p. 295).
- How can children use the technology independently, alone, and with other children? (A cadre model often develops when some children become resources for a particular procedure.) [**Procedural note:** Consider introducing technical procedures to small groups and monitoring them periodically.]
- How does the material add to the children's concrete knowledge base? For example, children can scan their block construction picture onto the computer (Clements & Sarama, 2010).
- Are children having plenty of time for large-muscle movement activities and social interaction?
- How does the experience connect with manipulative materials?
- How does it introduce, demonstrate, or help children learn something worthwhile?
- How does the particular experience help transfer understanding to other situations?
- How are ethical values championed?
- How are visuals and animations integral to story lines?
- How does software content blend with other classroom activities?
- What provisions can you make so that children can feel comfortable with the medium?

- How do girls as well as boys have equal access, so both may gain a sense of comfort in using the computer? With the youngest children, and those with less exposure at home, perhaps comfort and familiarity with the medium are reasonable initial goals.
- Is the software gender-equitable, gender-neutral (AAUW, 2000)?
- How does the software depict cultural diversity and people of different abilities?
- What are the opportunities for cooperative work among children? A computer may invite use by dyads or small groups who are working together on a problem or game, quite as much as with one child serving as the single mouse mover, although others typically look on. Smart boards permit the ease of using a touch-screen, with which more than one child can collaborate actively to share the screen (Plowman, Stephen, & McPake, 2010).
- What meaningful learning can the computer present? On the one hand, the imagery of *indirect progress* (a Dynamic-Theme) can take place when a player might sacrifice a turn in order to make progress in a computer game just as in a board game of checkers. On the other hand, the graphics in a LOGO format might more flexibly represent *indirect progress* than would numerous variations on paper.
- How do you justify the expenditure in relation to other budget needs and priorities? Parental and community views are sometimes persuasive considerations regardless of how you answer this question.

The reverse of guidelines for computer use would be criteria for rejection of software, namely when the software is equivalent to an electronic worksheet which, by its nature, is a test requiring single, correct answers. "Research suggests that most computer-based intervention programs are not effective at raising reading achievement . . . because so many . . . are, literally, worksheets" (Allington, 2009, p. 169). If you want children to practice, then use software that builds in the practice for purposes of playing a game that has some meaning. This criterion parallels the use of criteria for fine-quality literature in order to develop meaningful connections for skills (Neuman, 2010). The standards of national learned societies also support the guidelines mentioned as well as critical, creative, and ethical uses of software.[1]

Many pre-kindergarten children will need your support because they need some ability to identify numerals and differentiate at least a few keys on a keyboard if they are to use a computer independently. You might also need to scaffold by setting up the cursor on the desktop so children can point and click; perhaps provide hand-over-hand support, or simply be nearby.

You can scaffold computer use by color coding the on–off switch and show children how to click and drag the cursor (Plowman, Stephen, and McPake, 2010, pp. 84, 85–86). "Guided interaction" extends scaffolding to planning and intentional teaching as follows:

> *Indirect interaction* includes access, help, modeling, monitoring, planning a balance in curriculum, a range of activities, differentiating instruction, and placement . . . *Direct interaction* includes demonstration, support by your presence, enjoying together, explaining, reading, prompting, providing feedback, modeling, and intervening by taking turns.
>
> *(Stephen & Plowman, 2008, pp. 644, 646)*

Similar outlooks include "immersion with guidance" (Gee, 2007, p. 167) and "guided participation . . . an attempt to keep individual, interpersonal, and cultural processes simultaneously in focus" (Rogoff, Mistry, Goncu, & Mosier, 1993, p. 5). These views are similar to the Zone of Proximal Development (Vygotsky, 1978), and the teacher's role as "mediator" (Feuerstein, Feuerstein, & Falik, 2010).

Children can scaffold each other when they work in pairs. They can be more independent when you place icons on the computer desktop. You can readily assess their attentive or off-task behavior in order to decide when an activity is relevant or appropriate. For example, if you need to remind children to return to a task, you might suspect that the activity is beyond their comprehension, too restrictive, or occurring at the wrong moment.

During center time, two children at a time are able to sign into each computer on a clipboard schedule in the area. Kindergarten children and some younger ones can sign in; most pre-kindergarten children recognize their name and some can place a mark next to their name. Young children are able to engage in some of the activities that appear in Box 11.3.

BOX 11.3 ACTIVITIES WITH ELECTRONIC TECHNOLOGY

- *Electronic toys.* Pre-kindergarten children are able to press a numeral in order to move a vehicle a particular number of spaces. [**Procedural note:** When you tape vehicle lengths on the floor, children can plan and count the number of lengths that the vehicle travels.] Some toys require a player to press a green "go" button to begin a page with audible words and music (see LeapPad Learning Systems, 2003).
- *Physical activity software.* Players might follow increasingly complex directions and touch a dance mat or interact with the screen on Nintendo's WiiFit.

- *iPod Touch and iPhone.* Kidpix version 4 downloads to iPods. Some pre-kindergarten children are able to touch and drag an icon in order to interact with a song in English or another language, animate items, or record a song such as *Wheels on the Bus* by Duck Duck Moose (http://childrenstech.com).

- *Digital cameras and video cameras as teaching devices.* An electronic historical record provides imagery that sticks, long after isolated bits of information fade (*revisiting*, a condition for learning). The documentation serves to organize isolated, discrete moments in time (see Edwards, Gandini, & Forman, 1998; Worth & Grollman, 2003). It is noteworthy that stability regulation in some cameras can help someone whose hand trembles.

- *Computer graphics.* Graphics and clip art can augment a child's own drawing and writing. [**Procedural note:** An adult or older child usually needs to open and close the program.] Pre-kindergarteners are able to use such programs as Kidpix, Crayola Make a Masterpiece, and Paint to develop their own graphics, perhaps after hearing a related story. Some kindergarten children are able to use graphics and story-making software, such as Kidpix Studio 3.

- *Photo journals.* Children can scan their drawings and writing into the computer. They take delight in sharing their work. Not only do the creators feel accomplished, but other children feel motivated to look at the products. Along with related graphics, "this method can be especially satisfying for children with fine motor disabilities because it can compensate for imprecise fine motor skills" (Bergen, 2008, p. 94). A variation of journals is PETS, a Personal Electronic Teller of Stories (Druin, 1999). It is a collaboration between adults and children who design a storytelling environment that uses robots the children can control. Also, older children can serve as e-buddies and help to post work on a school district's website.

- *Documentation.* Software such as HyperStudio and BuildAbility includes flexible features that help children customize their drawings and writings. Children feel motivated to read their "classroom books" when the interactive process is meaningful and collaborative. Another software product, Kidpix Deluxe 4, provides a range of interactive flexibility, bilingual English/Spanish capacity, and support in documentation for portfolios. Educators also consider these features easy to use and "ideal for working with children with special needs or utilizing a theme-based curriculum" (Center for Best Practices in Early Childhood Education, 2007).

- *Interactive literature-based software.* Some books on the computer make it possible to highlight text, change the text color, or animate illustrations in order to focus attention. Some books are read aloud in a language other than English. Riverdeep Living Books Library (http://www.river deep.net.products/livingbooks/index.jhtml) offers selections from among early childhood mainstays as well as other software.

- *Computer games and interactive computer games.* Many traditional board and card games now have computerized versions on the Internet. In addition, games software can offer some authentic situations, enabling children to use their imaginations and learn about different subjects without memorizing facts out of context. Players learn and remember information in order to play the game. For example, a game for advanced kindergarteners is Zoo Tycoon, where players can own and run a zoo, purchase animals, build exhibits, cater to visitors, design environments, solve problems, and expand activities (Shaffer, 2006, p. 6).

- *English language learners.* To support English language learners, there is a database of interactive games, translators, songs, rhymes, books, listening activities, pronunciation, vocabulary, games, puzzles, videos and more (http://www.everythingesl.net). Translation programs on the Web include Babelfish and Google Translator (Skeele & Russo, 2009).

- *Internet research.* Kindergarteners with their teacher "used the Internet to research an animal, and then used the computer to draw the animal. Then they used the computers to record short story voice-overs" (McHenry, 2010).

- *Interactive conferences and exchanges.* Interactive technology permits classes to see and speak with one another in real time. In addition, there is a website that posts children's work, KidPub (http://www.kidpub.org/kidpub/). [**Procedural note:** As with all such interaction, teachers plan together with one another and with their children in order to reduce waiting time and to assure focused, fine-quality interchanges.]

As you plan, think about the different experiences with computers that children have at home. Some have no access. In contrast, the access of one middle-class 5-year-old to electronic technology is impressive (S. Popovchak, personal communication, 2010). The 5-year-old uses an X-Box, PlayStation, and Nintendo DS; DVD player; iPod; digital camera; electronic toys and musical instruments. Among her computer games are Leapfrog for Kids; Jumpstart for Kids; and television-related sources from Nickleodeon; Noggin; and PBSkids. Some of the games she plays include Build a Bear; Dora the Explorer; Cooking Mama; Imagine Teacher; Brain Age; Daily Training Sweet Life; Battleship; Sorry; and Wii

Bowling and Singing-along. (Other software that is popular with young children includes Edmark, Sunburst, Broderbund, and Scholastic products.)[2]

You will need to resolve the ongoing issues of how to use time; select quality software; and provide access to technology. It is important to keep in mind that the number of computer software choices, no less than books, continues to grow. The Center for Best Practices in Early Childhood (2007) at Western Illinois University provides detailed reviews about a range of software interactivity that relate to content, design, and usability (http://www.wiu.edu/itlc/). Internet sites also deal with just about every topic you and your children might wish to pursue. *It is important to limit the time for vicarious activities so that young children can continue to develop their 3-dimensional constructions and social interaction.* The discussion below about IWBs extends this subject.

The Computer as an Interactive Electronic Whiteboard (IWB)

Some researchers suggest that computers are less useful for pre-kindergarten than IWBs that use touch controls (Plowman, Stephen, & McPake, 2010). Children who use the computer need to coordinate the mouse and cursor. One child controls the mouse. One or more other children become onlookers and could comment, but the screen has limited visibility. With the IWB, using touch alone, more than one child can participate at the same time and together create a construction or play a game.

Some teachers and children engage in *choral reading* with an IWB. When you project a poem or song on the board, you can point to each word as you do on a paper poster or reveal one word at a time. You can also easily engage in a rhyme "trick" by changing a letter or word. After demonstrating how to do it, invite children to suggest alternative rhymes. In a similar way, kindergarten children can play with changing a phoneme in simple words, as they might do with cards, magnetic letters, or felt board letters: for example, they transform "cat" to "fat" to "hat" to "mat."

You can model the use of the Internet to locate information, photographs, videos, and games with an IWB. IWBs already make possible virtual trips to wild animal reserves and aspects of the cycle of food production services; and children who live in the plains can enjoy virtual visits to mountains and see other climatic conditions.

IWBs offer the possibility for social networking, including real-time communication with applications such as Skype. When available and carefully planned by the teachers, children are able to show each other work products, including role-plays. Teachers and children can view the same read-aloud session and teachers can learn from one another.

Other issues to consider are the following:

1. sequence of technical skills—the touch-screen can be an assistive device for children with special needs (Plowman, Stephen, & McPake, 2010; Cooper, 2005);

2.   degree and amount of adult tutoring in use of the electronics;
3.   type of software content;
4.   sequence of concepts within the software; and
5.   degree and amount of necessary adult support.

The issue of content is significant. At home, for example, many 4-year-old boys play computer games with violent content that demand speed, accuracy, and competition. At school, teachers typically try to build community (rather than competition) and problem-solving skills (rather than violence) in order to help all children feel competent and successful. A general goal is to develop concepts and skills in ways that challenge but do not frustrate children. Thus, all children would have the chance to learn how to use the equipment for educative purposes, with comfort and fluency.

Assistive Technology and Assistance

Assistive technology could help children with disabilities in a number of ways when you match the device to the needs of each child. These devices offer children opportunities to build more independence, self-regulation, and participation in the classroom community.

Notice how many switches a child would need to use and the physical demands of the type of switch or the body part—such as a finger, foot, or nose—that an individual would need in order to activate a switch. Helpful devices include electronic items such as "voice synthesizers, Braille readers, switch-activated toys . . . [as well as] low-tech tools . . . for example, special handles on utensils and paint brushes, or a handle attached to a stuffed animal, allow a child to grasp without help. Pillows and bolsters make it easy to interact with peers during circle time" (Mulligan, 2003, p. 1; also includes details of related websites). There are some low-tech stability devices to help children draw and play games, such as page turners for books (a piece of sponge or felt); high-tech adaptive devices, such as switches, touch-screens, IntelliKeys; and specialized software (Skeele & Russo, 2009). For example, Swype permits fingers to slide from letter to letter instead of striking them, and ThickButtons enlarges needed keys as you go.

While technology might ease interactions with other children, "it can provide well-structured tasks that are always individualized and offer appropriate, patient feedback, and also provide exploratory and language experiences . . . It can help teachers work with and track children's progress on Individualized Education Programs" (Clements & Sarama, 2003, pp. 35, 38–39).

Scholars also suggest that children with learning difficulties can benefit from the use of ICT because it helps them to focus on activities (Skeele & Russo, 2009). Pre-kindergarten children with and without disabilities can benefit from an emergent literacy technology approach (Hutinger, Bell, Daytner, & Johanson, 2005). "An emergent literacy approach stresses that written and oral language develop concurrently and interrelatedly from birth . . . [It is] 'purposeful' [and] interactive with others" (Neuman, 2001, p. 4). *Although children comfortably integrate interactive, meaningful, literature-based software, researchers do not recommend using computers for isolated drill and letter practice.*

As technology becomes more miniaturized, diversified, and faster, young children as well as adults find that the way things work becomes increasingly less visible. However, when children interact with other children during socio-dramatic play and 3-dimensional constructions, they build the distinction between play and reality (Bateson, 1972). Therefore, these electronic contexts challenge early childhood educators to consider what other resources to provide, to whom, and when. Therefore, the next sections of this chapter explore related issues about hands-on design technology (engineering) as well as the place of science education.

Reflections on Interactive Computer Technology

We continue to hear both concerns about and acclaim for the use of ICT with young children (see McCarrick & Ming, 2007). A commonsense outlook suggests that ICT is part of today's culture and a tool that deserves the same attention as any other. At the same time, it makes sense to keep perspective and retain the important 3-dimensional activities with concrete materials that young children's brains require in order to develop fully.

On the one hand, for young children, this means keeping a clear and whole-some level of challenge which will differ among individuals. It means

- having hardware that is part of a classroom center for use during an activity period;
- selecting applications and software that fit the criteria of quality for any literature or games that you value;
- providing ongoing attention to the progress and socialization that take place in this center as you do in other classroom centers; and
- finding ways to collaborate with children to represent their experiences with new media.

On the other hand, computers—no less than other formats—are opportunities to expand and represent the learning of skills and concepts. Researchers tell us what is possible. Our job is to learn what children can teach us they need by observing and interacting with them. We continue to assess what children can do and need to learn, scaffold with next steps, and differentiate instruction.

Children view technology as prestigious and feel motivated to persevere because they see older children and adults with mobile e-technologies. At the same time, we need to be cautious not to blur the line between children's and adults' play with the media, and push children beyond their childhood.

The speed of technology does not mean that young children need to be speeded up by policy that dictates getting children "up to speed." Time compression might take place behind us but it need not detract from savoring the moment and providing enriched, deep, and caring experiences for young children—experiences that will actually get children up to speed, at their varied paces. Design technology, discussed in the next section, is a domain in which children can continue to be fully active learners at their varied paces.

Design Technology as 3-Dimensional Engineering

Is a technician connecting your new flat-screen television? Are carpenters framing a new building in your neighborhood? Children (and adults) enjoy seeing how they work, how the job progresses, and what the results look like, as well as what the tools, machines, and products can do.

The "industrial arts" of the electrician, carpenter, architect, and engineer form part of the DT process. DT activities counter the magical quality of invisible processes. DT as 3-dimensional engineering marries the arts and science. Children have opportunities to figure out how things work and how they can create them. For example, block building is a model of DT as youngsters build enclosures or mazes for their class pet. Battery and light bulb constructions as well as simple forms of Lego Robotics can help kindergarten children construct electrical power connections. DT begins in the 3-dimensional and 2-dimensional arts and con-structions. It also helps to make science more visible for young children.

Woodworking

Among the variety of industrial arts, *woodworking* is a part of early education. Pre-kindergarten children are able to engage in woodworking successfully. When you judge that children are following safe classroom routines and traffic patterns after several months in school, you could begin to open a carpentry center. Woodwork is prestigious and certainly a privilege that can be available only to those children who show that they can use the tools safely. [**Procedural note:** Woodwork should be in a space separate from traffic in order to house a maximum of two children who are able to work safely with a close adult presence.]

Children are able to plan verbally and sketch a plan for their woodworking. A minimal provision of items for woodworking includes soft pine wood, a strong vise, large-head nails, adult-size hammers and crosscut saws, sandpaper on blocks, glue, a ruler, pencil, paper, and goggles. [**Procedural note:** Adult-size tools are easier to use because their weight and size help children achieve more balance and control as they work.] Children learn to hold the hammer near the end of the handle and move from the shoulder; they learn to apply leverage when they extract a nail with the hammer. Children learn that they need to draw the saw across the wood, held in a vise, toward themselves several times in order to establish a groove. Then they can learn to apply a light, downward, rhythmic motion to saw the wood.

It is noteworthy that the American Association for the Advancement of Science advocates the use of tools within the broader scope of materials suitable for design technology during the early years (AAAS, 2009, p. 278). When children use tools, they have direct experiences with the principles of physics. As with other acquired skills, some children will need more direct help than others.

In the beginning, children are quite content to hammer large-headed nails into a block of soft wood. [**Procedural note:** You will see which children need you to start hammering the nail into the wood so that they can continue.] Later, when they use more wood pieces of varying sizes, they face the problem of finding just the right size of nail to hold the pieces together. If you have precut wooden wheels and dowels, you create another reason for children to measure carefully in order to attach the wheels so that they will turn together. They need to measure lengths of wood that can help them execute their plans, however simple they may be. Although pre-kindergarten children usually build up or out with woodworking, some will begin to create enclosures. Consider the parallel pathways of block building, discussed in Chapter 4.

Offer children dignity and respect for their work. For example, you can provide sandpaper so that they can make a smooth product. [**Procedural note:** Sandpaper is easier to use when it is tacked to a hand-sized block of wood or attached to a commercial sandpaper holder.] Another way to show valuing of their products is to have a nail-set available to sink nails below the surface of the wood, creating a finished look. Children sometimes like to paint their work. You might also consider displaying finished pieces on a colored-paper or cloth background.

Other Media

Wood is one medium for design technology. Looking at other media might suggest some ideas for design and construction. At different times, and at just the right moment, other materials might include craft sticks; pipe cleaners; wire coat hangers; hoops; toothpicks; drinking straws; cardboard; paper bags; paper plates; string; rope; socks; materials for stuffing; small boxes; colored vinyl tape; glue; Styrofoam; plasticene; Crayola Model Magic; cloth; buckram; felt; weaving and sewing materials; rolled-up newspapers; simple machines; wires, batteries, switches and small light bulbs; and Lego Robotics. Box 11.4 provides some examples of DT activities which young children are able to use.

BOX 11.4 EXAMPLES OF DESIGN TECHNOLOGY ACTIVITIES

- *Hats.* Children enjoy designing and constructing hats for classroom toys or for the pleasure of creating a joyful product for their own use.
- *Puppets.* They design and create puppets using paper plates, paper bags, and stuffed socks.
- *Masks.* They solve the problems of designing, trying on, and decorating masks. Inspiration for mask-making might come from hearing stories and thinking about costumes in relation to global holidays, as well as a teacher returning from Mardi Gras with an assortment of masks.
- *Airplanes and other vehicles.* Children use slotted cardboard as well as wood, using nails and/or glue, to design and build airplanes or trucks, inspired by extended study of transportation or a trip to the local supermarket in relation to a study of the food cycle.
- *Mobiles and built-up sculpture (stabiles).* Children create and decorate mobiles from coat hangers, hoops, and other items, using wires and tape. They also design, glue, and then paint collections of small boxes, cardboard cylinders, wood scraps, and/or rolled-up newspapers. They face challenging problems with balance as well as design and texture. Teachers also challenge different children with the problem of using the same number of items, such as tongue depressors or craft sticks, to create different glued sculptures. Stabile constructions built from a clay or Styrofoam base with interesting collections of clean junk provide opportunities for children to experiment with various materials, including plastic drinking straws. Kindergarten children are able to solve the balance problems of creating a stand-up flag with drinking straws and plasticene (J. Johnson, 2003).
- *Cooperative rug weaving.* Using a large homemade loom, kindergarten children take turns designing, selecting, and using lengths of yarn and rope, strips of cloth, and crepe paper to complete a colorful wall hanging with which to decorate their block-building area.
- *Habitats.* Children are able to design houses to protect story characters (Hetland, Winner, Veenema, & Sheridan, 2007).
- *Insulation.* Children enjoy trying a variety of methods and materials to wrap ice cubes in order to keep the ice cold for longer periods of time. Pre-kindergarteners notice that more ice takes longer to melt than less ice. Notice how this observation might build toward a sense of measuring time.
- *Pulley system.* Kindergarteners are able to work out ways to set up a classroom pulley system with a basket and figure out the limits of transporting objects and messages across the classroom.

- *Bridge building.* Children use uncooked spaghetti and adhesives to replicate bridges.
- *Simple machine exploration.* Children enjoy dismantling simple machines, such as an old wind-up clock, cassette player; or small household appliances, such as a spray mister or food grinder (Prairie, 2005, pp. 285–287). [**Procedural note:** Maintain a separate container with a photograph and label for each machine.]
- *Ramps and pathways.* Children build ramps for specific purposes, using different inclines and materials as they explore distance and speed. Box 6.5 includes a detailed discussion of ramps.
- *Domino happenings.* Kindergarten children can plan constructions that build on one another and create an aesthetic collapse as a finale.
- *Lego Mindstorms Robotic Kit.* Kindergarten children who use this kit "[learn] about physics, math and engineering concepts" (Bers, 2008, pp. 110, 111). They also build "their own town and . . . a bus stop at each house. Along the way they [learn] cartography, [practice] their budding reading and writing skills and [have] animated discussions about friction [and forces] . . . and design optimisation to improve the performance of their buses" (Erwin, Cyr, & Rogers, 2000, pp. 188, 181).

It is fair to say that when children design meaningful robotic projects, they can connect concrete objects and ideas with computers. In general, DT inquiry projects grow naturally out of children's questions. You have only to keep your eye on their activities and catch their questions. Then you have an opportunity to help them plan and locate the materials they need in order to launch their inquiry projects.

Although not presented as such, many inquiry projects of varied duration culminate with representations that could include DT constructions. For example, educators report that youngsters are able to plan, design, and build their own versions of a letter carrier's mail bag, a hospital, a movie theater, and a giant butterfly rendering (Helm, Beneke, & Steinheimer, 2007). Children's interest and motivation provide the impetus for these representations along with their drawing and writing. Before-and-after Web graphics can serve to document the children's development of related knowledge.

Three-dimensional collages are also part of the continuum of DT. Art educators recommend demonstrating the use of tape

to make the paper stand up and connect to other paper, but the rest is up to the children. All sorts of great things happen: Hats, forts, houses, and jewelry suddenly appear. Some learners spend most of the class punching holes in the paper and trying out brass fasteners. New tools are exciting and deserve practice.

(Douglas & Jaquith, 2009, pp. 68–69)

Arrange for youngsters to share their construction products as well as processes with classmates, other classes, and families. Photographs that document the process and product lend themselves to binding into a class book that circulates to families. Include an introductory statement about the significance of these projects.

DT also can be a hook into learning for the apathetic or hesitant child. Children can move at their own paces. Many play themes that children represent in their socio-dramatic and construction play serve as a basis for extended project development with a well-paced, thoughtful teacher scaffold (see Fromberg, 2002, for a variety of children's play themes). For example, you might ask, "What would you like to find out about . . .?" "Should we visit a farm or a bakery first?" The follow-ups to field trips often lend themselves to DT constructions.

Putting Design Technology in its Place

Technology does not replace existing modes of learning. Teachers use technology to extend and expand learning options, for example with film clips, to interact with children in other classes, or to videotape children's work and actions.

When you integrate technology, you employ the same conditions for early learning that include 3-dimensional activity, construction, and further inquiry, representation, and communication. A learned society recommends "higher-order thinking skills," including the ability to:

- Demonstrate creativity and innovation
- Communicate and collaborate
- Conduct research and use information
- Think critically, solve problems, and make decisions
- Use technology effectively and productively

(ISTE, 2007, p.1)[3]

Another learned society supports this statement: "Where possible, [children] should be encouraged to improve their ideas, but it is more important that they develop confidence in their ability to think up and carry out design projects. When their projects are complete, students can tell what they like about one another's designs" (AAAS, 2009, p. 36).

Socio-cultural issues surface in DT studies. In particular, girls are under-represented in science, technology, engineering, and mathematics (STEM) studies. In an attempt for all children to have equivalent aspirations, there are some ideas to influence broader participation in STEM fields, beginning with perceptions of young children. Among conscious efforts, you might provide some of the following opportunities:

> Hang posters that show a variety of people doing math and science in interesting ways . . . Bring in people from the business world or local universities, especially women, to educate students about the opportunities in STEM fields . . . Have [children] . . . explore what they are good at instead of following stereotypes.
>
> *(Ullman, 2010, pp. 1, 6)*

In addition, label children "scientists, physicists, astronomers, chemists, geologists, biologists, mathematicians, and geographers" as well as "authors" and "artists" in the context of classroom activities.

Reflections on Design Technology Education

Now that there is an increasing "transition" to a digital era, it is particularly relevant to consider the foundation of STEM to rest in 3-dimensional experiences. Youngsters need experiences that build the images and knowledge to help them understand how the world works. Beyond preparation to participate in a digital world, children have the opportunity to experience some degree of control over their environment when they can thoughtfully manipulate concrete objects. The feeling of control also helps children to build the self-regulation that contributes to being a civilized participant in community life.

Activity-centered Science Education

Early science education builds out of young children's curiosity and sense of wonder. Science studies include biological (life), physical (physics and chemistry), and geological (earth and space) sciences. The learning standards of science organizations emphasize the *transfer* of knowledge, which is similar to the mathematical standard of understanding quantitative *relationships*. Science inquiry is described throughout earlier chapters and parts of this book, particularly the Dynamic-Themes in Part II which integrate opportunities for children to learn about the physical world along with using their language, mathematical, and artistic literacy skills.

You might raise the matter of enough time to teach science as an inquiry process when literacy and mathematical skills are the emphasis of standardized test scores and national core standards. You might perceive that some administrators are rushing these limited skills achievements. However, young children are highly motivated to study, measure, calculate, draw, write, and read about the biological, physical (physics and chemistry), and geological world. Their scientific literacy knowledge and other literacy skills grow as you share their wonder, and respect their questions and theories. There are more than enough direct experiences for learning throughout the day—consider the block-building area, among others—whether or not labeled as science, technology, or mathematics. There are many opportunities for you to provide verbal harmony in the form of descriptions, and to raise thoughtful questions. For youngsters who are learning English, the activity orientation of science study helps to build a concrete focus for language development because children can connect vocabulary with events.

When you create a center that serves as a science laboratory, you add a focus to the ongoing integrated study of science and technology, as is shown in Box 11.5.

BOX 11.5 THE SCIENCE LABORATORY: CHANGING THE FOCUS OF CONTENTS

- *Physical world contents*, e.g., magnets, transparent water containers, eye droppers, funnels, pulleys, levers, simple machines (some educators recommend recycled liquid bottles with pumps (Chalufour & Worth, 2005, p. 19) and transparent pipes (Brooks, 2011; Worth & Grollman, 2003), sponges and paper towels.
- *Biological world contents*, e.g., plants, cuttings, seeds, seedlings, sea shells, spray bottles, insects and animal life, a mirror.
- *Geological world contents*, e.g., sand, rocks of different texture, hardened lava, balance scales, flashlight, and magnifying lenses.
- *Objects* to manipulate, explore, use playfully, compare, sort, and classify.
- *Measurement tools*, e.g., rulers, a variety of timers, measuring cups, and a stethoscope.
- *A table, chairs*, enough for six to eight children, and storage shelves that set off the area.
- *Writing materials*, including graph paper, clipboards, and relevant nonfiction trade books.
- *A sign* to identify the area as the science laboratory.
- *Safety accessories*, such as non-latex gloves and goggles.
- *Picture- and word-task cards.*

Science studies, including DT and ICT, become activity-based learning experiences when everyone uses the tools of the scientists. For example, while all sciences use measurement tools, physicists measure how objects move through space and time; while biologists and geologists also measure changes and use classification systems.

Scientific inquiry for young children often begins with observations that stimulate questions; this parallels the nature of *exploration*, finding out what things can do. The next step includes studying what happens when some change takes place; this parallels the nature of *play*, finding out what you can do. Indeed, scholars suggest this general sequence of scientific inquiry (Brooks, 2011; Chalufour & Worth, 2003; Kamii & DeVries, 1993; Lansdown, Blackwood, & Brandwein, 1971). When you make intentional plans for science education, you understand the value of building on children's many implicit, prior experiences in nature. "Young . . . students are likely to profit from study in areas in which their personal, prior experience with the natural world can be leveraged to connect with scientific ideas" (Duschl, Schweingruber, & Shouse, 2007, p. 119). The sections that follow discuss biology, chemistry, and physics education, in turn.

Understanding Biology (Life Sciences) as Classification

Consider a possible field trip outdoors or a nature study indoors (Chalufour & Worth, 2003). The synthesis of methods in science inquiry suggests a line of questions—consistent with the integrated conditions for learning in early childhood that were discussed in Chapter 3. Some questions that can help to focus a life science field trip are the following:

- What do you know about [plant/insect/animal]?
- Where might we look for them? What might we see?
- What do you see? Who saw something else? What questions do we have?
- What might we do to find out? What might be some other ways?
- What might we find later on from looking at books and Internet sources?
- How could we record with drawing/writing/photography?

At a time when many children's outdoor activities are limited (Louv, 2005; Rivkin, 2006), it is particularly important to include nature study, even if just beyond the classroom. It is noteworthy that one psychologist adds *Naturalist Intelligence* to the list of multiple intelligences that also includes: *Musical* (right brain), *Bodily-Kinesthetic* (motor cortex, each hemisphere, opposite sides), *Logical-Mathematical* (frontotemporal lobes for logical deduction; visuospatial for areas in parieofrontal for numerical calculation); *Linguistic* (Broca's brain; grammar; left cerebral cortex for right-handed); *Spatial* (posterior right cerebral cortex); *Interpersonal* (frontal lobe; problem solving); and *Intrapersonal* (lower area of frontal lobe) (Gardner, 2006).

As we think about biological concepts, we need to keep in mind that humans can perceive things most clearly when two features—movement and contrast—are present. (These features are components of *induction*, a condition for learning) Among these conditions, consider that a contrast is structural—for example, an unknown figure set against a known background, where the unknown figure represents a new single variable. By the same token, consider that movement is functional.

For example, when there is a sufficient contrast between the figure and ground structures, children can perceive the interrelation of these structures as movement. For biologists, function and structure are undergoing continual change and self-regulation because they are both processes: "What are called structures are slow processes of long duration, functions are quick processes of short duration" (Bertalanffy, 1960, p. 134). Regulator genes, for example, function as "stable, self-consistent patterns" (Waldrop, 1992, p. 107). Making these processes explicit for yourself can help you plan activities so that children can learn about biology. In effect, from their perspective, children experience contrasts between figure and ground, between slower and quicker phenomena.

Among the major concepts in biology are life changes, adaptation, and variety; these are broad categories that suggest many types of activity. The purpose of this section is to share some of the approaches and activities that represent these categories in the form of experiences to which young children can be receptive. Figure 11.1 provides a conceptual planning map for using the concepts in biology instruction.

Box 11.6 presents several criteria you might use to decide which activities fit the children in your class.

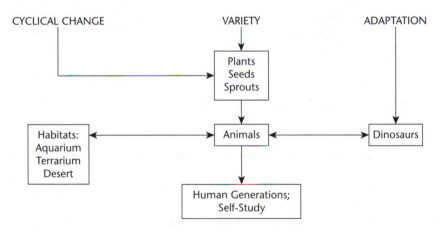

FIGURE 11.1 Conceptual Planning Map in Biology

BOX 11.6 CRITERIA FOR SELECTING BIOLOGY ACTIVITIES

- *Gregariousness.* Which processes or concepts can you investigate with the most gregarious activities? More gregarious activities help children suggest and generate possible ties with other related activities.
- *Appeal.* Which activities are the most exciting and attractive to pursue?

For example, it is ridiculous to initiate a study of snakes or mealworms if they make your stomach dance. Hatching chicks, guinea pigs, hermit crabs, peeper frogs, or fish provide equivalent opportunities to study growth concepts.

- *Resources.* For which activities do you have the most ideas, materials, and resources?
- *Receptivity.* In which directions do your children show greatest interest and capacity?
- *Opportunities to participate.* What opportunities might help different children participate with different degrees of involvement and commitment?
- *Representativeness.* Which activities most clearly represent an underlying Dynamic-Theme or part of a Dynamic-Theme? (See Chapter 5.)

Seeds and Sprouts You can collect seeds, including those in fruits and vegetable snacks. Wheat berries, mung beans, rice, and lima beans are other seeds you might collect. Children can use them on separate occasions in some of the ways outlined in Box 11.7.

BOX 11.7 ACTIVITIES WITH SEEDS

- *Classify* seeds according to one contrasted variable at a time, such as texture (rough/smooth), color (green/yellow), shape (curved/pointed), or size.
- *Create collage patterns* with seeds. Children can write or dictate descriptions of the products.
- For peas, *predict* the number of seeds in a handful of pods, shell them, and list how many you find in your set of pods, the largest number and the smallest number in a single pod, and the most frequent number.
- Notice any *symmetrical patterns* when you open the fruits and vegetables, and chart which seeds were or were not aligned symmetrically.
- You can offer *a collection of other objects that look like seeds* and ask, "What might these be?" "How do we know they are seeds?" "How do we know they are not seeds?" "How might we find out?" Accept all responses. Children might plant the various samples. **[Procedural note:** Attach a sample item to a stick with transparent tape so that it stands in the soil

or plastic bag where you planted the sample. Transparent bags and cups permit careful observation of changes.]
- *Predict* how many days it might take the seed to sprout.
- Create a class *Growing History Book* to which children add their drawings, dictation, and invented spelling.
- *Scaffold.* Describe events that take place in context, modeling vocabulary such as seeds, pollen, roots, stems, flowers, and stamens; symmetrical; and textures.

With any plants, it is important to vary such elements as water, heat, light, and plant food, *one at a time.* It is also relevant, for example, to *predict* what might happen when adding water alone or water *and* plant food, with all other variables remaining the same. When you control one variable at a time, children are able to construct their learning. Box 11.8 describes some ways to vary growth conditions on separate occasions that create *surprise/cognitive dissonance* (condition for learning). Predict and compare findings for each variable condition.

BOX 11.8 COMPARE CONDITIONS TO VARY SPROUT GROWTH WITH SURPRISES

- *Medium.* Grow seeds in water, dry soil, damp soil, as well as on a paper towel or a sponge. [**Procedural note:** Tape clear plastic bags that contain wet paper towels and mung beans or lima beans on the window.] Predict and chart predictions about sprouting time at the start and compare findings.
- *Distance.* Plant seeds in soil close together and farther apart.
- *Depth.* Vary how deeply you plant the seeds. Measure and record.
- *Location.* Place some plants in the dark and others on a sunny window sill.
- *Direction.* Using two transparent containers, plant several seeds in the usual way, but turn one container on its side and another upside down.
- *Moisture.* Vary the amount and frequency of watering, and keep a record with the children.
- *Nutrition.* Give some or no plant food.
- *State.* Predict and see what happens when you plant half a seed, a frozen green pea, or a raw green pea.
- *Measure.* Predict, compare, and measure the growth of different sprouts under each condition. Begin with nonstandard, then use standard measures.

> • *Record.* Use a chart to represent the findings. Label and date each variable. Photograph early and later.
>
> [**Procedural note:** It takes less time and management effort, and creates more in-depth discussion, when you work with a group of four–six children at a time.]

It helps to focus *surprise/cognitive dissonance* when you study one condition of growth at a time. Whichever activities you decide to use, keep in mind that the major purpose is to keep open the questions, the wonder, the imagination, and the excitement, rather than to provide a predigested set of statements for children to hear and repeat. *In this way, they will learn more about how plants grow and function, along with the rich vocabulary that you use during activities.*

Animals   Caring for animals creates an opportunity for children to learn about safety as well as to develop feelings of responsibility, nurture, and reverence for life. Box 11.9 outlines related activities.

BOX 11.9 ANIMAL STUDY ACTIVITIES

- *Measuring* the girth and length and/or weighing a young animal every two weeks for about two months is an exciting survey activity. [**Procedural note:** If your school has limited resources, perhaps you can exchange aquariums, terrariums, animals, and findings with another class, and revisit them later in the year.]
- Children can compile *class books of drawings* while observing animal growth. As they talk about their observations and drawings in small groups, they can build perspective-taking skills. [**Procedural note:** Children's drawings provide a way to assess what they understand.]
- Children document field trips that focus on animals or insects with digital photography and clipboard drawing and tallying; and add shared writing when they return to the classroom.
- Children *classify* elements in the aquarium according to their own criteria, including the following:
  - living things (plants, animals); nonliving things (water, a liquid; a pebble, a solid); once-living things that are no longer alive (waste products);
  - large and small objects;

- • slow-moving and fast-moving things;
- • animals that have fins or shells.
- Some kindergarten children can *classify* and *compare* the breathing rates as a fish moves its gills. They can compare their findings with the breathing rates of other classroom pets as well as humans.
- Children with an interest in dinosaurs enjoy *classifying* their different limb structures, teeth, and running capacities of vegetarian as opposed to flesh-eating dinosaurs. One knowledgeable group even *voted* for their favorite dinosaur. (Children's fascination with dinosaurs is an example of how emotional and aesthetic concerns influence motives for cognitive attention. They can deal with the subject of dinosaurs both playfully and for purposes of classification within the context of their own imagery.)
- *Computer software.* Kidpix Deluxe 4 software offers the flexibility to select and integrate "habitat backgrounds, animals or insects, and plants or objects for a particular habitat"; pairs or groups of children can integrate, revise, and print their drawings, written work, and photographs (Center for Best Practices in Early Childhood Education, 2007). Pre-kindergarten children enjoy software products that also include books, such as Sammy's Science House and the Magic School Bus. (See also Box 5.1.)

Box 11.10 describes a few adapted measurement ideas to suggest to children.

BOX 11.10 MAINLY MEASUREMENT CHALLENGES

- • Measure, with string, your height, width, and girth.
- • Measure the distance between your knee and the ground.
- • Measure the length of your cubit (elbow to middle fingertip).
- • Compare the length of your left and right feet.
- • Count how many beads, pegs, or other objects you can pick up in your right hand. What about your left hand?
- • How much water can you displace in a transparent container with each hand in turn immersed to the wrist? [**Procedural note:** Mark the water line with tape before and after the immersion.]
- • Kindergarten children can briefly tally their wrist pulse or heartbeat with a stethoscope.
- • Compare the different hair colors of people in the classroom, as relevant.
- • What colors can you see at the greatest distance?

- What colors can you see in the dark? What difference does sunlight make?
- What can you see when you look at a ruler in a transparent jar full of water?
- What can you see through Jell-O?
- What can you see when you look at a leaf/newsprint through a magnifying glass/a drop of water/a drop of oil/various layers of plastic wrap?
- Compare and sort out transparent, opaque, and translucent objects. Which are easier to see? Where? With a flashlight?
- How can you change the way things look with mirrors? (This activity might tie in with the earlier explorations of symmetrical patterns of seeds in foods.)
- What can you see with a periscope?
- How much can you smell and hear? Compare different smells. Identify sounds of objects that someone drops. Identify sounds of different actions, such as pouring water, rubbing sandpaper, or blowing bubbles through a straw. [**Procedural note:** Provide contrasts within these activities.]
- What are the warmest/coolest places indoors? How do living beings keep themselves warm or cool? (This may even lead to exploring the school's heating and cooling systems, tracing pipes, vents, or other conduits. Some people may say that we are too far from classical biology, but we achieve understanding in its broadest and most useful sense through such networking and exploration of connections—the way in which our brains work.)

(Adapted from Richards et al., 1976a, 1976b)

Pre-kindergarten children are receptive to hearing labels for parts of a 3-dimensional skeleton and measuring the phalanges, patella, clavicle, femur, rib, skull, and spine (L. Davey, personal communication, 2009). Their families are most impressed when children use the term "phalanges" as they wiggle their fingers.

Children also experience *surprise/cognitive dissonance* when they handle apple slices before and after washing their hands. When they see mold growing on the unwashed slices, their careful handwashing before eating becomes quite self-motivated.

Understanding Chemistry as Collaboration

Chemistry really concerns cooperation among the component elements of matter in such a way that chemical processes often seem to become *more than the sum*

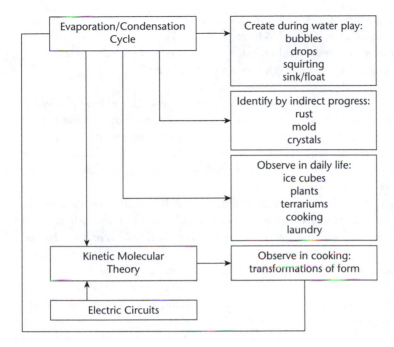

FIGURE 11.2 Conceptual Planning Map in Chemistry

of their parts. This is also known as *synergy,* the Dynamic-Theme discussed in Chapter 7. Figure 11.2 shows a conceptual planning map for chemistry instruction that reflects synergy.

Transformations are the focus of instruction in chemistry. For example, young-sters see transformations of the parts into new forms, whether apples become apple sauce; dry corn turns into sprouts or popcorn; or heavy cream becomes whipped cream and eventually butter. Sensitive teachers tie experiences in synergy to other activities. These kinds of experiences lend themselves to recording with photo-graphs, drawings, and charts. Picture–word recipe charts become part of the literacy program; and stick-figure and word directions on task cards have a place in the science laboratory.

The Evaporation–Condensation Cycle and Other Water Exploration
Particularly when we approach the study of the behavior of particles that we cannot see unaided, we need to integrate the study of chemical properties with concrete activities. A kindergarten group can enjoy predicting the outcome of a drying "race" between paper towels that are flat, folded, or crunched, as well as which materials might dry more quickly or slowly indoors and outdoors. Children's experience with only a part of the cycle will help them build toward broader understanding. It is useful to develop and use open-ended questions in these investigations:

- What do you see? (This is worth lots of time.)
- What happened when . . .? What else?
- What do you suppose might happen . . .? What are some other ideas?
- How might we find out? What are some other ideas?

Ice cubes are fun to have on occasion at the snack table. If you have a snowfall, take the opportunity to look carefully at the snow outdoors; bring some indoors and try to find different ways to keep some snow frozen longer and how to melt some faster. Children enjoy bringing snow into the classroom, placing some on ice cubes, leaving some in a bowl, comparing and predicting the rate of melting (*surprise/cognitive dissonance*).

Consider developing a survey chart during a week in which you measure the height of the outdoor snow in the same location, then the water each day, and record the amounts with a length of yarn or a ruler. As children compare lengths, they will raise important questions, such as, "What happened? Where did it go?" Also, children wonder at a parallel activity when you mark a puddle with chalk immediately after a rain shower and then after some hours or the next day.

At another time, mark the height of water in a transparent container at the same time each day, to add both drama and precision, as you predict and compare each day (*surprise/cognitive dissonance*). If you heat the snow or ice in a pot, consider using heat-proof glass with a cover so that the children can see the steam and then the condensation form. Consider asking a few children to signal the moment of change with a rhythm instrument. [**Procedural note:** For safety, scholars recommend the use of goggles during any such science or cooking activity (Brooks, 2011).] At other times, tossing pebbles in a pond, looking at clouds, or connecting light switches all offer similar moments of phase transition, which you might highlight as contrasts. Such activities begin to create for children a sense of the frontiers of scientists' studies in the field of chaos and complexity theory (see Fromberg, 2010). Indeed, when you give them a chance, youngsters are willing to share with enthusiasm their observations and theories about the nature of such changes.

Clothing does become wet in school from time to time, and there are occasions when children might launder socio-dramatic play clothes. If there is a reasonable moment, ideally not planned grandly ahead of time, you might take the time to consider with the small group involved in the activity which fabrics seem to dry more quickly. It would be good to have cotton, nylon, silk, corduroy, wool, and plastic items handy.

This activity can lead to a written chart with a sample of each of three or four labeled items in the *predicted* order of drying time and, after the *activity*, a rank order of the *comparison*. You can record as a shared writing activity such statements as: "The nylon was the first to dry. The silk dried faster than the cotton shirt. The wool sweater took the longest to dry."

Other water exploration activities include squirting water into a tub, using containers of different shape, size, and size of opening. Ask children to make predictions and compare their findings. Encourage them to observe the following events (see also Elementary Science Study, 1971; Chalufour & Worth, 2005; Brooks, 2011; Worth & Grollman, 2003):

- Notice which openings water squirts out of more quickly.
- Determine how high the container needs to be before the stream either becomes wiggly or turns into droplets.
- Notice the differences when you use funnels, straws, eye droppers, and syringes.
- Watch what happens when two streams meet as they fall.
- Using a balance scale and identical transparent containers, weigh different liquids, such as water, juices, oil, and milk.

If the occasion arises at a birthday party, you might ask children to describe what they see as they look at the candles. Just looking is an adequate activity, as long as you accept what they say. While we have moved away from the discussion of evaporation and condensation, it is worth mentioning one other role of water that many teachers study: that is, water as an aspect of the weather. You might compare the quality of precipitation, such as heavy or light rain, drizzle, and snow.

Temperature   Teachers help children become conscious of the temperature by using comparisons, outlined in Box 11.11.

BOX 11.11 COMPARING TEMPERATURE

- Which is the warmer or cooler object (comparing objects in the classroom)?
- Which glass of water is warmer (comparing water poured from the same source and then placed in the sun or in a shaded corner of the classroom)?
- Which materials (woolen mitten, wooden ruler, and steel fork) seem to be more or less warm?
- Whose hands are warmer or colder?
- How can we try to warm up the cooler hands?

Ice cubes are popular with young children. After exploring, sucking on, and building with ice cubes, pre-kindergarteners can happily focus on some questions.

- *Expect.* Will the large or small container of ice cubes melt first?
- *Experience.* Children fill transparent containers, set a timer, and return later.
- *Compare.* Children experience surprise when they find the results. Then, they *predict* which materials might keep the ice cubes cold for a longer period of time.
- *Experience.* They wrap small transparent cups of ice cubes with a variety of materials, e.g., fleece, newspapers, plastic bags, aluminum foil, and so forth.
- *Compare.* Then, they compare their findings with their predictions by referring to the predictions on the pre-wrapping chart.

[**Procedural note:** If, after exploring and building with ice cubes, children already have figured out that the ice cubes in the larger container are likely to take longer to melt, move to the later insulation activity.]

Provide *contrasts* when children play with melting and freezing water, with and without salt. At different times, provide one new variable at a time, such as melting a large and small ice cube in the air; ice cubes of equal size in the air or cool water; in cool or warm water; in a closet or on a window sill in the sun; and on the radiator or a heated cooking surface.

Children can meet the challenge of creating coverings and containers to slow down the melting process and then can attempt to create coverings to speed up the melting process. They predict and compare how water looks when frozen in plastic ziplock bags, transparent cylindrical and square-edged transparent plastic containers. Youngsters discuss with awe the dramatic bursting of the plastic cover in a container that was filled to the top with water before freezing. They represent their predictions and experiences in survey charts, drawings, and writing, according to their skills.

Children need to understand the notion of density somewhat if they are ultimately to understand temperature as well as evaporation–condensation. Concepts of density grow from their daily experiences with balance scales and water play. The child who has time to study a straw sinking into a thick milkshake and says, "Oh, look, like quicksand," is learning about density just as she does when she takes delight in slopping through mud. Experiences with foods, plant textures, the bathtub, and blowing soap bubbles are related, as are rush–hour train trips, packed elevators, and popular buffet tables.

Kindergarten children can survey and seriate food and plant densities using straws and lenses. Pre-kindergarten children are able to survey traffic density.

Bear in mind that young children can gain more when they actually do things physically in ways that grow out of their inquiries, rather than merely observing a demonstration. A worthwhile activity is worth repeating for others, as they become receptive. At the same time, not everybody needs to have participated in each activity. *Remember, different children doing different things at different times can have equivalent experiences.*

Because temperature is abstract and changeable, it is not as accessible to measure as something like length. Therefore, it is helpful to use nonstandard representations and analogies. An example of nonstandard representation would be marking a large thermometer by color designations—red for hot, yellow for medium, and blue for cold. Some teachers provide thermometers of varying size.

When you introduce a *personal analogy*, children have a chance to learn about temperature personally and aesthetically by role-playing and moving. "When you get into bed at night and the sheets are cold, what does your body do?" "When you get into bed and it is a hot, sticky night, what does your body do?" The mercury (or other substance) in the thermometer thus becomes more accessible to the young child, as children empathize their way toward understanding. Moreover, with digital thermometers in children's lives, there is less reference to liquid thermometers. The digital thermometer, similar to the digital clock, is more abstract than the liquid thermometer or the analog clock. The molecular activity of mercury bridges chemistry and physics.

Understanding Physics as the Movement of Objects Through Space and Time

Physicists study and measure how objects, waves, and particles of matter move through space and time within the limitations of specific conditions. Young children have similar interests in how things move and why events take place.

"Humans have never lost interest in trying to find out how the universe is put together, how it works, and where they fit in the cosmic scheme of things . . . All humans should participate in the pleasure of coming to know their universe better" (AAAS, 2009, p. 48). Children generally take for granted the daily cycle of light and dark. At the same time, they wonder and develop intuitive notions about the unseen physical forces in the world. For example, Albert Einstein credited the roots of his development of the theory of relativity not with advanced mathematical calculations but with the pictures in his head (Sullivan, 1974), the images that young children develop. Today, scientists at the frontiers of the field continue to wonder about and study the forces of gravitation and magnetism (Overbye, 2010).

Scaffolds   Young children directly experience the impact of the unseen forces of gravitation and magnetism as well as the forces of air pressure and centrifugal force. Chapter 6 details examples of children's learning about the contrasts and interactions of forces in physics. You can develop activities to help them find the language to focus on these forces. Young children can begin to move along the path of scientists in intuitive ways as they *first look* at how things function and *then try to change* some aspect of a physical situation (Kamii & DeVries, 1993). Within an activity-based learning environment, youngsters are able to move beyond observing and manipulating to wondering and beginning to make connections. You are able to assess what children are figuring out about physics when you see what they do, hear the questions they ask, and notice the connections they make.

You do not need to plan activities that focus only on one force and pursue it to the ends of human knowledge; nor do you need to make explicit to children the interaction of these forces, regardless of the children's receptivity. Plan concrete experiences as you go along, taking into account children's reactions. Bear in mind that, were any other group of children to begin with the same set of materials, the actual experience would most likely be different. Therefore, each year that you work with different children will be a chance for you to build together a unique fingerprint in time. In studying the physical world, youngsters particularly enjoy using flashlights, as is discussed below.

Light Flashlights are prestigious in young children's culture. They enjoy exploring light closer and farther from an object and seeing how the light makes their fingers glow. Youngsters are able to classify how their hands look when they shine the flashlight against their skin. They are able to classify items that they can (1) see through clearly (transparent), (2) see through unclearly (translucent), or (3) not see through at all (opaque). After you model using the flashlight to sort a few items into separate containers, while labeling each item as transparent or opaque, children are able to follow up with other materials. [**Procedural note:** As with any classification activity, children begin with the greatest contrast (transparent–opaque) and later add another variable (translucent).] Some items that pre-kindergarten children are able to sort are the following: green leaf; aluminum foil; window glass; waxed paper; tissue paper; lightweight cloth; heavy cloth; ice cube; jar of water; wood; construction paper; your hand; and an egg. It is noteworthy that families tend to be impressed when children accurately use the words "transparent," "opaque," and "translucent." Indeed, beyond pointing, children's accurate use of language is a form of assessment.

Assessment

Young children make their connections and build their theories about science when you use the conditions for learning, including physical contrasts, inductive comparisons, and predictions that they compare with their findings (surprise/ cognitive dissonance). They engage in science-related activities in the biological, chemical, and physical world through these kinds of direct activities with concrete materials.

National professional societies provide standards for studying science and technology. Science standards include unifying concepts and processes in science; science as inquiry; physical, life, earth and space science, and technology; science in personal and social perspective; and the history and nature of science (NSTA, 2003). Technology literacy content standards include the study and design of the designed world (Dugger, 2007). This chapter and preceding chapters have discussed activities related to many of these broad areas and skills dealing with technology and science education relevant to how young children learn.

Scholars make the distinction between "practical vs. conceptual knowledge" (DeVries & Sales, 2011, p. 30) and suggest that young children are developing practical knowledge when they use concrete materials. When you want to figure out what children learn, you have only to see how they use materials. You would be talking with them, asking them what they saw, how they changed things to make a difference, and what they might do next. Occasionally asking them to talk about their activities with other children or adults and drawing or writing about their activities can offer additional insight into their ideas.

Reflections

This chapter consists of a sampling of ideas around computer, design technology, and science education to which young children are receptive. There are numerous print and electronic publications that offer activities directed to teachers of young children. As you come across these resources, it is useful to keep in mind some general principles:

- Select authentic experience in which you can support the children to participate with choices and increasing independence.
- Think about how to raise the just-appropriate question that might help them focus on a significant observation or possible next step.
- Improvise props with found materials.
- Above all, resist the "cute" as well as the memory-and-spit-back fact-stating that is empty of meaning.

You can integrate the conditions for learning in early childhood when you promote literacy in computer use, design technology, and science education. In addition, you provide reasons for children to connect their learning to mathematics and measurement as well as language and the arts. As you sequence activities, consider planning activities in adjacent time frames that represent a Dynamic-Theme. When children engage in activities that represent a Dynamic-Theme, there is potential to support their capacity to make and retain meaningful connections. You can integrate both proficient content and meaningful inquiry when you provide engaging experiences in an activity-based learning environment. The next chapter discusses literacy in mathematics, the natural partner of technology and science education.

12

LITERACY IN MATHEMATICS

Cooperative Experiences

Introduction

A kindergarten child was counting the corners of a huge cardboard carton. He was engaged in this dramatic activity but continuously lost count. When an observer suggested to his teacher the possibility of scaffolding the activity by offering the child a Post-it note to place at each corner and then count the notes, the teacher replied, "That is not in the program."

This activity was part of a published sequence of activities in a playful, game-centered program that used mainly concrete materials. As the incident illustrates, it is important to resist becoming overly dependent on any published sequence and method. Instead, look at and listen to the children and then adapt.

As you adapt ideas from mathematical materials published for use with young children, you might consider giving priority to those activities that provide opportunities for developing meaningful concepts when

- you can integrate with real, rather than contrived or "cute," activities;
- provide children with opportunities to figure out their own strategies, using the integrated conditions for learning, especially *induction; surprise/cognitive dissonance; and physical Eexperiences*;
- leave time for children to share the different strategies they use (*social interaction*). You might view with healthy hesitation tasks that require you to cut out lots of uniform patterns.

This chapter establishes a context for learning and then discusses the foundations of mathematics in motor activity, rules, and relationships. The *grammar* of mathematics includes the *elements* of space and shape (geometry) as well as size (including numbers), and the *contrasting* ways in which children learn how they function. The discussion integrates what to teach with how you might teach it.

Literacy in Mathematics

Mathematics is a discipline that schools typically view as a tool or a skill. It is often taught as if it were an end in itself, although children can learn mathematics as they apply it to the study of many social and physical phenomena. This chapter discusses mathematics as an applied body of constructions and activities. Educators agree that a meaningful integration of mathematics study helps children to develop a positive disposition to learning and using mathematics (Atkinson, 1992; Common Core State Standards Initiative, 2010b; Commission for Teaching Standards for School Mathematics, 1991; Jensen, 1993; Snow & Van Hemel, 2008; Stoessinger & Edmunds, 1992).

Inasmuch as children come to school with plenty of quantitative event knowledge (Baroody, 2004; Bowman, Donovan, & Burns, 2001; Schwartz, 2005), young children are more capable than previously thought. Therefore, your job is to build bridges from children's informal knowledge when they solve real quantitative problems until they are able to use the conventional language of mathematics, grouping, and representation. A similar development occurs in the *inductive* ways that children learn to speak, read, and write, as discussed in Chapter 10.

As is the case with any skill, mathematics requires intentional teaching when you gradually provide *contrasting* variables. Your art as a professional teacher is to provide practice in a variety of engaging, active formats that make sense to children. "Mathematics is a participant sport. Children must play it frequently to become good at it . . . Both modeling and feedback can come from other students as well as adults, and feedback also sometimes comes from the situation" (Cross, Woods, & Schweingruber, 2009, p. 125). Philosopher-mathematicians also view learning mathematics as an *inductive* "game" with rules (Whitehead & Russell, 1910). Among other strategies, therefore, constructions and games, discussed later, support the development of mathematical knowledge.

One of the big public relations problems in kindergarten and pre-kindergarten is finding a way to teach mathematics that will satisfy parents that teachers are doing serious business, even though workbooks and ditto sheets are not the core of the program. In order to communicate the seriousness of our purpose, we must present our program so that parents and other educators can understand that mathematics education takes many forms. Toward this end, it is useful to establish a visible mathematics center that includes many of the components we will discuss in the following section. The mathematics center described in Box 12.1 can provide a focus for the particular attention that skill-building needs.

BOX 12.1 THE MATHEMATICS CENTER

A physical space is labeled "Mathematics Center." It should contain the following:

- Mats upon which to use each set of concrete materials, in order to define work space for many small pieces in a set.
- Storage space.
- Writing and drawing materials with a date stamp.
- Kindergarten mathematics notebooks.
- Standard measures, such as a cup, ruler, meter stick, and tape measure.
- Pan balance and balance-beam scales with accessories, such as labeled boxes of buttons pine cones, wooden cubes, washers, and so forth.
- One or two tables and six to eight chairs.
- Floor space as an alternative area to use materials.

Concrete materials often include the following, labeled and stored in transparent containers:

- Beads and laces.
- Pegs and peg boards; geoboards and rubber bands.
- Parquetry blocks.
- Wikki Stix.
- Sand/water table and accessories: transparent containers of different shapes that hold the same volume; transparent measuring cups and spoons of varying sizes; transparent funnels; transparent tubes of varying length and diameter; squirting bottles; and a rotary beater. Sponges and cloths to ease cleanup.
- Color cubes [Exploration, and Color Cube Task Cards Prekindergarten+ (Learning Resources, 1988, 1993)].
- Unifix/linking cubes.
- Sequential pattern cards (pre-kindergarten: Developmental Learning Materials Teaching Pattern Blocks; kindergarten: Geoboard Activity Cards: Primary (Barson, n.d.)). [**Procedural note:** To keep cards in sequence, punch holes in them and secure them in a ring binder.]
- Commercial and teacher-made games, such as board games and card games.
- Centimeter graph paper, writing tools, and related books.
- Muffin tins, plastic egg cartons, and other containers for sorting and building patterns.

- Nonstandard measures, such as tongue depressors, drinking straws, yarn, and strings of different thickness and texture.
- Tool tote trays for related materials so that children can move them easily to a table, a mat on the floor, or outdoors.

Additional manipulative materials that are worth having, even if you build your stock by adding a few each year, would be the following:

- Attribute blocks, or their generic equivalents.
- Cuisenaire rods.
- Picture and word task cards in sequence.

[**Procedural note:** The contents are renewed, replaced, revised, and retired as needed so that children can focus without clutter.]

Aids in Teaching Mathematics

Mathematics Notebooks

Each child should have a personal mathematics notebook labeled as such, with the child's name. The notebook can begin as a set of blank, unlined pages with an oak tag or construction paper cover. Content might include drawings, photographs, and attached lengths of yarn, straws, or paper with labels. The notebook records children's measurements and findings for revisiting and celebrating progress. Many kindergarten children can copy a line of text early in the school year, and most feel comfortable using invented spelling to record their experiences. Keep in mind that mathematics is an applied tool and many activities will relate naturally to children's measurements and other quantitative studies of physical and social events.

Activity File

Keep a personal file of cooperative mathematics ideas, including games. Word processing makes it easy to add new ideas and to revise the sequence of activities.

Bulletin Boards and Displays

Label bulletin board and hallway displays with captions, such as "Pre-Kindergarten Math Study in February," and present concrete formats of children's work. Young children provide us with fresh, reasonable ways to represent their data collection (see Whitin, Mills, & O'Keefe, 1990).

Camera

Photograph children engaged in cooperative mathematics with concrete materials or as they record findings in their notebooks. Photographs with captions and children's comments that also show the sequence of events provide important opportunities to *revisit* experiences. Children enjoy talking about photographs, and families appreciate seeing them. The discussion that follows highlights the foundations of mathematical development in motor activity, rules, and relationships within an interactive environment.

Cooperative Mathematics

Pre-kindergarten and kindergarten children learn mathematics best when they engage in concrete activities with other children. Working together, they use mathematics as a tool to solve the natural problems that arise in their encounters with the physical and social worlds. Contained in this approach are two important, interrelated assumptions for teaching that influence mathematics activities. The first is that children should have legitimate opportunities for *social interaction* (condition for learning) in connection with their active learning of mathematics. They learn about quantity as they *contrast and compare (induction)* physical relationships.

The second assumption is that young children should have opportunities to participate in activities that create *surprise/cognitive dissonance* (condition for learning). Indeed, children's *social interactions* create more opportunities for cognitive dissonance as they *predict, observe,* and *compare* their views with those of others. When they encounter other children's varied viewpoints, they could extend their own view and de-center from it.

Organizing and Grouping for Instruction

Cooperative mathematics can flourish when you work with children in small-group activities that use contrasting materials that children can then pursue independently in dyads, just as you do in reading or science instruction.[1] The all-day schedule provides time to organize in this way while leaving time for other worthwhile experiences.

You might begin with a brief (eight minutes or less) problem using concrete materials that offer a comparison and/or expectation. While children follow up work in the mathematics center, you would circulate and *revisit* the center to assess and support what they are doing. You would record which children participate in the pre-planned groups. You might also group together children of different abilities—for example to reinforce the procedures of a game.

Foundations in Motor Activity (Indoors and Outdoors)

Mathematics concepts depend upon visual–spatial relationships that children experience in the physical world. Children develop visual–spatial skills when they have many and varied experiences, including music and movement, large muscle games, and building activities in which they explore 3-dimensional space. When you notice some children who need more exposure to these kinds of activities, you can try to extend the time those children will spend in a center. [**Procedural note:** You might (1) invite a child or children to work with you in a particular motor activity at a specific time and (2) physically move near the child or children who are in an area where they might improve visual–spatial skills.]

Collaborative games can help children build the visual–spatial skills they use to imagine mathematics. Researchers and educators find that group games, skills games with marbles, and tag games provide important support for building mathematical concepts (Clements & Sarama, 2009b; Cratty, n.d.; Kamii & DeVries, 1993; Zan & Geiken, 2010).

Particularly in an all-day program, it is important to schedule more than one opportunity for such large muscle activity each day. Young children can learn as they enjoy activities with one-to-one correspondence; and concrete experiences with concepts including larger than, smaller than, any, some, either–or, biggest–smallest, pairs, groups of two, sets or two, and simple seriation. They play with sorting and classifying, class inclusion, class exclusion, and pattern building.

Pattern Building

A first step is building patterns with 3-dimensional materials, such as playing with children standing up and sitting down in different patterns. Children are able, first, to recognize patterns, then build patterns, extend patterns that others have begun, add to and subtract from patterns, and describe patterns. As very young children build patterns as simple as abab, abcabc, or aabb while stringing beads or straws of different colors, they are building and representing quantitative knowledge; and both patterns and representation are among the standards of the National Council of Teachers of Mathematics (NCTM, 2000). Another way is to build patterns with objects, such as colored toothpicks, that children sort by color and glue in patterns as well as different shapes (Wohl & Gainer, 1996, p. 69). It is interesting that researchers have found that, after 3-dimensional pattern building, children are able to create more patterns when they manipulate patterns on computers (Moyer, Niezgoda, & Stanley, 2005). These findings reinforce the "abstraction ladder" continuum that progresses from concrete to visual to symbolic representation (Hayakawa, 1949).

Foundations in Rules (Number and Operations)

In order to play games, children voluntarily use and learn to understand the relationships of rules in mathematics (Bodrova & Leong, 2007; Kamii & DeVries, 1980). "Mathematics is a participant sport. Children must play it frequently to become good at it . . . Both modeling and feedback can come from other students as well as adults, and feedback also sometimes comes from the situation" (Cross, Woods, & Schweingruber, 2009, p. 125).

Simple ball games as well as board games help children build toward a sense of codifying rules. Attribute blocks, color cubes, and colored loops are useful as children build a notion of rules. The guessing game in Box 8.8 is an example of children setting rules for one another. Box 12.2 describes a sequence of activities for building rules.

BOX 12.2 A CONCRETE ACTIVITY SEQUENCE FOR BUILDING RULES

Build Sets

A basket containing cubes of many colors is present. Lay out a red loop and a blue loop so that they do not touch. "Let's pretend that this is a red playground and that this is a blue playground. The rule is that I can put red cubes in the red playground and blue cubes in the blue playground. Here are two loops. What cubes can you put in the green loop? In the yellow loop?" Children place cubes.

Build Intersecting Sets

Lay out the red loop and the blue loop so that they overlap each other in part. "I can put red cubes in the red part and blue cubes in the blue part. Now, there is this part (overlapping) which is both blue and red. Let's put cubes in it. Which ones can be in there? Now use the green and yellow playground loops."

Build Class Exclusion

Lay out the red loop and the blue loop. "Guess what rules I am using." Place blue cubes in the red playground loop and red cubes in the blue playground loop. "Here is a green playground loop and a yellow playground loop. Place the green and yellow cubes, using the same rule that I just used." Then, "Make up your own rule and let us try to guess what it is."

> After building these activities over several sessions, you might place cubes outside, but adjacent to, the same-color loops. A "People Sorting" game uses a similar procedure (Downie, Slesnick, & Stenmark, 1981, p. 28). Children themselves enter or leave a large loop of yarn laid out on the floor. They base their movement upon some attribute, such as wearing something green or not wearing glasses. They guess one another's rules.

Color Matrices

Playing with color matrices is a helpful parallel activity. Children might begin by looking at a pattern of cubes, have someone remove a cube, and then guess which cube is missing. When you reverse two cubes in a matrix, children can attempt to locate the change for one another. In addition to playing with rules, children are developing scanning skills. (Scanning skills help in reading as well as in the ubiquitous standardized tests.)

Games

Since mathematics is a rule-bound occupation, as are group games, children need to have opportunities to explore and test rules in many games that they play. Research indicates that children develop an understanding of rules as they live through repeated social interactions and get feedback from their peers (Piaget et al., 1965). Children often experience *surprise/cognitive dissonance* in a new perception when they experience such feedback from others.

Young children use rules in games, but they might apply them incompletely, although with confidence. Therefore, they need repeated opportunities to test the rules, see how they work, make and play with rules, and see how their actions affect other people.

For teachers who feel the pressure of tests results, it is noteworthy how little time it might take you to engage in games that support mathematical learning. For example, researchers find that playing number board games for just two to four minutes with pre-kindergarten children from low-income homes across four fifteen-minute sessions over two weeks significantly increases their numerical estimation proficiency (Siegler & Ramani, 2008). Others report that pre-kindergarten children make significant progress in sequencing and subitizing (number sense) after four to six brief, engaging sessions with game formats in sequencing and subitizing as well as overall progress in shape identification and composition; and they can manipulate objects directly or on a computer that enhances "more sophisticated numerical strategies and the development of spatial imagery" (Clements & Sarama, 2007, p. 156). In addition to fixing puzzles, researchers report opportunities to reverse, rotate, or turn over pieces in order to complete a task—all actions that build images of space (Clements & Sarama, 2007, p. 157). Kindergarten children also make progress in their spatial relationships after as few as eight sessions across a four-week period (Casey, Erkut, Ceder, & Young, 2007).

Gender Differences in Mathematics Achievement

The parallel between the rules of children's games and the rules of mathematics is too important to ignore. This is particularly true with respect to boys, who traditionally are more involved with group sports, building with large floor blocks, and woodworking activities that tend to improve visual–spatial development. It is no surprise that some research has found that boys seem to achieve better than girls in mathematics after the elementary school years because they come to school with different patterns of socializing and game preferences, particularly those using spatial relations (Maccoby & Jacklin, 1974; Serbin, 1978). It is important to be aware of these factors and plan for girls as well as boys to build with large blocks, engage in group sports and rule-bound games, and continue their woodworking and other problem-solving activities. During planning sessions and when you circulate around the classroom, encourage all the children to participate in cooperative mathematics.

There are general research trends that summarize an immense number of related studies and are subject to some exceptions. For example, when pre-kindergarten girls and boys experience a research-based mathematics curriculum that includes numerical and spatial tasks and block building, girls as well as boys flourish (Cross, Woods, & Schweingruber, 2009, p. 182; Clements & Sarama, 2008a). Girls in particular benefit from the use of storytelling that integrates spatial reasoning (Casey, Erkut, Ceder, & Young, 2007). Therefore, it makes sense to plan for all children to have visual–spatial experiences, and to give extra help to those who need it. You will find related games throughout this chapter. In addition, a variety of commercial and teacher-made games are discussed in the section dealing with numbers and operations.

Foundations in Relationships of Space, Shape, and Size

In mathematics, you are helping children to understand *relationships* in space, shape, and size and to develop the ability to represent these relationships through symbols. Young children learn best when you isolate one variable at time, such as space or shape or size. For example, if *comparing* sizes, then space, shape, and color would be identical; if *comparing* shapes, then space, size, and color would be identical. It is simply easier for youngsters to *induce* a concept when they have a clear comparison between a familiar property and a single fresh property. Learning mathematics with meaning is more than acquiring a rapid command of "number facts" and basic arithmetic computation. Machines are better able than people to do that. *Comparing* numbers and understanding *relationships* provide a stronger foundation for mathematics than rote counting and memorizing verbal statements about numbers.

Standards

The standards of the National Council of Teachers of Mathematics recommend moving beyond only technical, rote approaches to encouraging teachers to help children develop "mathematical power . . . [which includes] the ability to explore, conjecture, and reason logically; to solve non-routine problems; to communicate about and through mathematics; and to connect ideas within mathematics and between mathematics and other intellectual activity" (Commission for Teaching Standards for School Mathematics, 1991, p. 1).

The Council's definition of "mathematical power" is congruent with the *Common Core State Standards for Mathematics* (Common Core State Standards Initiative, 2010b) as well as the integrated and meaning-based approaches to curriculum design that include Dynamic-Themes and the conditions of learning.

Other ways in which national standards are compatible with this book's outlook include their egalitarian concern that "every" child should have access to a respectful learning environment in a setting where children's voices are present along with the teacher's voice. While not dictating how to teach, the Common Core standards also underscore the importance of helping children to develop a disposition to engage in mathematics.

A disposition to engage in mathematics (or verbal) literacy activities makes the difference between seeking out opportunities to use literacy skills or avoiding them in school and thereafter. Researchers have found that children whose teachers feel comfortable with mathematics achieve more in the subject and have more positive attitudes toward it (Karp, 1988; Beilock, Gunderson, Ramirez, & Levine, 2010). Consider your own mathematics autobiography, present attitudes, and what enthusiasms you convey. Consider how you can relate to the notion of mathematics as a body of games with rules, games which mathematicians both play and create: "The really profound changes in human life all have their ultimate origin in knowledge pursued for its own sake" (Whitehead, 1911, pp. 19–20). Play, the arena in which children feel empowered, is "pursued for its own sake." If the roots of your personal discomfort with mathematics begin with the sense of "required work" rather than playfulness and choice, then perhaps you might reflect on your playfulness index.

Children will need help in building positive dispositions and expectancies, in understanding how and when to use the tool that mathematics is, and in applying computational skills where they are relevant. Objects, task cards, and books, whether employed separately or in combination, do not insure that children will learn. You need to juxtapose elements of space, shape, and size, some of which are detailed in the following sub-sections, at the proper times, with adequate preparation and appropriate follow-up activities.

Space

Young children explore space in a variety of ways. They collect data from visual and plastic arts, building with blocks, and construction activities. When they try to fit into boxes, tunnels, toys, last year's coat, father's shoes, or an area near the teacher, they also learn about space.

Topology   Topology is a good way to study spatial properties. It relates to the "existence of permanence in the midst of change" (Guillen, 1983, p. 153), whether in the arts, psychology, politics, economics, or physics. For example, the sizes of markings on a deflated balloon will change when you inflate the balloon, but the topological relations—relative ordinal positions among any set of points on the markings—remain the same. Children learn this kind of spatial order through repeatedly transforming actions that bend, twist, or stretch, just as they learn to recognize a particular person intuitively on the basis of a profile view (Clements & Sarama, 2009b; Copeland, 1984; Piaget & Inhelder, 1976; Sauvy & Sauvy, 1974). The baby's development of object permanence is the root of both the social and physical components of this development.

Some of the activities that help children build this intuitive sense of spatial order include work with clay, yarn, rubber bands, and other malleable materials. The actions children perform—molding, tying, sewing, weaving, stretching, compressing, and so forth—foster the acquisition of early geometric concepts.

Children also reconstruct concepts of *enclosure* and *boundary* through some of these activities, as well as through building with blocks, puzzling over mazes, and engaging in various mapping activities, such as those that involve color cubes and colored loops. Experiences that call upon children to differentiate by categories—such as part of/not a part of; inside/outside/on; and before/after/between—provide excellent opportunities for *inductive* learning of these ideas. Jumping games in front of, next to, and behind one another also add to the vocabulary of English language learners.

Proximity and *continuity* concepts can develop through countless daily activities that involve tying knots, stringing beads, and various science activities with evaporation and condensation. Such learning grows whenever an experience calls for being close/far away, in front/behind, above/below, or to the left/right.

Children's sense of topology develops intuitively before their sense of relative length and number of surfaces or angles emerges. You help them extend and deepen their topological experiences when you provide concrete materials that children can *transform*, and when you plan activities in which they can feel and see *contrasts* in texture and appearance. Children also need a chance to talk about what they are seeing and feeling as they are using materials.

Examples of topological activities appear in Box 12.3. These activities focus on *contrasts* and *changes*. For example, pouring is a most concrete example of change. It is especially important to provide children with containers of varied shapes and sizes as well as a series of containers of standard size gradations, which will help them learn about volume. Children acquire the concept of conservation of quantities with objects only after many experiences in which they observe and create transformations of shape, size, and space that are reversible in real, social settings.

BOX 12.3 TOPOLOGICAL ACTIVITIES

- Tie, twist, or weave yarn or raffia with two adjacent colors or textures. These activities help to sharpen the sense of proximity.
- Build patterns cooperatively with a friend using beads, blocks, stickers, or geoboards, first back-to-back and then comparing patterns—a potential *surprise/cognitive dissonance* experience.
- Touch an unseen object in a "mystery box" and match it with corresponding pictures to sharpen images of boundaries.
- Engage in large muscle creative movement activities with props such as hoops, ropes, disks, and cloth, to help develop a feeling for boundaries, enclosures, and proximity.
- Rotate shapes and objects, and play with symmetrical signs to stimulate relative thinking (Waters, 1973; Cross, Woods, & Schweingruber, 2009).
- Describe children's actions while they turn, rotate, and flip 2-dimensional jigsaw-puzzle pieces.
- Create a poster of children's photos with captions in different spatial relationships, such as Jorge is under the table; Ed is on the chair; Rosa is in front of Serge (adapted from Schiller & Peterson, 1997, p. 22). Personalizing the photos also supports English language learners.
- For English language learners, the "Don't Let It Drop" game invites children to balance a small object, such as an index card or soft toy, on their heads. The teacher suggests increasing challenges, such as, "Sit on a chair; sit on the floor; sit under the table; stand up;" and so forth (Gordon, 2007, p. 82).
- When children try to fit the most unit blocks into four shoeboxes, they might record an estimate of how many blocks and *predict* which among four methods is most efficient (adapted from Macdonald, 2001). The four methods are: (1) standing up the blocks; (2) laying them flat; (3) laying them on their sides; and (4) piled in a heap. *Experience*: pairs of children take turns filling each box and tallying how many could fit using each method. Then they can *compare* their findings with their predictions (*surprise/cognitive dissonance*).

- Pour water, sand, or beans through funnels, sieves, and transparent tubes, into containers.
- Play "Hide-And-Go-Seek" in relative location games with dioramas. For example, a toy figure, "Mr. O," functions as a puppet, describing to anyone trying to find him whatever he sees from his location (Karplus & Thier, 1967). Kindergarten teachers and children are able to *play* with the observer notion, placing objects in front of "Mr. O" and setting him on both stationary and moving vehicles. Young children can deal with an imaginary observer on much the same level as an imaginary friend they can blame for misdeeds. The outside observer points up for children that, depending upon your viewpoint, there may be more than one way to describe a situation. The *surprise/cognitive dissonance* in this tension between viewpoints is an important turning point in learning. Pre-kindergarten teachers can also rotate dioramas that include 3-dimensional trees, a house, and a garage while children compare and match the arrangement with pictures (Lavatelli, 1970).
- Place a blanket over a table so that children can move under, over, around, and next to the setup.

Scaffold: You help to extend meaning when you describe activities using a variety of descriptive vocabulary. A vivid children's book that uses topological terms—such as *Over, Under, and Through* (Hoban, 1973)—can reinforce learning after children engage in related activities.

Youngsters also enjoy exploring images with mirrors. In addition, they are able to use computers to transform objects on the screen in ways that help build mental images. Researchers do not recommend that computers be used exclusively for individual drill, but do recommend that computer manipulation can support spatial learning. The process underlying these manipulations of viewpoint contributes to the kindergarteners' later construction of place value when they compose and combine shapes; and they can turn, flip, resize, glue, and even cut shapes to create objects for their pictures (Clements & Sarama, 2008b, pp. 130–134). These spatial concepts also relate to the shapes of objects and can build toward the imagery of scientific models, such as chemical structures.

Shape

Children can explore shapes in a variety of ways. They build discrimination skills when they match and compare similar and different shapes, and series of shapes whose sizes vary. When they fit shapes into corresponding openings, they are ready to solve 2-dimensional and, in kindergarten, 3-dimensional puzzles. Researchers find that pre-kindergarten children gain competence in identifying and applying visual concepts after engaging in the following activities: they look at and discuss shapes; engage in tasks to develop their visual memory; and recreate shapes with a variety of materials (Eylon, Razel, Ben-Zvi, & Somech, 1990). Such tasks appear to increase children's spatial skills and their IQ scores (Clements & Sarama, 2006).

Geoboards Circular or triangular as well as square geoboards are useful. Youngsters move from creating rubber band designs on peg boards to geoboards. Wherever possible, it is useful for two or more children to work together when they are independent of the teacher. Kindergarten children can rotate a figure on matching geoboards and *compare* them (Burton et al., 1991). Sharing sequenced teacher-made or selected commercial picture task cards, they can work on parallel, equivalent geoboards and later on boards that have different proportions—an experience in topology. Then the children can compare their parallel work—another occasion when they are likely to encounter *surprise/ cognitive dissonance*.

Youngsters can explore how many different three-, four-, five-, or six-sided figures they can create on the geoboard. When comparing shapes and sizes, they can replicate street signs, such as the octagonal stop sign.

Youngsters build up their sense of parts and wholes as well as imagery for division and fractions when they bisect a geoboard with another rubber band. Researchers contend that part–whole relationships are important in mathematical operations (Casey, Erkut, Ceder, & Young, 2007; Clements & Sarama, 2009a, 2009b). As children select geoboard shapes for drawing, they add to their representational repertoire. Related activities include walking, hopping, crawling, skipping, and jumping around shapes outlined on the playground or the floor as well as representation with a "turtle" using LOGO on the computer (Burton et al., 1991).

Various ways of exploring shapes also include considerations for patterned shapes. Patterns of shapes might range from children alternating sitting and standing formations to geoboard rubber bands to pattern blocks or cubes. Patterns in turn help children build number concepts.

Tangrams Tangrams are puzzle patterns composed of seven shapes that children can assemble in numerous ways. The puzzle requires children to move outside of preconceived frames of reference and proceed through *indirect progress* (a Dynamic-Theme), using trial-and-error manipulation. Tangram puzzles are difficult to do when children (or adults) begin with the seven pieces and try to replicate the preprinted patterns. For example, to complete the puzzle, players need to turn, reverse, rotate, or flip the parts in order to create the whole. However, there is a helpful set of cards with a sequential approach to building

Tangrams that begins with two shapes rather than seven (Elementary Science Study, 1976); Clements & Sarama (2009b) recommend a similar adaptation. Using a series of cards, the puzzle proceeds with controlled variables until children reach seven shapes. Some 4- and 5-year-olds surge through the sequential cards with great zest!

In addition to controlling variables, there are a number of steps that help children develop the *indirect progress* skills that make it possible to work with all seven shapes. Box 12.4 describes steps that are also useful with cubes, cards, and parquetry blocks.

BOX 12.4 TANGRAM SEQUENCE FROM CONCRETE TO VISUAL

1. There is a one-to-one correspondence between the printed pattern outline, which is marked for each piece. Children place each piece on its outline. The sequence begins with two pieces and adds one piece at a time.
2. There is a one-to-one correspondence only within the printed outline, which is not marked for each piece. Children place the pieces within the outline.
3. Using the same-size outline, children assemble the pieces *next to* the outline.
4. Children assemble the pieces *next to* a smaller-size outline.

When you control the variables and increase them gradually, most kindergarten children are able to move into Box 12.4's third step. A few children may be able and interested enough to pursue the less concrete fourth step.

Particularly for children with perceptual difficulties, it is very important to control variables and analyze tasks so that they have an abundance of experience similar to the first two steps in Box 12.4. Materials in the first two parts of the sequence provide self-correction which affords the players a sense of empowerment and *competence* (condition for learning).

Attribute Blocks   When some children need to study shape, it is useful to compare two shapes as the only variable, while color and size are the same. This method is useful whenever you want children to perceive an individual variable, whether in the study of mathematics, reading, or science.

However, even before children acquire labels for shapes, they can sort them into same or different containers. As they do so, you can name the shapes. Children will probably learn most labels easily in this incidental way. Your control of new variables creates "figures" that contrast with children's "backgrounds." [**Procedural note:** These activities have the most impact when you work with small groups and individuals.]

Size

Relative size and absolute size form still another relationship for study. Young children notice phenomena such as the size of a group of children or a portion of strawberries, the length of a truck, the height of a building, and how much is enough money for an ice cream. They are concerned with being bigger than or smaller than; having more than and receiving less than or fewer than; and having the least or the most. These concerns reflect daily life and pave the way toward understanding numbers and counting. Researchers, for example, note that 96 percent of kindergarten children can solve quantitative problems when they are couched in terms of their experiences—for example, "How many won't get . . .?" —as compared to the 2 percent who respond correctly to "How many more birds . . .?" (Hembree & Marsh, 1993). Clements & Sarama's research (2009b) supports this finding. Consider that this is one way that children reflect their personalized grasp of the economic problem of scarcity in a mathematical sense.

Fractions   Children's concept of fractions also develops out of everyday experiences that deal with relationships. They learn to share half of multiple materials, such as blocks; then half of a single fruit. Their movement education activities involve patterns with body parts in 4/4 then 3/4 rhythm. Consistent with other learning, images of fractions begin with hands-on, concrete materials. Beyond dividing concrete materials, a board game such as Auntie Pasta's Pizza deals with visual matching of halves, quarters, and thirds.

To create an *Amish quilt design/fraction quilt*, some kindergarten children, using a paper square, can mark the midpoint on each of four sides. Using a straight edge, they can line up these midpoints and draw lines connecting them. By folding along the lines they draw, they can create squares within a square. Coloring each set of patterns with a different color highlights the pattern. Different color patterns represent different fractions.

Kindergarten children also enjoy making *snowflake designs*. They are able to use an equilateral triangle of paper and mark the midpoint on each side to create three line-segments. Coloring each set of patterns with a different color highlights the pattern.

When you inoculate children with an image for a concept, they are less likely to become infected by rote formulas. Researchers recommend that teachers focus on fractions as a particular quantity (Siegler et al., 2010). After children learn to read whole numbers, some kindergarten teachers show what fractions look like when written in the context of quantities less than a whole.

Seriation/Ordering   Other experiences help children to construct their under-standing of size relationships. As they classify materials and have many experiences with one-to-one correspondence, their seriation skills can grow. The ability to seriate depends on the relationship of the part to the whole, as in meaningful counting. When children compare sizes, they build the capacity to count-on rather than re-count by rote each time. Indeed, one scholar has found that a quarter of pre-kindergarten children in a content-rich, center-based program are able to count-on (L. Davey, personal communication, 2010). Some useful seriation activities appear in Box 12.5.

BOX 12.5 SERIATION/ORDERING ACTIVITIES

- *Match keys to padlocks.* Keys and padlocks tend to have prestige in the culture of early childhood. As the number of items increases, you can encourage children to seriate, beginning at first with large and small locks, then with three locks, and adding items as children seem ready for more. They are using their working memory when you add a third lock. In effect, they need to keep in mind *smaller than, larger than,* and *still larger than* the preceding lock. In a similar way, you might *match jars with lids* (Kaltman, 2009). [**Procedural note:** You might find that different children are able to seriate more or fewer items, with three items the limit for many 4-year-olds.]
- *Pour materials.* Children decide how much water, sand, or beans to pour into transparent cups and then seriate each in turn. [**Procedural note:** This is different from asking a child to fill the cup with a bit less or more. It is best when children can decide independently how much to pour and thus experience a degree of control. Then they can make comparisons as they seriate.]
- *Compare the weight of a guinea pig against other objects,* using a balance scales—predict–do–compare (*surprise/cognitive dissonance*). Then place objects in order that weigh more and weigh less.

Seriation and Time   Time is invisible, and it is difficult for children to under-stand the relationship between distance, motion, and time (velocity).

For psychological time or physical time, children are able to reconstruct the sequence of events and the causal order of some events by comparisons and with the if–then reasoning of "lived" time. In this sense, children construct the reality of time (Piaget, 1969). Many kindergarten children are able to identify analog clock time "on the hour." However, digital clocks add a layer of abstraction.

It is probably sufficient to focus on a picture–word sequence of daily events and, when relevant, simply use a sand timer to accompany children's activities. Young children need such concrete formats, rather than a daily teacher ritual that approaches calendar worship which bypasses children's capacity to understand. They derive more meaning from thinking about how many days until an important event rather than counting days simply for the sake of counting. Educators suggest additional concrete ways to build concepts of past, present, and future by planning events and creating formats that have meaning to youngsters (Beneke, Ostrosky, & Katz, 2008; Schwartz, 2005). However, youngsters do learn to recite the days of the week and months of the year much as they do the alphabet.

Measurement   In the course of solving problems of size, young children are able to use nonstandard measures to find out more about themselves—their heights and weights, the length of their feet, the length of their strides.

For example, they can create a class book titled

> *Measuring Our Hands and Feet.* Let each child make a handprint and a footprint on a large sheet of paper. Help children to use links of Unifix cubes to figure out how long their hands and feet are. Write a sentence for each child. Sarah's hand is five links and her foot is eight links. Staple the book together and read it often.
>
> *(Neuman & Roskos with Wright & Lenhart, 2007, p. 117)*

IMAGE 12.1 Height Measurement of Blocks with Language Experience Chart

Youngsters can measure "How many children hold hands to meet around a big tree?" Then, "How many hands around the smaller tree?" Tally helpers record the number of children, and kindergarten children can compare the number of hands.

Children can use nonstandard measures such as strings, blocks, crayons, a favorite doll, or other objects of their choice. They are also able to compare size and density by using balance scales, perform float-or-sink activities, predict distances when rolling objects along varied inclined planes, and kindergarten children can use a meter stick to mark the arc of a pendulum. These activities flow into graphic representations.

Measuring activities, because they employ some tool, prove to be active and involving for young children. Mathematics educators suggest a sequence of measurement activities in various categories, beginning with nonstandard, direct measures of length and later with standard, indirect measurements of temperature (Cruikshank, Fitzgerald, & Jensen, 1980). After length, they recommend, in order, the measurement of area, volume, weight, and time. Others also note that measurement of lines precedes area (Clements & Sarama, 2009a, p. 10). These activities support meaningful scientific and social studies.

A direct, nonstandard measure is the most fundamental form, that is a = b, because measurement defines the relationship between a phenomenon and the measuring tool. Many examples are integrated and some others would be "What objects are longer than this book?" or "What is shorter than this doll?" Such experiences lead to considering "How much longer/shorter is this one?" on the way to number operations.

Kindergarten children can measure the area of a surface by cutting a paper outline of one object and comparing the outline with a second object. You would need a similar indirect measure, however, to test the relationship between a bookcase and a closet, since it is unwieldy to move the bookcase each time you might want to establish if it could fit into the closet. Rather than remove all of the books and move the case, kindergarten children might be able to come up with a suggestion for using an indirect continuous measure, such as a length of string: thus, a = b, b = c, a = c.

In order to create *surprise/cognitive dissonance*, consider suggesting that children select a set of nonstandard items with which to measure a particular length or area.

If different children use smaller or larger items in their set, then there will be discrepancies in their findings, which they would discuss. Children demonstrate how their emotional sense of fairness leads their learning, "It's not fair. She used smaller blocks to get more." They might come to see that few and many units make comparisons difficult when measuring the same length or area (Wilson & Rowland, 1993). In this way, they come to construct the need for standard measures when they experience *surprise/cognitive dissonance*.

Your role as teacher is to integrate each new variable gradually and to help children with the needed language as they engage in activities. Over time, children refine gross observations and approximations as they make predictions, repeat observations, try out new actions, and revise their views. When children have opportunities to work in these ways, their learning develops via the healthy tensions of *surprise/cognitive dissonance*. Two activities in which pre-kindergarten and kindergarten children experience cognitive dissonance with the conservation of quantity appear in Boxes 12.6 and 12.7.

BOX 12.6 COGNITIVE DISSONANCE IN THE DIRECT MEASURE OF VOLUME I

- *Purposes.* Invite children to predict, observe, and compare. Create the possibility for cognitive dissonance.
- *Materials.* Two transparent jars of the same size, one low and wide, one tall and thin; measuring cup; paper strip taped along the length of each of two jars; rice; marker.
- *Organization.* A group of six to eight children works with the teacher.
- *Procedures.* Pour one measuring cup of rice into a jar, shake it down, and mark the height on the paper strip. Empty the contents into the second jar and mark the height.
  - Ask the children what they see when they compare the lengths on the markers in different jars. What might have happened? Accept all answers and consider them seriously.
  - Repeat estimates and measure a few times. [**Procedural note:** This is important because some children may not be able to conserve a quantity when it changes in appearance. Repetition gives children the chance to discover that the discrepancy does not exist because of incorrect measurement.]
- *Representation.* Children can record their findings in their mathematics notebooks as drawings and direct measures of tape length.

(Adapted from Baratta-Lorton, 1976, p. 136)

BOX 12.7 COGNITIVE DISSONANCE IN THE DIRECT MEASURE OF VOLUME II

- *Purposes.* Encourage children to predict, observe, and compare. Create the possibility for *surprise/cognitive dissonance.*
- *Materials.* Two eight-ounce transparent containers, one low and wide, one tall and thin; brown paper sacks; identical beads or marbles.
- *Organization.* A group of six to eight children with the teacher.
- *Procedures.* Place a brown paper sack with a hole in the top over each of the containers. Ask a child to drop a bead from each hand into each of the holes in the paper sacks, at the same time. Ask the child, "Are you putting the same number of beads in each jar?" [**Procedural note:** When they can see the beads, children may deny that both containers have the same amount of beads, but invariably give conservation of quantity responses when they cannot perceive the unequal level of the beads in the containers.]
- Repeat a few times, occasionally alternating using the paper sacks and leaving the containers uncovered. Eventually the *discrepancy* between the responses they give in the two situations becomes apparent to them, and they say excitedly, "It's got the same; I put the same in each jar! It doesn't matter how it looks."

(Adapted from Lavatelli, 1970, p. 112; see also Burk, Snider, & Symonds, 1992, p. 144)

Balance Scales   Using balance scales is another activity in which children can experience *surprise/cognitive dissonance.* You can ask 4- and 5-year-old children to sort heavy and light objects by touch, observing the balance scales' movement for feedback. You can ask them to guess, for example, which would be heavier—a small metal object or a large piece of Styrofoam. When they look at the Styrofoam, they might *predict* that it will be heavier; but when they *test* it on the scales they find that the smaller metal object is heavier—a moment of *surprise/cognitive dissonance.* They can verify their observations by repeated testing. When contrasts take place between appearance and performance, children notice and raise questions. These same kinds of contrasts may be evident in their science study, for example when they use magnets or compare flotation in fresh and salt water. Kindergarten children are independently able to graph a comparison between their predictions and their findings after balancing objects on the scales. The children's cognitive development progresses through the dialectical imagery of *contrasts/conflicts* (Dynamic-Theme).

IMAGE 12.2 Balance Scale and Surprise/Cognitive Dissonance "Predict-and-Really" Chart

Children also build the concept of equality (=) when using the balance scales, similar to their intuitive experiences when they balance on a seesaw. For example, kindergarteners imagine and test "What weighs more/the most/the same?" "How many cubes might balance scissors/a book/a crayon?" In a similar way, they compare and count units of water volume: "How many small cups fill the large cups? How many large cups fill the box? How many small cups fill the box?"

Through the shared, underlying imagery within these active experiences, children build their isomorphic (similar) understandings; these images then smooth the way for learning other meaningful concepts that underlie different surface forms (Dynamic-Themes). Number lines alone do not substitute for such direct opportunities to construct the meaning of equality; and when adults expect children to use the equals sign before building understandings, they perceive it to mean "action to be completed" or "the end is coming up" in relation to calculations (Ginsburg, Lee, & Boyd, 2008).

Estimations These various physical problem-solving activities help children cross the bridge into numbers and calculations. Estimations and probabilities continue the process.

Almost any activity can begin with estimations. Children are able to estimate/predict such items as how many red, yellow, and green apples might be in a basket; how many Unifix cubes tall a popular classroom material might be; and whether a guinea pig's girth is longer or shorter than a particular length of yarn. You should begin with smaller quantities and gradually increase the variables. Children then graph their *predictions* and *compare* their findings by counting. Some kindergarten children can use a place value chart with tokens to count beyond ten.

Many teachers help children begin to count by sorting. For example, children can use M&M or Gummy Bear candies or Miniature Chocolate flavors wrapped in different paper. On a paper grid, sort by color or type of chocolate. On a second grid, represent each color or flavor within each square with Post-it notes of the same color or the wrapping from each chocolate. Of course, you would control the total number of items in order to sequence children's counting, for example beginning with ten, and later with twenty, items.

In general, after young children think of numbers in groupings (sets), they are able to advance their sense of number for problem solving. Researchers recommend a sequence for solving problems with numbers as follows: begin with tallies; then change to quantity; then manipulate parts in relation to the whole; then equalize and compare; then change the unknown (Baroody & Standifer, 1993). A sequence for solving problems with words includes beginning with children's natural spoken descriptions of concrete materials; then pictorial materials; then mathematics language; then written symbols. Games, discussed later, are helpful in constructing such activities.

Young children, in effect, best develop their number sense and counting within real contexts. Educators recommend that setting the table or matching objects one-to-one builds concepts of cardinality as well as one-to one correspondence (Clements & Sarama, 2009a; Schwartz, 2005). In pre-kindergarten, kindergarten, and the primary grades, there is currently considerable engagement in counting the 100 days of school and then celebrating with many different collections of 100 objects. Reflect on how much of an enjoyable thing is sufficient.

Representation in the Development of Relationship Concepts

Children build an important foundation for mathematical concepts when they understand the relationships of space, shape, and size, but it is not an end in itself. Beginning with surveys, the activities that follow can prepare children to manipulate and represent relationships with symbols.

Surveys (Measurement and Number) and Counting

Surveys grow naturally when you classify and seriate activities, and they are good ways to investigate relative size. The survey is a useful activity because children can be active, work cooperatively, set problems, suggest ways to represent findings, and use both nonstandard and standard measures, as they are able. Children from diverse backgrounds can learn similar concepts and receive practice through various forms whether you classify the content as science or social science.

Counting Surveys also require counting. Children need lots of practice in counting in order to move beyond comparing more than or less than, bigger or smaller, heavier or lighter. You will be counting in the context of everyday events that include how many children can engage in an activity or how many items are available to share. A sequence to develop quantitative counting takes practice.

"Verbal counting" rather than rote counting occurs over years (Clements & Sarama, 2009a, p. 24). At first, children can only say some numbers in words, but not necessarily in sequence. Then they learn to count verbally by starting at the beginning and saying a *string* of words, but they do not even hear counting as separate words. Next they *do* separate each counting word and learn to count up to ten, then twenty, then higher. Only later can children start counting from any number, known as the "Counter from N (N + 1, N − 1)" level. Even later, they learn to skip count and count to 100 and beyond. Finally, children learn to count number words themselves (e.g., "count on"). Among other developments, "they also learn (a) to coordinate verbal counting with objects . . . and (b) that the last counting word names the cardinality of ('how many objects in') the set" (Clements & Sarama, 2009a, p. 26; see also pp. 30–39).

Children's literature reinforces environmental counting. (See the list of Related Children's Books for this chapter.)

Planning a "counting walk" (Copley, 2010, p. 153) with partners in and around the school adds variety to the practice of counting. Each pair of children could count a particular item, such as doors, windows, wastebaskets, chairs, tables, or flags. They

> record their findings on sticky notes, making up to five tally marks per note. For example, a pair of children documenting the number of doors in the school may find that there are twenty doors. These children return to the classroom with four sticky notes labeled "Doors," each note having five tally marks. When children are finished counting, all of the sticky notes are stuck to the classroom's chalkboard, and the children discuss how to organize their results. The children assign items to categories such as Furniture or Things That Can Be Opened. The results are used to make graphs.
>
> *(Copley, 2010, p. 153)*

Surveys are an essential way to integrate mathematics with meaningful content. For example, a study of apples in the autumn integrates social studies with mathematics.

1. Provide a container with red, yellow, and green apples. Ask children to estimate how many apples, fewer than thirty, might be in the container. Then have a child count the apples in groups of ten as another child maintains a tally in groups of ten for all to see.

2. Children survey their favorite color of apple and represent it on a graph. Summarize the findings with a language–experience chart: for example, seven children like red apples.
3. Pairs of children *estimate* the circumference of an apple and cut a piece of yarn.
4. Children see if their yarn is longer, shorter, or the same. Then they hang their yarn on a chart that sorts the three estimates.
5. Ask pairs of children to estimate the number of seeds in their apple and mark the number on a piece of paper or with a tally of pegs.
6. Ask the children to *predict* how many seeds, fewer than twenty, they might find in their respective apple. Cut open the apples and children count the seeds. (See also Inter–Group Experiences: Apple Seeds in Chapter 8.)

Surveys can provide data that might help children transform their thinking as well as their attitudes. They integrate social science research, mathematics, and literacy. From a mathematical perspective, various survey ideas that young children can use successfully appear in Box 12.8.

BOX 12.8 SURVEY ACTIVITIES

- Birthdays each month among children in the group. (This is an engaging first survey of the year.)

[**Procedural note:** When reasonable, use horizontal surveys to reinforce left-to-right reading.]

Favorite or preferred . . . Children self-evaluate each week, when relevant, their favorite/least favorite:

- Writing tool (pencil, maker, pen, crayon, etc.) [**Procedural note:** Pre-kindergarten children use actual objects to represent a "real" graph before using 2-dimensional formats.]
- Activity center
- Story books this week
- Children's actual snacks, such as fruits, vegetables, or baked goods on a large floor graph
- Food in general—cookie, ice cream flavor, or snack in school
- Preferred age (older, younger, same)
- Color (in general, or sneaker or shoe color, etc.)
- Bedtimes
- Vehicle to drive (truck, automobile, spaceship, motorcycle, etc.)
- Television program

- Family size
- How many letters in your name?
- "When I grow up I would like to be . . . (career choices)
- How many cards can you hold in each hand?
- How high can you leap to place paint from your hand onto a chart?
- How many cars of each of several colors are in the parking lot? Which color is the least present? Which color is the most popular?
- How many cars, trucks, motorcycles, and so forth, pass the school during several five-minute time samplings? (Use a sand timer.) Use pegs or a tally to keep track. [**Procedural note:** This is ideal for a collaborative small-group, independent activity.]
- Number of children wearing long or short sleeves today (or shoes, sneakers, or sandals)
- Ways that parents travel to work (walk, automobile, train, bus, motor-cycle, bicycle, etc.)
- Ways that children in class travel to school (walk, bus, automobile, etc.)
- Parents who smoke or do not smoke. Adults in school who smoke or do not smoke (or other yes–no sorting)

Organizing Surveys While young children enjoy participating in and collecting data for surveys, not everybody needs to participate in every survey. Having the entire group sit while each child places a marker next to his or her birthday month or favorite snack can take a very long time, during which most of the children could be doing more productive things than watching the seemingly eternal repetition. Many teachers find that working with a group of about eight children provides enough repetition to represent the communal process, while it avoids too much waiting, which could create demands on the teacher to manage children's inattentive or disruptive behaviors. Then, the whole group might gather to count and summarize the data on a language-experience chart. Keep in mind that *different children doing different things at different times might have equivalent experiences with surveys.*

Some teachers begin with 3-dimensional "real" graphs that use small objects to represent choices, such as magnets of different shape, miniature vehicles, animals, snacks, or people. They then use photographs or pictures and labels of items such as book jackets, musical instruments, foods, television logos, depending upon the subject of the survey. Colors or shapes, and then words, serve to follow behind and match children's skills. This sequence follows Hayakawa's (1949) "abstraction ladder."

After the children have participated in a variety of surveys, pairs of pre-kindergarten children might be ready to cooperate in collecting data independently.

IMAGE 12.3 Real Graph of Class Food Preferences

First, you would plan together the purposes of the survey with the partners and discuss their suggestions for recording what they find. For example, if the survey involves asking individual classmates in which area of the classroom they prefer to work, pairs of children would need some guidelines about when they should approach another child or when it would be intrusive. Before they begin, they would need to agree about answers to the questions in Box 12.9.

BOX 12.9 PLANNING SURVEY FORMAT WITH CHILDREN

- How will we keep a tally (marks on a two-column clipboard or moving pegs from one basket to another)? How will we take turns asking and recording: e.g., mark under "yes" or "no"?
- Who will do what? In what order?
- Will the same person do each task throughout the activity? If we take turns, how do we switch roles?
- When will we have enough samples?
- When will we be finished?

[**Procedural note:** During an activity time, the easiest independent tally activity for pre-kindergarteners is simply to mark "yes" or "no" to a preference between two items. The paper is held in place on a clipboard.]

When developing a survey with a group of children, it is useful to ask them to *estimate* what they are likely to find. [**Procedural note:** As relevant, it is useful to suggest a limited range of numbers within their capacity.] Realistic estimations initially are phrased in terms of more than, less than, the most, the fewest, and so forth, as well as actual numbers. Solicit their suggestions for ways to record their predictions. After all, there is evidence that pre-kindergarten children can invent their own symbolic representations (Atkinson, 1992; Whitin & Whitin, 2010). After recording their *predictions*, the children enjoy the anticipation that builds until they can *compare* their original projections with the actual results.

In addition to recording predictions, you and the children will need to select a way to represent the findings in graphic form. Whether using a horizontal or vertical bar graph format, each section of a grid represents one response. Be sure that each token—whether it is a card, sticker, tooth outline, marking, or photograph of a child—is the same size for each datum. This is important so that anybody who looks at the graph or chart can make comparisons easily. Box 12.10 is an example.

BOX 12.10 GRAPH OF A SURVEY OF LOST TEETH

Lost more than 1 tooth X X X X X
Lost 1 tooth X X X X X X X
Not yet lost a tooth X X X X X X X X X

The next step is to develop a language-experience/shared writing chart of some sort that describes and analyzes the survey. For example,

- 5 children lost more than 1 tooth.
- 7 children lost 1 tooth.
- 9 children did not lose a tooth.
- Most children did not lose a tooth.

Before you know it, kindergarten children are using, comparing, and writing numerals.

While estimations and surveys are one form of activity in which numbers burst into life, there are a number of other approaches that nourish that development.

Number and Operations

Cuisenaire Rods   Cuisenaire rods use visual, spatial, and tactile senses. They are rods with different colors. Rods of the same length are the same color with a *relationship* of one centimeter through ten centimeters. They help young children move from concrete manipulation of materials to dealing with quantitative relationships and actions with numbers.

It is useful to nail an edge of quarter-round molding (or the equivalent, such as a tray) onto one table in the mathematics center, so that the rods cannot slide off easily. It makes sense to use this area for small-group instruction. After two to ten minutes of instruction, you can leave the children with ten to twenty minutes of follow-up activities that are both independent and cooperative, while you circulate and revisit.

At the outset, children need plenty of time to explore freely and build usual and unusual structures with the rods, which should be set out in the mathematics center for several weeks or longer. This activity might be sufficient for many pre-kindergarten children and a few kindergarten children. During the exploratory time, some children may sort them by color intuitively, and some may notice that the rods of the same color are also of the same length—or you might describe what they are doing. When you observe any pattern building, you might begin with one group of those children to play a grab-bag game in which each person has a brown paper sack, described in Box 12.11.

BOX 12.11 GRAB-BAG OF RELATIONSHIPS

- "Pick up a white rod, feel it, and place it in your bag. Now, pick up an orange rod, feel it, and place it in your bag." [**Procedural note:** The greatest contrast exists between the white (1 cm) and the orange rod (10 cm), thus assuring a successful initial experience. Children build a tactile and mental image of quantitative relationships.]
- "Shake them up. Now you can see with your fingertips. Pick out the white rod. Put it back."
- "Now pull out the orange rod. Put it back. That was easy for you."
- "Next, pick up a red rod, feel it, and add it to the bag. Shake it well. Now, pull out a white rod. Put it back. Now, pull out a red rod. Look at that! You can see with your fingertips."
- And so forth.

[**Procedural note:** Teachers render these activities in a playful manner: "Think about what your imagination saw while you felt inside the bag . . . Oh, you really found it!"]

Fingertip retrieval with three lengths of rods as described in Box 12.11 may be enough for one instructional episode. Keeping it brief and seeing that children feel successful means that they will look forward to the next session in which you begin the same way, then gradually add a yellow rod (5cm); on another occasion the green rod (equivalent to three white rods or a red and a white); and on still another occasion, the purple rod (equal in length to two red rods). [**Procedural note:** Before adding a rod to the grab-bag, repeat the earlier sequence of activities, and assess that children have fully felt each rod, before moving forward.]

At a separate time, after reinforcing the tactile relationships with the grab-bag game, you might ask children how they could tell somebody who is not in the grab-bag group their methods for tactile retrieval. As relevant, when children are using the rods, the questions in Box 12.12 can help children develop quantitative relationships.

BOX 12.12 SOME FOCUS QUESTIONS TO SCAFFOLD RELATIONSHIPS WITH RODS

- What can you build with these rods?
- What can you build with the purple rods? (Ask about other colors.)
- Which rods are the same length?
- Which rods are longer than the green? Let's put them in this box. Which rods are shorter? (Ask about other colors).
- If the light green rod were a train and you used red rods and white rods as cars in the train, what different patterns of cars could you make?
- If the purple rod were the length of your train, what different combinations of cars could you use to equal the length, the same length, as your purple train?
- What if the yellow rod were the length of your train? (Ask about other colors when you have assessed that children appear ready for more challenge.)

[**Procedural note:** Remember to raise questions only after children have explored and played with the rods for several weeks, and as relevant to their activities.]

Five-year-olds can comfortably spend as long as twenty minutes substituting two rods for one. They are ready to hear you casually describe this process: "When we put these together, we call it adding their lengths." As children *compare and contrast* lengths, it is clear that there are differences among individuals. Some may need weeks, while others may spend months exploring and making patterns with the rods. The materials may help, but they do not substitute for children's personal construction of the relationships. The ultimate recognition is in the child, not in the materials.

At the very least, it makes sense to offer varied materials and activities. After you and the children explore many possibilities with trains, you might have some centimeter graph paper and colored markers or crayons handy so that children who want to do so can pick their favorite train to record in their mathematics notebook.

At this point, many kindergarten children are on the threshold of manipulating numerals, if they have not already done so spontaneously. The use of graph paper as a discontinuous form provides children with a *contrast* to the continuous form of the rods. Printed materials offer suggestions for using graph paper with rods, for playing with "trains," and for engaging selectively in cooperative games (Davidson, 1995; Ito, 2010). The children may experience a touch of *surprise/cognitive dissonance* in the game Filling Spaces with Rods. In this activity, two or more kindergarten children back-to-back can completely fill a limited area with rods, transform the rods in that area so that they lie end to end, and then *compare* their patterns at various stages with the patterns of other.

Whenever children can predict, transform materials, and *compare and contrast* their results, there is an opportunity to make new connections. Materials provide an additional benefit because children can arrive at their conclusions through *comparing contrasts* and the basic problem-solving technique of trial and error, in this case with some inevitable *inductive* discoveries. You will notice that children who have more opportunity for inductive learning also acquire a stronger sense of power and comfort with quantitative issues. Their findings are not based on an authority figure decreeing a "correct answer," but on their own constructed understandings, which they can verify by returning to the materials. This process builds a *sense of competence* (condition for learning).

After manipulation, train construction and other active pursuits, some children may be ready to consider addition, typically with plus-one. While they add, they can use the Cuisenaire rods as a self-checking device that confirms whether the mental construction is true or false. You may find that some kindergarten children are able to engage in this concrete activity with understanding by mid-year.

Initially, children will spend plenty of time playing out the combinations of plus-one and doubles of numbers (Kamii with Houseman, 2000). At each new phase, it is useful to begin instruction with the rods or other concrete materials and then to have them available for self-checking. You will find that it is easy to individualize instruction within your instructional groups because you can pose different problems to different children. This can be helpful for individuals who are returning to school after an illness or for those who need more time or special help with a procedure. This kind of approach is useful within the Response to Intervention (RTI)/differentiated instructional model because assessment and sequence are apparent in ongoing, specific ways. (Discussion of RTI appears in Chapter 14.)

Kindergarten children tumble into number operations when they engage in the kind of activity that follows: "Let's estimate how many Unifix cubes tall the dinosaur figure is." Children stack the cubes next to their dinosaur toy figures. "How many Unifix cubes tall is Trachodon? Tyrannosaurus Rex? How many more cubes tall is Tyrannosaurus Rex?" Children stack cubes and count. "How many fewer cubes tall is Trachodon?" (M. Silberman, personal communication, 1998).

In addition, young children enjoy singing and tapping the number song "This old man, he played one / He played knick knack on his thumb / With a knick knack, paddy whack, give a dog a bone / This old man is rolling home . . ." The type of counting that takes place in this sort of folk song develops as social knowledge. However, children happily build the vocabulary to describe their experiences.

Commercial and Teacher-made Games

Games are useful to help youngsters understand numbers and the operations of addition and subtraction. There are several "grammars" or varieties of games that children use successfully. Among these are card games, action games, and board games with cards, spinners, dice, or tokens. You might also adapt stories with a die, *predictions*, and *comparison*: for example, *Rosie's Walk* (Hutchins, 1968); *Ten, Nine, Eight* (Bang, 1991); and *The Legend of Spookley the Square Pumpkin* (Troiano, 2003). Moreover, "Vygotskians argue that games provide an opportunity to develop resilience in the face of temporary setbacks" (Bodrova & Leong, 2007, p. 137). Children take turns and persevere while playing. Teacher-designed game formats are also discussed in Chapter 10. Mathematical games with objects are discussed in the following sub-sections.

Card Games You can create a simple Concentration/Memory/Pairs game that matches cards of dots with cards containing numerals, using the rules outlined in Chapter 10. Some kindergarten children can match two sets of dots on one card with their total as a single set of dots on another card. This early addition activity requires strong visual memory skill. An advanced game would provide two numerals on one card to match their total on another card. A variation is to use ordinary adult playing cards for Pairs games. To start, select cards with fewer numbers. Using either numerals or suits, children seek pairs of the same quantity after the cards are placed face down.

Teachers usually begin to use adult playing cards with part of the deck when children can identify numerals. Two children at a time can independently play a "more-than" or "less-than" game variation of War. Another name for this *compare* game is One More (Clements & Sarama, 2009a, p. 51). This card game might use cards numbering up to ten. It is a game of chance in which players match pairs of numbered playing cards to see which is greater. [**Procedural note:** To reduce the variables, begin with cards numbering up to five. To increase the variables, play with two decks of cards numbering to ten.] Researchers have found that 6-year-olds can successfully play a game of Double War in which they make sums with two cards, using a deck that has limited values (Kamii with Houseman, 2000).

Dominos requires that children match equivalent sets of dots on wooden or plastic pieces; and you can sometimes find or create domino cards. After instruction, kindergarten children are able to play Go Fish, in which they ask each other for a particular card by number in order to collect and discard pairs of identical cards.

Board Games Researchers have found that playing number board games benefits the numerical knowledge of low-income children (Ramani & Siegler, 2008). Board games encourage counting by using dice, spinners, and tokens. They require counting to move along the board or you could adapt a color-card format, such as Candyland, to use numerals. As children play, you could scaffold by appreciating, "Look, how many can you/did you move? How many more until . . .?" [**Procedural note:** Some children need help in maintaining the sequence of the parts and path that tokens can move.]

An African board game, commercially available as Kalah, Owari, or Mankalah, encourages kindergarten children to plan ahead. You can make the game board easily out of a regular twelve-hole (two-by-six) egg carton, with an attached "bowl" or box at each end made from two halves of the upper part of the carton. To begin the game, there are three or four beans (or pebbles) in each of the twelve "pots," six of which "belong" to each of two children. On each turn, one player empties one pot from her side of the game, placing one bean in each succeeding pot, moving clockwise. When a bean enters a bowl, it is out of the action. The person who ends up with nothing but empty pots on her side finishes first. You can make the game easier by using half the egg carton and fewer beans/pebbles. As children play, they learn to anticipate strategies and intuitively begin to add and subtract. [**Procedural note:** Some children need help to start placing only one bean in each succeeding pot. After you show a few pairs of children how to play and assess that they understand the rules, they can show others how to play (with your intermittent monitoring).]

Pre-kindergarten children begin to play checkers, while some kindergarten children are able to play chess. These games call upon children's spatial imagery and working memory.

Games with Objects In another game, teachers use lima beans or commercial items, painted on one side, to play with probability and adding.

1. Toss five (later more) lima beans, painted on one side, onto a tray or felt cloth.
2. *Predict* the pattern of colors before tossing (*experience*) and place colored stickers on graph paper.
3. *Compare* findings with predictions (*surprise/cognitive dissonance*).
4. *Represent* the finding with colored stickers underneath the prediction with a one:one correspondence.

Children have the opportunity to see the different combinations of colors that can add up to five or six or another number of beans. The use of *hanging links* in two colors can be a dramatic representation of the commutative nature of numbers and can help children move toward understanding the equals sign (Copley, 2010, pp. 80–83). Children create combinations of two link colors up to five. You place each combination in sequence on a wire hanger in symmetrical order, showing all combinations of five, and later six–ten.

Partners take turns in a fingertips combination game with Unifix cubes (Richardson, 1984, p. 87). Child 1 places cubes on the fingertips of both hands. Child 2 records on graph paper the cubes on each hand. Child 1 changes the number of cubes on each hand and Child 2 records the new combination. Children figure out different combinations of a set number of cubes, initially a total of five, then up to ten and more as children are able. Games with bowling pins also use counting.

Out-of-sight Games Mystery "feely" bags can help children build a number sense and practice counting. Fill each of several bags with a different number of uniform objects, such as beans, beads, cubes, or token bears. After feeling and counting the objects in one bag, children feel for the same number of objects in another bag to find a match. Then they add one more item to the bag and feel their way until they touch a match in another bag.

An advanced use of out-of-sight objects with pre-kindergarten children is the Bears in a Cave game (Copley, 2010, p. 60). Begin with five visible objects; place some out of sight; and children guess how many are missing. You might also reverse the process and children guess how many more objects have been added. A variation on the out-of-sight objects game uses a spinner or task cards and Unifix cubes (adapted from Richardson, 1984, p. 87). Task cards or the spinner could direct players as follows: "Find a bag with more or less than [a number]." "Find two bags equal to [the number]."

Flannel boards lend themselves to manipulating pieces. You can create patterning games, combining sets, and adding or subtracting items. You can also use the flannel board to extend folk tales that deal with numbers. CD-Roms are yet another source for commercial early mathematical games (Neuman & Roskos with Wright & Lenhart 2007, p. 111). Websites provide ideas for mathematical games with computer manipulations.[2]

A summary of research on the effectiveness of mathematical instruction identifies advantageous factors relating to achievement as follows: hands-on activities; using everyday events to practice counting; choices among activities; talking about the activity and reflecting on the process; presenting and debating strategies; playing mathematical strategy games; and applying mathematical skills to solve problems (Heuser, 2002, pp. 74, 76, 93).

Pathways, Assessment, and Scaffolds

When you see how children manipulate a thoughtful sequence of concrete materials, you can assess what they understand.

When you find that a child does not understand a particular concept, reduce the activity by one variable in order to support the child's *sense of competence* (condition for learning). When you return to the activity a week or three weeks later, intervening experiences might have prepared the child to be ready for the next steps. For example, if a child with two sets is counting by ones, you might scaffold by commenting, "You really know that first amount, so here is one more. Now, how many do you have altogether?" Youngsters' ability to "count-on" might be erratic for a while before they apply the concept consistently. Other scaffolds when you confer with children might include asking, "How did you find that?" "Who used other ways to find the same thing?" "This is a pattern. What's your pattern?" "What's a different way to create patterns with that number of . . .?"

When children share their findings, it is not necessary to announce, "No," or "That's wrong." Your attitude tells the children that there could be more than one way to solve a problem and that you respect their effort and thinking. Their *sense of competence* that grows from our respect for their thinking has the potential to keep open the learning process. In this way, you also build a caring community. At the same time, you can assess what concepts they understand. Keep in mind that tomorrow lies ahead for 4- and 5-year-olds.

Your image of the progression of mathematical concepts from simple to complex guides your ability to assess what children are able to do and what they can do next with your help. Educators generally agree about the pathways of early mathematical development, outlined in Box 12.13. The sequence of complexity provides a guide to assessing children's understanding and planning relevant activities.

BOX 12.13 PATHWAYS IN EARLY MATHEMATICAL DEVELOPMENT (ADAPTED FROM CLEMENTS & SARAMA, 2009A)

- *Recognizing numbers and number sense (subitizing):* Pre-Explicit Number; Number Sense, e.g., "Subitizing introduces basic ideas of cardinality— 'how many,' ideas of 'more' and 'less,' ideas of parts and wholes and their relationships, beginning arithmetic, and in general, ideas of quantity . . . the building blocks of mathematics" (p. 10).
- *Counting:* Pre-Counter (random number names); Counter (chant); Reciter (up to 5, then 10); Correspondent (one-to-one); Counter (Small Numbers, "how many?"; up to 20, may write numerals up to 10); Producer

---

(contextual counting); Counter and Producer (10–30); Count backwards from 10; to Verbal and Object Counter from N (N + 1, N – 1).

- *Comparing, ordering and estimating numbers:* From one-to-one to Mental number line (to 10).
- *Addition and subtraction (emphasizing counting strategies):* Pre-Explicit; Nonverbal; Small Number (less than 5, then 8); Make It N (count-on); Find Change (missing addend); Counting Strategies (count-on and counting up to 20).
- *Composing number and addition and subtraction:* Pre-Part–Whole Recognizer; Inexact Part–Whole Recognizer; Composer to 4, then 5, 7, 10, and doubles to 20.
- *Shapes:* "Same Thing" Comparer; Shape Recognizer—Typical, then "Similar"; Shape Matcher—More Shapes; Sizes and Orientation; Combination Shape; Recognizer; *Classifying.*
- *Addition:* Nonverbal; Small Number (up to 5); Find Result (up to 10); Find Change (including add on); Counting-on (conceptually embedding smaller within larger number).

Scaffolds. The authors suggest games and activities with materials, similar to those discussed above, along with related computer games to reinforce these concepts. (See also http://www.gse.buffalo/edu/org/buildingblocks/.)

A similar sequence consists of the following: one-to-one correspondence of objects; pairs; sort, classify, seriate; estimate, grouping and sets; numbers and counting; operations; and measurement (Snow & Van Hemel, 2008). Still another list of early mathematical strands to consider are the following: number and operations; geometry and spatial sense; measurement, data and probability; algebra (patterns); skip counting, 2, 5, 10; counting 1s and 10s; hundred chart; join and separate; addition; counting–on and –back; facts for 10; doubles and near doubles; subtraction; equals sign; and estimation (NBPTS, 2010).

It is noteworthy that children's skills fluctuate. For example, pre-kindergarten children might not always count objects accurately while kindergarten children count objects accurately most of the time and choose counting as a tool. It is important to notice if children align nonstandard as well as standard measuring tools at the start of the object. It is worth reiterating that constructions with objects and games help children develop the imagery they need to understand quantitative relationships.

Based upon research findings, educators further recommend that

Young children need to be able to touch and move objects to give an accurate demonstration of their understanding of the concepts. Assessments using still pictures on a piece of paper are likely to underestimate their mathematical understanding, as they may be better able to solve problems when they are allowed to move actual objects around physically.

> Since young children's primary experience with numbers focuses on counting, any assessment of number sense should examine how children count groups of objects. Assessment should include asking the child to count to measure their knowledge of number sequence names and rote counting, assessing the child's understanding of one-to-one correspondence between objects and counting and of cardinality. Similarly, assessment of spatial sense and reasoning (geometry) should involve observation of children engaged in activities using shapes. Assessment of children's understanding of measurement in early childhood should begin with asking them to make direct comparisons of different attributes of objects. For classification and sorting, children should be provided with materials or objects and asked to create their own groups and describe their reasoning . . . [T]heir understanding should be evaluated based on their reasoning, not solely by the evaluator's criteria. Assessment items for mathematical reasoning should be embedded in other content topics.
>
> *(Snow & Van Hemel, 2008. pp. 117–118)*

For example, look at how children use shapes. Ask them to create their own groups of materials and how they made the decision to group them. You might ask children to count a number of objects; to draw the number of objects; to extend a model pattern of objects; to count backwards; to count *any* group of objects. Children's active use of objects as well as friendly, integrated interviews can provide both caring and effective formats for systematically assessing their achievements. Other scholars suggest the following: it is possible to see how children use comparative terms after showing them objects that are bigger, smaller, lighter; to see how children order a set of objects according to size, weight, and length; and how they solve problems that involve collecting and analyzing data (Neuman & Roskos with Wright & Lenhart, 2007, pp. 109 ff).

The need to provide support for your activity-based learning environment in the time of standards indicates the relevance for such systematic collection of information (see Schwartz, 2005; Schwartz & Copeland, 2010). For example, teachers typically ask children to show how they sort objects by shape; or by color, then by size, then by both. One educator recommends using a spinner that could point to red–blue–yellow or, in other contexts, a spinner divided into plus or minus (Copley, 2010, p. 95). Using a spinner can make this kind of assessment feel like a game rather than an interrogation.

Reflections

You might wonder why it is worth the time and effort to plan many concrete experiences with young children. After all, they can memorize number facts and, later, use calculators to get the "right" answers. To use calculators, consider that they would need to know when and how to use them. To do so requires that they understand the *relationships* between events and the rules underlying mathematical operations. Young children do not need to define the rules denotatively but they can learn to function within mathematical systems, as is evidenced by a body of significant research. Again, the research supports the notion that children acquire early mathematical concepts when they engage in direct experiences with manipulative materials and game formats.

Researchers find that teachers of lower-income children recommend more direct instruction while teachers of higher-income children recommend more integrated learning of mathematics; both groups of teachers agreed that instruction should be enjoyable, without pressure, built upon children's interests, and different formats for children who have different capacities (Lee & Ginsburg, 2007).[3] Therefore, it is a particular service to children from low-income families to provide experiences, such as board games, that many children from middle-income families experience before arriving at school.

Indeed, it is possible to envision a mathematics and literacy education that adapts to children when you have an image of the pathways and phases of mathematics development. There is a growing consensus among researchers that, since young children have many experiences with quantity and shape outside of school settings, with children from middle-income families generally privileged, early childhood teachers can do no harm by providing intentional teaching of mathematics in the child-friendly ways described (Bowman, Donovan, & Burns, 2000; Casey, Erkut, Ceder, & Young, 2007; Clements & Sarama, 2004, 2007, 2009a, 2009b; Cross, Woods, & Schweingruber, 2009; National Mathematics Advisory Panel, 2008; Schwartz, 2005).

The research-based consensus is that the major areas of number sense (subitizing), number, and geometry are relevant for young children—in ways that match how they learn—a view that is consistent with national standards. In particular, children need to understand the relationships between quantities and the ways in which procedures can represent transformations (National Mathematics Advisory Panel, 2008).

Images come first; computation follows. There are times when schools expect children to memorize steps in computing numerals mechanically without any roots in the children's brains. However, when youngsters have experiences with 3-dimensional materials, they increase their capacity to imagine how to manipulate quantities. The Dynamic-Themes activity-based learning environments focus on relationships and transformations that provide children with reasons to use mathematics while they are building their knowledge and fluency.

It is apparent that young children enter pre-kindergarten with quantitative experiences and knowledge, and that early childhood teachers can successfully engage young children in mathematics learning in both integrative activities (described in many chapters of this book) and intentional, focused teaching using the conditions for learning. As with any skill, children need focused practice in systematic, sequenced activities that can help them build knowledge, a *sense of competence*, and fluency.

Mathematics education, no less than language education, has ridden a pendulum between formal drill and situational, meaningful learning. You could integrate mathematics with social studies- and science-related experiences. You could create essential questions for which children would apply mathematical skills. You could create playful ways to practice skills while incidentally providing social knowledge, such as counting and topological vocabulary. The next chapter suggests systematic ways to schedule time for this type of activity-based learning environment.

PART IV

Planning, Assessment, and Community Connections

This part of the book provides an overview of how to schedule teaching and learning across a year and all day. It opens with Chapter 13: Planning a Year, Month, Week, Day, and Moment. Planning the schedule relies on assessing what children know and can do, which is the focus of Chapter 14. The focus of assessment is to figure out the next steps to help children build their understandings. In turn, assessment, teaching, and learning integrate how socio-cultural and family contributions to children's learning blend with your teaching, the subject of Chapter 15. Although these subjects interconnect, words and print require a linear presentation of these non-linear processes.

13

PLANNING A YEAR, MONTH, WEEK, DAY, AND MOMENT

Introduction

The pre-kindergarten child schedule-helper-of-the-week says, "We just finished story time. I'm turning over the books card. The next activity is outdoors!"

In preparation for youngsters to take responsibility for following a daily schedule, you could prepare a laminated picture-and-title card for each activity of the day before school begins. Then you would help them practice turning and replacing the cards. When individual schedule-helper children become acquainted with the schedule and words, the cards could include only titles.

Before the first day of school, check off a personal list that includes some of the items listed in Box 13.1.

BOX 13.1 BEFORE THE FIRST DAY OF SCHOOL

- Arrange furniture and set apart centers.
- Label interest centers, prepare materials, and set up hooks or Velcro to indicate the safe number of participants.
- Plan the first day, and days, with alternative ideas to reduce or increase challenges and choices.
- Prepare laminated cards for each activity to place in the daily pocket chart schedule.
- Prepare laminated in–out sign-in cards with each child's photograph and name for daily attendance.

- Prepare name tags for each child.
- Label children's personal closets and storage.
- Prepare bulletin boards with some enticing photos from prior years with brief captions.
- Place growing plants.
- Prepare a welcome message for families.
- Prepare teacher-made phonemic and mathematics games ready for use later.

IMAGE 13.1 Class Helper Pocket Chart

You would plan the general schedule for the moment, day, week, month, and year. However, within that structure, listen and observe carefully to detect ways in which to support children's possible choices and needs. When children feel empowered by choices, they are likely to be self-directed and attentive to experiences. When you plan activities with the imagery of Dynamic-Themes in mind, you could provide equivalent underlying images that include different degrees of challenge and participation. *In these sensitive ways, you can try to match experiences that maintain a balance between what children need, are capable of doing with support, and want or might prefer.*

Building a Caring Community

First Days of School

During the first few days, you might meet a pre-kindergarten child who ducks under his mother's skirt at the door. An administrator could advise his mother to wear trousers to school. In that way, the child could be tempted to see the happy things that other children are doing in order to ease his transition. You might also encounter parents who have a push–pull reaction: that is, "Another kiss before you go . . ." It is helpful to plan ahead to help children who are attending any school for the first time or for those who might have anxiety about the transition to a new classroom in the "big" school. Keep in mind that a child who is upset or crying has feelings worthy of our respect.

You can expect that a few kindergarten children and many pre-kindergarten children as well as immigrant children may be coming to school for the first time. Attachment theory reminds us that healthy children develop a secure emotional connection with a caring adult (Bowlby, 1988; Honig, 2002). The next section discusses some successful, alternative ways that schools could use to ease the initial transition to a new setting.

Initial Adjustment to School

Plan together with the assistant teacher/teacher aide how to work consistently with children and parents. Everyone needs to know the areas for which they are responsible so that there are no location or time gaps in supporting the children. Box 13.2 lists ways to support a smooth adjustment.

BOX 13.2 PROCEDURES TO SUPPORT A SMOOTH ADJUSTMENT

- Some schools arrange teacher home visits before school begins. With permission at registration or at a home visit, teachers take separate digital photos of the parent/guardian and the child. [**Procedural note:** Children feel welcome when their photograph and name are present on their name tag, locker/cubby, and attendance card.]

- Find out about possible allergies and who will meet the child at the end of the day. Procedures for other arrangements and emergency contacts need to be clear and written.

- School policies often include a brief questionnaire or family interview, with translation as needed. Parents have a chance to share information about allergies, other health issues, earlier group care and education experiences, after-school childcare arrangements, and other important information. There may be questions about children's favorite toys, games, television shows, computer experience, public library use, reading experiences, or travel experience, as well as other siblings or family pets. This is an important opportunity to collect emergency contact information as well as permission for field trips and digital photographs of their children at work.

- When possible, each child and family member visit before the school year begins (or before the preceding school year ends) to meet the teacher(s) and see the classroom's temptations; this gives children a sense of predictability and control.

- A familiar adult (parent, grandparent, or caregiver) and child meet briefly with a small group and the teacher(s) in the classroom and tour the classroom, using selected materials. This is particularly helpful if children will come on a school bus.

- Children see the location of the "family waiting room" on their way to the classroom to spend an hour or two with a small group of children and the teacher.

- On another day, provide selected materials. Some children find comfort in manipulating play dough or clay.

- Try keeping each child engaged in an activity, particularly looking ahead to easing transitions when children might be likely to miss their family member.

- If a child is inconsolable, you might walk him/her to the family room to receive reassurance that the adult is waiting, and possibly take back to the classroom something from the family member, such as keys or a scarf.

- If a child continues to need additional support, the family member might return to the classroom and sit against a wall. [**Procedural note:** Ahead of time, all family members would be instructed not to help the child with materials in the classroom but to direct the child to the teacher for help.]
- One program suggests that children could have a family picture to keep in the classroom (Epstein, 2009, p. 32).
- "An interactive family bulletin board allows children to match their pictures with those of their parents; this is another way to demonstrate attachment when parents and children are separated" (Good, 2005, p. 79).

Some ideas for first day activities include providing name tags for everyone; singing a favorite movement–activity song such as "If you're happy and you know it clap your hands . . ." Then keep changing: for example, "cross your arms," "touch your toes/nose/neck/shoulder," "tap your knee," "smile a smile," "whisper hello," and so forth. Use your imagination and invite the children's ideas. An alternative is a finger play such as "Where is thumbkin? Here I am. Here I am. How are you this morning? Very well, thank you. Run away." Then, "pointer," "middle finger," "ring finger," and "pinky." Some teachers introduce a class puppet. Others read a brief book at the end of the day. Some teachers provide a decorative mystery bag or box and model how to ask for clues (L. Davey, personal communication, 2009).

Show children the three, four, or five activity centers that you set up ahead of time and *briefly* begin to demonstrate the planning, transition, and circulating process. Children might independently use tabletop materials, such as bead stringing and peg boards, jigsaw puzzles, play dough, drawing with stunning markers, Lego table, and library center. Some teachers provide each child with their own name card and invite them to write their name on whiteboards or a 5 × 8–inch card.

Plan with the whole group, and ask children to raise their hands (practice this) to select a starting activity: for example, "Four people [hold up fingers and count] can fit at the Lego table," and so forth. Ask children to raise their hand when they finish an activity so that you can appreciate it and help them plan their next activity. Then, using a brisk pace, send a few at a time to each activity by calling names, type of shoe, or birthday month. [**Procedural note:** This prevents pushing and sets a calm tone.] Circulate constantly, nodding and encouraging. Then help them plan their next activity. Keep a positive focus on routines as you let the children know how happy you are to meet them. [**Procedural note:** Model using a low-pitched, calm tone as you address children, keeping eye contact with all of them. After they disperse, avoid calling across the room, but speak quietly to each group as you circulate. These methods help establish a healthy sound level.]

During the first six to eight weeks, you will circulate and reinforce routines and smooth transitions. At the same time, you have a chance to become acquainted with individuals and assess what they might need to learn next. As children become increasingly independent with routines and traffic patterns, you are able to engage increasingly in small-group and individual instruction. After you establish routines, you can build up activities that represent a Dynamic-Theme and thread related activities throughout the year. As you help children knit their caring community, you can use classroom-proven approaches to build coherence, discussed below.

Continuing to Build a Caring Community

We/Us   When you focus on we/us rather than I/me, you convey the sense that "We are together in this place." When you plan many small-group and pair-share activities, it is easier for children to feel part of a class community than if most of the time is devoted to whole-group activity; and choices empower them to feel ownership within the community. As you add activity centers, the children take on rotating classroom jobs, such as turning over the schedule card, counting out napkins for the snack table, and replacing materials that they can understand will help them to find things the next time they need them.

Young children sometimes need help to remain focused on a topic. You might notice everyone talking about transportation when a child offers information about the sweater his aunt is knitting for him. If you were to ask, "What reminded you about the sweater?" the child might talk about the green wool which is the same color as the truck delivering food to the supermarket. Therefore, trying to assess the connections that a child makes can often be a challenge. Sometimes, you might simply comment, "Thanks for sharing." While respecting the syncretic connections that a child makes, and focusing on ideas and respect for one another, Box 13.3 lists some of the comments you might use during a group discussion.

BOX 13.3 GROUP FOCUS ON SHARING IDEAS

- Build up we/us: e.g., "Tell *us* . . ." "This is *our* classroom, *our* jobs, *our* materials . . ." Reduce "I/me," " I want you to . . ."
- "*Let's* listen to what Dina has to say."
- "Think about what he's saying. When did something like that happen to you?"
- "*Let's* find out what she is going to say? I wonder what she is going to tell *us*."
- "Who has a different idea?"

- "What do you have to tell *us*?"
- "*Let's* see if he agrees with you."
- "Imagine how far that would go."
- "What do you think about that?"
- "*Let's* see what might happen next."
- Use positive, appreciative language: "It's wonderful to see how interested you are. Hold on to your idea and tell *us* when she finishes." (Alternative: "You can hold the talking stick/teddy bear after she finishes.")
- "Think first."
- "Please stay in your own space." (Alternative to begin the session: "Everybody imagine that you are in a bubble.")

[**Procedural note:** When you believe that a child needs redirection, it is useful to speak privately to the child in order to avoid the possibility that others might categorize and scapegoat the targeted child.]

Educators find that they can "build a culture of inquiry and collaboration . . . [when they] look at children's work with groups of children. For example, compare and contrast living things by highlighting the different ways they have been represented. What did you notice? How did you find that out?" (Chalufour & Worth, 2005, p. 136).

You can also build a sense of trust and caring, along with self-regulation, when you appreciate their work by encouraging and validating without evaluating:

- "That was hard to do but you did it."
- "It's great when you try out new ideas."
- "You are working so carefully."
- "You really are thinking about how to figure that out."
- "You figured out how to slide down."
- "You really seem to understand that."
- "See how much you get done when you think first."
- "You took the initiative when you . . ."
- "That looks complicated. What did you do first?"

When children hear only "Good job/How nice/I like it"—evaluating without validating—they could depend on external motives and reduce their self-motivation. Share *why* you appreciate their actions.

Share Classroom Jobs   All children share in maintaining the classroom with specific jobs that rotate. One kindergarten teacher (Kuhn, 2009) compiled the list of jobs that appears in Box 13.4.

BOX 13.4 CLASSROOM HELPER JOBS

- Attendance (Check that everyone turned over their attendance card on arrival and count children present and absent)
- Lunch count
- Milk delivery
- Schedule card-changer and substitute (Turn down the card for each completed activity and turn up the card for the next one)
- Calendar
- Line leader
- Door holder
- Hand-out
- Collect items
- Custodians
- Snack table helper (If you have a whole-group snack, this person might set out the correct number of napkins)
- Room inspectors
- Lights
- Plants
- Pattern leader (One child claps a rhythm for the assembling children to join while the teacher finishes helping a small group or individual)
- Pet caretakers (For example, pet caretakers follow a picture–word chart: "Feed George and Ralph [class ferrets]; Give George and Ralph fresh water; Clean the ferret cage; Feed Scooby and Sandy [hermit crabs] food and biscuits; Give Scooby and Sandy their water; and Feed the goldish"]

Friend of the Day/Star of the Week   Some teachers invite one child at a time, perhaps once every few days, to be "Our Friend of the Day." Other children in the group state something nice about the focus child. Of course, the children know that there will be a time for each of them to become the subject. [**Procedural note:** This might be an opportunity to reinforce the notion of the alphabetic sequence of the first letters of children's last names. In another method, children draw a raffle of numerals that sets the order in which they become a "Friend (or "Star"), or the subject of a "Biography Display." The numerals organize the sequence of each child's "stardom."] A group of pre-kindergarten children and their teacher can discuss what a good friend does and create a dictated chart of the children's comments (G. Mauro, personal communication, 2010).

Some procedures for the "Star of the Week" are as follows:

- Day 1. Bring photographs to share.
- Day 2. Sit in the teacher's rocking chair.
- Day 3. Show and tell about the photographs.
- Day 4. Pick read-aloud for the day.
- Day 5. Pick the name of the next "star" out of a cup.

(Adapted from D. Popovchak, personal communication, 2010)

Of course, the cup is empty after all the names have been selected.

Biography Display   Other teachers create a bulletin board that focuses on one child each week. The bulletin board includes a photograph of the child. The teacher asks the child's family for information and photographs about their history, such as location and date of birth, baby and toddler photographs if available, names of siblings, favorite food(s), playthings, and pastimes.

Birthday Parties   Some teachers ask families to include all boys, all girls, or all the children in out-of-school birthday parties. In this way, everyone can feel included. Some schools, mindful of health concerns and obesity, have policies concerning what foods to bring to birthday celebrations; they share with parents the celebration schedule and nutritious menu recommendations, along with important information about food allergies. When birthday candles are present, children happily count the number as each candle is placed on the cupcake (or in a holder, if a cake is not present) and happily count backwards as you remove each candle. The birthday child wears a "birthday hat." Another initiative is that family members provide not cupcakes but a book for the class library (G. Mauro, personal communication, 2010.) "You can even provide a master list of titles from which caregivers can choose" (Fountas & Pinnell, 2006, p. 242).

Pair-share and Pairs-share   Kindergarten children are able to share and exchange their interest in a particular book with another child. They might do so by talking as well as drawing and writing about their book. Another form of pair-share is for children to discuss with one another possible solutions to an issue before sharing with a larger group. Children are also able to exchange their mathematical solutions, using concrete materials. A teacher who plans many interviews with community workers includes pair-share activities during the whole-group interview process (Rogovin, 2001). In this way, all children have the chance to participate actively and express their own ideas. With your support, some kindergarteners later in the year are able to participate in book clubs to share their pleasure in reading about similar topics of interest, including nonfiction.

Cooperative Sharing of Items or Out-of-school Experiences If you have ever sat through a forty-minute whole-class show-and-tell session, you might reflect on how tedious it is for the listeners and how difficult it is for some of the child presenters. A different format for a "cooperative show and tell" is to "Invite all pairs (or groups) to converse quietly at the same time: twelve children talk to their partners and then they reverse roles. [You can follow up with pairs placing their objects for others to view. Then,] Ask the children to visualize what they might draw and write about before the pairs (or groups) move to journal writing" (Swan, 2009, p. 20).

Each One Teach One Children often show one another how to engage in a game or computer technique. For example, pre-kindergarten children can show one another how to play checkers and memory-card games. Kindergarten children are able to show one another how to assemble a 3-dimensional wood puzzle.

Variety and Delights One educator describes a pictorial "message board" on which pre-kindergarten children can see pictures of some new materials, and special or distinctive things to take place that day (Epstein, 2009, pp. 75, 77). A child might bring information such as "My grandfather had a birthday party." You might add an illustration with caption to the message board and announce someone's birthday or the birth of a sibling.

A classroom also needs occasions for "delights" as well as special shared celebrations and events. Multicultural holidays provide opportunities. Another approach appears in a film that depicts a huge, stuffed giraffe visiting the lunch crowd, to the children's delight (Reggio Emilia, 1987). Youngsters also enjoy interviewing adults, and appreciate seeing and hearing performances of different instruments and music, some of which represent different cultures.

Problem Setting and Solving Interpersonal Problems Children need to feel safe in order to feel part of a caring community. Ask youngsters, "What do you think we can do to make sure that happens?" (Kohn, 1996, pp. 110–111). It is clear that the discussion of classroom dilemmas is essential in a setting where children can feel safe to share their thinking with acceptance in a supportive environment.

A small-group discussion provides an opportunity for children to talk about and solve problems in their community, such as running in the classroom, not helping at cleanup time, not sharing, or not taking turns. You might introduce a problem by using typical strategies for beginning a group time: for example, telling a story; reading a hidden message; using props such as puppets, photographs of feelings, or pictures to focus on the problem. Youngsters ably deal with issues such as loss, fairness, and aggression. They can share experiences, and reflect on important questions, such as: "What things about a person make you want to be his friend?" "How could we solve our disagreements without hitting?" "When did someone help when you needed help?"

After children offer different solutions, they might role-play alternatives (McCaslin, 1980; Shaftel & Shaftel, 1983). When you *revisit* the problem later you can decide which ideas work and which need modification. The satisfaction of dealing with issues as a group ("*We* solved the problem!") further builds the children's sense of belonging to a vital and meaningful community.

When youngsters participate in setting and solving problems, they have the chance to recognize patterns and make connections, and hence see things in new ways. Among the devices that help us to see things in new ways are analogies. The intentional use of analogy can serve as a tool that helps children learn, create, and set and solve problems because analogies help us locate some familiar elements and fresh ideas upon which to build solutions.

You can work at solving problems with *direct analogies*, in which children draw on parallels to increase their understanding (for example, to highlight a behavioral problem, "What animal acts like that?"). You could also use *personal analogies*, in which children imagine that they have "become" the animal or object and indicate how they think or what they can do in their analogous role. It is useful for you to explore with the children how the analog is like or unlike its referent, in order to suggest new possibilities.

Values questions often arise. Questions such as the following also tend to encourage children to consider alternative viewpoints:

- What might have made that important or worthwhile to them? When might they have begun to see it that way?
- What would you have done if you were there?
- How might you help them to find a peaceful/happy/honest solution?
- What are some things she bought that you wouldn't buy? Why? What would be more important for you to buy?
- What might happen if you/they felt differently?
- How might they do it differently next time?
- If that happened to you, what might you think/do/plan?
- When do some people tell lies?
- What might make him feel friendly toward you?
- When might you choose to do it that way?

[**Procedural note:** In the expanded interaction that is likely to result from such questions, you may find that, after planning half a dozen questions, only one or two fit into a particular session because children raise other relevant issues for you to follow up.]

In trying to solve a social problem, young children may focus on a surface variable from their own viewpoint rather than address the essential factors. Piaget's (1950) concept of decentration reflects this interaction of affect and cognition and supports the notion that "logical thought is necessarily social" (p. 164). Both he and Vygotsky (1978), from their distinct perspectives, recognize that thinking becomes more flexible through social interaction. Therefore, your role as a questioner who welcomes children's questions and curiosity is pivotal.

When teachers help children build rules together and explore analogies, children tend to become more independent as they come to see other points of view (DeVries & Zan, 2003). Some teachers simply tell children the rules. Others ask them to participate in planning before the children understand the need for rules. In this case, "Children may view rule making as another exercise in trying to figure out the right answer or say what they think the teacher wants to hear. The rules that they suggest may not reflect a real understanding of the need to treat others in moral ways" (DeVries & Zan, 2003, p. 65). Still other groups develop rules after group discussions about a particular event or issue. Even if rules are hung up for all to see, keep in mind that children are still learning how to play with the rules of games and are incomplete classifiers. Consider patience when you compare children's abilities with those adults who are able to verbalize a code of rules but might show quite different behavior on waiting lines. Therefore, we need to adapt to each situation, and sometimes to individual needs.

Separate Plans for Individuals Despite your best plans, there might be an occasion when the same pre-kindergarten child during read–aloud disrupts the remainder of the group, all of whom seem to be fully engaged. It is reasonable to plan beforehand separately for an individual who needs a different experience. You might observe that "Paul" is able to focus better when he uses play dough at a table during story time. When he hums loudly and another adult signals him to be quiet, you might hear him say (adjusting the play dough), "OK. I'll turn down my iPod." At the same time, it is apparent that Paul hears every word and sees every picture. Whenever a mischievous Curious George (Rey, 1973) story appears, he might announce that he is ready to be with the group—and he is. If you were to have a rule that everyone must sit for story time, then Paul could create a major disruption of the group's focus. Therefore, a flexible plan for him will help everyone. The other children accept the routine because they simply enjoy story time.

Assessing Group Size or Composition Youngsters send signals that you can notice when a group is too large or too small for a particular activity. Either situation tells you that you should try to adjust group size. For example, if a group is too large, children might persist in the following behaviors:

- pay attention to other children rather than the activity;
- lose the sequence of activity;
- be reluctant to participate in discussion;
- ignore or not follow group focus comments, gestures, or directions.

(A child might also be misplaced in the group, either not yet ready for the activity focus or beyond it.)

You might feel:

- uncertain of specific progress of individuals;
- pressure to provide more than the time allows;
- concern about too little chance for child participation.

(Sometimes one child less or a particular child less might improve communication.)

Your perceptions help you adapt each moment against the background of each day and beyond.

Sequence of Activities

Although you plan the daily sequence of activities, you should flexibly expand or reduce a particular part of your class schedule. An exception is the need to accommodate schedules with others in the school who might share outdoor or indoor playground or gymnasium space. Lunch service, arrival, and departure times are also fixed. There is an outline below of some ways that some teachers sequence and schedule events, and organize and manage time.

Experiential Activity-based Daily All-day Schedule

Entry Routines   (10–15 minutes, dependent upon bus service or none) For example, greet, health look over, each child moves personal attendance card and stores clothing and backpack as relevant.

Group Planning   (10–20 minutes, with briefer meetings early in the school year) Build in opportunities for a mini-lesson to focus on a Dynamic-Theme, specific literacy or mathematical concept, such as estimation games that require counting or uses of space. Children might also learn to use new equipment. In addition, some educators suggest offering children a choice of books that you would read to them (Diffily & Sassman, 2002).

The HighScope Foundation uses a variety of engaging activities successfully to assist children in planning. For example, pre-kindergarten children hold tickets which they use to "board a class train" to tour centers with a teacher, state a plan, and remain in a center. Another approach creates tabletop paper tracks toward a picture of each center, and small groups of children move their miniature cars toward the picture of their center of interest and state their plans (HighScope Press, 2009). After the plan and activities, some would share what they had done, hence the "plan–do–review" format.

Activity Centers (60–90 minutes) *Provisions*: socio-dramatic activity with literacy materials; construction—floor blocks, with literacy materials; 3-D tabletop constructions; 2- and 3-D puzzles; library; thematic center; science laboratory with literacy materials; mathematics materials; draw/write; art studio—some educators recommend daily access to drawing materials, paint, and clay (Wright, 2003); water/sand/oats measurement table; woodworking; computers/interactive white-board table. Children also use activity center time to pursue longer-term inquiry or construction projects that grow out of their Dynamic-Theme activities and/or design technology work. (Consider that most of what you do indoors can be moved outdoors, weather permitting, such as drawing, building, and dancing. You can also adopt a tree and plant a garden.)

Teacher's instructional area is for brief, small-group or individual meetings (interspersed with circulating). Snack table is set up mid-way. *Whole- or small-group sharing after cleanup* (except for ongoing projects that remain in place as needed). **[Procedural note:** Some teachers hoist a flag or place a closed sign on floor blocks and socio-dramatic play during the first twenty minutes of activity time in order to encourage all children to focus on sedentary activities. They set the time on a paper-plate clock hung beside the wall clock. Pre-kindergarten children quickly learn to recognize when the clock hands match.]

Music and Movement (30–40 minutes) Indoors or outdoors.

Whole-group Read-aloud and Discussion (15–25 minutes)

Outdoors and Lunch (40–50 minutes) Schools that schedule playground (recess) before lunch find that children eat and drink more (Montana Office of Public Instruction, 2003; Parker-Pope, 2010). **[Procedural note:** Before lunch, in order to support a calm transition after lunch, some teachers plan with children the reading material that they will use upon their return to the classroom.]

Quiet Time (20 minutes) Some pre-kindergarteners might need a nap. This is an opportunity for independent reading on individual mats.

Planning and Center Time with Moderate Activities (50–60 minutes) Teacher circulates and works in turn with small instructional groups in reading, writing, mathematics, or Dynamic-Theme concepts dealing with sciences or social sciences. Children engage in a variety of self-paced activities, excluding large muscle activity such as floor blocks or woodworking.

Whole-group Activity or a Special Event (20–35 minutes) Social studies discussion/planning or viewing a brief related video clip; shared writing; creative dramatics; planning a trip; recounting and recording a trip; or taking a brief trip in or around the school. Other activities might be group games; movement education; and read–aloud/poem/singing.

Dismissal Time   (10–15 minutes) The day ends with singing, clapping rhythms or syllables of names, riddles, poetry, and so forth. [**Procedural note:** Before children leave, ask them to review what they have done as a group. This helps youngsters anticipate the language they will need in order to answer adults' questions, including, "What did you do today?" Also, it is routine to count all the children any time you leave or return to the classroom.]

Weekly Schedule

- *Whole-group meeting time.* Three or four new, brief mini-lessons: for example, survey books read during the week; plan for, introduce, or discuss a class animal; share a new center theme, props, or provisions; new shared writing; new song; or new movement activity that explores space.
- *Provide three, four, or five new books in the library center* (Neuman & Roskos with Wright and Lenhart, 2007, p. 31).
- *Create one or more surveys.*
- *Special day.* Dynamic-Theme-related activities, including a significant science or social studies focus. There also are opportunities to integrate literacy, mathematics, and arts activities. Plan an adult-supervised food preparation or cooking activity in which small groups rotate their participation during the activity center time.
- *New concepts.* Two or three new mathematics concepts and games at each of three or four levels of difficulty—with concrete materials. Two or three new, contrasting decoding games at each of three or four levels of difficulty. Three new art/craft media for individualized interpretation.
- *Gather and assemble materials in baskets or tool carriers for the forthcoming week.*

Weekly or Bi-weekly Schedule

- *Interview* someone with a different career, talent, or travel experience to share; invite a resource person, for example someone with a new baby to observe and measure, and returning months later.
- *Review your records* of children's participation in centers or instructional groups in order to help plan, such as regrouping for a particular skill or identifying children who need more time in an under-used center.

Monthly to Six-week Schedule

- Socio-dramatic and construction center thematic *prop addition, recycling, or revisiting.*

- *Refresh reading materials* in the class library and *software* in the computer center.
- *Freshen materials and presentations* in all centers.
- Build in a *celebration/delight*.
- *Field trip*, within the school, just beyond the school, or to another location to support ongoing Dynamic-Theme projects: for example, post office cycle; food cycle (e.g., farm to market, bakery, restaurant); production–consumption resources (e.g., lumber yard, cabinetmaker's workshop or sculptor's studio); transportation-related locations (e.g., garage, airport, bus or train station); natural resources (e.g., pond, river, lake, forest, beach, or farm); or any reasonable suggestions from children. Fresh imagery can emerge from trips.

Yearly: Dynamic-Themes and Revisiting Across Months

Time for Dynamic-Themes   Dynamic-Themes weave throughout the year after the opening weeks of school. They do not start on Monday and end on Friday as do units, discrete themes, or some projects.

Outside pressure for narrow skills and fact-stating make some teachers feel that there is "not enough time" to do many of the active, participatory experiences mentioned in this book. "However, to be successful, students need carefully struc-tured experiences, scaffolded support from teachers, and opportunities for sustained engagement with the same set of ideas over extended periods of time (weeks, months, even years)" (Duschl, Schweingruber, & Shouse, 2007, p. 338). The American Association for the Advancement of Science advocates for *integration* of learning in *integrated planning, interconnected knowledge,* and *coherence* (AAAS, 2009, p. 303).

Successful teachers select plans based upon a combination of factors. They consider community resources such as a construction site; and terrain, such as trees, prairie, mountains, beach, semi-arid, or water sources. When they focus on the underlying images of Dynamic-Themes and cluster activities around a Dynamic-Theme, they remember that *different children doing different things at different times can have equivalent experiences.* Equally, the *same children doing the same things at the same time might be having different experiences.* Another corollary is that *not everyone must do every single classroom activity every time.*

Time Management Minute-to-Minute   After group planning, children par-ticipate in centers.

- *Activity periods* (at least once and sometimes twice a day) during which small groups and individuals work in self-organized and interactive experiences. **[Procedural note:** Children learn early in the year about their choices of activities when they finish an activity. For example, they can find an open hook or Velcro dot that marks an opening in a center. Each day, they are able to draw/write; read; fix a puzzle; or pull a scroll out of the "grab-bag" that you create with challenges. The grab-bag might hold brief activities, such as a connect-the-dots puzzle; a pattern to continue building; a cutting and assembly puzzle task; or a paper maze.]

- *Fleeting teaching* (1–2 minutes) during an activity period with small groups or individuals.
- *Small- or whole-group demonstrations and instruction* (5–12 minutes.) You would leave children with a follow-up activity.
- *After an activity period, individuals or small groups share* with the whole group or in small groups their discoveries, constructions, drawings, or writing.

Lesson Plan for Your Private Use

- *Materials* to collect [**Procedural note:** Each day, placing materials ahead of time in tool carriers or baskets eases immediate entry into the activity.]
- Two or three questions to open that ask children to wonder, "What might happen if . . .?"
- *Plan a more complex and a less complex activity and question* to adapt to children and use only if needed.
- Ask children to suggest a *follow-up*: e.g., "What are some ways we might . . .?" (This also serves to assess learning.)
- *Close down* with a next-step or follow-up activity.
- Specify where children will go and how they will get to the *next activity* when done.
- Consider how to assess children's learning.

This sort of brief lesson plan helps to prepare each day for the following activities:

- Whole-group meeting and times for intentional instruction, such as mini-lessons, read-alouds, movement education, and group problem-solving or problem-preventing discussions.
- Small-group intentional instruction and helping children re-plan during activity periods.

Half-day and All-day Issues

Although all-day schedules in the U.S. continue to expand, half-day and mixed-day programs continue to function. Teachers who make the transition to all-day schedules reflect on feeling less rushed. They perceive that more in-depth study is possible, that they can complete some activities, such as field trips, in a single day without the loss of focus if children would otherwise have to re-focus on another day. A summary of research on all-day and half-day programs finds the strongest impact on achievement of children from low-income homes (Crosser, 2005, pp. 64–65; National Education Association, 2008). Moreover, there is less retention in kindergarten.

Transition to a Half-furnished House

Transition to the all-day schedule is like moving into a half-furnished house. Rather than doubling the number of kitchens or duplicating furnishings, you would have the space to spread out what you need and want. You might also decide that your former furnishings no longer match the architecture.

You could use the opportunity to transform the focus of classroom time during the longer day. The additional time provides opportunities for longer time blocks, more in-depth conversations and assessment, and more opportunities to help children make connections between Dynamic-Theme activities. In short, the pace and rhythmic balance of options, challenges, socialization, and enriched productivity can change the pace and content of each day. However, if you already offer a worksheet, paper-and-pencil program focused mainly on number skills and phonics, it would make sense to rethink the half-day uses of time before expanding the time to a meaningful, activity-based, full-day schedule.

Reflections

After the initial weeks of living with your group, and surviving some inevitable off-key moments, you have built the confidence to choreograph plans for small groups and individuals and feel like a virtuoso who can hit some high notes. Sometimes, your work with children has the feeling of "flow" (Csikszentmihalyi, 1996) when time seems irrelevant and you feel fully immersed in the joy of knowing the children and living the moment. You are multi-tasking, thinking, rethinking, and trying to adapt flexibly to the daily developments, occasional spills, and emergencies. Nevertheless, it is sincere work, work in planning differentiated experiences for children with varied needs; assembling, stocking, storing, displaying, and using many varied materials; continually seeking new book titles and software for each child's particular interests; wearing comfortable footwear to survive the movement while bending to speak eye-to-eye, being constantly aware of the entire room; monitoring coverage by a teacher aide or student participant; and juggling administrative paperwork.

Style in teaching is having control over your alternatives (Whitehead, 1929). Chapter 3's integrated conditions for learning in early childhood, combined with your planning and sequencing with Dynamic-Themes, provide a wide range of combined alternatives that could contribute to your teaching style. Consider reflecting on your own work and the alternatives you, rather than anyone else, can control when you close the classroom door.

Wherever you are on your sincere working journey, there is likely to be a next step and another one after that one. The great joy of working with young children can be the predictable unpredictability and feeling light-on-your-feet along the way. It is a reason to smile when you think about going to work.

14

INTEGRATING MULTIPLE FORMS OF ASSESSMENT

Introduction

A pre-kindergarten child, Alma, carries a wooden jigsaw puzzle, turns it upside down, and continues to walk away from the pieces hitting the floor. Then she drops the puzzle frame on a table and, in passing, pinches Bette, who begins to weep. The teacher focuses on the crying child and says to nearby children, "Bette is crying because she is hurt. Let's hug our friend Bette to help her feel better. She needs to know that her friends are sorry to see her hurt because friends do not like to see their friends hurt. We're friends in this class." When the other children hug Bette, Alma voluntarily joins the other children in hugging her. The teacher settles Bette back at the table with other children. Then she has a private chat with Alma and walks her to the easel.

Alma's teacher made an assessment based on many similar observations before this event and unsatisfactory results with earlier interventions. She learned that Alma and her family were homeless immigrants from a violent country, living out of shopping bags, and sleeping in the homes of different families every few nights. Moreover, Alma recently learned to speak English. In the past, when she was destructive and aggressive, staff members berated her and gave her "time out." The punitive attention for her angry behavior did not change her behavior. Staff members discussed the situation with an adviser who took into account the child's cultural context. First, they decided to have a consistent adult engage her in activities and try to anticipate transitions in order to prevent aggressive contact with other children. They thought that she needed a safe sense of attachment to a significant adult as well as support to spend enough time with activities so that she might feel satisfied and competent. Second, they modeled positive behavior with supportive language, as described above. Two weeks of diligent anticipation, monitoring, and positive focus on classroom activities nearly eliminated Alma's hostile episodes.

Social and emotional relations are only one among many assessments you make continuously in an early childhood classroom. Assessment is something that you do all the time, connecting children with one another, ideas, and skills. You make multiple assessments as you multi-task; it a creative part of your work. The challenge of the predictably unpredictable nature of working with young children offers part of the job satisfaction.

360-Degree Assessment, Learning Pathways, and Learning Standards

Even though you are continuously assessing learning, there is a need for this separate assessment chapter because of the current competitive environment of accountability with standardized tests. Actually, the major purpose of assessment is to help you decide what to teach next based on what children know, are able to do, to what they are receptive with your support, and within the skills and content that you value. Therefore, assessment for purposes of scaffolding learning is integrated throughout the preceding chapters.

This chapter focuses on the multiple ways to plan and scaffold instruction through assessment based on the elements within domains, children's pathways of learning, and the integrated conditions for learning in early childhood. Figure 14.1 outlines a model for assessment that continuously recirculates.

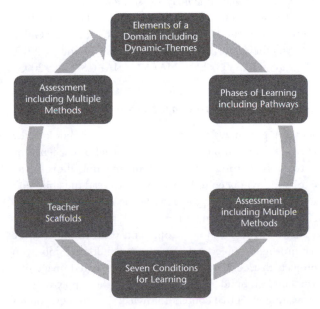

FIGURE 14.1 A Continuous Model for Assessment in Early Learning and Teaching

Whether or not you consciously connect your goals for instruction with a particular standard, most wholesome activities for young children fulfill one or another of the formal learning standards of your state or professional associations or, now, the national standards. Learning standards change and goals are likely to continue to evolve because of economic and political influences. When you look at your children, you might identify additional goals and teach accordingly. At the same time, your vision of how young children make progress along the phases of learning is tempered by the knowledge that immediate progress may not be visible until later. The best that you can do is expose children to rich, meaningful experiences to which they appear to be receptive.

The learning standards of major professional associations are embedded within activities presented throughout this book. Regardless of standardized tests and subject-matter standards, you remain with the children along with the time, resources, and repertoire of practices and alternatives that you have to figure out how to support the next steps of children's learning. Regardless of the Monday after children might have had an enervating weekend at home, the Friday energy level, or the dreary weather, you still need to figure out how to support the next steps of children's learning.

In order to evaluate children's accomplishments within each domain, you might think about how individuals demonstrate their particular achievement of knowledge at progressive levels: (1) related; (2) concrete; (3) connected; (4) applied; or (5) creative grasp. However, teaching is no guarantee that children will learn. Therefore, scholars concur and recommend that we can build upon young children's learning when we *integrate multiple forms of assessment that are ethical, valid, and reliable* (Copley, 2010; Crosser, 2005; Edwards, Gandini & Forman, 1998; Epstein, Schweinhart, De Bruin-Parecki, & Robin, 2004; Gestwicki, 2007; Gullo, 2005; Helm, Beneke, & Steinheimer, 2007; Mindes, 2011; Owocki, 2010; NAECTE/NAECS/SDE, 2005; NAEYC, 2009; NAEYC/NAECS/SDE, 2003).

Concrete, Active Experiences Make Assessment Observable

The many concrete, active experiences detailed throughout this book make assessment directly observable. Children indicate a relevant level of challenge by their engagement or distraction. During a whole-group meeting, how many requests to leave for the toilet do you need to hear in order to read the children's behavior? Perhaps the activity is too lengthy, too easy, or too difficult—or several children legitimately need to leave at the same time.

When children have many questions about a topic and want to know more about guinea pigs or what fire-fighters need to learn in order to do their jobs, you might follow up with projects that connect activities with the shared image of a Dynamic-Theme. In turn, children build skills sequentially as they apply them in activities that also build toward conceptual content knowledge. This viewpoint is consistent with how the brain functions to make connections.

The brain functions by holistic connection-making. Young children benefit from the *plasticity* of the brain, the capacity to develop more and stronger connections. The brain also engages in *pruning*, the cleansing of pathways with unused connections (Gopnik, Meltzoff, & Kuhl, 1999). Think about opportunities that children might have as well as those that they could miss during time with you. Therefore, it is important to keep open learning pathways so that children can strengthen their meaningful connections through engaging, rich, and varied activities with embedded vocabulary.

When you organize experiences around connections rather than isolated bits of information, it is easier to remember events (Luria, 1968; Piaget & Inhelder, 1973). In turn, experiences that flow later can dock with earlier perceptions to connect, build upon, and retrieve them. When you value curiosity, you are likely to assess and extend a moment with that value in mind. For example, when children rush to look out the window at a passing fire truck, how do adults assess the moment? A functionary might say, "Get down from that chair. You'll hurt yourself." A professional (valuing curiosity) might steady the chair and ask, "What did you notice? When have you seen a fire truck before? What do you want to know about . . .?" (Adapted from B. Nilsen, personal communication, 1994.)

A Focus on Holistic Connection-making

Many researchers recommend that assessing young children's learning "should be expanded beyond those traditionally emphasized (language, literacy, and mathematics) to include others, such as affect, interpersonal interaction, and opportunities for self-expression . . . [as well as] . . . other currently neglected domains, such as art, music, creativity, and interpersonal skills" (Snow & Van Hemel, 2008, p. 3). It also makes sense to consider how children understand social science and science concepts. The purpose of any assessment builds in next steps for using what you learn in order to continue instruction (NAEYC/NAECS/SDE, 2003). Beyond waiting for children to demonstrate connections they make, you can ask them questions, such as those listed in Box 14.4.

Life comes to us as a whole, and young children learn through physical, socio-emotional, aesthetic, and cognitive experiences that weave many forms. This chapter continues by outlining some developmental phases of strands in the weave and then discusses many ways to assess children's learning along with issues that impinge on adaptive teaching.

Assessment Domains

Young children learn in integrated ways. The integrated, activity-based Dynamic-Themes curriculum offers meaningful opportunities to integrate mathematical, language, artistic, and technological literacy within activities that build concepts. *Integrated activity offers a time-saving benefit, because you can use time efficiently when you assess multiple domains within specific conceptually rich experiences.*

As you figure out what children might be able to do, you systematically extract specific assessments from a variety of integrated experiences. The checklist in Table 14.1 can help record children's participation in experiences within the full range of domains you intend.

TABLE 14.1 Checklist of Activities Across the Curriculum

	Number of Activities					
	1	*2*	*3*	*4*	*5*	*6*
Dynamic–Themes:*						
Cyclical Change						
Contrast/Conflict						
Synergy						
Other						
Multicultural Studies:						
Book Themes						
Holiday Themes						
Inter-Group Experiences						
Two-Way Bilingual						
Social Studies:						
History						
Geography						
Economics						
Political Science						
Technology & Science:						
Computers						
Design Tech.						
Biology						
Chemistry						
Physical						
Mathematics						
Arts Media:						
Music						
Movement						
Visual/Plastic						
Creative Drama						
Language Literacy:						
Writing						
Reading						
Phonemics						
Play & Imagination						
Self-regulation						
(Executive Function)						

Note: * Children have the potential to perceive the underlying imagery of a Dynamic-Theme after exposure to at least three or four representative activities.

With ongoing assessment by all adults in the classroom, pause every few weeks to review your checklists, notes, children's comments, digital photographs, and children's products. This process might help you see if individuals might need additional experience or attention. Specific phases of 3-dimensional construction and other domains, ideas for intentional teaching of concepts, and scaffolds appear in preceding chapters. In summary, your support can take many forms that include such actions as nodding appreciatively, pointing to an item, asking a question, showing how to do something, providing a material, making a suggestion, offering help, inviting another child to participate, and simply giving a child additional information.

Two domains merit specific attention because they can offer nurture and optimism across the curriculum—play and self-regulation (executive function). The discussion continues with an outline of ways to assess and support each domain.

Play and Assessment

Whenever children are active and talking, you have a chance to learn what they can do. Educators and researchers with an informed eye assess children's social and academic competencies by observing their play (Coplan, Rubin, & Findlay, 2006; Fromberg, 2002; Gullo, 2005; Mindes, 2011). An informed eye sees the progression of skills in play with objects as well as social play. Children's play reveals increasing complexity of themes and skills as children have reasons to apply skills, as outlined in Box 14.1.

BOX 14.1 PLAY PATHWAYS AND SCAFFOLDS

Play with Objects

Youngsters progress along the following continuum:

- Realistic use of objects.
- Imaginative use of objects.
- Substitution of objects.

Scaffold: Model aspects of the next phase in parallel play or bring a child model nearby. Provide verbal harmony, describe the child's activity as well as your model activity: "I wonder if my make-believe dog is hungry."

Social Play

Youngsters progress along the following continuum (see Parten, 1932; Coplan, Rubin, & Findlay, 2006, p. 79, for "Play Observation Coding Sheet"):

- Onlooker.
- Solitary.
- Parallel play, mainly.
- Interaction with others.

Scaffold: Model aspects of the next phase in parallel play or bring a child model nearby. Provide verbal harmony, describe the child's activity as well as your model activity.

(See Wolfberg, 2009, on scaffolds for children with autism.)

- Rough-and-tumble play.

Scaffold: Observe facial expression and posture to anticipate and avert possible tipping into aggression. Suggest another direction for the group: "How might they use all that power to build a sports stadium/theater?" Or: "Let's talk about your characters/plans during group time." Then role-play alternative suggestions for resolving issues/problems (following Paley, 1984; Levin & Carlsson-Paige, 2005).

Socio-dramatic Play

Youngsters typically engage in episodic play and progress along the following continuum.

Communication

- Mainly gestures with an occasional phrase
- Directions and statements reflect increasingly complex grammar
- Negotiations, including social competence in entering a play group as well as deciding on pretend roles and script development.

Scaffold: Model entry into the play framework by offering a service or an idea for use in the action. Ask a child to try to join by bringing a new prop, becoming a visitor from a relevant place, such as "I just came from the drug store with some strong bandages." Use or add literacy forms, such as labels, signs, tickets, menus, receipts, lists, and so forth, as relevant.

Overview of Integrated Mathematics

- Grouping.
- One-to-one correspondence.
- Counting.

- Adding-on; removing.
- Adding together.

Scaffold: Ask or demonstrate comparisons, matching one-to-one correspondence with objects, counting, and measuring as relevant. Count items on receipts. Add together sets of items. Comment: "I wonder which is larger/ which weighs more/how many more players we need." "How many would we be if another friend came?" Compare sizes of blocks. "How many small blocks could fit on this large one?" "How many more/fewer do we need?"

Content

- Imitative.
- Repetitive action.
- Actions and talk are integrated with script.

Scaffold: "Become" a role in the action. Model new vocabulary and sentence complexity. "Suppose he didn't give up. What might happen if he tried something new?" "What might he hope for?" "Where might he go?" "Who could he ask?"

- Variety of themes.

Scaffold: Change props that relate to other aspects of study. Model new vocabulary and sentence complexity.

- Requesting props/literacy support.

Scaffold: Provide requested follow-up.

- Expanding themes.

Scaffold: Acknowledge and reflect aloud about their sophistication: "You've really been thinking about . . ." "Are you sure you're not in second grade?" "You figured out how to do that." "What else do you need to make that happen?"

- Duration of play episodes.

Scaffold: Wonder: "What might happen if . . .?" "What else could he do?" "Where else might he go?"

> • Connecting to social studies or science concepts/Dynamic-Themes.
>
> *Scaffold:* Add experiences related to a Dynamic-Theme during the play and on various occasions. Model entry into the play framework by offering a service, such as creating a sign, providing literacy materials or a prop that relates to the play script. (See also Chapter 3.)

Assesment of Executive Function, Including Self-regulation Skills and Attitudes/Predispositions

As young children interact with others, raw emotion, and the way they control their impulsivity, is apparent. Researchers have found that such self-regulation supports mathematical and some literacy skills (Matthews, Ponitz, & Morrison, 2009). The body of research on *brain* function also supports the notion that emotion, self-motivation, and social and cognitive skills interact (see Box 3.4). "The frontal lobe is the brain's executive control system, responsible for planning, organizing, and sequencing behavior for self-control, moral judgment and attention . . . [When] children . . . do things, . . . [they thicken] the fibres connecting neurons in this part of the brain, and the more the person is stimulated, the more the fibres will thicken" (Sigman, 2008b, p. 7).

The related body of research on executive function is also relevant to understanding how children develop, as follows:

> Executive function (EF), also known as fluid cognitive ability . . . comprises cognitive processes utilized in response to novel stimuli . . . [T]he cognitive processes involved in executive function include the ability to hold information in mind in working memory, inhibit incorrect responses, and sustain or switch attention for the purposes of goal-directed action. Generally speaking, executive function refers to effortful cognitive processes as opposed to relatively automatic aspects of cognition associated with crystallized knowledge and declarative memory (memory for information that has been learned). Measures of effortful control, inhibitory control, and attention-shifting in preschool predicts mathematical and literacy skills in a study of Head Start children . . . [E]xecutive function plays a critical role in the development of social, language, and academic skills [and] interacts with health, language, academic approaches to learning, and socioemotional [*sic*] adjustment.
>
> *(Snow & Van Hemel, 2008, pp. 109–110)*

Moreover, an extensive review of research concerning executive functions and self-regulation generally concludes that these functions are essential in wholesome and successful learning (Galinsky, 2010). It is noteworthy that kindergarten teachers value children's motivation and their self-regulation, outlined in Box 14.2, as more important than information alone.

BOX 14.2 EXECUTIVE FUNCTION COMPONENTS AND SCAFFOLDS

Working Memory Capacity

- Looks ahead.
- Checks back and compares.
- Keeps past and future in mind.
- Makes connections between ideas.

Scaffold: Place samples of next step and preceding step next to the task at hand. Model your thinking out loud as you figure out a mathematics problem or read for comprehension. Play games that reveal *surprise/cognitive dissonance* after expectations. Engage in the *plan–do–review* process (HighScope Press, 2009). "Consider asking pairs of children to share a game of 'wait-to-respond': 'Think of three words that end like "bear." When I give the signal, Partner A will tell the words to Partner B.' This type of direction requires the child to formulate an answer, but the child is not allowed to immediately respond . . . During the wait-to-respond time, students must rehearse the answer and hold it in working memory. Retrieval from working memory for initial concentration improvement requires a verbal response" (Nevills & Wolfe, 2009, p. 80).

Controls Behavior/Inhibits Impulses (Self-regulation)

- Aggression, such as pushing, grabbing, hitting. Saying, "You can't play."

Scaffold: Model support for victim. Comment: "That hurts." "Please use words to say what you need." "You can tell her that it hurts. Don't do it. Say it with words." "You can't say you can't play" (Paley, 1992). Also, plan for children to have real choices as they build a sense of control and autonomy within the classroom community.

- Takes turns, shares, collaborates, takes initiative.
- Perseveres.
- Communicates feelings with drawing/writing/words.

- Postpones impulse.
- Self-motivated; independent in teacher's absence (see DeVries & Zan, 1994)

Scaffold: Acknowledge with verbal descriptions: "Good friends take turns/ share/collaborate/cooperate." "You're really thinking about that, and it shows." "You're figuring out how to think first." Model courtesy: "Please/ Thank you. I'll wait until you finish/you're ready. It really pays to put in the time to figure that out."

Adaptation; Attention-shifting Capacity

- Transitions.

Scaffold: Prepare children with notice. First, help needy children shift focus. Use a prop, such as a "magic" puppet or a stuffed toy. A rubric for thinking about adaptation follows:

- Hesitant approach to new materials.
- Curious.
- Proactive.
- Takes initiative.
- Creative.
- Transforms ideas.
- Transforms attitudes.

Scaffold: Reduce a variable. Plan and pace activities next to one another in order to help children make connections. Model intermediate steps. Describe children's behavior while reinforcing purpose: "You're finding friends, planning ahead." (Additional description of problem-solving discussions appears in Chapter 13.) While self-regulation and self-motivation within school and life are valuable, it is worthwhile to consider the question: "Are these assignments really worth doing?" (Kohn, 2008, p. 175).

One scholar identifies eight components of self-regulation (Zimmerman, 2008). It is possible to see how the seven integrated conditions for learning in early childhood (see Chapter 3) intersect with the components of self-regulation. Table 14.2 illustrates these connections.

Three particular conditions for learning—*surprise/cognitive dissonance*; *play*; and a sense of *competence*—support all eight components of self-regulation. The four

TABLE 14.2 Self-regulation and Integrated Conditions for Early Learning

Conditions for Learning	Self-regulation Components							
	Active Engagement	Imagery	Goal Setting	Personal Initiative	Perseverance	Adaptation	Self-concept	Self-control
Comparison/Induction	x	x	x	x		x	x	
Surprise/Cognitive Dissonance	x	x	x	x	x	x	x	x
Concrete Materials/Physical	x	x		x	x	x	x	
Social Interaction	x	x		x	x	x		
Play and Imagination	x	x	x	x	x	x	x	x
Revisit	x	x			x	x		x
Competence	x	x	x	x	x	x	x	x

other conditions for learning also intersect with some of the self-regulation components. It is possible to imagine how children's ability to make choices and their sense of competence contribute to the growth of confidence and personal empowerment. In turn, you support children's sense of competence when you more nearly match instruction for different children with their capacity to learn. Consider that teachers who provide these integrated conditions for early learning or could modify their classrooms might support an increase in self-regulated learning.[1] [**Procedural note:** Some teachers modify their classrooms to promote self-regulated learning by reducing one transition at a time while adding one choice at a time.]

However, talking about assessment for the purpose of instruction can only be a bare outline of the complexity of moment-by-moment decisions. After all, children come to school with a wide range of varied experiences and skills. When you have systematically helped to organize routines and traffic patterns to support children's independence, you are more likely to succeed both in supporting their executive function and in assessing the different learning needs of different children in order to guide their development. This discussion continues with a look at assessing and addressing special learning needs.

All Children and Children with Disabilities

"Special education is not a categorization but a continuum of development" (Brooks, 2011, p. 152). Each child presents us with distinct skills and experiences. Within a socio-cultural Vygotskian framework,

> There is a complex, nonlinear relationship between learning and develop-ment. The exact relationship between learning and development may be different for each child and for different areas of development. Teachers must constantly adjust their methods to accommodate the learning and teaching process for each child. This is a great challenge for all educators.
>
> *(Bodrova & Leong, 2007, p. 13)*

Moreover, each child's growth is not a straight line but oscillates. Young children need time to percolate their experiences. However, you can see how they change in small steps as children apply skills, make connections, and burst with occasional insights. Some children exceed expectations about what might be reasonable development and need additional challenges. However, when you believe that children need special help to make progress in their learning, you should consider plans to intervene.

Response to Intervention (RTI)

The Response to Intervention practice is a formal procedure, mandated in some states, to help children improve their scholastic achievement by specifying different degrees of support for their learning. A purpose of this support system is to minimize referrals to special education. It is part of some elementary school practice, beginning in first grade, and there is talk of extending services to younger children (VanDerHeyden & Snyder, 2006). For example, there is a detailed collection of strategies for kindergarten reading instruction within the RTI framework, based on a formative assessment model that uses multiple formats (Owocki, 2010). "The Recognition and Response system is an emerging early childhood practice designed to help . . . respond to learning difficulties in young children . . . beginning at age 3 or 4" (Coleman, Buysse, & Neitzel, 2006, pp. 7ff). A similar piece of legislation is the use of federal funds for formal early intervention services to serve young children who are identified with disabilities. Therefore, this chapter makes a brief mention of this assessment procedure.

It is fair to say that RTI is a form of differentiated instruction. "It is recognized that many students with learning difficulties struggle with organization or 'executive' tasks. These difficulties may include time management, ability to recall information, and planning everyday jobs and future events" (Skeele & Russo, 2009). An outline of the three-step, tiered RTI system follows.

All children receive Tier 1 instruction: a center-based model can work for teachers who differentiate instruction within activity-based learning environments. Support teams can assist classroom teachers by sharing specific ways to work with individuals.

A subset of children who need additional help receive small-group intervention in Tier 2 for a particular skill, often in a pull-out format. However, the classroom teacher could provide

> supplemental instruction right away, before any referrals are made. The supplemental instruction is connected to what is already happening in the classroom, ensuring coherence and consistency. And the instruction often occurs with peers in the classroom, as an expected part of the classroom day. This brings a sense of normalcy to the notion that some students need extra support.
>
> *(Owocki, 2010, p. 5)*

For example, after working four times a week for one hour each time, one child moved out to Tier 1 while another child moved to Tier 3. Also, a policy in one county expects that eligible English language learner children would receive Tier 2 support before qualifying for Tier 3 (Zehr, 2010). In any case, "Approximately 10 to 15 percent of students are designated for Tier 2 instruction . . . Approximately 5 to 10 percent of [these] students are designated for Tier 3 instruction" (Owocki, 2010, p. 4).

A few children who need intensive one-on-one instruction receive Tier 3 or the special education service. Families typically participate in the decision-making process with an interdisciplinary team of school personnel who develop an individual education plan. Screening instruments often verify this level of service.

A central feature of RTI is progress monitoring "on a regular basis to determine the effectiveness of the intervention" (Snow & Van Hemel, 2008, p. 34). A factor to consider is whether the monitoring instruments narrow the focus of intervention to meet the scope of what is testable. Inasmuch as RTI responds to a concern that children "catch up" to norms, children who exceed norms receive less attention. Another perspective proposes that gifted and talented children receive similar systematic progress monitoring for next steps. However, the more that all children make progress, the wider will be the spread of skills. One critic suggests that, "to actually catch up to their achieving peers, most struggling readers need to double or triple their rate of reading acquisition" (Allington, 2009, p. v). For the youngest children, this might mean building their oral language skills by engaging in conceptually rich activities.

Beyond small-group and individual attention, it is important to use remediation methods that differ significantly from the methods that did not help children in the first place. With limited financial resources, the issue of offering all children equivalent assessment and enrichment remains a future policy question. Some teachers, however, experience RTI as a way to slow down the process of providing special services beyond the classroom as teachers are exhorted to "Try this for six weeks and let's see what happens," then something else, then yet another strategy (S. Lederman, personal communication, 2010).

Standardized Tests

Inasmuch as standardized tests exist, young children can benefit from your help in order to learn paper-and-pencil test-taking skills. Show them how to scan across a row and move from the top to the bottom of a page. Show them the techniques of filling in the box or circle, or drawing lines across the page to match objects.[2]

Scholars and policy-makers recommend that assessment should be in a child's first language (NAEYC, 2009; McAfee & Leong, 2011, p. 108; NAECTE/NAECS/SDE, 2005; Pew, 2007). While this recommendation might appear to be self-evident, some local policies do not take language into account when they rank schools and school districts. Federal policy directs that children deserve to be in a "least restrictive environment." "The overrepresentation of young minority group children and dual-language/English-language learners in special education classes and their underrepresentation in programs for gifted and talented children is a frequently cited example of bias" (McAfee & Leong, 2011, p. 17, citing Burnette, 1998; Snow & Van Hemel, 2008).

The point is that "we can't 'skill and drill' our way to *innovation*. Standardized testing produces standardized skills. Our standards–driven curriculum, especially in our urban schools, is not preparing children to be innovators at the highest technical levels that will pay off most in a high-tech global economy" (Gee, 2007, p. 3, citing Shaffer). Researchers comment that

> Standardized tests represent the most formal extreme of the assessment continuum because they place the greatest constraints on children's behavior [and instead, recommend] "repeated measures design" because young children on assessment tasks will fluctuate according to mood and environment, as well as their rapid and sporadic development . . . 1. Assessment should not make children feel anxious or scared. 2. Information should be obtained over time. 3. An attempt should be made to obtain information on the same content area from multiple and diverse sources, especially when repeated instances of data gathering are not feasible (e.g., due to time or budgetary constraints). 4. The length of the assessment should be sensitive to young children's interests and attention spans. 5. Testing for purposes of program accountability should employ appropriate sampling methods whenever feasible.
>
> *(Epstein, Schweinhart, De Bruin-Parecki, & Robin, 2004, pp. 5, 8)*

Results of standardized tests can be more reliable when youngsters are acquainted with the adult administering the test. It is also reasonable to provide adaptive formats. For example, an instrument for young children that evaluates only language and number skills can provide both developmental guidelines and performance formats (Meisels, Xue, & Shamblott, 2008, p. 968).

Transfer of Learning

Indeed, important learning that leads to transfer and use of knowledge may not be on standardized tests (Brooks, 2011). A child's competence and understanding that leads to transfer may not be on the type of test that measures isolated facts and narrow skills, although those facts and narrow skills are easier to identify. If you value the transfer of learning, then you could assess children in your classroom as they apply knowledge directly; observe the things about which they are curious; and listen to the questions they ask.

Although pre-kindergarten children are not exempt, kindergarten teachers are feeling increasing pressure to prepare children for tests of discrete skills and information. Some teachers feel that they need to narrow the curriculum to fit the tests. Some nearly eliminate significant social studies, socio-dramatic play, exploratory science studies, construction play and design technology, and representational arts, except for report writing. Such teachers drill children ready-or-not with rote learning to be used for spit-back parroting of facts-on-demand. Such teachers often complain that the children are difficult to manage. Indeed, verbal interaction analysis in such classrooms has found that the majority of teacher language and time is devoted to re-focusing attention when young children are merely being honest in their behavior. *With mainly management up front, meaningful teaching and learning take a back seat.*

Not only does the scope of the curriculum become subordinated to the tests, but the cultural richness of society suffers a loss. This pressure sometimes leads to a loss of focus on helping children build a strong foundation for the development of self-regulation and skills that help to communicate understanding.

So, the current model of high-stakes standardized tests does not fit the way young children develop and learn and typically does not provide you with information about what to do next. Many of these tests do not evaluate some of the most significant learning that includes attitudes toward school, the capacity to apply knowledge and skills to solve problems, use imagination constructively, make connections, consider alternatives, collaborate, and feel competent.

We turn now to another issue tied to evaluating children's readiness for pre-kindergarten and kindergarten—the issue of who might attend and when they might attend.

Redshirting and Retention

In light of research findings about the great range of capacity within any chrono-logical age group, it is a constant wonder that adults continue to be concerned with the starting age for school. Some school districts (and parents), however, expect that progress toward early technical reading—with or without meaning—is the single criterion for "success" and that it is best to invest in "older" children. Despite contradictory research (Shepard & Graue, 1993; Snow & Van Hemel, 2008), such districts keep raising the age of entry to school, as if all children might behave as one; and some parents "redshirt" their children by keeping them out of school for an extra year. It would be better to regard "readiness" to read as an emerging lifelong state. If you take this view, then your job as teacher boils down to interpreting a child's skill at a given time and providing experiences at the next level of challenge.

Across the United States, for example, the cut-off month for 5-year-olds' kindergarten entry in different states ranges from June to December. In any case, 91 percent of children in the United States are 5 years of age at the start of the school year (West, Denton, & Reaney, 2000). "While older children do initially perform better academically, these positive outcomes are limited and fade out in the early grades" (Vecchiotti, 2001, p. 18). Policy that is based on research supports "a commitment to universal school readiness" (NAEYC, 2004, p. 1).

Even if all children were born on the same day, they would enter schools with different learning needs. The issue is that schools need to be ready to educate all children by differentiating instruction to fit how young children learn.

Retention is another practice that affects youngsters. It is noteworthy that teachers perceive impulsive children with limited self-regulation skills as less ready to be promoted. Other screening methods include testing youngsters before pre-kindergarten or kindergarten to figure out if they might move on to kindergarten or first grade, or be retained in kindergarten or a transitional class. Researchers and advocates consistently recommend against the use of readiness tests for this purpose (Shepard & Graue, 1993; Shepard & Smith, 1986; Snow & Van Hemel, 2008, p. 31, citing NAECS/SDE, 2000). Children, however, are being kicked out of preschool: "It's like taking sick people out of the hospital" (Child Care Information Exchange, 2008, citing W.S. Gilliam).

Researchers point out that young children do not always test well, for reasons already mentioned. Moreover, the pace of development is erratic, and these years represent rapid growth. A professional teacher's observations generate a huge amount of valid information within an activity-based learning environment because children have many opportunities to demonstrate their understanding by the ways in which they transfer their learning and make connections. For example, children's acquisition of skills, concepts, and capacity to focus are self-evident: "Observation aimed at understanding the meaning students construct and how they construct it leads to well-rounded instruction that keeps phonics and fluency *in the service of* comprehension" (Owocki, 2010, p. 23). In effect, *compared with the millions of dollars spent on standardized tests, the professional early childhood teacher's observations are a great bargain.* The discussion below focuses on how teachers can assess learning.

Assessment for the Purposes of Learning

Assessment to help children learn also includes your own self-reflection. For example, when you listen to an audiotape of the comments and questions that you ask during discussions and individual conferences with the children, you might notice some patterns. If you want children to speak more than one-word responses to questions, then you would want to expand your questioning techniques. This is a form of "inquiry" or "research" into your own teaching. At the same time, you are using many opportunities to figure out what children already know and can do and what it is that they might need to know and do next.

Observation   Observation begins when you greet each child in the morning and intuitively experience his or her mood, energy level, or state of health. Observations continue as you circulate and teach throughout the day, assessing what children accomplish, where they need help, and what they need to learn next. More systematic observation may take place after identifying, for example, one child's need, whenever he is nearly finished with an activity, for help in planning a transition to the next activity. It is noteworthy that a statistical analysis supports the reliability of systematic observation in assessing reading and mathematics ability of pre-kindergarten children (Meisels, Xue, & Shamblott, 2008). Researchers also find that teacher observations "correlate highly with objective measures of children's academic performance" (Gullo, 2005, p. 85).

Record Keeping   When you find a child who has problems with other children or with work, and you are not sure what to do, it may be helpful to keep brief anecdotal records about problem moments for a week or two, in order to gather information. [**Procedural note:** To see if there are some patterns or triggering events, see if you can identify possible precipitating factors and try to notice and appreciate the child's moments of acceptable behavior. Simply describe what you notice.] When you review your notes after a week or two, a pattern of behavior and a possible alternative way of working may emerge. Sharing such records with other teachers might also provide fresh ideas for handling a problem.

Record keeping in a decentralized classroom reflects the center-based activities as well as whole-group accomplishments. Box 14.3 lists some ways to collect information to help identify levels of participation and then compare progress.

BOX 14.3 RECORD-KEEPING FORMATS IN AN ACTIVITY-BASED LEARNING ENVIRONMENT

- *Plan learning center time:* Record activity selections and who begins in which activity.
- *Small-group and individual direct instruction:* List children for each group.
- *List individuals in an indexed loose-leaf record book:* Duplicate a list of materials. Check off attainments. Note next steps. Record findings from individual conferences with children. (Consider how hand-held e-technology could streamline your record keeping.)
- *Center sign-in:* Collect notes at each center with a "clipboard and chart to fill out quickly" (Smutny & Von Fremd, 2010, p. 73).
- *Event sampling with four-for-the-day (or any number) on a systematic basis:* Jot down a few things about the activities of a few children each day. Record an activity and particular progress: e.g., independence; duration of attention; new connection. Store in each child's folder.
- *Individual folders* of selected, dated, and collected sample drawings, paintings, dictated stories, writings, and drawings/photographs of constructions.
- *Journals, notebooks or portfolios of individual children:* Mathematics notebooks record such items as nonstandard measures and then standard

---

measures of growth progress in plants; or children's matching of patterns and objects.

- *"Wonder boxes"* or equivalent boxes for index cards or envelopes: Individual children record (or dictate) questions about which they wonder (Heard & McDonough, 2009, pp. 65–66; AAAS, 2009). [**Procedural note:** Verbal or written questions can serve as starting points for planning "inquiry committees" for extended projects.]
- Each child's *center time clipboard/planning sheet* to start each center time.
- *Rubrics* can help you assess children as they role-play, draw, write, construct, and calculate—sample early, ongoing, and later work.

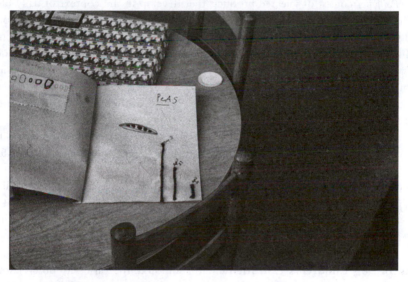

IMAGE 14.1 Science–Mathematics Notebook, Recording Pea Sprout Measurements

Product Samples and Portfolios   When looking at children's behavior and the products that they create, you can gain additional insight into how to work with them. An urban pre-kindergarten teacher reports saving children's easel paintings through the autumn, dating them, and binding them with a ribbon in December to take home on the bus for the holiday season. She was surprised to realize that one gregarious child had *never* painted. When she told him about it and said that "now" was the time to paint, he enthusiastically did so. [**Procedural note:** You might consider a timely periodic portfolio review to prevent a similar surprise.] The writing attempts and artwork of pre-kindergarten children also show their coordination, perseverance, and representational accomplishments, and reviewing this material may also suggest ways to plan new experiences. The drawings and 3-dimensional constructions can also provide insights into the perspectives of English language learners.

On another note, scholars find that the drawings and play of children who have been sexually abused may reveal their victimization (Koblinsky & Behana, 1984). Socio-dramatic play also serves as a window through which to see a child's perspective and event knowledge. Anecdotal records of such play and occasional audiotaping, videotaping, and photographs provide other kinds of "product" samples. Such items, collected for each child over time, also serve as documents to create "portfolio assessment" formats instead of only summative report cards and standardized tests.

Portfolios consist of selected products that develop in the context of daily life. The contents of a portfolio reflect your learning goals for the children. You, together with the children, can decide which samples of art, writing, constructions, photographs of projects, dictated stories, and audiotapes of retold stories to include. You might also decide to include anecdotal records as well as interviews with children concerning their reactions to events, their preferences, and other observations. "The portfolios are a more dynamic record of child practice than records of formal screening tests and other measures" (Mindes, 2011, p. 325).

The contents represent each child's progress across the program. It is useful to have a checklist for areas to include in the portfolio along with the dates (McAfee & Leong, 2011). It is useful to share this material with other professionals—such as the teacher next year and school administrators—as well as families. "Portfolios fulfill most of the basic purposes of classroom assessment" (McAfee & Leong, 2011, p. 118; see sample checklists and forms; there are also portfolio formats online that you might decide to use).

Recording Children's Comments   In addition to the variety of observations and records, recording children's comments over time can reveal the ways they think about classroom activities. You might decide to focus on a particular classroom center and domain of study. The children's comments can help you to assess the connections they make as well as when to challenge them with new materials or activities.

The next section presents some other ways for children to share their perspectives.

Opportunities to Share: Discussions, Conversations, and Conferences as Assessment

Discussions typically take place with a large or small group; conversations with a small group or individuals; and conferences with an individual about a specific work product or event. These are opportunities for children to share what they intend as well as for you to learn more about what they think. It is also a time when both of you might build upon each other's ideas. Therefore, it is useful to retain ways to capture the moment with a note or photograph. Some teachers carry hand-held computers to record notes easily (Helm, Beneke, & Steinheimer, 2007). The unplanned as well as planned moments are chances to find noteworthy information. Your goal-based internal (or external) spreadsheet checklist supports the assessment process (see Table 14.1).

Question Strategies Promote Sharing Ideas, Assessing Learning, and Transfer of Learning

Think about questions as opportunities for contributions, sharing, and finding out what others are thinking, rather than reciting answers. Questions you ask can help children expand their oral and written language as well as stimulate their general comprehension and critical thinking. Box 14.4 lists questions that focus on soliciting committed content.

Committed Content

Committed content elicits children's attitudes, opinions, personal reactions, and evaluations. Children are willing to talk about ideas that are important to them when the content grows out of their experiences. When they talk about their experiences, their ideas tend to generate expanded language which can help you assess their understanding as well as the complexity of speech. Honest questions concerning children's experiences can also help to expand their oral and written language as well as focus their comprehension and critical thinking.

In order to extend their thinking possibilities, it is useful to *reduce* reliance on yes-and-no and informational questions whose answers you already know. Instead, *increase* questions that are descriptive, comparative, evaluative, predictive, and explanatory. You might find that fascinating discussions ensue when you raise a question and then consider the procedures that follow. [**Procedural note:**

- *Pause* for children to think and form a response, retaining eye contact, and nodding encouragingly.
- *Listen* thoughtfully to children's comments.
- *Build on their content with follow-up questions:* "What happened/might happen next?" "What else happened?" "What happened before?" "What might you do next time?" *Clarify their meaning:* "Did you mean that . . . ?" "What if . . . ?" "What might someone else think about that?" "Who has another idea?"]

BOX 14.4 QUESTION STRATEGIES TO PROMOTE SHARING OF COMMITTED CONTENT, ASSESSMENT OF LEARNING, AND TRANSFER OF LEARNING

- YES–NO: "Did you . . .? Was it . . .? Could you . . .? Will you . . .?" Questions that begin with these openings invite a yes–no response. Instead of: "Do you have something to add?" *Consider:* "What else can you add?" *Consider:* If you really want a "yes" response, then be direct: "Please take this."

- INFORMATION: "Which one was first? What color was . . .? What happened when he . . .?" *Consider:* When you request information about what children know, continue accepting ideas after the "correct" contribution. Ask different children, "How did you decide that?" "How did you get that idea/answer?" If children need information in order to engage in a discussion, offer the information instead of asking them to guess the "correct" information. When you ask for information such as "What did you find out?" continue accepting ideas after the "correct" contribution; different children provide somewhat different perspectives. [**Procedural note:** You can use a similar approach whether discussing story comprehension, social problem solving, or mathematical problems. Children's perceptions provide additional *assessment* information on which to base future instruction.]

- DESCRIBE: "Tell us about a time when . . .? When did something like this happen to you? How did you do that?" *Consider:* Questions such as "How did you/were you/could you . . .?" Eliminate the need for yes–no construction. Note that "feel" questions such as "How did you feel?" tend to elicit one-word responses. Instead, focus on: "What were you/might she . . . be thinking/planning/wishing?" [**Procedural note:** When teachers ask young children "What do you wish?", if you do not want to hear about a trip to Disneyland, consider a focus: "What would you wish that could help that person be safe/happy/have friends?" and so forth.]

- EXPLAIN: "Why might he have done that? Why do you think so?" *Consider:* Young children need concrete situations and informational background to deal with explanations. They often respond as if you had asked for a description.

- COMPARE: "How is it like that? How is it not like that? Which might be a better idea for you?" *Consider:* The paired use of similar and different is a powerful condition for learning and provision for teaching. *Contrasts help to make perception possible.*

- CHOOSE/EVALUATE: "Which do you prefer? What is more important to you?" *Consider:* These questions open up the possibility to explore "whys." "What helped you decide?"

- GUESS/PREDICT: "What do you think this book might be about? What do you suppose he was thinking/planning? What do you think might happen next? What do you wish could happen?" *Consider:* It is important to use conditional language such as "might," "could," and "suppose" in order to signal that you expect to learn about alternative views and interpretations.
- INFER: "If she did that, then what do you suppose might happen? If that broke, then what might she want to do?" *Consider:* The if–then construction is more complex than prediction.
- CHILDREN ASK QUESTIONS: "What questions do you have? What do you/we need to find out/know?" *Consider:* Such questions grow more easily out of a concrete, situational context such as a journal, book, problem, or issue.

[**Procedural note:** Keep in mind that you can learn a lot when children build on one another's ideas. Therefore, be aware if you repeat everything one child says, then the other children have less reason to listen to one another. The exception would be when you re-state to model expanded language use, and when your tone invites a child to confirm or expand an idea.]

A classic sequence of questions that elicit concrete or abstract thinking is "Bloom's taxonomy" (Bloom et al., 1956). The idea of a hierarchy suggests to some educators that the most abstract, logical forms of thinking are more worthwhile than more intuitive, concrete forms. However, consider that all forms of thinking are nested within one another, just as our brains connect concrete, motor, intuitive, emotional, and logical dimensions. Therefore, attempt to keep open the interactive flow through your activity-based learning environment.

You support community building when you look at the child who is speaking while nodding to others to listen to the speaker. In addition, consider that youngsters might hesitate to speak up in a whole-group setting if they have learned at home not to be the center of attention.

Children's comments and other sample assessments emerge from many sources when you envision the connections between domains. Table 14.3 suggests a framework with which to evaluate conceptual/content learning across the curriculum, and Table 14.4 suggests a sample for marking progress across one domain. When you want to evaluate what children understand, you could observe the dimensions of (1) discriminating concrete ideas; (2) making connections;

TABLE 14.3 Overview Framework to Evaluate Pathways Across Domains

Pathway Dimensions	Domains								
	Dynamic-Theme: Cyclical Change	Dynamic-Theme: Contrast/Conflict	Dynamic-Theme: Synergy	Multicultural Themes; Social Studies	Arts	Language	Sciences; Technology	Math	Self-regulation; Socio-dramatic Play
Discriminates Concrete Ideas									
Makes Connections									
Applies Thinking									
Creative Construction									

TABLE 14.4 Sample Framework to Evaluate Pathways within a Domain

Pathway Dimensions Development	Domain Activities—Dynamic-Theme: Cyclical Change			
	Activity 1	Activity 2	Activity 3	And so forth . . .
Concrete				
Connections				
Applications				
Creative				
Constructions				

(3) applying thinking; and (4) creative constructions (adapted from Yelland, Lee, O'Rourke, & Harrison, 2008, Appendix I). As a practical matter, these dimensions are "performances of understanding" (Gardner, 2006, p. 126).

When working with young children, it is particularly relevant to look for evidence of achievement in many forms and at different paces. Whether or not they function with concrete materials, visual forms, or some symbolic forms, their development is likely to follow an irregular profile. For some activities, they might progress into making connections and applying their learning to new examples. For other activities, they might be able to create constructions of their own designs. Even when their comments suggest that they understand, you might find that asking children to draw what they mean could reveal somewhat unique ideas.

The main focus of the Dynamic-Themes approach is to teach for knowledge and understanding; this includes and subsumes facts and skills. Scholars agree that learning in order to understand, generate ideas, ask questions, wonder, critique, communicate, and collaborate are essential skills for the present and future (Gardner, 2006; Kaku, 1997; Yelland, Lee, O'Rourke, & Harrison, 2008). In turn, professional early childhood teachers recognize that young children are sufficiently capable and self-directed to absorb and extend what a caring, truly intellectual, action-based learning environment can provide. Professionals are valued producers, not merely consumers of curriculum. At the same time, learning standards and published teachers' guides can be partners in your teaching if you retain the initiative to adapt activities selectively to the different children with whom you work at a pace that matches their capacity to learn.

Reflections

This chapter has discussed the connections between young children's learning content and skills and their social and emotional development of self-regulation. Young children develop at different rates, based in part on their experiences before school. The purpose of assessment is to help you plan instruction. However, neither assessment nor instruction assures learning. Your assessment braids together children's experiences, your teaching, and plans for ongoing teaching and new learning. Professional, specifically prepared early childhood teachers are able to adapt instruction to the learning needs of different children. They have the capacity to provide many different formats to help children perceive Dynamic-Themes and learn skills while retaining hopeful attitudes toward their learning in school.

Individual children develop and learn at their own pace, which tends to be erratic, and they demonstrate their progress in a variety of ways. Therefore, it is important to use many ways to assess and document their progress. These varied forms of documentation can also provide the evidence to support your activity-based, content-rich Dynamic-Themes curriculum. These images differ from high-stakes evaluation tests that examine minimalist reading and arithmetic skills and rote information.

If you imagine yourself as a visitor from another galaxy, you might infer that the current focus on evaluation is a type of pill. That is, if youngsters correctly complete the tasks on standardized tests, then they are all right and so are their principals and teachers. However, it is helpful to remember that all pills have side-effects. So, there are some choices to make. On the one hand, pills have the benefits of being fast and easy to swallow, and they appear to give short-term relief. However, they often have harmful side-effects or trade off one ill for a different one. At the same time, weighing myself daily or annually does not affect how I balance nutrition and exercise; nor does it help my weight goals. On the other hand, planning and eating a wholesome diet with enough exercise and rest demands making thoughtful decisions, taking the time to follow up, self-regulation, and often trusting that the effort will result in middle- and long-term benefits.

Consider children's rights and simple civil liberties. A form of sanctioned child abuse is present in classrooms that cajole and press young children to sit quietly for long periods for paper-and-pencil tasks or drill them in rote information tasks that are easy to evaluate. This kind of ongoing managerial manipulation might have short-term impact. Such practice calls upon children to use only a small part of themselves; minimalist expectations are likely to yield limited future outcomes.

However, there is no need to become enslaved to the future. It is quite legitimate for valid activity that challenges children in present time to focus on present time. Many activities and wholesome social experiences that offer children the chance to explore, compare, and play will serve children eventually. At the very least, they are likely to embrace learning with a contagious enthusiasm because attitude change takes more time than memorizing a word.

It is reasonable to expect that achievement will vary, because the more instruction children receive, the more variable will be the range of attainments. *One size continues* not *to fit all!*

15

WORKING WITH FAMILIES, COMMUNITIES, AND COLLEAGUES

Introduction

Hector had trouble focusing on drawing and writing in kindergarten. So you can imagine how surprised his teacher was when she saw him on a busy city street, selling shopping bags and making change.

This chapter deals in turn with ways to build bridges between school and home as well as the subsequent teacher, school administration, and community. There is also a discussion about the issues of transition from half-day to all-day programs.

A central issue in education is how all participants might feel empowered. Children who feel trusted to make the choices you offer them experience a sense of respect and possibility. "Service learning" projects that involve children in helping others within their community add to their sense of empowerment and affiliation with the process of school learning. For example, young children are able to participate in the Common Cents activity of the Penny Harvest (Gross, 2010; Pernu & Maloy, 2010). Children also build bridges of trust and caring when they interview adults. Adult participants who leave an interview with buoyant feelings can help to support the commitment of children as well as adults to an active educational process.

Family Involvement

Parents usually fall totally in love with their children even before they see them for the first time. It is self-evident that parents typically wish each of their children to have the best possible education. They want you to know who their children are; care about helping their children learn; and offer rich educational experiences in which youngsters can feel successful.

Families simply want their children to have great expectations for their lives. Those families who can afford it attempt to secure what they deem the best education for their children. Some send their children to private schools whose websites offer cultural enrichment, integrated learning projects, in-depth studies, and creative opportunities to think and represent experiences. And their children's education does not appear to limit performance on standardized tests.

Imagine if that educational privilege were available to benefit all children.

Students exposed only to test-prep workbooks and memorized information have little opportunity to engage in reflection, critical thinking, and imaginative problem solving. To become the kind of people that the world needs, those schools would need to re-focus on exploration, inquiry, and a rich curriculum in place of test-prep, so that all parents can realize great expectations for their children.

Scholars remind us that "Schools will need to be more family-friendly . . . Transformations of readiness definitions and assessment will also occur as programs are implemented for younger children" (Pianta, 2007, p. 3). Personnel in successful programs for young children, particularly children from immigrant families and low-income families as well as children of color, also report working effectively with their families (Campbell et al., 2002; Ladson-Billings, 1994, 1995; Temple & Reynolds, 2007; Schweinhart et al., 2005). These programs help teachers build upon the strengths that children bring to school. Family contacts can also help identify possible health needs and connect families with services.

It is worth noting that your goals for children might differ from those of their families. For example, consider how to help the parents from a patriarchal society understand that their daughter is an able scholar. Might some families value protecting their healthy pre-kindergarten children, feeding them, buttoning their jackets, carrying them to school, and postponing their independence? Consider how to share your goal that children build independent skills. For example, some Latino families value interdependence over independence, and prefer to speak their birth language at home with their children and other family members (Maldonado & DeBello, forthcoming). Might some families teach their children to respect elders by lowering their eyes during greetings? Might some families teach their children to avoid attention within a group? Might some families expect a high degree of cleanliness?

As global boundaries shrink, it makes sense to think about each family's distinct ways to teach about social relationships and category systems. For example, Israeli teachers report being puzzled by some immigrant children's comments and socio-dramatic play. They created a "Look to the East" project and invited parents of young children to school festivals in order to teach the Western-oriented teachers what families taught their children at home (N. Nir-Janiv, personal communication, 1976). The teachers learned that North African immigrant families taught a distinct category system; families stored household materials, not by function, but by the container shape, such as placing together liquid detergent and juice. Also, their folk tales focused on themes of modesty and fatalism. Some North American children of color also conclude that there is no point in planning too far beyond the present (Erickson & Mohatt, 1982; Ogbu, 1978).

In Brazil, in order to help reverse the fatalistic perceptions of illiterate adults in an agrarian society so that they saw themselves as individually worthwhile and capable of learning to read, an adult literacy educator helped the adults view themselves as being powerful and capable (Freire, 1970). Therefore, when adults assume that they will never learn to read or attend college, and that they will always struggle to subsist, children—even in the United States—also learn not to have educational expectations.

These insights suggest that we try to understand family perspectives and their goals for children before dismissing a child's idea or behavior. Moreover, it is ethical and worth the effort of trying to understand parents' cultural perspectives (Genishi & Goodwin, 2008; NAEYC, 2009, citing Gonzales-Mena). Therefore, consider the following insight: "The teacher is no longer merely the one who teaches, for the teacher is also taught in dialogue with the students. And the students, while being taught, also teach. In this way, teacher and students become jointly responsible for a process in which all of them grow" (Freire, 1973, p. 53). When you consider the implicit as well as explicit goals of families, you can add value to parent conferences.

Parent Conferences

Family involvement, for example, could help youngsters when you have concerns about bullying and detect signs of depression that might grow out of a sense of pessimism. There is strong support for children to develop a feeling of *competence* and optimism, however, when you integrate the conditions for learning in early childhood.

Individual Family Conferences: An Extra Pair of Hands at Home

Meetings with individual families two to four times a year to share their children's accomplishments and the ways of working with them are traditional. When parents speak a language other than English, schools send translated messages and arrange for a translator, sometimes an older child, to be available. [**Procedural note:** It is helpful to confirm each meeting.]

Immigrant families as well as English–speaking families may fear that you will judge them and that their child reflects on their competence. Therefore, thoughtful planning for these meetings can help all of you feel satisfied. Begin with a friendly welcome and try to have adult-size chairs. Moreover, when you complete a successful meeting with parents, there is the potential for you to envision an "extra pair of hands at home" to help out.

A *sandwich* approach to conferring with a parent(s) or guardian is the following:

- *Bottom bread*. They will want to understand that you notice their children, respect, and appreciate them. Share the purpose and format of the conference: "This is a time for us to learn about Melvin at school and at home so we can work together to help him develop. I can tell you how much I enjoy seeing him learning so much/being a wonderful friend/building with blocks." Ask them what they want to know about their youngster at school. Begin and close with descriptions of their child's activities in class, the progress of their development, and their strengths. This might be a time to review their child's portfolio. Share samples of the child's work and digital photographs of the child in action. Refer to anecdotes to bring your descriptions alive.
- *Filling*. The filling of the sandwich might include asking what the child likes to do at home and how the family deals with the child. You might share what you have found to be the most helpful and effective ways of working with their child. You might ask them if they notice a particular behavior at home about which you have questions or concerns, and how they deal with it: for example, "I've noticed that [describe particular events.] Have you noticed this at home?" You might ask them what questions they have about the program.
- *Top bread*. The close of the conference might include something that you will be working on with the children in the future. Conclude with a positive appreciation of their child and how much you welcome meeting them at other times.

Use only positive language that emphasizes the child's progress and strengths. If you find that parents express angry reactions or suggestions about which you are unsure, it might calm the situation by listening thoughtfully to their comments. You might restate their suggestion to confirm that you heard what they said: "Let's see if I understand what you mean . . ." Then, try to defuse the moment by suggesting that you will think about their concerns and be in touch soon to follow up. If a parent is upset, you might try saying, "I'm sorry you are upset. Tell me more so I can see if I can help." Be open to hearing and responding to criticism with patience and concern. You don't have to acknowledge blame to be concerned! (L. Davey, personal communication, 2010).

Another good idea is to follow up the conference with a note or telephone call. Many teachers also communicate with families through e-mail. Telephone conferences might be the best way to reach some families, now that most parents work outside the home.

For children with disabilities or special needs, you would participate in individual education plan conferences alongside consultant specialists. You and your colleagues will plan the specialized next steps for individual children ahead of time.

Report Cards

Some districts feel strongly that pre-kindergarten and kindergarten should have report cards. One format is two letters, with the first describing each child's participation and progress—"Your child could do . . ., can do . . ., and will do . . . next"—and the second a general letter about class activities and events. Sometimes a rubric with the general letter describes participation in different domains, as follows: "Frequent, Often, Sometimes, Making Progress, Emerging, Rarely, Plans for Ongoing Support."

However, it makes as much sense to grade young children on their knowledge as it does to grade them on their eye color because there is little that they are able to change about either condition. After all, "young children are not motivated to complete tasks for external reasons (e.g., good grades)" (Snow & Van Hemel, 2008, p. 116). Indeed, negative feedback is detrimental to children's self-concept and motivation to pursue scholarly activities.

> Unlike traditional assessment where children are supposed to get everything correct, dynamic assessment starts at the point where a child is having difficulty performing or is making many errors. Dynamic assessment provides information at both levels of ZPD [Zone of Proximal Development]; the lower, or unassisted level and the upper, or maximally assisted level. It integrates assessment with responsive teaching.
>
> *(McAfee & Leong, 2011, p. 53)*

In a sense, the "rhythm" of ZPD is the fluctuating transition between competence and performance.

The Issue of Family Homework

You also can connect with families by recommending activities to share with children at home. It is clear that working parents have limited time with their children. Some of them might have unhappy memories of their own schooling. Some arrange full after-school schedules for their children of sports, music, art, science, a second language, and religious classes. Whatever the situation, drilling children at home is no more useful than drilling them at school. However, you might involve families in active learning experiences that are collaborative and still leave plenty of time for children to play outdoors, visit friends, share family fun, and watch the clouds. Some examples follow.

Mathematics Family Homework

Let parents know what you are doing in mathematics education at meetings and parent conferences, as well as with occasional notes/emails. Messages need not be any more complicated than this example:

Dear Fiske Family,

Ray weighed and measured the hamster today and wrote it up in the Math Book. It was exciting to see Ray's enthusiasm.

Sincerely,

If everyone has e-mail, families welcome an occasional digital photograph.

Each week, kindergarten teachers in one school district send home a ziplock bag, labeled "Math Homework." The bag might contain a simple instruction, such as: "Count together how many pieces of mail came to your home each day this week and help your child write the number each day on the enclosed form." Parents of pre-kindergarten children can deal with "We have used the piece of yarn in this bag to measure some objects in school. Please help your child find three things at home that are the same length as the yarn. Please send two objects to school that are the same length as the yarn." For parents with limited English proficiency, teachers should arrange to have messages translated. Teachers can also send home different homework with different children so that the children can feel competent and enjoy a sense of ownership (see Vatterott, 2009). Develop ideas cooperatively with other teachers, and use them optionally.

You can use the same technique in studying family size over generations, and the result is often an engrossing kindergarten social science research project. Again, send letters home to the parents to enlist their cooperation, as follows:

Dear Parents (kindergarten),

We are making a survey of families at school. Please have your child make a mark for each brother and sister that you have.

Parent's brothers:_____and sisters:_____

Parent's brothers: _____and sisters:_____

Dear Parents,

We are comparing generations of families at school. Please have your child make a mark for each brother and sister of his/her grandparents.

Parent's grandparent's brothers:_____and sisters:_____

Parent's grandparent's brothers:_____and sisters:_____

Parent's grandparent's brothers:_____and sisters:_____

Parent's grandparent's brothers:_____and sisters:_____

Begin with the data from the children's immediate families, graphing the results of the survey and then describing the findings. Then you can graph and describe the result of the parents' families and then the grandparents' families. Did the sizes of families in different generations in your class change or remain the same? Children might also create an individual family comparison as well as a group study of generations. What patterns exist in different families? Such surveys apply mathematics to social science research. They also integrate writing skills when you describe the findings.

Do be sensitive to the possibility that you may have parents who represent alternative families, or are otherwise uncomfortable with messages from school. Be sure to talk about the homework task with children beforehand and read the precise message to them before they take home their homework bag.

"Backpacks" are another way to involve families.

Literacy

Literacy backpacks or story sacks might include simply a class-made book or article in English or another language for parents and children to read together. A backpack, tote bag, or portfolio can be an exciting way for parents to learn about the power of your comprehensive, active literacy approach. Once or twice a month, depending on your resources, children take home an actual backpack for a week's time that includes activities for them to do at home with their parents. Each backpack focuses on a topic and includes the following items: a letter to the parents (see Box 15.1); a list of projects (see Box 15.2); four to six children's books and one or two articles or pamphlets about literacy for parents; some writing or other materials, as seem appropriate for the family; and a photograph of the contents of the backpack.

Backpacks are sometimes funded through parent–teacher association, school district, or teacher association mini-grants, or by local businesses. If you are interested in developing this form of playful, interactive collaboration with parents, begin with one backpack and add one to your collection every month or two. Before you know it, you may have as many as twenty. Some recommendations that focus on a committed issue with dynamic possibilities are such topics as "Friendship and Rejection," "Brave and Frightened," "Competing and Cooperating," "Angry and Happy Feelings," "Saying Goodbye and Moving In," "Wishes and Fears," and "Growing Up and Holding On." (See the Dynamic-Theme clusters of multicultural books in Chapter 8's Related Children's Books list for additional ideas.)

BOX 15.1 A LETTER TO PARENTS ABOUT BACKPACKS

Dear Parents:

Welcome to the world of Backpack Projects!

Enclosed you will find several books, novelty items, and a poem pertaining to the backpack topic.

You will have a week to linger over and enjoy the books. During the week you are hosting the backpack your child, and any members of the household who wish to get involved, will be working on a project.

The backpacks will be signed out on a Thursday and will be returned the following Thursday. If Thursday falls on a school holiday, return the backpack and project the next day school is in session.

Each backpack will contain a journal in which I would like you to write down the process you went through to do your project. You may also wish to write any other comments you or any family members would like to make about your child's efforts. Keep the project enjoyable for both you and your child.

In each backpack you will find an "adult" reading book or article for your reading pleasure. You may also address any question you have about the "adult" reading in the journal.

A pictorial inventory has been taken for each backpack. A copy of this picture will be enclosed in each backpack.

Thank you for your efforts in this matter.

Sincerely,

BOX 15.2 BACKPACK PROJECTS FOR CHILDREN

1. Pretend your teacher runs a bookstore, design a poster to advertise a book, to hang in her bookstore.
2. Make a map or pictorial timeline of one of the books.
3. Model a character from a story in clay.
4. Construct a diorama to represent a scene from a story.
5. Use paper, cardboard, wire, pipe cleaners, to recreate a character from one of the stories.
6. Make a mobile of characters from the books.
7. Create a pie plate movie of scenes from a book: Divide a paper plate into fourths; each part should have a scene; fasten a second plate on top with a brass fastener; cut out a section so one fourth is visible; top plate rotates to show scenes.

8. Write a letter to a friend, or family member, telling them about your favorite book.
9. Design a T-shirt advertising a book or character you love.
10. Write a poem to accompany a story.
11. Write a letter to the author of your favorite book.
12. Create a stick puppet character using popsicle sticks or straws; retell the story using your puppet.
13. Record yourself reading one of the stories.
14. Write what you think or imagine happened to the characters before the story began.
15. Create an ad for your favorite book. The ad will be used to entice other children to read your favorite book.
16. Plan a menu for the characters that you have read about in the backpack. Prepare a shopping list of what they need to buy for that menu.

(*Source:* Used with permission of Mary C. Quinn)

You might include supplies in the backpack for those at-home activities that require resources such as clay, paper plates, and fasteners or pipe cleaners. Another activity, a "Family Literacy Dig," asks children and their families to identify print in the home; then, children bring to school and share small sample items, such as labels (Owocki, 2010, p. 61).

Science Kits

One nursery school sends home a teacher-made pillow case with drawstring closings that contains concrete materials and instructions for a science topic (Chelsea Free Nursery School, 2006). Topics include exploring water properties, magnets, and sorting rocks, and the pillow case might contain implements for exploring garden life. Each kit visits for one week (see also Ritz, 2007).

Mystery Bag/Box

Children can take turns bringing home a prestigious mystery container. They bring to school an object from home in the container for others to guess after they provide some clues. You can assess their capacity to provide clues and to guess with increasing strategies beyond focus gambling. This process can continue to support community building and language development.

Social Studies

A "Family Time Capsule" consists of families collaborating by placing representative items in a container (Quinn, Fisher, & Garriel; & Novelli, 1994, p. 35). Among the items might be photos of family members, home, pet(s), outlines of feet, heights of family members, favorite foods, and future dreams of each person.

Newsletters

Paper or electronic newsletters also serve to maintain contact.[1] The periodic newsletter is a place to share classroom events and one or two ideas that families might do at home. It is also a place to state why the events are important to the children's intellectual and socio-emotional development. Families welcome knowing titles of books you read aloud and recommendations for a few library books that they might share. You could also include the words to a song or poem that the children enjoy (see also Gestwicki, 2010).

Newsletters typically describe science projects, welcoming a class pet, or survey results, and list children's comments after field trips. In addition, some educators recommend sharing ahead of time forthcoming activities, including supportive ideas of activities for families to do at home (Chalufour & Worth, 2004). Invite families to participate in special projects, trips, celebrations, talk about their work, and simply to arrange appointments to visit.

Some other newsletter topics include listing each child's dictated comment about subjects, such as the following:

- What I like to do in school (or children's drawings about their favorite activity with a caption).
- What I like to do after school.
- Things that make me happy.
- Children's trip drawings and photographs with their comments.
- I can . . . (with children's drawings).
- What are we thankful for?
- Collection of children's dictated similes (as short as . . .; as strong as . . .) or poems, such as haikus or cinquains.
- Family comments about a class visit or reaction to a newsletter issue.
- Information about a particular activity, such as studying ramps or evaporation–condensation.
- Favorite computer software or new books.

Other newsletter resources relate to programs in health departments or hospitals, such as subsidized programs to quit smoking or give inoculations. If you notice families with younger children at home or expecting a baby, the *New Parents Kit* (University of California-Berkeley, 2001) is relevant.

Another feature of your newsletter could be a notice about one or two community cultural activities that families might enjoy together on weekends. Libraries offer story times and Internet access; community centers offer Internet access; parks, community organizations, and agencies occasionally schedule family events; high schools and colleges offer dance, drama, and music productions. You might be fortunate to work near a museum devoted to children, the arts, or sciences. When you share such opportunities with families, they might well become your partners in providing an intellectual education.

Family Open-house Meetings

Evening meetings traditionally combine open-house formats with some programs that the parent–teacher association plans. Topics might include issues of consumer advertising targeted at children, relating to how girls, boys, and ethnic groups receive distinct messages. Resources for such a meeting appear on the website of the Campaign for a Commercial-Free Childhood (http://www.commercialfree childhood.org).

You could explain to families how activity-based learning environments that include 3-dimensional learning and play help children to develop the self-regulation that is so valuable to school success. Increasingly, with the miniaturization of technology, you can bring many digital photographs and brief videotapes of *all* the children's engagement in significant activity to underscore and interpret important learning.

Open School Night, Family Breakfast, and Special Occasions

A parent advisory committee for your classroom can help plan and organize details for volunteers as well as open school nights or special occasions. Parent members can also provide timely information about community events. Faculty members could share samples of adaptive software[2] and everyday objects that children could use adaptively; and issues dealing with computer-game and television violence.

Families are also impressed when pre-kindergarten teachers present brief videotapes of children role-playing folk tales after mid-year when their language development is clear. Educational researchers remind us that U.S. families typically focus at home on language literacy (Clements & Sarama, 2009a, p. 237). Therefore, it is also helpful to engage them in ideas for counting and measuring at home with their children. In addition, parents (and other educators) appreciate seeing photographs of children's block building, and hearing explanations about the mathematical and scientific importance of construction activities. To economize, one educator recommends that families should "Save boxes of various sizes and let your child build with them" (MacDonald, 2001, p. 53).

Families also enjoy seeing children's science and art exhibits with 2- and 3-dimensional items, and captions are helpful. Parent workshops can deal with what to expect from emergent readers; why schools appreciate invented spelling; and the power of socio-dramatic play. Remember to ask parents about topics of interest to them.

As you look at open-house evening meetings, you might notice that parents of the youngest children come more often than parents of older children. Therefore, you should always make parents feel welcome in the school at these events. Share ideas with the goal of having them return. (See also the Family Museum and Immigration Timeline sub-section in Chapter 8.)

Classroom Visits and Volunteers

Some schools provide a regular schedule of classroom visits during the day and others solicit family volunteers. Volunteers need orientation about what to do, along with flexibility. It makes sense to match the person's skill with an activity. Show them how to support a particular activity, such as using a computer; playing a mathematics game with four children; or cooking with a small group (provide a picture–word recipe). Encourage, appreciate, and thank each volunteer.

Families can staff voting booths for children during a simulated presidential election. Early childhood teachers might also contact community agencies to invite volunteers and guest readers from among local empty-nesters and retirees. [**Procedural note:** It is sensible to work with school administrators whenever you plan to communicate outside the school.] Then children participate in drafting thank-you notes to the volunteers.

Some teachers post the seven conditions for learning (see Chapter 3) with a brief rationale for each volunteer or visitor to see. Others create a horizontal display that lists a new activity for each day of school and post it on the wall. Families find out more about the rich organization and content of your classroom when you place signs on learning centers, clearly mark places to store materials, and label thematic book boxes.

When family members visit your classroom, they learn about the many ways that children learn literacy and mathematics skills. For example, you might enlist a visiting adult to represent seriation as follows: As children practice lining up by size, they include all adults in the room. Children delight in comparing the sizes of adults. Also, ask children to estimate how many people (up to ten or twenty) could fit into a hoop. When the children protest that it is unfair to include an adult, they are building their sense of the need for a standard measure. (You can explain these purposes to the visitor.) Inasmuch as families like to see how you appreciate their children, you can also become a credible model of many ways in which you help their children build independence and interact with others.

Working with Colleagues to Solve Problems

When you feel stumped by an issue with children or families, it helps to share ideas with colleagues. For example, if you and your colleagues see increasing numbers of children arriving with family problems, you might agree to focus on the strengths with which children come to school before looking at areas to improve. What would the preferred behavior look like when the problem is solved? Provide and discuss objective observational documentation of children in order to consider alternative ways to interact.

In addition, plan ways to organize and share resources with one another. For example, after six weeks, the fish in your classroom might become invisible to the children who move on to other concerns. Exchanging the animal(s) with another colleague can refresh animal study. In turn, when you bring back the fish, children often find a fresh level of interest and new insights.

When you develop games and other materials with other teachers and share copies of the materials, you are advertising how you teach concepts and skills. This also helps you to learn ideas from them that you could selectively adapt for your children.

Working with Self-development Helps Working with Everyone Else

Whether you have been working with young children for many years or are starting out, there is a next step in figuring out what to do and how you might prefer to do it if you were able. After setting aside policies, budgets, administration, last year's teacher, families, your own personal stressors, Mondays, Fridays, dreary weather, and after the summer break, the mirror continues to show you the one person who can help you.

You can help yourself in quite a few ways. You can refine your questioning skills and group focus comments. Some teachers find that it helps to target a particular skill. One way to do this is simply to audiotape (or videotape) discussions or conferences and listen to your own comments. It is useful to use guidelines such as those in Boxes 10.8, 13.3, and 14.4. When you jot down verbatim some of your questions or comments, you might be surprised to find that you exceed your expectations. At the same time, you might reflect that, if you could replay the moment, you would word a comment differently. Many teachers are able to refine the quality of interactive content after they have got over hearing all the "OK"s; or all of the occasions when they repeated what each child said; or referred to everyone as "boys and girls" instead of using gender–neutral language. You might have a transformative and satisfying experience when you identify what you want to continue to do and what you want to modify.

Explaining Conditions for Activity-based Learning to Administrators

Some schools have websites on which teachers post their school e-mail addresses, display announcements, and document classroom events. These websites supplement classroom and hallway displays of children's work.

School administrators and the teacher next year, no less than parents, might need to understand your integrated, inquiry-based, activity-based learning environment. Share examples of what you are doing with your children to integrate important learning standards as well as the results of research that support this practice.

Advertise Your Program with Relevant Research

The sum of relevant studies suggests that young children who participate in an integrated, experiential model do as well academically on standardized tests of skills as children in a more teacher-directed, skills-oriented approach. Within the context of a rapidly changing technological global society, it also makes sense to integrate rich cultural opportunities with the skills that children will need to thrive.

However, researchers have found that children in activity-based learning environments achieve: improved positive attitudes toward school; concept development; improved self-regulation and executive function; and more flexibility in solving problems (Jerrold, 2010). A related study finds that kindergarten children whose teachers are prepared to teach an integrated, inquiry-based approach score higher in their state's standardized tests (Strasser & Sepolcha, 2009). The findings of these studies confirm other longitudinal findings (Bodrova & Leong, 2007; Campbell et al., 2002; Marcon, 1992; Reynolds, Temple, Robertson, & Mann, 2001; Schweinhart et al., 2005; Stipek, Feiler, Daniels, & Milburn, 1995). The longitudinal studies of these early interventions also find fewer problems among secondary school students. In addition, they support an economically valuable societal investment in child-centered, conceptually rich, and engaging programs.

It is worth looking at some possible contributing factors that appear in one kindergarten study (Fromberg, n.d.). Public school kindergarten teachers with equivalent experience would plan to teach the same concepts with the same activities on the same day. School administrators report that they are diligent in equitably assigning children who might need additional support. The differences in evaluations appear in Table 15.1.

Such research findings strengthen support for activity-based learning environments that include both Dynamic-Themes and the integration of representational language, mathematical, cognitive, physical, artistic, social and emotional skills. Increasingly, with the miniaturization of technology, you should be able to show colleagues electronic portfolios that document and interpret children's engagement in significant activity.

TABLE 15.1 Small-group Compared with Whole-group Instruction

	Model A	Model B
Statistical standardized test scores	Significantly higher	Significantly lower
Group work	Four small groups, alternating independent activities	Whole-group demonstration with more management time
Duration of activities	Same	Same
Child participation	In-depth talk	Listening to demonstration[3]
Picture–word representation	Always	Occasionally
Children's perception of progress in school interviews	Significant perception of progress; positive expectations of differences	Neutral perceptions of progress and expectations

Transitions

Many teachers begin to share classroom goals at a family orientation during registration time and on the first day of school. Teachers also discuss policies, such as arrival and departure arrangements; snack and lunch policy; and donated materials. At the end of the year, they help children close down the year by creating a class address book and class photograph as the children move from pre-kindergarten to kindergarten, or kindergarten to first grade. Another project might be a patchwork quilt that includes dated, scanned drawings and paintings selected each month with a child's handprint on one square (adapted from Matricardi & McLarty, 2005, p. 110).

Next year's teachers might visit your classroom or see video clips to get an orientation about how you organize and work with your group. These contacts require administrators' help to organize "preparation time" for teachers' dialogue. Your other collaborations with colleagues throughout the year can also aid a smoother transition for the children. In effect, *work tactfully, eloquently, and persuasively to push back against push-down*. In addition, whenever possible, it is particularly helpful to discuss with the school administration ways to assign children equitably to next year's sections.

If you are planning to move from a half-day program or mixed schedule of alternating full and half days to an all-day program, there are some budget issues to consider:

- *Additional classroom space*. Furnishing a new classroom may cost $10,000.
- *Additional salaries*. An additional teacher and aides for each room and lunchroom aide salaries and fringe benefits.

- *Additional expendable materials.* The arts and writing consumables double in cost for each classroom.
- *Other provisions.* Lunchroom services may need to be increased. Check the height of the cafeteria counters to make sure that young children can see what food is available and can manage their trays (J. McGinn, personal communication, 1984). Young children need more time at lunch than the general population.
- *Transportation.* The midday bus service budget will be smaller. Additional children will use the existing bus service at the start and end of the school day.
- *State aid.* It may be possible to gain additional state aid.

During the first year or so, some families might elect to send their children during a half day. After that, virtually all families send their children all day. Administrators, however, reserve the right to furlough a few children who might need additional adjustment time for half the day.

Working families welcome having to make fewer childcare transitions and transportation arrangements (National Education Association, 2008). Teachers welcome the opportunity to become better acquainted with half the number of families and children. They do not, however, welcome pressure to rush children beyond their levels of challenge. On a positive note, the all-day schedule provides time to pursue activities in greater depth and with a sense of continuity.

Reflections

Education that is intellectual means acquiring knowledge-for-understanding and cooperation among people rather than only knowledge-for-information and memorized facts. Worthwhile content knowledge-for-understanding and co-operation includes *using* knowledge and skills.

On the one hand, the relationship between learning and teaching is complex; and there is simplicity in complexity. That is, it is simple once you teach in ways that children can learn. At the same time, you recognize and accept that your interaction with children is predictably unpredictable, a simple understanding that recognizes the complexity of the learning process in an activity-based learning environment. On the other hand, simple solutions may lead to minimal results.

Early education is a public relations nightmare because young children learn big ideas, knowledge, and skills through social, emotional, physical, and aesthetic means. Therefore, an important part of our work as early childhood educators is to find ways to communicate the significance of an activity-based learning environment to families, community members, and colleagues.

In order to maintain support for an intellectually rich, engaging education, we need to learn how to advertise the quality of complex education for knowledge and understanding. Some of the features include showcasing positive models, personalizing communication to different audiences, and providing message and "product" redundancy. Stakeholder audiences can integrate saturation of key messages such as the following:

- Block constructions build visual and spatial skills that help children learn mathematics, chemistry, and physics.
- Good citizens learn to collaborate and adapt during socio-dramatic play.
- Good readers and writers begin with lots of good talk about important ideas.
- Children who have choices gain the power to become independent and feel motivated to persevere.
- Different children doing different things at different times can have equivalent experiences.
- Expanded brain development and thinking feed on diets of varied, content-rich nourishment.
- Content-rich experiences for children are likely to meet, and possibly exceed, learning standards. Therefore, the idea is to fit teaching to children's learning, not to fit children to minimalist standards and tests.

Youngsters can connect and use ideas when teachers provide an activity-based Dynamic-Themes curriculum, using the seven integrated conditions for learning in early childhood. Real experiences in an activity-based learning environment can leave ethical, caring teachers and competent children both satisfied and thirsting for more.

For some needy youngsters, your classroom might become a relatively stable, nurturing, benevolent part of their lives. The year they spend with you is your chance to create a distinctly human and satisfying learning experience so that they can retain the potential to envision great futures in their lives.

ENDNOTES AND RELATED CHILDREN'S BOOKS

An asterisk after an entry in the Related Children's Books sections indicates that some kindergarten children and a small number of pre-kindergarten children will be able to read this book for themselves.

Preface

1. The term "activity-based learning environments" is adapted from "action-based learning environments" (S. Schwartz, personal communication, 2009).
2. Trans-disciplinary trading zones (Galison, 2003) provide an integrating image for learning. In a parallel way, "Unifying Concepts" in science education pull together ideas for constructivist planning (Brooks, 2011).

1. An All-Day Kindergarten and Pre-Kindergarten

Related Children's Book

de Paola, T. (1975). *Strega Nona*. Englewood Cliffs, NJ: Prentice-Hall.
Rey, H.A. (1973). *Curious George*. Boston: Houghton Mifflin
Sendak, M. (1963). *Where the Wild Things Are*. New York: Harper & Row.

3. Seven Conditions for Learning in Early Childhood

1. It is noteworthy that researchers recommend that early experiences with sharing and comparisons could build toward an understanding of fractions (Siegler et al., 2010).
2. Jean Piaget's developmental theory points to a similar progression: (1) sensori-motor/physical experiences; (2) perceptual imagery; (3) concrete concepts; and then (4) abstract/symbolic thought (Piaget, 1950).

4. Hands-On Learning Ties to Concept Development

1. Some people say that young children have short attention spans. We need to ask, "To what?" Quite the opposite, children demonstrate long attention spans to activities that invite their curiosity and match their conditions for learning.
2. Researchers consider the mathematical standards of number sense and spatial awareness related to geometry as crucial for young children's mathematical development (Clements & Sarama, 2009a).

Related Children's Books

Adler, D.A. (1999). *How tall, how short, how faraway?* New York: Holiday House.
Barton, B. (1981). *Building a house.* New York: Penguin.
Begaye, L.S. (1993). *Building a bridge.* Flagstaff, AZ: Northland.
Fortunato-Chisena, P. (2009). *Big digs and construction sites.* New York: Parachute Press.
Gibbons, G. (1996). *How a house is built.* New York: Holiday House.
Grifalconi A. (1986). *The village of round and square houses.* Boston: Little, Brown.
Hayward, l. (2001). *Jobs people do: A day in the life of a builder.* New York: DK Publishing.
Kleven, E. (2010). *Welcome home, mouse.* Berkeley: Tricycle Press.
Macken, J.E. (2008). *Construction tools.* Mankato, MN: Capstone Press.
Thomas, M. (2001). *A day with a bricklayer.* New York: Children's Press.

Websites

Bob the builder, www.bobthebuilder.com, games, puzzles, and activities; www.kenken kikki.jple_index2., machines in building, pictures, games, and activities.

Part II

1. Physicists, biologists, other scientists, economists, and artists at the frontiers of their fields in the sciences, complexity and chaos theory, are dealing with similar specifically unpredictable, nonlinear issues (American Association for the Advancement of Science, 2009; Gleick, 1987; Mitchell, 2009; Robertson & Combs, 1995; L.A. Smith, 2007). They are studying turbulence, the moments when states of matter change, and the outlines of rough and smooth things that they can measure. They are finding ways to measure the rough edges of the world, like broccoli and jagged shorelines, thinking about *fractals* (McDermott, 1983) and the patterns of scroll waves (Briscoe, 1984; Sullivan, 1985). Scientists are discovering that these apparently chaotic, nonlinear, unpredictable events follow a deeper, predictable, underlying pattern that they can express in nonlinear ways.

5. Dynamic-Theme Experiences: Cyclical Changes

Related Children's Books

Asch, F. (1985). *Bear shadow.* New York: Simon & Schuster.
Barner, B. (2001). *Dinosaur bones.* New York: Chronicle.
Brown, P. (2009). *The curious garden.* New York: Little, Brown & Co.

Burton, V.L. (1988). *The little house.* Boston: Houghton Mifflin. (Originally published in 1942.)

Carle, E. (1970). *The very hungry caterpillar.* New York: G.P. Putnam's Sons.

Carle, E. (1991). *A house for hermit crab.* New York: Simon & Schuster.

Cole, J. (1996). *The magic school bus: A book about the water cycle.* New York: Scholastic.

Cole, J. (1999). *The magic school bus plants seeds.* New York: Scholastic.

de Paola, T. (1995). *The cloud book.* New York: Scholastic.

Fowler, A. (2001). *From seed to plant.* New York: Holiday House.

Garland, S. (1998). *My father's boat.* Illus. T. Rans. New York: Scholastic.

Gibbons, G. (1993). *From seed to plant.* New York: Children's Press.

Gilman, P. (1992). *Something from nothing.* New York: Scholastic.

Glaser, M. (1983). *Does anyone know where a hermit crab goes?* Boston: Knickerbocker.

Gordon, M. (2008). *A drop of water.* Boston: Houghton Mifflin/Walter Lorraine Books.

Halfman, J. (20007). *Hermit crab's home: Safe in a shell.* Norwalk, CT: Soundprints.

Hall, D. (1997). *Ox-cart man.* Illus. B. Cooney. New York: Viking.

Harris, N.A. (2009). *A year at a construction site.* Minneapolis: Millbrook Press.

Heine, H. (1983). *The most wonderful egg in the world.* New York: Atheneum.

Helldorfer, M.C. (1994). *Gather up, gather in: A book of seasons.* Illus. V. Pederson. New York: Viking.

Heller, R. (1987). *Chickens aren't the only ones.* New York: Grosset & Dunlap.

Jonas, A. (1982). *When you were a baby.* New York: Greenwillow.

Jonas, A. (1983). *Round trip.* New York: Greenwillow.

Krauss, R. (1945). *The carrot seed.* New York: Harper & Row.

Krauss, R. (2007). *The growing story.* Illus. H. Oxenbury. New York: HarperCollins (originally published 1945).

Macken, J.E. (2008). *Flip float fly: Seeds on the move.* Illus. P. Paparone. New York: Holiday House.

Miles, M. (1971). *Annie and the old one.* Boston: Little, Brown & Co.

Moncure, J. (1990). *How seeds travel: Popguns and parachutes.* Newtown, PA: Child's World.

Moss, M. (2005). *This is the tree.* Brooklyn, NY: Kane/Miller

Numeroff, L.J. (1985). *If you give a mouse a cookie.* New York: Scholastic.★

Olivieri, S.M. (2009). *Elena's big move.* Austin, TX: Synergy Books.

Rohman, E. (1994). *Time flies.* New York: Scholastic.

Rosenberry, V. (2003). *The growing-up tree.* New York: Holiday House.

Ryder, J. (1982). *The snail's spell.* Illus. L. Cherry. New York: Bradbury Press.

Schlein, M. (1953). *Fast is not a ladybug.* Illus. L. Kessler. New York: Scott.

Selsam, M. (1980). *All about eggs.* Illus. S. Fleischer. Reading, MA: Addison-Wesley.

Shimberg, E. (2007). *Herman, the hermit crab.* Yarmouth, ME: Abernathy House.

Stevenson, R.L. (1961). "My shadow." In *The child's garden of verses.* New York: Platt & Munk. (Originally published in 1885.)

Taback, S. (1999). *Joseph had a little overcoat.* New York: Scholastic.

Ungerer, T. (2005). *Snail, where are you?* Maplewood, NJ: Blue Apple Books.

Websites

Snails facts at http://www.weichtire.at/Mollusks/Schneck/lkand/weinberg/pte_snails.html; hermit crab facts at http://ezinearticles.com/?Interesting-Hermit-Crab-Facts&id=1943644.

6. Dynamic-Theme Experiences: Contrasts and Conflicts (Dialectical Activity)

1. The issue of context in science is particularly relevant in order to overcome the tendency to become complacent with "truths." A few daring individuals, seduced more by questions than by the prevailing politics of their time, push the frontiers of knowledge. We may, however, never know (or find out only much later) about the many who suppress their questions or discount their intuitions or findings because of their socio-historical situations. While Galileo's work is one well-known example of a society's exercise-with-blinders, it may be that some of today's so-called "alternative" medicines are among contemporary blind-sided phenomena. The physical sciences, long thought to be fixed and reliable, ironically chronicle political limitations on theory (Hawking, 1988; Sobel, 1999).

Related Children's Books

Barkan, J. (2006). *What is density?* New York: Children's Press.
Bloom, S. (2007). *A splendid friend, indeed.* Honesdale, PA: Boyds Mill Press.
Bradley, K.B. (2001). *Pop! A book about bubbles.* New York: HarperCollins.
Branley, F., & Vaughan, E. (1976). *Mickey's magnet.* New York: Crowell.
Challoner, J. (1998). *Floating and sinking.* Austin, TX: Raintree Steck-Vaughn.
Clark, E.C. (2002). *Mim's book of opposites.* London: Andersen Press.
Cole, J. (1999). *The magic school bus ups and downs: A book about floating and sinking.* New York: Scholastic.
de Paola, T. (1977). *The quicksand book.* New York: Holiday House.
Dyer, W.W., with Tracy, K. (2009). *How what you say can get in your way.* Illus. S.H. Budnik. Carlsbad, CA: Hay House.
Havill, J. (1986). *Jamaica's find.* Illus. A.S. O'Brien. Boston: Houghton Mifflin.
Joosse, B.M. (1991). *Are you my mother?* San Francisco: Chronicle Books.
Krensky, S. (2004). *Bubble trouble.* N. Richland, TX: Aladdin.
Lamorisse, A. (1956). *The red balloon.* Garden City, NY: Doubleday.
Niz, E.S. (2006). *Floating and sinking.* Mankato, MN: Capstone.
Raschka, C. (2000). *Ring! Yo?* New York: Dorling Kindersley.
Rosinsky, N. (2002). *Magnets: Pulling together, pushing apart.* New York: Picture Window Books.
Schreiber, A. (2003). *Magnets.* New York: Grosset & Dunlap.
Spelman, C.M. (2000). *When I feel angry.* Illus. N.Cote. Morton Grove, IL: Albert Whitman.
Stein, D. (2005). *How to make monstrous, huge, unbelievably big bubbles.* Palo Alto, CA: Klutz.
Viorst, J. (1994). *Rose and Michael.* New York: Atheneum.

7. Dynamic-Theme Experiences: The Whole Exceeds the Parts (Synergy)

Related Children's Books

Backstein, K., & Mitra, A. (2009). *Blind men and the elephant.* Newton, KS: Paw Prints.
Beaty, A., & Roberts, D. (2007). *Iggy Peck, architect.* New York: Abrams Books.

Bertrand, D.G. (2010). *The party for Papa Luis/La fiesta para Papa Luis*. Houston, TX: Pinata Books.

Brown, M.W. (1947). *Stone soup*. New York: Charles Scribner's Sons.

Charles, R.P.E. (2009). *Sometime my Mommy and me*. Georgia: Revolutionary Disciples Media.

Davis, A., & Petricic, D. (1997). *Bone button borscht*. Buffalo, NY: Kids Can Press.

de Paola, T. (1978). *The popcorn book*. New York: Holiday House.

de Paola, T. (2009). *Strega nona's harvest*. New York: G.P. Putnam's Sons.

Demi (1990). *The empty pot*. New York: Henry Holt.

Flood, N.B. (2008). *The hogan that Great-Grandfather built*. Flagstaff, AZ: Salina Bookshelf.

Flournoy, V. (1985). *The patchwork quilt*. New York: Dial Books for Young Readers.

Gershator, D., & Gershator, P. (2005). *Kallalloo! A Caribbean tale*. Tarrytown, NY: Marshall Cavendish Children's.

Jonas, A. (1984). *The quilt*. New York: Greenwillow.

Kimmel, E. A. (2004). *Cactus Soup*. Illus. P. Huling. Tarrytown, NY: Marshall Cavendish Children's.

Kroll, S. (2006). *The biggest valentine ever*. Illus. J. Bassett. New York: Scholastic.

Landau, E. (2003). *Popcorn!* Watertown, MA: Charlesbridge.

Lewis, R., & Zong, G. (2010). *Oran Peel's pocket*. New York: Abrams Books.

Lionni, L. (1989). *Swimmy*. New York: Scholastic.

Low, A. (1994). *The popcorn shop*. New York: Scholastic.

McCloud, C. (2006). *Have you filled a bucket today?* Illus. D. Messing. Northville, MI: Ferne Press.

McFarland, C. (1998). *Cucumber soup*. Golden, CO: Fulcrum.

Milway, K.S. (2008). *One hen: How one small loan made a big difference*. Illus. E. Fernandes. New York: Kids Can Press.

Perrow, A. (2010). *Many hands: A Penobscot Indian story*. Rockport, ME: Down East Books.

Plune, I. (1980). *The Bremen-town musicians*. Garden City, NY: Doubleday.

Polacco, P. (1988). *The keeping quilt*. New York: Simon & Schuster.

Ringgold, F., & Cameron, D. (1998). *Dancing at the Louvre: Faith Ringgold's French collection and other story quilts*. Berkeley: University of California Press.

Segal, J. (2006). *Carrot soup*. Illus. J. Segal. Chicago: Margaret K. McElderry.

Southgate, V. (Retold) (1970). *The enormous turnip*. Loughborough: Wills & Hepworth.★

Wood, D. (1998). *Making the world*. Illus. Y. Miyaki & H. Miyaki. New York: Simon & Schuster.

Young, E. (2002). *Seven blind mice*. New York: Philomel Books.

Zemach, M. (1989). *All God's critters got a place in the choir*. New York: E.P. Dutton.

8. Social Studies, Multicultural, and Egalitarian Experiences

Related Children's Books

Rites of Passage

Bunting, E. (1989). *The Wednesday surprise*. New York: Clarion Books.

Child, L. (2004). *I am absolutely too small for school*. New York: Candlewick Press.

Diakité, P., & Diakité, B.W. (2006). *I lost my tooth in Africa*. New York: Scholastic Press.

Felt, S. (1950). *Rose too little*. Garden City, NY: Doubleday.

Gonzalez, D.C. (2010). *The red umbrella*. New York: Random House.

Heide, F.P., & Gilliland, J.H. (1990). *The day of Ahmed's secret*. New York: Lothrop, Lee, & Shepard.

Kim, J.U. (2003). *Sumi's first day of school ever*. New York: Viking Juvenile.

McCloskey, R. (1986). *One morning in Maine*. New York: Viking. (Originally published in 1952.)

Mills, D., Crouth, J., & Denham, S. (2003). *The wibbly wobbly tooth*. London: Mantra.

Sis, P. (2000). *Madlenka*. New York: Francis Foster.

Sisulu, E.B. (1997). *The day Gogo went to vote: South Africa, April 1996*. Cape Town: Tafelberg.

Wurm, K., (2006). *Truman's loose tooth*. Illus. M. Chesworth. Appleton, WI: Spirited Pub.

Yashima,T. (1986). *The umbrella*. New York: Puffin.

English as a Second Language

Choi, S.N. (2001). *The name jar*. New York: Knopf.

Levine, E. (1995). *I hate English!* New York: Scholastic.

Media, J., & Vandenbroeck, F. (2004). *My name is Jorge*. Honesdale, PA: Boyd Mills Press.

Pak, S. (2001). *Dear Juno*. New York: Puffin.

Recorvits, H., & Swiatkowska, G. (2003). *My name is Yoon*. New York: Farrar, Straus, & Giroux.

Dealing with a New Baby

Alexander, M.G. (2005). *Nobody asked me if I wanted a baby sister*. Watertown, MA: Charlesbridge.

Bunting, E. (2001). *Jin Woo*. Illus. C.K. Soentpiet. New York: Korea.

de Paola, T. (1999). *The baby sister*. New York: Putnam Juvenile.

Keats, E.J. (1998). *Peter's chair*. New York: Viking Juvenile.

Krishnaswami, U. (2006). *Bringing Asha home*. Illus. J. Akib. New York: Lee & Low.

Look, L. (2001). *Henry's first moon birthday*. Illus. Y. Heo. New York: Atheneum.

Wholesome Family Relationships

Balgassi, E.C. (2000). *Halmoni's day*. Illus. R. Hunt. New York: Dial Books.

Cheng, A. (2000). *Grandfather counts*. Illus. A. Zhang. New York: Lee & Low.

Hegamin, T.C. (2009). *Most loved in all the world*. Illus. C.A. Cabrera. Boston: Houghton Mifflin.

Katz, K. (2006). *Best ever big sister*. New York: Grosset & Dunlap.

Look, L. (1999). *Love as strong as ginger*. New York: Atheneum.

Look, L. (2006). *Uncle Peter's amazing Chinese wedding*. Illus. Y. Heo. New York: Simon & Schuster/Atheneum.

McCain, B.T. (2001). *Grandmother's dreamcatcher*. Illus. S. Schuett. Park Ridge, IL: Albert Whitman.

Mendoza-Roas, G. (2007). *My family and me/Mi familia y yo*. Wheaton, IL: Me+Mi.

Onyefulu, I. (2007). *Here comes our bride: An African wedding story*. London: Frances Lincoln.

Polacco, P. (1998). *Chicken Sunday*. New York: Putnam & Grosset Group.

Polacco, P. (2001). *The keeping quilt*. New York: Aladdin Paperbacks.

Rylant, C. (1993). *The relatives came.* New York: Aladdin Paperbacks.

Schick, E. (1999). *Navajo wedding day: A Dine marriage ceremony.* Tarrytown, NY: Cavendish.

Soto, G. (2006). *Too many tamales.* New York: Putnam & Grosset Group.

Velasquez, E. (2001). *Grandma's records.* New York: Walker Books.

Walker, D. (2009). *Mama says.* New York: Blue Sky Press.

Modern Families

Bunin, C., & Bunin, S. (1992). *Is that your sister? A true story of adoption.* Wayne, PA: Our Child Press.

Igus, T. (1996). *Two Mrs. Gibsons.* Illus. D. Wells. San Francisco: Children's Book Press.

Lamperti, N. (1999). *Brown like me.* Norwich, VT: New Victoria.

Rounce, R. (2009). *Pancakes with chocolate syrup.* Staten Island, NY: Xlibris.

Schmitz, T. (2008). *Standing on my own two feet.* New York: Penguin.

Simon, S. (2003). *All families are special.* Illus. T. Flavin. Park Ridge, IL: Albert Whitman.

Vigna, J. (1987). *Mommy and me by ourselves again.* Morton Grove, IL: Albert Whitman.

Economic Issues Affect Families

Bauer, C.F., (1981). *My mom travels a lot.* Illus. N.W. Parker. New York: Warne.

Credle, E. (1934). *Down, down the mountain.* New York: Thomas Nelson.

Demi (1997). *One grain of rice.* New York: Scholastic.

Hazen, B.S. (1983). *Tight times.* New York: Puffin.

Hegamin, T. (2009). *Most loved in all the world.* Boston: Houghton Mifflin.

Hernandez, M.A. (1999). *Erandi's braids.* Illus. T. de Paola. New York: Penguin.

McBrier, P. (2004). *Beatrice's goat.* Illus. L. Lohstoeter. New York: Aladdin.

Mitchell, M.K. (1998). *Uncle Jed's barbershop.* New York: Aladdin.

Viorst, J. (2002). *Alexander, who used to be rich last Sunday.* Ottawa, IL: Reddick Library.

Williams, V.B. (1984). *A chair for my mother.* New York: Harper Trophy.

Loss

Havill, J. (1989). *Jamaica's find.* New York: Scholastic.

Jonas, A. (1986). *Where can it be?* New York: Greenwillow.

Willems, M. (2004). *Knuffle Bunny: A cautionary tale.* New York: Hyperion.*

Willems, M. (2007). *Elconejito Knuffle: Un cento aleccionador.* New York: Hyperion.*

Overcoming Obstacles

Bloom, S. (2001). *The bus for us.* New York: Macmillan/McGraw-Hill.

Choi, S.H. (1993). *Halmoni and the picnic.* Illus. K.M. Dugan. New York: Houghton Mifflin.

Edwards, M. (2004). *Papa's latkes.* Illus. S. Schuett. New York: Candlewick Press.

Friedman, I.R. (1987). *How my parents learned to eat.* Boston: Houghton Mifflin.

Hoffman, M.A. (1991). *Amazing Grace.* New York: Dial Press.

Say, A. (2008). *Grandfather's journey.* New York: Sandpiper.

Suen, A. (2008). *Helping Sophia.* Minnesota: Abdo Consulting Group.

Young, E. (1996). *Lon pop po.* New York: Putnam Juvenile.

Friendship

Cohen, M. (2008). *Will I have a friend?* New York: Star Bright Books.

Cummins, J. (2002). *Country kid, city kid.* New York: Henry Holt.

DeCosta, D. (2001). *Snow in Jerusalem.* Illus. C. Van Wright & Y. Hu. Park Ridge, IL: Albert Whitman.

English, K. (2004). *Hot day on Abbott Ave.* Illus. J. Steptoe. New York: Clarion Books.

Ludwig, T. (2008). *Trouble talk.* New York: Tricycle Press.

McAllister, A. (2005). *Just like sisters.* New York: Atheneum.

Munsch, R. (1999). *We share everything.* New York: Scholastic.

O'Neill, A. (2007). *Estella's swap.* New York: Lee & Low.

O'Neill, A. (2008). *The worst best friend.* New York: Scholastic.

Rodman, M.A. (2005). *My best friend.* Illus. E.B. Lewis. New York: Puffin.

Tingle, T. (2006). *Crossing Bok Chitto: A Choctaw tale of friendship and freedom.* El Paso, TX: Cinco Puntos Press.

Emotions and Bullying

Criserll, P.K. (2008). *Stand up for yourself and your friends.* Illus. A. Martini. Middleton, WI: American Girl.

Keats, E.J. (1998). *Where the wild things are.* New York: Harper & Row.

Munson, D. (2000). *Enemy pie.* New York: Chronicle.

Parr, T. (2000). *The feelings book.* Boston: Little, Brown.

Smith-Mansell, C. (2004). *Stop bullying Bobby.* Illus. S Riggio. Far Hills, NJ: New Horizons Press.

Tetik, B. (2009). *If you are mad say it with words.* New York: BookSurge.

Harvest

Atwell, D. (2006). *The Thanksgiving door.* Sandpiper, UT: Riverside.

Brown, M. (1973). *Stone soup.* New York: Atheneum. (Originally published 1945.)

Jackson, E.B., & Ellis, J.D. (2000). *The autumn equinox: Celebrating the harvest.* Brookfield, MA: Millbrook Press.

Kindersley, A. (1997). *Children just like me: Celebrations.* New York: DK.

Lin, G. (2010). *Thanking the moon: Celebrating the mid-autumn moon festival.* New York: Knopf Books for Young Readers.

Pfeffer, W., & Bleck, L. (2006). *We gather together: Celebrating the harvest season.* New York: Dutton Children's.

Uk-Bae, L. (1999). *Sori's harvest moon day: A story of Korea.* Norwalk, CT: Soundprints.

Sacrifice/Repenting

Heiligman, D. (2007). *Holidays around the world: Celebrate Independence Day.* London: Marshall Cavendish.

Katz, K. (2007). *My first Ramadan.* New York: Henry Holt.

Taylor, C.A. (2002). *Juneteenth: A celebration of freedom.* Greensboro, N.C.: Open Hand.

Wikler, M., Groner, J.S., & Schanzer, R. (1991). *In the synagogue.* Rockville, MD: Kar-Ben Copies.

Zucker, J., & Barger, J. (2003). *Four special questions: A Passover story*. Hauppauge, NY: Barron's.

Zucker, J., & Barger, J. (2004). *Fasting and dates: A Ramadan and Eid-ul-fitr story*. Hauppauge, NY: Barron's.

Heroes/Heroines/History

Anderson, L. (1976). *Mary McLeod Bethune*. Illus. W. Hutchinson. Champaign, IL: Garrard.

Greenfield, M.M. (1977). *Mary McLeod Bethune*. Illus. J. Pinkner. New York: Thomas Y. Crowell.

Lindeen, M. (2009). *Marie Curie: Scientist*. Illus. R. Sprunger. Edina, MN: Magic Wagon.

McCormick, L. W. (2006). *Marie Curie*. New York: Scholastic.

Mortensen, L. (2008). *Marie Curie: Prize-winning scientist*. Illus. S.M. Jaekel. Minneapolis, MN: Picture Window Books.

Schaefer, L.M., & Schaefer, W. (2005). *Marie Curie*. Mankato, MN: Capstone.

Fischel, E. (2005). *Mahatma Gandhi*. Illus. R. Morgan. Mexico: S.N. Ediciones.

Mitchell, P. (1998). *Gandhi: The father of modern India*. Illus. M. Mitra. Oxford: Oxford University Press.

Shaw, M. D. (2004). *Gandhi, India's great soul*. Illus. S. Marchesi. Woodstock, VT: SkyLight Paths.

Cooper, F. (2004). *Jump: From the life of Michael Jordan*. New York: Philomel Books.

Houghton, S. (2002). *Michael Jordan: The best ever*. Mankato, MN: Capstone Press.

Kirkpatrick, R. (2001). *Michael Jordan, basketball superstar*. Illus. R. Kirkpatrick. New York: Powerkids Press.

McCormick, L.W. (2007). *Michael Jordan*. New York: Children's Press.

Adler, D.A. (1990). *A picture book of Martin Luther King, Jr*. Illus. R. Casilla. New York: Scholastic.

Bauer, M.D., & Smith, J. (2009). *Martin Luther King, Jr*. New York: Scholastic.

Brown, J.A. (2005). *Martin Luther King, Jr*. Milwaukee, WI: Weekly Reader Early Learning.

Marzollo, J. (2006). *Happy birthday, Martin Luther King*. Illus. J.B. Pinkney. New York: Scholastic.

Patrick, D.L. (2003). *A lesson for Martin Luther King Jr*. New York: Aladdin.

Schlank, C.H., Metzger, B., & Kastner, J. (1990). *Martin Luther King, Jr.: A biography for young children*. Mt. Rainier, MD: Gryphon House.

Trueit, T.S. (2007). *Martin Luther King Jr. Day*. New York: Children's Press.

Adler, D. A. (2009). *Honest Abe Lincoln*. Illus. J. Wallner. New York: Holiday House.

Feinstein, S. (2004). *Read about Abraham Lincoln*. Berkely Hgts, NJ: Enslow.

Fontes, J., & Fontes, R. (2009). *Abraham Lincoln*. New York: Dorling Kindersley.

Hall, M., & Martinez, M. (2009). *Abraham Lincoln: 16th U.S. president*. Edina, MN: Magic Wagon.

Mayer, C. (2008). *Abraham Lincoln*. Chicago: Heinemann Library.

Pingry, P.A., & Britt, S. (2005). *Discover Abraham Lincoln: Storyteller, lawyer, president*. Nashville: Ideals Children's Books.

Winters, K., & Carpenter, N. (2006). *Abe Lincoln: The boy who loved books*. New York: Aladdin Paperbacks.

Adler, D.A. (1993). *A picture book of Rosa Parks*. Illus. R. Casilla. New York: Holiday House.

Baker, C., & Hunt, R. (2004). *Let's read about—Rosa Parks*. New York: Scholastic/Cartwheel.

Benjamin, A., & Beier, E. (1995). *Young Rosa Parks: Civil rights heroine*. Mahwah, NJ: Troll Associates.

Chanko, P., & Ramsey, M.D. (2007). *Rosa Parks: Bus ride to freedom*. New York: Scholastic.

Klingel, C., & Noyed, R.B. (2002*). Rosa Parks*. Chanhassen, MN: The Child's World.

Pingry, P.A., & Walker, S. (2008). *Meet Rosa Parks*. Nashville, TN: Ideals Children's Books.

Roop, P., & Roop, C. (2005). *Take a stand, Rosa Parks*. New York: Scholastic.

Geography

Fanelli, S. (2001). *My map book*. New York: Harper Festival. (Originally published in 1995.)

Jonas, A. (1983). *Round trip*. New York: Greenwillow.

Lock, D. (2009). *Homes around the world*. Newton, KS: Paw Prints.

MacDonald, G. (1971). *The little island*. Illus. L. Weisgard. Garden City, NY: Doubleday.

McCloskey, R. (2010). *Blueberries for Sal*. Newton, KS: Paw Prints. (Originally published in 1948.)

9. Literacy in Music, Movement, and the Arts

1. The lyrics of many folk songs appear on the websites of poet-composers and singers.
2. Labanotation is a written format that records the figures, directions, levels, and pace of dance movements.
3. Some teachers use role-playing in folk tales as a way to help children practice saying "No" in situations involving child abuse or drugs (Lynn, McGinn, & Wohlstadter, personal communication, 1991). "Scared and Hurt" (Kuhmerker, 1984) briefly summarizes many of the issues in child abuse, which you might adapt to role-playing. See also *Caps for Sale* (Slobodkina, 1989), *The Pied Piper* (Jacobs, 1968), and *The three billy goats gruff* (Ashjornsen, & Moe, 1991; Galone, 1981).

Related Children's Books

Ashjornsen, P.C., & Moe, J.E. (1991). *The three billy goats gruff*. Illus. M. Brown. San Diego, CA: Harcourt Brace Jovanovich.

Christensen, C. (2001). *Sky tree: Seeing science through art*. Illus. T. Locker. New York: HarperCollins.

de Paola, T. (1989). *The art lesson*. New York: G.P. Putnam's Sons.

Galone, P. (1981). *The three billy goats gruff*. Boston: Houghton Mifflin Harcourt.

Jacobs, J. (Ed.) (1968). *Pied Piper and other fairy tales*. Illus. J. Hill. New York: Macmillan.

Yenawine, P. (1991). *Lines*. New York: Delacorte.

10. Literacy in Oral Language, Writing, Reading, and English Language Learning

1. Irene Fountas and Gay Pinnell present useful lists of "leveled" books for emerging readers in the Appendix of *Guided Reading* (1996) and in *Leveled Literacy Intervention* (2008). In addition, see their related *Benchmark Assessment System* (2010a).

Related Children's Books

Brown, M.W. (1973) *The noisy book*. Illus. R. Thomson. New York: Scroll Press.★
Cowley, J. (1990). *Mrs. Wishy-washy*. San Diego, CA: Wright Group. (Originally published in 1980.)★
Flack, M. (1968). *Ask Mr. Bear*. New York: Macmillan. (Originally published in 1958.) ★
Hoberman, M.A. (1978). *A house is a home for me*. Illus. B. Fraser. New York: Viking.★
Keats, E.J. (1963). *Where the wild things are*. New York: Harper & Row.
Melser, R., & Cowley, J. (1986). *The big toe*. Illus. M. Bailey. San Diego, CA: Wright Group. (Originally published in 1980.)★
Milne, A.A. (1957). *Winnie-the-Pooh*. Illus. E.H. Shepard. New York: Dutton.
Numeroff, L.J. (1978) *A house is a home for me*. New York: Scholastic.★
Numeroff, L.J. (1985). *If you give a mouse a cookie*. New York: Scholastic.★
Slobodkina, E. (1989). *Caps for sale*. New York: Scholastic. (Originally published in 1947.)★
White, E.B. (1968). *Charlotte's web*. Illus. G. Williams. New York: Dell.

Poetry

Adoff, A. (1974). *My black me*. New York: E.P. Dutton.
Giovanni, N. (Ed.) (2008). *Hip hop speaks to children: A celebration of poetry with a beat*. Naperville, IL: Sourcebooks. (See especially Greenfield, E. "Books," p. 28; Zephania, B., "For word," p. 29; Giovanni, N. "The Rosa Parks," p. 38.) (With audio CD.)
Hopkins, L.B. (Ed.) (2004). *Wonderful words: Poems about reading, writing, speaking, and listening*. New York: Simon & Schuster Books for Young Readers. (See especially Merriam, E., "Metaphors," pp. 10–11.)
Milne, A.A. (1958). *The world of Chrisopher Robin*. Illus. E.H. Shepard. New York: Dutton. (Originally published in 1924.) (Includes *Now we are six* and *When we were very young*. See especially "Happiness," p. 10, and "Sand between the toes," p. 87.)
Stevenson, R.L. (1961). *The child's garden of verses*. New York: Platt & Munk. (Originally published in 1885.) (See especially "My shadow," p. 39; "Bed in summer," p. 61.)
Taberski, S. (Ed.) (1996). *Morning, noon and night: Poems to fill your day*. Illus. N. Doniger. Greenvale, NY: Mondo.
Yolen, J., & Peters, A.F. (Eds.) (2007). *Here's a little poem: A very first book of poetry*. Illus. P. Dunbar. Cambridge, MA: Candlewick Press. (See especially Milne, A.A., "Halfway downup," p. 16; Livingston, M.C., "Just watch," p. 17; Wells, R., "Your birthday cake," p. 22; Yolen, J., "Recipe for green," pp. 54–55; Mayer, G., "Paper songs," pp. 70–71; Hughes, L., "April rain song," pp. 74–75; Prelutsky, J., "Baby in a high chair," p. 23; Stevenson, R.L., "The swing," pp. 64–65.)

11. Literacy in Computers, Design Technology, and Science: Issues and Opportunities

1. The International Society for Technology in Education (ISTE, 2007) highlights the need for children to analyze, critique, create, communicate, collaborate, problem solve, and develop informational fluency in order to make wholesome decisions. The National Council of Teachers of English (NCTE, 2009) adds concern for "ethical responsibility" in using technology.
2. Commercial software is plentiful and development is ongoing. New titles and features will continue to emerge. The point of mentioning specific titles in this book is to share

criteria for selecting materials. Ideally, your own choices of software will depend on the experiences you estimate that children bring to school and how you might scaffold those experiences with meaningful and custom-tailored activities.

3. It is noteworthy that the NAEYC technology policy statement was under revision at the time of writing (2011), a reflection of the attempt to maintain currency with the expansion of technology and design technology. Along with the *Common Core State Standards*, the National Council for Social Studies includes attention to standards for science, technology, and society.

12. Literacy in Mathematics: Cooperative Experiences

1. Most teachers traditionally provide reading instruction for small groups, often "three reading groups." Most schools have remedial reading teachers who work mainly with boys, individually and in small groups. Most schools typically teach mathematics as a whole-group activity. Few schools have remedial mathematics teachers.

2. The NCTM website (http://www.nctm.org) and the National Library of Virtual Manipulatives website (http://www.matti.usu.edu/nlvm) are sources of many virtual manipulatives.

3. Administrator anxiety about test scores creates a preponderance of directive skill-and-drill practice with young, lower-income, urban children. It is worth considering the effect of such an approach upon the children's capacity to self-regulate and exercise executive function that depends upon the ability to use their imaginations and delay gratification. On another note, the directive and sedentary approach might negatively impact youngsters' motivation to participate in school activities.

Related Children's Books

You might adapt stories with a die, *predictions*, and *comparison*.

Bang, M. (1991). *Ten, nine, eight*. New York: Greenwillow.

Brown, M.W. (1999). *Another important book*. Illus. C. Raschke. New York: HarperCollins.

Brown, R. (2010). *Ten seeds*. London: Andersen Press.

Burns, M., (1994). *The greedy triangle*. Illus. G. Silveria. New York: Scholastic.

Crimi, C. (1995). *Outside, inside*. Illus. L.A. Riley. New York: Simon & Schuster.

Demi (1986). *Demi's count the animals 1–2–3*. New York: Grosset & Dunlap. (Rhyme to 20, then 100.)

Evans, L. (1999). *Can you count ten toes? Count to ten in ten different languages*. Illus. D. Roche. Boston: Houghton Mifflin Harcourt.

Feelings, M. (1971). *Moja means one: Swahili counting book*. New York: Dial.

Fleming, D. (1992). *Count!* New York: Henry Holt & Co. (To10, then by tens to 50.)

Gardner, B. (1987). *Can you imagine . . .? A counting book*. New York: Dodd, Mead, & Co.

Hoban, T. (1973). *Over, under and through, and other spatial concepts*. New York: Simon & Schuster.

Hong, L.T. (1993). *Two of everything: A Chinese folktale*. Morton Grove, IL: Albert Whitman.

Hutchins, H. (2007). *A second is a hiccup: a child's book of time*. Illus. K.M. Denton. New York: Arthur A. Levine. Scholastic. (Originally published in 2004.)

Hutchins, P. (1968). *Rosie's walk*. New York: Greenwillow.★

Jenkins, S. (2004). *Actual size*. New York: Houghton Mifflin.

Lionni, L. (1960). *Inch by inch*. New York: Astor-Honor. (Also bird vocabulary.)

McGrath, B.B. (1994). *The M&M's counting book*. Watertown, MA: Charlesbridge. (To 12, adding and subtracting.)

McMillan, B. (1991). *Eating fractions.* New York: Scholastic. (Whole, half, quarters.)

Mullins, P. (1998). *One horse waiting for me.* New York: Simon & Schuster Books for Young Readers.

Myller, R. (1962). *How big is a foot?* New York: Atheneum.

Schafer, K. (2002). *Penguins 123.* Chanhassen, MN: NorthWord Press.

Schlein, M. (1953). *Fast is not a ladybug.* Illus. L. Kessler. New York: Scott.

Schlein, M. (1954). *Heavy is a hippopotamus.* Reading, MA: Addison-Wesley.

Thong, R., & Lin, G. (2000). *Round is a mooncake: A book of shapes.* San Francisco: Chronicle Books.

Troiano, J. (2003). *The legend of Spookley the square pumpkin.* New York: Greenwillow.

Willems, M. (2007). *There is a bird on your head.* New York: Hyperion.

14. Integrating Multiple Forms of Assessment

1. Although your observations reveal children's capacity for executive function (EF) for formative assessment purposes, there are some tasks that researchers use to evaluate EF. Among tasks that measure the capacity to control impulsive behavior are the *Head-to-Toes Task* (Ponitz et al., 2008); the *Marshmallow Task* (Mischel, Shoda, & Rodriguez, 1989); and the *Peg Tapping Task* (Blair & Razza, 2007). The *Item Selection Task* (Blair & Razza, 2007) and the *Dimensional Change Card Sort* (Zelazo, 2006) ask youngsters to shift attention to different properties of the same items in order to measure adaptive flexibility.

2. There are ome evaluation instruments that focus on meaning in general. The *Benchmark Assessment System* (Fountas & Pinnell, 2010a) measures achievement in reading comprehension. The SRA *Real Math Building Blocks* (Clements & Sarama, 2007) parallels the Clements and Sarama (2009a) activity-based and games-related mathematics program for young children. The *ECERS-E-The Four Curricular Subscales Extension to the Early Childhood Environment Rating Scale (ECERS-R)* (Sylva, Siraj-Blatchford, & Taggart, 2010), *Teaching Strategies GOLD: Birth through Kindergarten* (http://www.TeachingStrategies.com/GOLD), and the *Boehm Test of Basic Concepts* (Boehm, 2001) evaluate general concept development in young children. In order to obtain a clear and relevant picture of children's learning achievement and potential, however, it is useful to assess their attitudes toward school.

15. Working with Families, Communities, and Colleagues

1. See Mitchell, Foulger, & Wetzel (2010) for ideas about how to use email with families.

2. Sources for planning family meetings include Haugland (1998) and Haugland & Wright (1997). Software to share could include Sunburst's (1998) *I-Spy* and *Thinking out Loud*, and the Learning Company's (1996) *Paint, Write, and Play*. See also other software publisher websites.

3. Participation in in-depth conversations is significant for developing literacy skills (Cazden, 1988).

REFERENCES

Adams, M.J. (2001). Alphabetic anxiety and explicit, systematic phonics instruction: A cognitive science perspective. In S.B. Neuman & D.K. Dickinson (Eds.), *Handbook of early literacy research*, (pp. 66–80). New York: Guilford Books.

Allington, R.L. (2002). *Big brother and the national reading curriculum: How ideology trumped evidence.* Portsmouth, NH: Heinemann.

Allington, R.L. (2005). Ideology is still trumping evidence. *Phi Delta Kappan 86* (6), 462–468.

Allington, R.L. (2009). *What really matters in Response to Intervention: Research-based design.* Boston: Pearson.

Althouse, R., Johnson, M.H., & Mitchell, S.T. (2003). *Colors of learning: Integrating the visual arts into the early childhood curriculum.* New York: Teachers College Press.

American Association for the Advancement of Science (AAAS) (2009). *Project 2061 benchmarks.*

http://www.project2061.org.org/publications/bsl/online [Retrieved July 10, 2010].

American Association of University Women Foundation Commission on Technology, Gender, and Teacher Education (AAUW) (2000). *Tech-savvy: Educating girls in the new computer age.* Washington, DC: Author.

Anderson, R.C., Hiebert, E.H., Scott, J.A., & Wilkinson, I.A.G. (1985). *Becoming a nation of readers.* Champaign: University of Illinois Press.

Archer, E. (2010). Personal communication.

Armstrong, T. (2004). Making the words roar: Reading strategies aimed at multiple intelligences can make literacy come to life for all students. *Educational Leadership 61* (6), 78–81.

Astington, J.W. (1993). *The child's discovery of mind.* Cambridge, MA: Harvard University Press.

Astington, J.W., & Pelletier, J. (2005). Theory of Mind, language, and learning in the early years: Developmental origins of school readiness. In B.D. Homer & C.S. Tamis-LeMonda (Eds.), *The development of social cognition and communication* (pp. 205–230). Mahwah, NJ: Lawrence Erlbaum.

Atkinson, S. (1995). Children making paper planes. In S. Atkinson & M. Fleer (Eds.), *Science with reason* (pp. 26–31). Portsmouth, NH: Heinemann.

Atkinson, W. (Ed.) (1992). *Mathematics with reason: The emergent approach to primary maths.* Portsmouth, NH: Heinemann.

Baines, E., & Blatchford, P. (2011). Children's games and playground activities in school and their role in development. In A.D. Pellegrini (Ed.), *The Oxford handbook of the development of play* (pp. 260–283). New York: Oxford University Press.

Baratta-Lorton, M. (1976). *Mathematics their way.* Menlo Park, CA: Addison-Wesley.

Barnes, D. (1981). Personal communication.

Barnes, R. (1987). *Teaching art to young children 4–9.* New York: Routledge.

Baroody, A.J. (2004). The developmental bases for early childhood number and operation standards. In D.H. Clements, J. Sarama, & A.-M. DiBiase (Eds.), *Engaging young children in mathematics: Standards for early childhood mathematics education* (pp. 172–219). Mahwah, NJ: Lawrence Erlbaum.

Baroody, A.J., & Standifer, D.J. (1993). Addition and subtraction in the primary grades. In R.J. Jensen (Ed), *Research ideas for the classroom: Early childhood mathematics* (pp. 72–102). New York: Macmillan.

Barrett, K. et al. (1999). *Science and math explorations for young children.* Berkeley: University of California Lawrence Hall of Science.

Barson, A. (n.d.) *Geoboard activity cards: Primary.* Ft. Collins, CO: Scott Resources.

Bateson, G. (1971). The message "this is play." In. R.E. Herron & B. Sutton-Smith (Eds.), *Child's play* (pp. 261–266). New York: Wiley.

Bateson, G. (1972). *Steps to an ecology of mind.* New York: Ballantine.

Bateson, G. (1976). A theory of play and fantasy. In J.S. Bruner, A. Jolly, & K. Sylva (Eds.), *Play: Its role in development and evolution* (pp. 119–129). New York: Basic Books.

Bateson, G. (1979). *Mind and nature.* New York: E.P. Dutton.

Beilock, S.L., Gunderson, E.A., Ramirez, G., & Levine, S.C. (2010). Female teachers' math anxiety affects girls' math achievement. *Proceedings of the National Academies of Sciences 107* (5), 1860–1863.

Beneke, S.J., Ostrosky, M.M., & Katz, K.G. (2008). Calendar time for young children: Good intentions gone awry. *Young Children 63* (3), 12–16.

Bergen, D. (2008). New technologies in early children: Partners in play? In O.N. Saracho & B. Spodek (Eds.), *Contemporary perspectives on science and technology in early childhood education* (pp. 87–104). Charlotte, NC: Information Age.

Bers, M.U. (2008). Engineers and storytellers: Using robotic manipulatives to develop technological fluency in early childhood. In O.N. Saracho & B. Spodek (Eds.), *Contemporary perspectives on science and technology in early childhood education* (pp. 105–125). Charlotte, NC: Information Age.

Bertalanffy, L. von (1960). *The problems of life.* New York: Harper & Row. (Originally published in 1952.)

Blair, C., & Razza, R.P. (2007). Relating effortful control, executive function, and false belief to emerging math and literacy ability in kindergarten. *Child Development 78* (2), 647–663.

Bloom, B.S., et al. (1956). *Taxonomy of educational objectives: The classification of educational goals: Handbook 1, cognitive domain.* New York: McKay.

Bloomfield, L., & Barnhart, C.L. (1961). *Let's read.* Detroit: Wayne State University Press.

Bodrova, E., & Leong, D.J. (2007). *The Vygotskian approach to early childhood education.* 2nd edn. Upper Saddle River, NJ: Pearson/Merrill/Prentice-Hall.

Boehm, A.E. (2001). *Boehm test of basic concepts.* 3rd edn. New York: Garland.

Bowlby, J. (1988). *A secure base: Parent–child attachment and healthy human development.* New York: Basic Books.

Bowman, B.T., Donovan, M.S, & Burns, M.S. (Eds.) (2001). *Eager to learn: Educating our preschoolers*. Washington, DC: National Academy Press.

Bransford, J.D. et al. (2002). Foundations of opportunities for an interdisciplinary science of learning. In K. Sawyer (Ed.), *Cambridge handbook of learning sciences* (pp. 19–34). West Nyack, NY: Cambridge University Press.

Bridge, S. (1986). Squeezing from the middle of the tube. In T. Newkirk and N. Atwell (Eds.), *Understandiing writing* (pp. 68–75). Portsmouth, NH: Heinemann.

Briscoe, M.G. (1984). Tides, solutions and nutrients. *Nature*, November 1, p. 15

Brooks, J.G. (2011). *Big science for growing minds: Constructivist classrooms for young thinkers*. New York: Teachers College Press.

Brown, R., & Bellugi, U. (1964). Three processes in the child's acquisition of syntax. In E.H. Lenneberg (Ed.), *New directions in the study of language* (pp. 131–161). Cambridge, MA: MIT Press.

Brown, S. with Vaughan, C. (2010). *Play: How it shapes the brain, opens the imagination, and invigorates the soul*. New York: Avery/Penguin Group.

Bruner, J.S. (1966). *Toward a theory of instruction*. Cambridge, MA: Harvard University Press.

Bruner, O., & Bruner, K. (2006). *Playstation nation: Protect your child from video game addiction*. New York: Center Street.

Buber, M. (1958). *I and thou*. 2nd edn. Trans. T.G. Smith. New York: Charles Scribner's Sons. (Originally published in 1923.)

Bullard, J. (2010). *Creating environments for learning: Birth to age eight*. Upper Saddle River, NJ: Merrill/Pearson.

Burk, D., Snider, A., & Symonds, P. (1992). *Math excursions K: Project-based math for kindergartners*. Portsmouth, NH: Heinemann.

Burton, G. et al. (1991). *Curriculum evaluation standards for school mathematics: Kindergarten book*. Reston, VA: National Council of Teachers of English.

Burton, J.M. (2001). Lowenfeld: An(other) look. *Art Education 54* (6), 33–42.

Butler, A. (1984). *Story box: Teacher's guide*. San Diego, CA: Wright Group.

Butler, A., & Turbill, J. (1984). *Towards a reading–writing curriculum*. Portsmouth, NH: Heinemann.

Calkins, L., & Louis, N. (2005). *Writing for readers: Teaching skills and strategies*. Portsmouth, NH: Heinemann.

Calkins, L., & Oxenhorn, A. (2005). *Small moments: Personal narrative writing*. Portsmouth, NH: Heinemann.

Calvert, S.L., Rideout, V.J., Woolard, J.L., Barr, R.F., & Strouse, G.A. (2005). Age, ethnicity, and socioeconomic patterns in early computer use. *American Behavioral Scientist 48* (5), 590–607.

Calvert, S.L., Strong, B.L., & Gallagher, L. (2005). Control as an engagement feature for young children's attention to and learning of computer content. *American Behavioral Scientist 48* (5), 578–589.

Cambourne, B. (1988). *The whole story: Natural learning and the acquisition of literacy in the classroom*. Richmond Hill, ON: Scholastic.

Campbell, F.A., et al. (2002). Early childhood education: Young adult outcomes form the Abecedarian Project. *Applied Developmental Science 6*, 42–57.

Carey, B., & Markoff, J. (2010). Students, meet your teacher, Mr. Robot. *New York Times*, July 11, 1, 18–19.

Carlson, S.M., Mandell, D.J., & Williams, L. (2004). Executive function and Theory of Mind: Stability and prediction from ages 2 to 3. *Developmental Psychology 40* (6), 1105–1122.

Casey, B., et al. (2008). The development of spatial skills through interventions involving blockbuilding activities. *Cognition and Instruction 26* (3), 269–309.

Casey, B., Erkut, S., Ceder, I., & Young, J.M. (2007). Use of a storytelling context to improve girls' and boys' geometry skills in kindergarten. *Journal of Applied Developmental Psychology 29*, 29–48.

Cazden, C.B. (Ed.) (1981). *Language in early childhood education*. Rev. edn. Washington, DC: National Association for the Education of Young Children.

Cazden, C.B. (1988). *Classroom discourse*. Portsmouth, NH: Heinemann.

Center for Best Practices in Early Childhood Education (2007). Website. Macomb: Western Illinois University. http://www.wiu.edu/itlc [Retrieved July 10, 2010].

Center for Research in Educational Policy (2009–2010). *Evaluation of the leveled literacy intervention: Year 1*. Memphis, TN: Author. http:www.memphis.edu/crep/pdfs/AERA_08.LLI.pdf [Retrieved November 11, 2010].

Centers for Disease Control and Prevention. (2009). *Childhood overweight and obesity*. http://www.cdc.gov/obesity/childhood/index.html [Retrieved January 19, 2010].

Chalufour, I., & Worth, K. (2003). *Exploring nature with young children*. St. Paul, MN: Redleaf.

Chalufour, I., & Worth, K. (2004). *Building structures with young children*. Minneapolis, MN: Redleaf.

Chalufour, I., & Worth, K. (2005). *Exploring water with young children*. St. Paul, MN: Redleaf.

Chelsea Free Nursery School (2006). *Science kits*. London: Author.

Chalufour, I. et al. (2004). The science and mathematics of building structures. *Science and Children 41* (4), 30–34.

Child Care Information Exchange (2008). Kicking children out of preschool. July 18. http://www.ccie.com/eed [Retrieved July 18, 2008].

Chomsky, C. (1971). Write now, read later. *Childhood Education 47*, 296–299.

Chomsky, N. (1965). *Aspects of a theory of syntax*. Cambridge, MA: MIT Press.

Chomsky, N. (1972). *Language and mind*. New York: Harcourt Brace Jovanovich.

Christie, J.F. (Ed.) (1991). *Play and early literacy development*. Albany: State University of New York Press.

Christie, J.F. (1994). Academic play. In J. Hellendoorn, R van der Kooij, & B. Sutton-Smith (Eds.), *Play and intervention* (pp. 203–213). Albany: State University of New York Press.

Christie, J.F., & Roskos, K.A. (2009). Standards, science, and the role of play in early literacy education. In D. Singer, R.M. Golinkoff, & K. Hirsh-Pasek (Eds.),. *Play=learning: How play motivates and enhances children's cognitive and social-emotional growth* (pp. 57–73). New York: Oxford University Press.

Chukovsky, K. (1963). *From two to five*. Trans. & Ed. M. Morton. Berkeley: University of California Press.

Clay, M.M. (1991). *Becoming literate*. Exeter, NH: Heinemann.

Clements, D.H., & Sarama, J. (2003). Young children and technology: What does the research say? *Young Children 58* (6), 34–40.

Clements, D.H., & Sarama, J. (2006). Early math: Young children and geometry. *Early Childhood Today 20* (7), 12–13.

Clements, D.H., & Sarama, J. (2007). Effects of a preschool mathematics curriculum: Summative research on the Building Blocks project. *Journal for Research in Mathematics Education 38*, 136–163.

Clements, D.H., & Sarama, J. (2008a). Experimental evaluation of the effects of a research-based preschool mathematics curriculum. *American Educational Research Journal 45*, 443–494.

Clements, D.H., & Sarama, J. (2008b). Mathematics and technology. In O.N. Saracho & B. Spodek (Eds.), *Contemporary perspectives on science and technology in early childhood education* (pp. 127–147). Charlotte, NC: Information Age.

Clements, D.H., & Sarama, J. (2009a). *Learning and teaching early math: The learning trajectories approach*. New York: Routledge.

Clements, D.H., & Sarama, J. (2009b). *Early childhood mathematics educational research: Learning trajectories for young children*. New York: Routledge.

Clements, D.H., & Sarama, J. (2010). New products from the Building Blocks project are available. http://www.gse.buffalo.edu/building blocks [Retrieved June 10, 2010].

Cole, E.S., & Schaefer, C. (1990). The teacher is the facilitator working between the piece of art and the child. *Young Children 45* (2), 35–38. [Based on the Feldman model: Feldman, E. (1970). *Becoming human through art*. Englewood Cliffs, NJ: Prentice-Hall.]

Coleman, M.S., Buysse, V., & Neitzel, J. (2006). *Recognition and response: An early intervention system for young children at-risk for learning disabilities: Full report*. Chapel Hill: University of North Carolina/FPG Child Development Institute.

Commission for Teaching Standards for School Mathematics (1991). *Professional standards for teaching mathematics*. Reston, VA: National Council of Teachers of Mathematics.

Common Core State Standards Initiative (2010a). Common core state standards for English language arts & literacy in history/social studies, science, and technology subjects. http://www.corestandards.org/assets/CCSSI_ELA%205Standards.pdf [Retrieved June 10, 2010].

Common Core State Standards Initiative (2010b). Common core state standards for mathematics. http://www.corestandards.org/the_standards [Retrieved June 2, 2010].

Cooper, H., Allen, A.B., Patall, E.A., & Dent, A.L. (2010). Effects of full-day kindergarten on academic achievement and social development. *Review of Educational Research 80* (1), 34–70.

Cooper, L.W. (2005). Developmentally appropriate digital environments for young children. *Library Trends 54* (2), 286–302.

Cooper, P.M. (2009). *The classrooms all young children need: Lessons in teaching from Vivian Paley*. Chicago: University of Chicago Press.

Copeland, R.W. (1984). *How children learn mathematics*. 4th edn. New York: Macmillan.

Coplan, F.J., Rubin, K.H., & Findlay, L.C. (2006). Social and nonsocial play. In D.P. Fromberg & D. Bergen (Eds.), *Play from birth to twelve: Contexts, perspectives, and meanings*. 2nd edn. New York: Routledge.

Copley, J.V. (2010). *The young child and mathematics*. 2nd ed. Washington, DC: NAEYC; Reston, VA: National Council of Teachers of Mathematics.

Cratty, B.J. (n.d). *Learning and playing*. Freeport,, NY: Educational Activities.

Cross, C.G., Woods, R.A., & Schweingruber, H. (Eds.) (2009). *Mathematics learning in early childhood: Paths toward excellence and equity*. Washington, DC: The National Academies Press [National Research Council].

Crosser, S. (2005). *What do we know about early childhood education? Research based practice*. Clifton Park, NY: Thomson Delmar Learning.

Cruikshank, D.E., Fitzgerald, D.L., & Jensen, L.R. (1980). *Young children learning mathematics*. Boston: Allyn & Bacon.

Csikszentmihalyi, M. (1996). *Creativity: Flow and the psychology of discovery and invention*. New York: HarperCollins.

Cullinan, B., & Galda, L. (1994). *Literature and the child*. 3rd edn. New York: Harcourt Brace Jovanovich.

Damasio, A. (1999). *The feeling of what happens: Body and emotion in the making of consciousness*. New York: Harvest.

Damasio, A. (2003). *Looking for Spinoza: Joy, sorrow, and the feeling brain*. New York: Harcourt.

Dansky, J.L. (1986). Play and creativity in young children. In K. Blanchard, W.W. Anderson, G.E. Chick, & E.P. Johnsen (Eds.), *The many faces of play* (pp. 69–79). Champaign, IL: Human Kinetics.

Davidson, J. (1995). *Using the Cuisenaire rods*. Chicago: ETA.

Davies, M. (2003). *Movement and dance in early childhood*. 2nd edn. Thousand Oaks, CA: Paul Chapman/Sage.

Davis, B., & Sumara, D. (2006). *Complexity and education: Inquiries into learning, teaching, and research*. New York: Lawrence Erlbaum/Taylor and Francis.

Davis, U. (1985). Personal communication.

DeBell, M., & Chapman, C. (2006). *Computer and Internet use by students in 2003: Statistical analysis report*. Washington, DC: Institute of Education Sciences National Center for Educational Statistics, U.S. Department of Education.

DeFord, D.E., Lyons, C.A., & Pinnell, G.S. (Eds.). (1991). *Bridges to literacy: Learning from Reading Recovery*. Portsmouth, NH: Heinemann.

Derman-Sparks, L., & Edwards, J.O. (2010). *Anti-bias education for young children and ourselves*. Washington, DC: National Association for the Education of Young Children.

DeVries, R., & Sales, C. (2011). *Ramps and pathways: A constructivist approach to physics with young children*. Washington, DC: National Association for the Education of Young Children.

DeVries, R., & Zan, B. (1994). *Moral classrooms, moral children: Creating a constructivist atmosphere in early education*. New York: Teachers College Press.

DeVries, R., & Zan, B. (2003). When children make rules. *Educational Leadership 61* (1), 64–67.

Dewey, J. (1933). *How we think*. Boston: D.C. Heath.

Dewey, J. (1958). *Art as experience*. New York: Capricorn. (Originally published in 1934.)

Diamond, A., Barnett, W.S., Thomas, J., & Munro, S. (2007). Preschool program improves cognitive control. *Science 318*, 1387–1388. Supplemental online material: www.devcog neuro.com/publications/science%20article%20-%20Diamond%20et%20al.pdf [Retrieved May 28, 2010].

Dickinson, D.K., & Neuman, S.B. (Eds.) (2006). *Handbook of early literacy research*. Volume 2. New York: Guilford Press.

Diffily, D., & Sassman, C. (2002). *Project-based learning with young children*. Portsmouth, NH: Heinemann.

Douglas, K.M., & Jaquith, D.B. (2009). *Engaging learners through artmaking: Choice-based art education in the classroom*. New York: Teachers College Press.

Downie, D., Slesnick, T., & Stenmark, J.K. (1981). *Math for girls and other problem solvers*. Berkeley: Lawrence Hall of Science, University of California.

Druin, A. (1999). *PETS, a Personal Electronic Teller of Stories*. College Park: University of Maryland Human–Computer Interaction Lab.

Dugger, W.E., Jr. (2007). The status of technology education in the United States. http://www.itea/...2010FinlandCygnaeusSumposiumStatusTechnologyEd.ppt [Retrieved November 20, 2010].

Durkin, D. (1966). *Children who read early*. New York: Teachers College Press.

Duschl, R.A., Schweingruber, H.A., & Shouse, A.S. (Eds.) (2007). *Taking science to school: Learning and teaching science in grades K–8*. Washington, DC: The National Academies Press.

Dyson, A.H. (1987). The value of "time off-task": Young children's spontaneous talk and deliberate text. *Harvard Educational Review 57* (4), 396–420.

Dyson, A.H. (1989). *Multiple worlds of child writers*. New York: Teachers College Press.

Edwards, C., Gandini, L., & Forman, G. (1998). *The hundred languages of children*. 2nd edn. Greenwich, CT: Ablex.

Edwards, L.C., Bayless, K.M., & Ramsey, M.E. (2005). *Music: A way of life for the young child*. 5th edn. Upper Saddle River, NJ: Pearson/Merrill/Prentice-Hall.

Egan, K. (1988). The origins of imagination. In K. Egan & D. Nadaner (Eds.), *Imagination and education* (pp. 91–127). New York: Teachers College Press.

Eisner, E. (2009). What do the arts teach? Presentation at Vanderbilt University. http://www.youtube.com/watch?v=h12MGuhQH9E [Retrieved December 12, 2010].

Elementary Science Study (1971). *Drops, streams, and containers*. New York: McGraw-Hill.

Elementary Science Study (1974). *Eggs and tadpoles teachers' guide*. New York: McGraw-Hill.

Elementary Science Study (1976). *Tangrams*. New York: McGraw-Hill.

Eliot, L. (2009). *Pink brain blue brain*. Boston: Houghton Mifflin Harcourt.

Epstein, A.S. (2009). *You, me, us: Social-emotional learning in preschool*. Ypsilanti, MI: HighScope Press; Washington, DC: NAEYC.

Epstein, A.S., Schweinhart, L.J., De Bruin-Parecki, & Robin, K.B. (2004). *Preschool assessment: A guide to developing a balanced approach*. Issue 7. New Brunswick, NJ: National Institute for Early Education Research/HighScope Educational Research Foundation.

Erickson, F., & Mohatt, G. (1982). Cultural organization or participation structures in two classrooms of Indian students. In G. Spindler (Ed.), *Doing the ethnography of schooling: Educational anthropology in action* (pp. 132–174). New York: Holt, Rinehart, & Winston.

Erikson, E.H. (1977). *Toys and reason*. New York: W.W. Norton.

Ervin, S.M. (1964). Imitation and structural change in children's language. In E.H. Lenneberg (Ed.), *New directions in the study of language* (pp. 163–189). Cambridge, MA: MIT Press.

Erwin, B., Cyr, M., & Rogers, C. (2000). *LEGO Engineer and Robo Lab: Teaching engineering with LabVIEW from kindergarten to graduate school*. http://www.ifee.dit.ie/articles/vol16-31/ijee1121.pdf [Retrieved May 25, 2010].

Espinosa, L.M. (2010). *English language learners/dual language learners: Getting it RIGHT for young children from diverse backgrounds: Applying research to improve practice*. Boston: Pearson.

Eviator, Z., & Just, M. (2006). Brain correlates of discourse processes: An fMRI investigation of irony and metaphor processing. *Neuropsychologia 44* (12), 2348–2359.

Eylon, B., Razel, M., Ben-Zvi, A., & Somech, A. (1990). *Cultivating visual cognition in young children*. Rehovot: Weizmann Institute of Science.

Fauconnier, G., & Turner, M. (2002). *The way we think: Conceptual blending and the mind's hidden complexities*. New York: Basic Books.

Ferreiro, E. (1991). Literacy acquisition and the representation of language. In K. Kamii, M. Manning, & G. Manning (Eds.), *Early literacy: A constructivist foundation for whole language* (pp. 31–56). Washington, DC: National Education Association.

Ferreiro, E., & Teberosky, A. (1982). *Literacy before schooling*. Trans. K.G. Castro. Exeter, NH: Heinemann.

Feuerstein, R., Feuerstein, R.S., & Falik, L.H. (2010). *Beyond smarter: Mediated learning and the brain's capacity to change*. New York: Teachers College Press.

Fields, J., Smith, K., & Lugaila, T. (2001). A child's day includes rules for T.V., extracurricular activities and organized care. Census Bureau reports. In *U.S. Census Bureau News*. Washington, DC: U.S. Department of Commerce.

Fisher, K., Hirsh-Pasek, K., Golinkoff, R.M., Singer, D.G., & Berk, L. (2011). Playing around in school: Implications for learning and educational policy. In A.D. Pellegrini (Ed.), *The Oxford handbook of the development of play*. New York: Oxford University Press.

Flemming, P. (1986). Writing and reading: The write way to read. In T. Newkirk & N. Atwell (Eds.), *Understanding writing* (pp. 93–100). Portsmouth, NH: Heinemann.

Fountas, I.C., & Pinnell, G.S. (1996). *Guided reading: Good first teaching for all children*. Portsmouth, NH: Heinemann.

Fountas, I.C., & Pinnell, G.S. (2006). *Leveled books (K–8): Matching texts to readers for effective teaching*. Portsmouth, NH: Heinemann.

Fountas, I.C., & Pinnell, G.S. (2008). *Leveled literacy intervention*. Portsmouth, NH: Heinemann.

Fountas, I.C., & Pinnell, G.S. (2010a). *Benchmark assessment system 1*. 2nd edn: *Assessment guide K–2*. Portsmouth, NH: Heinemann.

Fountas, I.C., & Pinnell, G.S. (2010b). Your reading resource center: Leveled reading. http://www.readinga-z.com/book.php?id-1232 [Retrieved September 20, 2010].

Freire, P. (1970). Cultural action and conscientization. *Harvard Educational Review 40* (2), 452–477.

Freire, P. (1973). *Education for critical consciousness*. New York: Seabury Press.

Fries, C.C. (1963). *Linguistics and reading*. New York: Holt, Rinehart, & Winston.

Fromberg, D.P. (1965). The reactions of kindergarten children to intellectual challenge. Doctoral dissertation. New York: Teachers College, Columbia University.

Fromberg, D.P. (1976). Syntax model games and language in early education. *Journal of Psycholinguistics Research 5* (3), 245–260.

Fromberg, D. (1982). Transformational knowledge: Perceptual models as a cooperative content base for the early education of children. In S. Hill & B.J. Barnes (Eds.), *Young children and their families* (pp. 191–206). Lexington, MA: Lexington Books.

Fromberg, D.P. (1999). A review of research on play. In C. Seefeldt (Ed.), *The early childhood curriculum: Current findings in theory and practice*, 3rd edn. (pp. 27–53). New York: Teachers College Press.

Fromberg, D.P. (2002). *Play and meaning in early childhood education*. Boston: Allyn & Bacon.

Fromberg, D.P. (2006). The power of play: Gender issues in early childhood education. In J. Koch & B. Irby (Eds.), *Gender play: Girls and boys in school*. Brunswick, NJ: Rutgers University Press.

Fromberg, D.P. (2010). How nonlinear systems inform meaning and early education. *Nonlinear Dynamics, Psychology, and Life Sciences 14* (1), 46–68.

Fromberg, D.P. (n.d.). A comparison of small-group compared with whole-group instruction in kindergarten. Unpublished study.

Fromberg, D.P., & Bergen, D. (Eds.) (1998). *Play from birth to twelve and beyond*. New York: Garland.

Galinsky, E. (2010). *Minds in the making*. New York: HarperCollins/NAEYC.

Galison, P. (2003). *Einstein's clocks; Poincare's maps*. New York: W.W. Norton.

Gallahue, D.L. (1993). Motor development and movement skills acquisition in early childhood education. In B. Spodek (Ed.), *Handbook of research on the education of young children* (pp. 24–41). New York: Macmillan.

Gardner, H. (1980). *Artful scribbles*. New York: Basic Books.

Gardner, H. (1982). *Art, mind, and brain: A cognitive approach to creativity*. New York: Basic Books.

Gardner, H. (2006). *Multiple intelligences: New horizons*. New York: Basic Books.

Gattegno, C. (1968). *Teaching reading with words in color*. New York: Educational Solutions.

Gee, J.P. (2007). *Good video games + good learning*. New York: Peter Lang.

Gelman, S.A. (1999). Concept development in preschool children. In American Association for the Advancement of Science (Ed.), *Dialogue on early childhood science, mathematics, and technology education* (pp. 50–61). Annapolis Junction, MD: Author; Washington, DC: U.S. Department of Education Educational Resources Information Center.

Genishi, C., & Goodwin, A.L. (Eds.) (2008). *Diversities in early childhood education: Rethinking and doing*. New York: Routledge.

Gestwicki, C. (2010) *Home, school, and community relations: A guide to working with families*. 7th edn. Boston: Cengage.

Gibson, L. (1989). *Literacy learning in the early years*. New York: Teachers College Press.

Ginsburg, H.P., Lee, J.S., & Boyd, J.S. (2008). Mathematics education for young children: What it is and how to promote it. *SRCD Social Policy Report 22*, 1–23.

Gitlin-Wiener, K. (1998). Clinical perspectives on play. In D.P. Fromberg & D. Bergen (Eds.), *Play from birth to twelve and beyond: Contexts, perspectives, and meanings* (pp. 77–92). New York: Garland.

Gleason, H.A., Jr. (1965). *Linguistics and English grammar*. New York: Holt, Rinehart, & Winston.

Gleason, J.B. (1981). An experimental approach to improving children's communicative ability. In C. Cazden (Ed.), *Language in early childhood education*, rev. edn. (pp. 77–82). Washington, DC: National Association for the Education of Young Children.

Gleick, J. (1987). *Chaos*. New York: Viking.

Goetz, E.M., & Baer, D.M. (1973). Social control of form diversity and the emergence of new forms in children's blockbuilding. *Journal of Applied Behavioral Analysis 6* (2), 209–217.

Goleman, D. (1995). *Emotional intelligence*. New York: Bantam.

Gombrich, E.H. (2006). *The history of art*. New York: Phaidon. (Originally published in 1950.)

Good, L. (2005). Snap it up! Using digital photography in early childhood. *Childhood Education 82* (2), 79–85.

Gopnik, A. (2009). *The philosophical baby*. New York: Farrar, Straus, & Giroux.

Gopnik, A., Meltzoff, A.N., & Kuhl, P.K. (1999). *The scientist in the crib: What early learning tells us about the mind*. New York: HarperCollins.

Gordon, T. (2007). *Teaching young children a second language*. Westport, CT: Greenwood/Praeger.

Gordon, W.J.J., & Poze, T. (1980). *The art of the possible*. Cambridge, MA: Porpoise Books.

Graves, D., & Stuart, V. (1985). *Write from the start*. New York: E.P. Dutton.

Gross, T. (2010). Service learning builds bonds to school for young learners. *Phi Delta Kappan 1* (5), 24–26.

Guillen, M. (1983). *Bridges to infinity: The human side of mathematics*. Boston: Houghton Mifflin.

Gullo, D.F. (2005). *Understanding assessment and evaluation in early childhood education*. 2nd edn. New York: Teachers College Press.

Hanline, M.F., Milton, M.F., & Phelps, P.C. (2001). A longitudinal study of the predictive relations among construction play and mathematical achievement. *Early Childhood Development and Care 167*, 115–125.

Harris, P.L., & Kavanaugh, R.D. (1993). *Young children's understanding of pretense.* Monograph of the Society for Research in Child Development No. 231, 58 (1).

Harste, J.C., Woodward, V.A., & Burke, C.L. (1984). *Language stories and literacy lessons.* Portsmouth, NH: Heinemann.

Hart, B., & Risley, T.R. (1995). *Meaningful differences in the everyday experience of young American children.* Baltimore, MD: Paul H. Brookes.

Haskell, L.L. (1984). *Art in the early childhood years.* Columbus, OH: Charles E. Merrill.

Haskins, J. (1991). *Count your way through the Arab world, China, Japan, Mexico.* New York: Carolhoda Books.

Haugen, K. (2007). Art to heart: Giving and receiving through art. http://mail.ccie.com/go/eed/1479 [Retrieved September 1, 2010].

Haugland, S.W., & Wright, J.L. (1997). *Young children and technology: A world of discovery.* New York: Allyn & Bacon.

Hawking, S. (1988). *A brief history of time: From the big bang to black holes.* New York: Bantam.

Hayakawa, S.I. (1949). *Language in thought and action.* New York: Harcourt Brace Jovanovich.

Heard, G., & McDonough, J. (2009). *A place for wonder: Reading and writing nonfiction in the primary grades.* Portland, ME: Stenhouse.

Heath, S.B. (1983). *Ways with words: Language, life, and work in communities and classrooms.* New York: Cambridge University Press.

Heffernan, V. (2010). Shift paradigm: The promise and peril of smart keyboards. *New York Times Magazine*, August 15, 18–19.

Helm, J.H., Beneke, A., Steinheimer, K. (2007). *Windows on learning: Documenting young children's work.* 2nd edn. New York: Teachers College Press.

Helm, J.H., & Katz, L. (2011). *Young investigators. 2nd edn.* New York: Teachers College Press.

Hembree, R., & Marsh, H. (1993). Problem solving in early childhood: Building foundations. In R.J. Jensen (Ed.), *Research ideas for the classroom: Early childhood mathematics* (pp. 151–170). New York: Macmillan.

Heroman, C., Burts, D.C., Berke, K., & Bickart, T. (2009). *Teaching strategies Gold™ assessment system: Child assessment portfolio.* Washington, DC: Teaching Strategies, Inc.

Hetland, L., Winner, E., Veenema, S., & Sheridan, K.M. (2007). *Studio thinking: The real benefits of art education.* New York: Teachers College Press.

Heuser, D. (2002). *Reworking the workshop: Math and science reform in the primary grades.* Portsmouth, NH: Heinemann.

HighScope Press (2009). *Plan–do-–review in action.* Ypsilanti, MI: HighScope Educational Research Foundation [DVD].

Hirsch, L. (Ed.) (1996). *The block book.* Washington, DC: NAEYC.

Hirsh-Pasek, K., Golinkoff, R.M., Berk, L., & Singer, D.G. (2009). *A mandate for playful learning in preschool: Presenting the evidence.* New York: Oxford University Press.

Hofreuter-Landini, E., & Krulock, L. (2010). The link between mind and movement. *The Intelligencer Wheeling News-Register*, February 12. http://www.news-register.net/page/content/detail/id/153339 [Retrieved February 14, 2010].

Holdaway, D. (1979). *The foundations of literacy.* New York: Ashton Scholastic.

Honig, A.S. (2002). *Secure relationships: Nurturing infant/toddler attachment in early care settings.* Washington, DC: NAEYC.

Hough, R.A., & Nurss, J.R. (1992). Language and literacy for the Limited English Proficient child. In L.O. Ollila & M.I. Mayfield (Eds.), *Emerging literacy* (pp. 137–165). Boston: Allyn & Bacon.

Hunt, J.M. (1961). *Intelligence and experience*. New York: Ronald Press.

Hutinger, P., Bell, C., Daytner, G., & Johanson, J. (2005). *Disseminating and replicating an effective emerging literacy technology curriculum: A final report*. U.S. Office of Special Programs Ideas that Work. http://www.wiu.edu/thecenter/elite [Retrieved March 20, 2010].

Hutt, C. (1976). Exploration and play in children. In J.S. Bruner, A. Jolly, & K. Sylva (Eds.), *Play: Its role in development and evolution* (pp. 202–215). New York: Basic Books.

Imhoff, M.M. (1959). *Early elementary education*. New York: Appleton-Century-Crofts.

Institute of Education Sciences National Center for Education Research (2007). *Organizing instruction and study to improve student learning: A practice guide*. Washington, DC: U.S. Department of Education. http://www.ies.ed.gov/ncee/wwwc/pdf/practiceguides/20072 [Retrieved May 24, 2010].

International Reading Association & National Council of Teachers of English (1996). *Standards for the English Language Arts*. http://www.ncte.org/libraryNCTEfiles/Resources/books/Samplr]StandardsDoc.pdf [Retrieved September 10, 2010].

International Society for Technology in Education (ISTE) (2007). *ISTE NETS for students*. http://www.iste.org/inhouse/nets/cnets/indes.html [Retrieved September 10, 2010].

Isaacson, W. (2007). *Einstein: His life and universe*. New York: Simon & Schuster.

Isenberg, J.P., & Jalongo, M.R. (2009). *Creative thinking and arts-based learning: Preschool through fourth grade*. 5th edn. Upper Saddle River, NJ: Pearson.

Ito, C.T. (2010). *Space, color, and mathematics*. http://www.ttac.odu.edu/Articles/cuisenai.html [Retrieved July 13, 2010].

Jensen, R.J. (1993). *Research ideas for the classroom: Early childhood mathematics*. New York: Macmillan.

Jerrold, R. (2010). A comparison of early childhood linear-academic and nonlinear-intellectual teacher methodologies. Doctoral dissertation. Cypress, CA: Touro University.

Johnson, D.W., Johnson, R.T., Holubec, E.J., & Roy, P. (1984). *Circles of learning*. Washington, DC: Association for Supervision and Curriculum Development.

Johnson, H.M. (1933). *The art of block building*. New York: John Day.

Johnson, J. (2003). *Early explorations in science*. London: Open University Press/McGraw-Hill.

Judge, J.S., Puckett, K., & Cabuk, B. (2004). Digital equity: New findings from the early childhood longitudinal study. *Journal of Research on Technology in Education 36* (4), 383–396.

Jukes, I., McCain, T., & Crockett, L. (2010). *Understanding the digital generation*. 21st Century Fluency Project. Thousand Oaks, CA: Corwin.

Kaku, M. (1997). *Visions: Science revolution for the twenty-first century*. New York: Basic Books.

Kaku, M. (2008). *Physics of the impossible*. New York: Doubleday.

Kaltman, G.S. (2009). *Hands-on learning!* Thousand Oaks, CA: Corwin Sage.

Kamii, C., & DeVries, R. (1980). *Group games in early education*. Washington, DC: National Association for the Education of Young Children.

Kamii, C., & DeVries, R. (1993). *Physical knowledge in preschool education*. New York: Teachers College Press.

Kamii, C. with Houseman, L.B. (2000). *Young children invent arithmetic: Implications of Piaget's theory*. 2nd edn. New York: Teachers College Press.

Karp, K. (1988). The teaching of elementary school mathematics: The relationship between how math is taught and teachers' attitudes. Doctoral dissertation. Hempstead, NY: Hofstra University.

Karplus, R., & Thier, H.D. (1967). *A new look at elementary school science: Science curriculum improvement study*. Chicago: Rand McNally.

Katz, L., & Chard, S. (2000). *Engaging children's minds: The project approach*. 2nd edn. Stamford, CT: Ablex.

Kean, E. (1998). *Chemists and play*. In D.P. Fromberg & D. Bergen (Eds.), *Play from birth to twelve and beyond* (pp. 468–472). New York: Garland.

Kindersley, A. (1997). *Children just like me: Celebrations*. Photos B. Kindersley. New York: DK Publishing.

Klingberg, T. (2006). Development of a superior frontal-intraparietal network for visuo-spatial working memory. *Neuropsychologia 44*, 2171–2177.

Koblinsky, S., & Behana, N. (1984). Child sexual abuse: The educator's role in prevention, detection, and intervention. *Young Children 39*, 3–15.

Kohl, M.A.F. (1984). *Scribble cookies*. Illus. J.McCoy. Bellingham, WA: Bright Ring.

Kohn, A. (1996). *Beyond discipline: From compliance to community*. Alexandria, VA: Association for Supervision and Curriculum Development.

Kohn, A. (2008). Why self-discipline is overrated: The (troubling) theory and practice of control from within. *Phi Delta Kappan 90* (3), 168–176.

Kohonen, T. (1989). *Self-organization and associative memory*. 3rd edn. New York: Springer-Verlag.

Krogh, S., & Morehouse, P. (2008). *The early childhood curriculum: Inquiry learning through integration*. New York: McGraw-Hill.

Kuhmerker, L. (1984). Scared and hurt. *Ms. magazine 12*, 69.

Kuhn, J. (2009). Setting up a kindergarten. PowerPoint presentation, November 17. New York: Hofstra University.

Laban, R. (1980). *The mastery of movement*. 4th edn. London: MacDonald & Evans.

Ladson-Billings, G. (1994). *The dreamkeepers: Successful teachers of African American children*. San Francisco: Jossey-Bass.

Ladson-Billings, G. (1995). *Other people's children: Cultural conflict in the classroom*. New York: The New Press.

Landeck, B. (1950). *Songs to grow on*. New York: Sloane.

Langer, S. (1953). *Feeling and form*. New York: Charles Scribner's Sons.

Langer, S. (1957). *Problems of art*. New York: Charles Scribner's Sons.

Lansdown, B., Blackwood, P.E., & Brandwein, P.F. (1971). *Teaching elementary science through investigative colloquium*. New York: Harcourt Brace Jovanovich.

Lasswell, H.D. (1958). *Politics: Who gets what, when, how*. New York: Meridian Books.

Lavatelli, C.S. (1970). *Piaget's theory applied to an early childhood curriculum*. Cambridge, MA: American Science and Engineering.

LeapPad Learning Systems (2003). Electronic toys. Vernon, IL: Author.

Learning Company, The (1996). *Paint, write, and play*. Software program. Minneapolis, MN: Author.

Learning Resources (1988, 1993). *Exploration and color cube task cards prekindergarten +*. Vernon Hills, IL: Author.

Lederman, S. (2010). Personal communication.

Lee, J.S., & Ginsburg, H.P. (2007). What is appropriate mathematics education for four-year-olds? Pre-kindergarten teachers' beliefs. *Journal of Early Childhood Research 5* (1), 2–31.

Leslie, A.M. (1995). Pretending and believing: Issues in the theory of ToMM. In J. Mehler & S. Franck (Eds.), *COGNITION on cognition* (pp. 193–202). Cambridge, MA: MIT Press.

Levin, D., & Carlsson-Paige, N. (2005). *The war play dilemma.* 2nd edn. New York: Teachers College Press.

Li, X., Atkins, M.S., & Stanton, B. (2006). Effects of home and school computer use on school readiness and cognitive development among Head Start children: A randomized controlled pilot study. *Merrill-Palmer Quarterly 52* (2), 239–263.

Lonigan, C.J., & Shanahan, T. (2008). *Developing early literacy: Report of the National Early Literacy Panel.* Washington, DC: National Center for Family Literacy.

Louv, R. (2005). *Last child in the woods: Saving our children from nature-deficit disorder.* Chapel Hill, NC: Algonquin Books.

Lowenfeld, V., & Brittain, W.L. (2006). *Creative and mental growth.* New York: Macmillan.

Luria, A.R. (1968). *The mind of a mnemonist.* Trans. L. Solotaroff. New York: Basic Books.

Lynn, F. (1991). Personal communication.

Maccoby, E.E., & Jacklin, T. (1974). *The psychology of sex differences.* Stanford, CA: Stanford University Press.

Macdonald, F. (2001). *Homes.* Discovering World Culture Series. New York: Crabtree.

MacDonald, S. (2001). *The complete guide to learning and playing with blocks.* Illus. K. Davis. Beltsville, MD: Gryphon House.

Malaguzzi, L., & Becchi, E. (1996). The city in the rain; From a puddle. In S. Spaggiari et al. (Eds.), *The hundred languages of children: The exhibit* (pp. 80–93). Reggio Emilia: Reggio Children.

Malaguzzi, L., & Petter, G. (1996). Shadowiness. In In S. Spaggiari et al. (Eds.), *The hundred languages of children: The exhibit* (pp. 118–129). Reggio Emilia: Reggio Children.

Maldonado, N.S., & DeBello, L.L. (Forthcoming). *Hispanic/Latino American children and their families: A guide for educators and service providers.* Olney, MD: Association for Childhood Education International.

Mallet, D. (1975). *Garden song.* New York: Cherry Lane Music Publishing (ASCAP).

Marcon, R.A. (1992). Differential effects of three preschool models on inner-city 4-year-olds. *Early Childhood Research Quarterly 7* (4), 517–530.

Mardell, B. (1999). *From basketball to Beatles: In search of a compelling early childhood curriculum.* Portsmouth, NH: Heinemann.

Matricardi, J., & McLarty, J. (2005). *Art activities A to Z.* Clifton Park, NY: Thomson Delmar Learning.

Matthews, J.S., Ponitz, C.C., & Morrison, J.S. (2009). Early gender differences in self-regulation and academic achievement. *Journal of Educational Psychology 101* (3), 689–704.

Mauro, G. (2010). Personal communication.

Mazurkiewicz, A.J. (1964). *New perspectives in reading instruction.* New York: Pitman.

McAfee, O., & Leong, D.J. (2011). *Assessing and guiding young children's development and learning.* 5th edn. Upper Saddle River, NJ: Pearson.

McCarrick, K., & Ming, X. (2007). Buried treasure: The impact of computer use on young children's social, cognitive, language development, and motivation. *AACE Journal 15* (1), 73–95.

McCaslin, N. (1980). *Creative drama in the classroom.* 3rd edn. New York: Longman.

McClelland, M.M., et al. (2007). Links between behavioral regulation and preschoolers' literacy, vocabulary and math skills. *Developmental Psychology 43* (4), 947–959.

McDermott, J. (1983). Geometrical forms known as fractals find sense in chaos. *Smithsonian 14* (9), 110–117.

McGhee, P.E., Etheridge, L., & Berg, N.A. (1984). Effect of toy structure on preschool children's pretend play. *Journal of Catholic Education 144,* 209–217.

McGinn, J, (1991). Personal communication.

McHenry, C. (2010). E-textbooks may soon be reality: Traditional hardbacks lost in wave of future. http://www.kxan.com/dpp/news/education/ [Retrieved May 19, 2010].

McLoyd, V. (1983). The effects of the structure of play objects on the pretend play of low-income preschool children. *Child Development 54* (3), 626–635.

McLuhan, M. (1963). We need a new picture of knowledge. In A. Frasier (Ed.), *New insights and the curriculum* (pp. 57–70). Washington, DC: Association for Supervision and Curriculum Development.

McPake, J., Plowman, L., & Stephen, C. (2010). Digitally divided? An ecological investigation of young children learning to use ICT. http://strathprints.strath.ac.ud/13319/ [Retrieved May 19, 2010].

Meisels, S.J., Xue. Y., &Shamblott, M. (2008). Assessing language, literacy, and mathematics skills with *Work Sampling for Head Start. Early Education and Development 19* (6), 963–981.

Miller, W.R. (1969). Language acquisition and reading. In J. Walden (Ed.), *Oral language and reading* (pp. 31–47). Champaign, IL: National Council of Teachers of English.

Mindes, G. (2011). *Assessing young children.* 4th edn. Upper Saddle River, NJ: Pearson.

Mischel, W., Shoda, Y., & Rodriguez, M.L. (1989). Delay of gratification in children. *Science 244* (4907), 933–938.

Mitchell, L.S. (1934). *Young geographers.* New York: John Day.

Mitchell, M. (2009). *Complexity: A guided tour.* New York: Oxford University Press.

Mitchell, S., Foulger, T.S., & Wetzel, K. (2010). Ten tips for involving families through Internet-based communication. *Spotlight on teaching preschools 2,* 56–59.

Montana Office of Public Instruction (2003). *Pilot project report: A recess before lunch policy in four Montana schools April 2002–May 2003.* Bozeman, MT: Author.

Montessori, M. (1965). *The Montessori method.* Trans. A.E.George. New York: Schocken. (Originally published in 1912.)

Morrow, L.M. (2009). *Literacy development in the early years: Helping children read and write.* Boston: Pearson.

Moyer, K.F., & von Haller Gilmer, B. (1956). Experimental study of children's preferences and use of blocks in play. *Journal of Genetic Psychology 89,* 3–10.

Moyer, P.S., Niezgoda, D., & Stanley, J., (2005). Young children's use of virtual manipulatives and other forms of mathematical representations. In W. Maslaski & P.E. Elliott (Eds.), *Technology-supported mathematical learning environments: 67th yearbook.* Reston, VA: National Council of Teachers of Mathematics.

MSNBC.com. (2004). More than 40 percent of N.Y.C. kids overweight: Researchers say 24 percent of urban children are obese. http://www.msnbc.msm.com/id/5868828 [Retrieved January 19, 2010].

Mulligan, S.A. (2003). Assistive technology: Supporting the participation of children with disabilities. *Beyond the Journal: Young Children on the Web.* http://www.naeyc.org/resources/journal [Retrieved May 29, 2010].

Nalim (1978). Untitled. In H. Brown, P. Lopate, D. Sklarew, & T. Vorsanger (Eds.), *The memories of kindergartners.* New York: Teachers and Writers Collaborative.

National Association for the Education of Young Children (NAEYC) (1996). Position statement: Technology and young children: Ages three through eight. *Young Children 51* (6), 11–16.

National Association for the Education of Young Children (NAEYC) (2004). *Where we stand on school readiness: Joint position statement on early childhood curriculum, assessment and program evaluation.* Washington, DC: Author. http://www.naeyc.org/files/naeyc/file/positions/ELL [Retrieved July 2, 2010].

National Association for the Education of Young Children (NAEYC) (2009). *Developmentally appropriate practice in early childhood programs serving children from birth through age 8.* 3rd edn. Washington, DC: Author.

National Association for the Education of Young Children & National Association of Early Childhood Specialists in State Departments of Education (NAEYC/NAECS/SDE) (2003). *Early childhood curriculum, assessment, and program evaluation: Building an effective, accountable system in programs for children birth through age 8 position statement with expanded resources.* Washington, DC: Authors. http://www.naeyc.org/files/naeyc/file/postions/CAPEexpand.pdf [Retrieved July 2, 2010].

National Association of Early Childhood Teacher Education & National Association of Early Childhood Specialists in State Departments of Education (NAECTE/NAECS/SDE) (2005). *Position statement on certification for teachers of children 8 years old and younger in public schools.* http://www.naecte.org [Retrieved September 1, 2006].

National Board of Professional Teaching Standards (NBPTS) (2010). *Early mathematics standards draft.* Arlington, VA: Author.

National Center for Educational Statistics (2004). *Full-day and half-day kindergarten in the United States: Findings from the early childhood longitudinal study, kindergarten class of 1998–1999.* Washington, DC: U.S. Department of Education Institute of Educational Statistics. http://www.nces.ed.gov/pubs2004web2004078.asp [retrieved December, 27, 2010].

National Council for Social Studies (2006). *National standards for social studies teachers vol. 1 rev.ed.* Silver Springs, MD: Author.

National Council of Teachers of English (2009). *Standards for the assessment of reading and writing.* Rev.edn. http:///www.ncte.org/announce/129117.html [Retrieved September 5, 2010].

National Council of Teachers of Mathematics (NCTM) (2006). *Curriculum focal points for prekindergarten through grade 8 mathematics: A quest for coherence.* Reston, VA: Author.

National Early Literacy Panel (2008). *Developing early literacy.* Washington, DC: Institute for Literacy.

National Education Association (2008). *Full day kindergarten helps close achievement gaps: A policy brief.* http://www.nea.,org/assets/docs/mf_PB12_FullDayK.pdf [Retrieved November 15, 2010].

National Mathematics Advisory Panel (2008). *Foundations for success: The final report of the National Mathematics Advisory Panel.* Washington, DC: U.S. Department of Education. http://www.ed.gov/about/bdscomm/list/mathpanel/ [Retrieved April 10, 2010].

National Scientific Council on the Developing Child (2004). Children's emotional development is built into the architecture of their brains. Working Paper No. 2. Cambridge, MA: Harvard University. http://www.developingchild.net [Retrieved February 16, 2010].

National Scientific Council on the Developing Child (2005). Exessive stress disrupts the architecture of the developing brain. Working paper No. 3. Cambridge, MA: Harvard University. http://www.developingchild.harvard.edu [Retrieved October 12, 2010].

National Scientific Council on the Developing Child (2008). The timing and quality of early experiences combine to shape brain architecture. Working Paper No. 5. Cambridge, MA: Harvard University. http://www.developingchild.net [Retrieved February 16, 2010].

National Science Teachers Association (NSTA) (2003). *NSTA Standards for Science Teacher Preparation.* http//www.nsta.org/pdf/nstastandards2003.pdf [Retrieved May 26, 2010].

Nelson, K. (1985). *Event knowledge: Structure and function in development.* Mahwah, NJ: Lawrence Erlbaum.

Nelson, K. et al. (1986). *Making sense: The acquisition of shared meaning.* Orlando, FL: Academic Press.

Neuman, S.B. (2001). Introduction. In S.B. Neuman & D.K. Dickinson (Eds.), *Handbook of early literacy rese*arch. New York: Guilford Books

Neuman, S.B. (2010). Lessons from my mother: Reflections on the National Early Literacy Panel report. *Educational Researcher 38* (4), 301–304.

Neuman, S.B., & Dickinson, D.K. (Eds.) (2001). *Handbook of early literacy research.* New York: Guilford Books.

Neuman, S.B., & Roskos, K. with Wright, T.S., & Lenhart, L. (2007). *Nurturing knowledge.* New York: Scholastic.

Nevills, P., & Wolfe, P. (2009). *Building the reading brain Pre-K–3.* Thousand Oaks, CA: Corwin/Sage.

Newkirk, T., & Atwell, N. (1986). Introduction. In T. Newkirk & N. Atwell (Eds.), *Understanding writing* (pp. 1–5). Portsmouth, NH: Heinemann.

Newman, J. (1984). *The craft of children's writing.* Portsmouth, NH: Heinemann.

New York Times (2010, January, 10). *Physics of the universe.* Author.

Nieto, S. (2010). *Language, culture and teaching: Critical perspectives for a new century.* 2nd edn. New York: Routledge.

Nilsen, B. (1994). Personal communication.

Nir-Janiv, N. (1976). Personal communication.

Nwokah, E., & Gulker, H. (2006). Emergent literacy for children with special needs: Developing positive interest in literacy experiences. *ACEI Focus on Infants and Toddlers 19* (1), 1–8.

O'Brien, M., & Bi, X. (1995). Language learning in context: Teacher and toddler speech in three classroom play areas. *Topics in Early Childhood Special Education 15* (2), 148–163.

Ogbu, J.U. (1978). *Minority education and caste.* New York: Academic Press.

Ogden, C.L., Flegal, K.M., Carroll, M.D., & Johnson, C.L. (2002). Prevalence and trends in overweight U.S. children and adolescents, 1999–2000. *Journal of the American Medical Association 288*, 1728–1732.

Overbye, D. (2010). Physicists' dreams and worries in era of the big collider. *New York Times,* January 26, p. D4.

Owocki, G. (2010). *The RTI daily planning book K–6.* Portsmouth, NH: Heinemann.

Paley, V.G. (1984). *Boys and girls: Superheroes in the doll corner.* Chicago: University of Chicago Press.

Paley, V.G. (1992). *You can't say you can't play.* Cambridge, MA: Harvard University Press.

Parker-Pope, T. (2010). Play, then eat: May shift gains at school. *New York Times,* January 25. http://www.newyorktimes.com [Retrieved January 25, 2010].

Parten, M.B. (1932). Social participation among preschool children. *Journal of Abnormal Psychology 27* (2), 243–269.

Pasnak, R. (1987). Accelerated cognitive development of kindergartners. *Psychology in the Schools 28*, 358–363.

Payne, L., & Kounios, J. (2009). Coherent oscillatory networks support short-term memory retention. *Brain Research 1247*, 126–132.

Pellegrini, A.D., & Galda, L. (1982). The effects of thematic-fantasy play training on the development of children's story comprehension. *American Educational Research Journal 19*, 443–452.

Pelletier, J., Reeve, R., & Halewood, C. (2005). Young children's knowledge building and literacy development through Knowledge Forum®. *Early Education and Development 17* (3), 323–346.

Perner, J. (1991). *Understanding and the representational world*. Cambridge, MA: MIT Press.

Pernu, D., & Maloy, K. (2010). Making the most of a penny. *Phi Delta Keppan 1* (5), 26.

Pew Charitable Trusts/Foundation for Child Development/The Joyce Foundation (2007). *Taking Stock: Assessing and improving early childhood learning and program quality*. http://ccf.tc.columbia.edu/pdf/Task_Force_Report.pdf [Retrieved May 25, 2010].

Piaget, J. (1950). *The psychology of intelligence*. London: Routledge & Kegan Paul.

Piaget, J. (1969). *The child's conception of time*. Trans. A.J. Pomerans. New York: Ballantine. (Originally published in 1927.)

Piaget, J. (1976). *The grasp of consciousness*. Cambridge, MA: Harvard University Press.

Piaget, J. & Inhelder, B. (1973). *Memory and intelligence*. New York: Basic Books.

Piaget, J., & Inhelder, B. (1976). *The child's conception of space*. Trans. F.J. Langdon & J.L. Lunzer. London: Routledge & Kegan Paul. (Originally published in 1956.)

Piaget, J. et al. (1965). *The moral judgment of the child*. Trans. M. Gabain. New York: Free Press.

Pianta, R.C. (2007). Early education in transition. In R.C. Pianta, M.J. Cox, & K.L. Snow (Eds.), *School readiness and the transition to kindergarten in the era of accountability* (pp. 3–10). Baltimore, MD: Paul H. Brookes.

Pica, R. (2004). *Experiences in movement: Birth to age 8*. Clifton Park, NY: Thomson Delmar.

Pinker, S. (2007). *The stuff of thought: Language as a window into human nature*. New York: Viking.

Plowman, L., Stephen, C., & McPake, J. (2010). *Growing up with technology: Young children learning in a digital world*. New York: Routledge.

Polanyi, M. (1963). *The study of man*. Chicago: University of Chicago Press.

Pollman, M.J. (2010). *Blocks and beyond: Strengthening early math and science skills through spatial learning*. Baltimore, MD: Brookes.

Ponitz, C.E.C., McClelland, M.M., Jewkes, A.M., Connor, C.M., Farris, C.L., & Morris, F.J (2008). Touch your toes! Developing a direct measure of behavioral regulation in early childhood. *Early Childhood Research Quarterly 23* (2), 141–158.

Popovchak, D. (2010). Personal communication.

Popovchak, S. (2010). Personal communication.

Prairie, A.P. (2005). *Inquiry into math, science, and technology for teaching young children*. Clifton Park, NY: Thomson Delmar.

Press, P. (1974). Personal communication.

Project Sex Equity in Education (n.d.). 101 ways to line up other than by sex. Poster. Sacramento: University of California.

Provenzo, E.F., Jr., & Brett, A. (1983). *The complete block book*. Photos M. Carleback. Syracuse: Syracuse University Press.

Quinn, M.C., Fisher, R., & Garriel, B.S., & Novelli, J. (Ed.). (1994). *12 Take-home thematic backpacks*. New York: Scholastic.

Raines, S.C., & Canady, R.J. (1992). *Story s-t-r-e-t-c-h-e-r-s for the primary grades*. Mt. Rainer, MD: Gryphon House.

Ramani, G.B., & Siegler, R.S. (2008). Promoting broad and stable improvements in low-income children's numerical knowledge through playing board games. *Child Development 79* (2), 375–394.

Ramsey, P.G. (2004). *Teaching and learning in a diverse world.* 3rd edn. New York: Teachers College Press.

Reggio Emilia (1987). *To make a portrait of a lion.* Videotape. Washington, DC: Reggio Children USA.

Reifel, S. (1984). Block construction: Children's developmental landmarks in representation of space. *Young Children 40* (1), 61–67.

Reifel, S., & Greenfield, P. (1982). Structural development in symbolic medium: The representational use of block constructions. In G. Forman (Ed.), *Action and thought: From sensorimotor schemes to symbolic operations.* New York: Academic Press.

Rey, H.A. (1973). *Curious George.* Boston: Houghton Mifflin.

Reynolds, A.J., Temple, J.A., Robertson, D.L., & Mann, E.A. (2001). Long-term effects of an early childhood intervention on educational achievement and juvenile arrest: A 15-year follow-up of low-income children in public schools. *Journal of the American Medical Association 285* (18), 2339–2346.

Richards, R. et al. (1976a). *Early experiences.* Milwaukee: Raintree-Macdonald.

Richards, R. et al. (1976b). *Ourselves.* Milwaukee: Raintree-Macdonald.

Richards, R. (1992). *An early start to energy and its effects.* Cheltenham: Simon & Schuster; Brattleboro, VT: Teachers' Laboratory.

Richards, R., Collis, M., & Kincaid, D. (1995). *An early start to science.* Cheltenham: Simon & Schuster; Brattleboro, VT: Teachers' Laboratory.

Richardson, K. (1984). *Developing number concepts using Unifix cubes.* Menlo Park, CA: Addison-Wesley.

Richgels, D.J. (2001). Invented spelling, phonemic awareness, and reading and writing instruction. In S.B. Neuman & D.K. Dickinson (Eds.), *Handbook of early literacy research* (pp. 142–155). New York: Guilford Books.

Ritz, W. (2007). *A head start in science education.* Arlington, VA: National Science Teachers Association.

Rivkin, M.S. (2006). Children's outdoor play: An endangered activity. In D. Fromberg & D. Bergen (Eds.), *Play from birth to twelve* (pp. 323–329). New York; Routledge.

Robertson, R., & Combs, A. (Eds.) (1995). *Chaos theory in psychology and the life sciences.* Mahwah, NJ: Lawrence Erlbaum.

Robison, H.S., & Spodek, B. (1965). *New directions in the kindergarten.* New York: Teachers College Press.

Rog, L.J. (2007). *Marvelous minilessons for teaching beginning writing, K–3.* Newark, DE: International Reading Association.

Rogers, S. (1982). *The field behind the plow: Songs from Fogarty's Cove.* Ontario: OPC Publications.

Rogoff, B., Mistry, J., Goncu, A., & Mosier, C. (1993). *Guided participation in cultural activity by toddlers and caregivers.* Monograph of the Society for Research in Child Development No. 236, 58 (8).

Rogovin, P. (1998). *Classroom interviews: A world of learning.* Portsmouth, NH: Heinemann.

Rogovin, P. (2001). *The research workshop: Bringing the world into your classroom.* Portsmouth, NH: Heinemann.

Rosenblatt, L. (1969). Towards a transactional theory of reading. *Journal of Reading Behavior 10* (1), 31–34.

Rosenblatt, L. (1978). *The reader, the text, the poem.* Carbondale: Southern Illinois University Press.

Rosenblatt, L. (1980). What facts does this poem teach you? *Language Arts 57* (4), 386–394.

Roskos, K., & Christie, J.F. (Eds.) (2002). *Play and literacy in early childhood: Research from multiple perspectives.* Mahwah, NJ: Lawrence Erlbaum.

Roskos, K., & Neuman, S.B. (2001). Environment and its influences for early literacy teaching and learning. In S.B. Neuman & D.K. Dickinson (Eds.), *Handbook of early literacy research* (pp. 281–292). New York: Guilford Books.

Routman, R. (2003). *Reading essentials: The specifics you need to teach reading well.* Portsmouth, NH: Heinemann.

Sanders, S.W. (2002). *Active for life: Developmentally appropriate movement programs for young children.* Washington, DC: NAEYC.

Sandkuhler, S., & Bhattacharya, J. (2008). Deconstructing insight: EEG correlates of insightful problem solving. *PLoS ONE (1). http://www.plosone.org* [Retrieved February 4, 2009].

Sauvy, J., & Sauvy, S. (1974). *The child's discovery of space.* Trans. P. Wells. Baltimore, MD: Penguin.

Sawyer, R.K. (2006). *Explaining creativity: The science of human invention.* New York: Oxford University Press.

Scarlet, W.G., & Nadeau, S., Salonius-Pasternak, D., & Ponte, I. (2005). *Children's play.* Thousand Oaks, CA: Sage.

Schank, R., & Abelson, R. (1977). *Scripts, plans, goals and understanding: An inquiry into human knowledge structures.* Hillsdale, NJ: Lawrence Erlbaum.

Schiller, P., Lara-Alecio, R., & Irby, B. (2004). *The bilingual book of rhymes, songs, stories, and fingerplays.* Beltsville, MD: Gryphon House. (Related website: http://www.wilderdom. com/games/descriptions/helloindifferentlanguages [Retrieved August 6, 2010].)

Schiller, P., & Peterson, L. (1997). *Count on math.* Illus. C.K. Noll. Beltsville, MD: Gryphon House.

Schirrmacher, R., & Fox, J. (2008). *Art and creative development for young children.* 6th edn. Belmont, CA: Wadsworth Cengage Learning.

Schrader, C.T. (1989). Written language use within the context of young children's symbolic play. *Early Childhood Research Quarterly 4* (2), 225–244.

Schrader, C.T. (1990). Symbolic play as a curricular tool for early literacy development. *Early Childhood Research Quarterly 5* (1), 79–103.

Schwartz, M. (n.d.). Untitled.

Schwartz, S. (2005). *Teaching young children mathematics.* Westport, CT: Greenwood/Praeger.

Schwartz, S.L., & Copeland, S.M. (2010). *Connecting emergent curriculum and standards in early childhood classrooms: Strengthening content and teaching practice.* New York: Teachers College Press.

Schweinhart, L.J., et al. (2005). *Lifetime effects: The HighScope Perry preschool study through age 40.* Monograph of the HighScope Educational Research Foundation No. 14. Ypsilanti, MI: HighScope Press.

Seefeldt, C. (1992). *The early childhood curriculum: A review of research.* 2nd edn. New York: Teachers College Press.

Serbin, L. (1978). Teachers, peers, and play preferences: An environmental approach to sex typing in the preschool. In B. Sprung (Eds.), *Perspectives on nonsexist early childhood education* (pp. 79–93). New York: Teachers College Press.

Shaffer, D.W. (2006). *How computer games help children learn.* New York: Palgrave Macmillan.

Shaftel, F.R., & Shaftel, G. (1983). *Role-playing for social values.* 2nd edn. Englewood Cliffs, NJ: Prentice-Hall.

Shagoury, R. (2010). Making reading meaningful. *Educational Leadership 67* (6), 63–67.

Shank, R., & Abelson, R. (1977). *Scripts, plans, goals, and understanding: An inquiry into human knowledge structures.* Hillsdale, NJ: Lawrence Erlbaum.

Shepard, L.A., & Graue, M.E. (1993). The morass of school readiness screening: Research on test use and test validity. In B. Spodek (Ed.), *Handbook of research on the education of young children* (pp. 293–305). New York: Macmillan.

Shepard, L.A., & Smith, M.L. (1986). Synthesis of research on school readiness and kindergarten retention. *Educational Leadership 44*, 78–86.

Shoda, Y., Mischel, W., & Peake, P.K. (1990). Predicting adolescent cognitive and self-regulatory competencies from preschool delay of gratification: Identifying diagnostic conditions. *Developmental Psychology 24* (6), 978–986.

Shore, R. (2008). *The power of pow! Wham! Children, digital media and our nation's future: Three challenges for the coming decade.* New York: The Joan Ganz Cooney Center.

Siegler, R., Carpenter, T., Fennell, F., Geary, C., Lewis, J., Okamoto, Y., Thompson, L., & Wray, J. (2010). Developing effective fractions instruction for kindergarten through 8th grade: A practice guide. Washington, DC: National Center for Education Evaluation and Regional Assistance, Institute of Education Sciences, U.S. Department of Education. http://ies.ed.gov/ncee [Retrieved October 11, 2010].

Siegler, R.S., & Ramani, G.B. (2008). Playing linear numerical board games promotes low-income children's numerical development. *Developmental Science 11* (5), 655–661.

Sigman, A. (2008a). *Does not compute: Screen technology in early childhood education.* Ruskin Mill Educational Trust. http://www.rmet.org.uk [Retrieved July 15, 2010].

Sigman, A. (2008b). *Practically minded: The benefits and mechanisms associated with a craft-based curriculum.* Ruskin Mills Educational Trust. http://www.rmet.org.uk [Retrieved April 21, 2010].

Silberman, M. (1988). Kindergarten artist studies. Unpublished paper. Hempstead, NY: Hofstra University.

Singer, D., Golinkoff, R.M., & Hirsh-Pasek, K. (Eds.) (2009). *Play=learning: How play motivates and enhances children's cognitive and social-emotional growth.* New York: Oxford University Press.

Singer, D.G., & Singer, J.S. (2006). Fantasy and imagination. In D.P. Fromberg & D. Bergen (Eds.), *Play from birth to twelve* (pp. 371–378). New York: Routledge/Taylor and Francis.

Singer, J.S., & Singer, D. (1979). The value of imagination. In B. Sutton-Smith (Ed.), *Play and learning* (pp. 195–218). New York: Gardner.

Skeele, R.W., & Russo, C. (2009). Students with learning difficulties: Web 2.0 resources for Response to Intervention (RTI). In T. Bastiaens, J. Dron, & C. Xin (Eds.), *Proceedings of the World Conference on E-Learning in Corporate, Government, Healthcare, and Higher Education* (pp. 1971–1980). Chesapeake, VA: AACE. http://www.editlib.org/p/32753 [Retrieved September 25, 2010].

Slavin, R.E. (1992). Grouping. In L.R. Williams & D.P. Fromberg (Eds.), *The encyclopedia of early childhood education* (pp. 394–396). New York: Garland.

Sleeter, C.E., & Grant, C.A. (2009). *Making choices for multicultural education: Five approaches to race, class, and gender.* 6th edn. New York: Wiley.

Sleeter, C.E., Grant, C.A., Nieto, S., & Fettes, M. (2007). Imaginative multicultural education: Notes toward an inclusive theory. In K. Egan, M. Stout, & K. Takaya (Eds.), *Teaching and learning outside the box* (pp. 126–137). New York: Teachers College Press.

Smilansky, S. (1968). *The effects of sociodramatic play on disadvantaged preschool children.* New York: Wiley.

Smith, F. (1978). *Understanding reading.* 2nd edn. New York: Holt, Rinehart, & Winston.

Smith, K. (1991). *Frank Lloyd Wright: America's master architect.* New York: Abbeville Press.

Smith, L.A. (2007). *Chaos: A very short introduction*. New York: Oxford University Press.

Smutny, J., & Von Fremd, S.E. (2010). *Differentiating for the young child: Strategies across the content areas PreK–3*. Thousand Oaks, CA: Corwin.

Snow, C.E., & Van Hemel, S.B. (2008). *Early childhood assessment: Why, what, and how*. Washington, DC: The National Academies Press.

Sobel, D. (1999). *Galileo's daughter: A historical memoir of science, faith and love*. New York: Walker.

Sowers, S. (1986a). Reflect, expand, select: Three responses in the writing conference. In T. Newkirk & N. Atwell (Eds.), *Understanding writing* (pp. 76–90). Portsmouth, NH: Heinemann.

Sowers, S. (1986b). Six questions teachers ask about invented spelling. In T. Newkirk & N. Atwell (Eds.), *Understanding writing* (pp. 47–54). Portsmouth, NH: Heinemann.

Spodek, B. (1962). Developing social studies concepts in the kindergarten. Columbia University doctoral dissertation. New York: Teachers College.

Sprenger, M. (2008). *The developing brain: Birth to age eight*. Thousand Oaks, CA: Corwin.

St. Exupery, A. de (2000). *The little prince*. Trans. R. Howard. Orlando, FL: Harcourt (Originally published in 1943.)

Steiner, G. (1970). *Language and silence*. New York: Atheneum.

Stephen, C., & Plowman, L. (2008). Enhancing learning with information and communication technologies in pre-school. *Early Child Development and Care 178* (6), 637–654.

Stipek, D., Feiler, R., Daniels, D., & Milburn, S. (1995). Effects of different instructional approaches on young children's achievement and motivation. *Child Development 66*, 209–233.

Strasser, J., & Sepolcha, H. (2009). *A snapshot of quality in kindergarten classrooms in low-income districts: Implications for policy and practice*. Trenton: New Jersey Department of Education.

Stoessinger, R., & Edmunds, J. (1992). *Natural learning and mathematics*. Portsmouth, NH: Heinemann.

Sullivan, W. (1974). A hole in the sky. *New York Times*, July 14, pp. 11ff.

Sullivan, W. (1985). Strange scroll-like wave is linked to biological processes. *New York Times*, January 8, p. C3.

Sulzby, E., Teale, W.H., & Kamberelis, G. (1989). Emergent writing in the classroom. In D.S. Strickland & L.M. Morrow (Eds.), *Emergent literacy: Young children learn to read and write* (pp. 63–79). Newark, DE: International Reading Association.

Sunburst Communication (1998). *Thinking out loud*. Software prgram. Minneapolis, MN: Author.

Swan, C. (2009). *Teaching strategies for learning in the early years*. Norwood, South Australia: Australian Literacy Educators' Association.

Sweet, M (1992). *Fiddle-I-fee: A farmyard song for the very young*. New York: Scholastic.

Sylva, K., Siraj-Blatchford, I., & Taggart, B. (2010) *ECERS-E: The Four Curricular Subscales Extension to the Early Childhood Environment Rating Scale (ECERS-R)*. New York: Teachers College Press.

Sylwester, R. (2000). *A biological brain in a cultural classroom*. Thousand Oaks, CA: Corwin.

Taberski, S. (2000). *On solid ground: Strategies for teaching reading K–3*. Portsmouth, NH: Heinemann.

Taberski, S. (2009). *Comprehension from the ground up staff development bundle*. Portsmouth, NH: Heinemann.

Teaching Strategies (n.d.). *Teaching Strategies GOLD: Birth through Kindergarten.* http://www.TeachingStrategies.com/GOLD.cfm [Retrieved April 14, 2011].

Temple, J.A., & Reynolds, A.M. (2007). Benefits and costs of investment in preschool education: Evidence from child–parent centers and related programs. *Economics of Education Review 26* (1), 126–144.

Terens, S. (1984). Personal communication.

Thorne, B. (1993). *Gender play: Girls and boys in school.* Brunswick, NJ: Rutgers University Press.

Tognoli, E., & Kelso, J.A.S. (2008). Brain coordination dynamics: True and false faces of phase synchrony and metastability. *Progress in Neurobiology 87* (1), 31–40.

Tompkins, G.E. (2011). *Literacy in the early grades: A successful start for prek–4 readers and writers.* 3rd edn. Boston: Pearson.

Torrance, E.P. (1952). *Guiding creative talent.* Englewood Cliffs, NJ: Prentice-Hall.

Turbill, J. (2001). *How to teach poetry writing.* London: David Fulton/Routledge.

Udall, N., (1996). Creative transformation: A design perspective. *Journal of Creative Behavior 30* (1), 39–51.

Ullman, E. (2010). Closing the STEM gender gap. *ASCD Education Update 52* (3), 1, 6.

University of California–Berkeley (2001). *New parents kit.* Berkeley: Author.

Urban Institute (2011). Children of immigrants data tool. http://datatool.urban.org/charts/datatool/chartbook.cfm? [Eetrieved January, 2011].

U.S. Department of Commerce, Bureau of the Census (2002*). Percent of population 3 to 34 years old enrolled in school, by race, ethnicity, sex, and age: Selected years, October 1980 to 2001.* Washington, DC: Author.

U.S. Department of Commerce, Bureau of the Census (2004). *Income stable, poverty up, numbers of Americans with and without health insurance rise, Census Bureau reports.* Washington, DC: Author.

VanDerHeyden, A.M., & Snyder, P. (2006). Integrating frameworks from early childhood intervention and school psychology to accelerate growth for all young children. *School Psychology Review 35* (4), 519–534.

Vatterott, C. (2009). *Rethinking homework: Best practices that support diverse needs.* Alexandria, VA: Association for Supervision and Curriculum Development.

Vecchiotti, S. (2001). *Kindergarten: The overlooked school year.* New York: Foundation for Child Development.

Vygotsky, L.S. (1962). *Thought and language.* Trans. E. Hanfmann & G. Vakar. New York: Wiley.

Vygotsky, L.S. (1976). Play and its role in the mental development of the children. In J.S. Bruner, A. Jolly, & K. Sylva (Eds.), *Play: Its role in development and evolution* (pp. 543–554). New York: Basic Books.

Vygotsky, L.S. (1978). *Mind in society: The development of higher psychological processes.* Ed. M. Cole, V. John-Steiner, S. Scribner, & E. Souberman. Cambridge, MA: Harvard University Press. (Originally published in 1934.)

Vygotsky, L.S. (1987). Imagination and its development in childhood. In R.W. Rieber & A.S. Carton (Eds.), *The collected works of L.S. Vygotsky* (Volume 1, pp. 339–349). Trans. N. Minick. New York: Plenum.

Waldrop, M.M. (1992). *Complexity: The emerging science at the edge of order and chaos.* New York: Simon & Schuster.

Walmsley, B.B., & Wing, D.R. (2004). *Welcome to kindergarten: A month-by-month guide to teaching and learning.* Portsmouth, NH: Heinemann.

Wanska, S.K., Pohlman, J.C., & Bedrosian, J.L.(1989). Topic maintenance in preschoolers' conversation in three play situations. *Early Childhood Research Quarterly 4* (3), 393–402.

Wardle, F. (2003). *Introduction to early childhood education: A multidimensional approach to child-centered care and learning.* Boston: Allyn & Bacon.

Waters, B. (1973). *Science can be elementary.* New York: Citation.

Wellhousen, K., & Kieff, J, (2001). *A constructivist approach to block play in each childhood.* Albany, NY: Delmar.

West, J., Denton, K., & Reaney, L.M. (2000). *The kindergarten year: Findings from the Early Childhood Longitudinal Study, kindergarten class of 1998–1999.* Washington, DC: U.S. Department of Education, National Center for Educational Statistics, U.S. Government Printing Office.

Whitehead, A.N. (1911). *An introduction to mathematics.* New York: Henry Holt.

Whitehead, A.N. (1929). *The aims of education.* New York: Mentor.

Whitehead, A.N., & Russell, B. (1910). *Principia mathematica.* Cambridge: Cambridge University Press.

Whitehurst, G.J., & Lonigan, C.J. (2001). Emergent literacy: Development from prereaders to readers. In S.B. Neuman & D.K. Dickinson (Eds.), *Handbook of early literacy research* (pp. 11–29). New York: Guilford Books.

Whitin, D.J., Mills, H., & O'Keefe, T. (1990). *Living and learning mathematics.* Portsmouth, NH: Heinemann.

Whitin, D.J., & Whitin, P.E. (2010). *Learning to read the numbers: Integrating critical literacy and critical numeracy in K–8 classrooms.* New York: Routledge/NCTE.

Wilson, P.S., & Rowland, R. (1993). Teaching measurement. In R.J. Jensen (Ed.), *Research ideas for the classroom: Early childhood mathematics* (pp. 171–104). New York: Macmillan.

Wittgenstein, L. (1958). *Philosophical investigations.* Trans. G.E.M. Anscombe. New York: Macmillan.

Wohl, M.F., & Gainer, C. (1996). *MathArts.* Beltsville, MD: Gryphon House.

Wohlstadter, K. (1991). Personal communication.

Wolfberg, P. (2009). *Play and imagination in children with autism.* 2nd edn. New York: Teachers College Press.

Wolfgang, C.H., Stannard, L.L., & Jones, I. (2001). Block play performance among preschoolers as a predictor of later school achievement in mathematics. *Journal of Research in Childhood Education 15* (2), 173–180.

Wormeli, R. (2009). *Metaphors and analogies: Power tools for teaching any subject.* Portland, ME: Stenhouse.

Worth, K., & Grollman, S. (2003). *Worms, shadows, and whirlpools: Science in the early childhood classroom.* Portsmouth, NH: Heinemann/NAEYC.

Wright, F.L. (1932). *An autobiography.* New York: Longmans.

Wright, S. (2003). *The arts, young children, and learning.* Boston: Allyn & Bacon.

Wyatt, L., & Seeger, P. (n.d.). *Wonderful friends.* http://wwww.lyricsmania.com/wonderful__friends__lyrics__pete__seeger.html [Retrieved February 28, 2010].

Wyman, E., Rakoczy, H., & Tomasello, M. (2009). Normativity and context in young children's pretend play. *Cognitive Development 24*, 146–155.

Yelland, N., Lee, L., O'Rourke, M., & Harrison, C. (2008). *Rethinking learning in early childhood education.* Maidenhead: McGraw-Hill/Open University Press.

Yonemura, M. (1969). *Developing language programs for young disadvantaged children.* New York: Teachers College Press.

Zan, B., & Geiken, R. (2010). Ramps and pathways: Developmentally appropriate, intellectually rigorous, and fun science. *Young Children 65* (1), 12–17.

Zaslavsky, C. (2003). *More math games and activities from around the world*. Chicago: Chicago Review Press.

Zehr, M.A. (2010). Tailoring lessons for English-learners: RTI to pay off in gains for English-learners: A California district gets results, and recognition using "Response to Intervention." *Education Week*, January 27. http://www.edweek.org/ew/articles/2010/01/22/19rtiells_ep.h29.html? tkn-SPVFZVcBAE3 [Retrieved February 1, 2010].

Zelazo, P.D. (2006). The Dimensional Change Card Sort (DCCS): A method of assessing executive function in children. *Nature Protocols 1* (1), 297–301. http://www.nature.com/natureprotocols [Retrieved October 11, 2010].

Zigler, E.F., & Bishop-Josef, S.J. (2004). Play under siege: A historical overview. In E.F. Zigler, D.G. Singer, & S.J. Bishop-Josef. (Eds), *Children's play: The roots of reading* (pp. 1–13). Washington, DC: Zero to Three Press.

Zimmerman, B.J. (2008). Investigating self-regulation and motivation: Historical background, methodological developments, and future prospects. *American Educational Research Journal 45* (1), 166–183.

Zubrowski, B. (1979). *Bubbles*. Illus. J. Drescher. New York: Beech Tree.

Zubrowski, B. (1990). *Balloons: Building and experimenting with inflatable toys*. Illus. R. Doty. New York: Beech Tree.

INDEX

Please note, ff. refers to intermittent presence of the preceding citation on several pages that follow.